THE ALCHEMY OF THEATRE

The Divine Science
Essays on Theatre & the Art of Collaboration

THE ALCHEMY OF THEATRE

～ THE DIVINE SCIENCE ～

Essays on Theatre & the Art of Collaboration

by

Lynn Ahrens, Edward Albee, Angelina Avallone, Jay Binder, William David Brohn, Adrian Bryan-Brown, Kathleen Chalfant, Cy Coleman, Nancy Coyne, Peggy Eisenhauer, Jules Fisher, Stephen Flaherty, Paul Gemignani, Rocco Landesman, Dick Latessa, Peter Lawrence, William Ivey Long, Terrence McNally, Tony Meola, Brian Stokes Mitchell, Cynthia Onrubia, Harold Prince, Chita Rivera, Gerald Schoenfeld, Susan Stroman, Robin Wagner, Wendy Wasserstein, and George C. Wolfe

EDITED BY ROBERT VIAGAS

PLAYBILL BOOKS

APPLAUSE THEATRE & CINEMA BOOKS

NEW YORK

THE ALCHEMY OF THEATRE—THE DIVINE SCIENCE
Essays on Theatre & the Art of Collaboration
Edited by Robert Viagas

Copyright © 2006 Playbill Books
All rights reserved

Book design by Mark Lerner

Library of Congress Cataloging-in-Publication Data:
The alchemy of theatre : essays on collaboration / by Lynn Ahrens ...
   [et al.] ; edited by Robert Viagas.
      p. cm.
   Includes bibliographical references and index.
   ISBN-13: 978-1-55783-698-4 (alk. paper)
   ISBN-10: 1-55783-698-1 (alk. paper)
   1. Theater. 2. Theater—United States. 3. American drama—History and criticism.
         I. Ahrens, Lynn. II. Viagas, Robert.
   PN2020.A55 2006
   792.01'5--dc22
            2006011322

Applause Theatre & Cinema Books
19 West 21st Street, Suite 201
New York, NY 10010
Phone: (212) 575-9265
Fax: (212) 575-9270
Email: info@applausepub.com
Internet: www.applausepub.com

Playbill Books
525 Seventh Avenue, Suite 1801
New York, NY 10018
Phone: (212) 557-5757
Internet: www.playbill.com

Applause books are available through your local bookstore, or you may order at www.applausepub.com or call Music Dispatch at 800-637-2852

SALES & DISTRIBUTION
North America:
Hal Leonard Corp.
7777 West Bluemound Road
P. O. Box 13819
Milwaukee, WI 53213
Phone: (414) 774-3630
Fax: (414) 774-3259

Europe:
Roundhouse Publishing Ltd.
Millstone, Limers Lane
Northam, North Devon EX 39 2RG
Phone: (0) 1237-474-474
Fax: (0) 1237-474-774
Email: roundhouse.group@ukgateway.net
Internet: www.halleonard.com
Email: halinfo@halleonard.com

Printed in China through Colorcraft Ltd., Hong Kong

"Collaboration is the biggest word in the theatre. It is the most important element in theatrical success.... The theatre is a welding of many arts into one. No one person can be efficient or talented in all of these arts, and if any man could write and produce and direct and act and play the music, shift the scenery, design the costumes and, in short, do everything that could be done on one stage and come up with what was literally a one-man show, he would still need one more thing: an audience. You cannot get away from collaboration."

—Oscar Hammerstein II,
from his Introduction to the compendium *Lyrics* (1949)

Thanks to all the great talents who gave so generously of their time and thought to the writing and editing of this project: Lynn Ahrens, Edward Albee, Angelina Avallone, Jay Binder, William David Brohn, Adrian Bryan-Brown, Kathleen Chalfant, Cy Coleman (and his assistant, Mark York), Nancy Coyne, Peggy Eisenhauer, Jules Fisher, Stephen Flaherty, Paul Gemignani, Rocco Landesman, Dick Latessa, Peter Lawrence, William Ivey Long, Terrence McNally, Tony Meola, Brian Stokes Mitchell, Cynthia Onrubia, Harold Prince, Chita Rivera, Gerald Schoenfeld, Susan Stroman, Robin Wagner, Wendy Wasserstein, and George C. Wolfe.

Plus all their hard-working assistants and secretaries who helped arrange their time and availability.

Special thanks to Catherine Ryan for her instrumental help in the preparation of the manuscript and Melissa Merlo for her assistance in exchanging final drafts with the essayists and tracking down photos.

CONTENTS

Collaborating with the Collaborators

In 2004, *Playbill* publisher Philip Birsh approached me about doing a book on the various interlocking crafts of Broadway. The idea was to coax masters in each area to describe their craft in their own words, illustrated with stories from their remarkable careers.

Mr. Birsh and I chose people from the innermost circle of each field, most of them legends; most of them people I had interviewed in the past, whom I knew to be thoughtful and articulate.

But beyond the notion of simply telling how people did their jobs, I thought the book should have a theme. What did these people have in common? It was this: their ability, despite their colossal talent and sometimes matching egos, to work with other artists, to allow their talent to melt into others' and form unexpected and sometimes alchemical alloys with those of their allies. After all, their greatest successes have come while combining their efforts with those of other artists.

Theatre has been called the most collaborative art form. Here is a group of people who have figured out how to achieve success in an environment where giant egos are locked up together under mounting financial and emotional pressure, and expected to deliver great art.

In this crucible they learn how to work together as a team, giving their best, and getting others' best back in return. They learn to collaborate.

The essence of drama may be conflict—but the essence of *creating* drama turns out to be cooperation.

METHODOLOGY

My methodology consisted of drawing up a list of dream candidates for each job on the list (multiple names in some cases), then contacting them in the name of *Playbill* and asking their cooperation. The premise drew near-unanimous participation and enthusiasm. Each participant was invited to write his or her own essay, with the editor's questions as guides, or not. Some did that. Most opted for Plan B, which was to take part in an extended interview with the editor, sometimes in multiple sessions, and then work with the editor sending text back and forth until an essay was fashioned.

In some cases, the strict essay form was waived. The thoughts of Ahrens and

Flaherty and Fisher and Eisenhauer were presented as conversations between two collaborators, to illustrate their partnership by the way they tell their shared story. Interestingly, both teams agreed to be interviewed only with their partners present.

The essays are arranged roughly in the order that the artists perform their functions. Every play starts with a writer putting a word on a page; therefore the writers come first, in the section called "Pen to Paper." The work is next taken up and reconceived for the stage by the producers and directors, who form the leadership for the eventual production. Their essays are included in the section called "Captains." Plays find their incarnation through actors, and these essays appear in the section titled "Their Hour Upon the Stage." The final section "Completion" includes essays by the designers and promoters of the show, ending with press agent Adrian Bryan-Brown, who gives his unique angle on a Broadway opening night, which seems a good place to conclude.

In general the essayists were pressed to give nuts and bolts, real-world solutions to common problems of collaborating. They almost always responded with anecdotes presented as parables of what to do, and what not to do.

The essays discuss several forms of collaboration, primarily the following:

1. Partnership Collaboration—A marriage-like artistic relationship between two people. These binary stars include Ahrens and Flaherty and Fisher and Eisenhauer, though others are described.
2. Leadership Collaboration—A relationship a person has with a group of artists organized and commanded by another, usually the director.
3. Collegial Collaboration—A web of relationships among artists of roughly equal status, who pool their knowledge and creativity.

The blocks of collaboration are often stacked in various combinations with others. For example, Ahrens and Flaherty working for Susan Stroman becomes a Partnership inside a Leadership. Each person on any given project may be participating in several kinds of collaboration simultaneously.

DIVAS

A common type to be encountered (generally in the third person) on these pages is the temperamental, tantrum-throwing diva, whose stories are presented as cautionary tales. The essayists rarely describe themselves as such divas. Nor are they. With just a few noteworthy exceptions, they preach a gospel of collegiality, mutual awareness, and mutual respect. But the overall experience seems to be that while fire-breathing divas and their male counterparts are scarcely an extinct species, the overall sea level of civility and mutual respect has risen over the past generation.

Behavior-wise, stars whose first-day ticket sales crash the ticket websites will always be able to get away with murder. But lesser pains in the kishkes simply don't get hired as much. A Darwinian hiring situation breeds for even tempers.

On the other hand, the absence of divas among the essayists in this book was also deliberate. No sense in asking notoriously poor collaborators to share their wisdom about collaboration.

PRECEPTS

Certain precepts emerge as themes in the essays.

- Successful collaboration consists in extending your personal ego into an ego for the project as a whole, which allows you to lose personal arguments while continuing to give your all for the project.
- Find your personal glory as part of a team.
- Respect your co-workers or, turning the notion around, refrain from treating them patronizingly or with unprofessional ignorance of what they do.
- Seek out ways to combine your talent with someone else's. The willingness to let go and allow something completely different and better to be created. In the arts, one plus one can equal three—if you let it.
- Keep an open mind. Allow yourself to be surprised by your collaborator.
- Let others have their "turn" winning an argument—unless it's a make-or-break for you. Pick your fights.
- But stand up for your art and integrity if pushed too far.
- Cultivate the ability to do well even when someone else's opinion has prevailed.
- Operate happily within one's position in the hierarchy.
- Superiors must allow everyone to have their moments.
- Understand how to show one kind of respect to those up the ladder, and another kind to one's equals, and yet another kind to one's inferiors.
- More technicians have helped to create than have autocratic directors.
- The scarcity of top talent has drained power from once-autocratic producers.
- Strive to balance art and commerce: wanting a show to have complete integrity, yet be a blockbuster hit. To challenge the audience and attract it at the same time.

- Be truly interested in other people. Find other people interesting and want to mix your creations with theirs.
- Many of the essayists said they'd never realized what they were doing was collaborating. To them collaboration means something very specific and circumscribed, usually like a composer working with a lyricist. In many cases, they only gradually accepted the notion that they were actually collaborating too. Some insisted they'd never thought about it, yet it was clear from their accounts that they had thought long and hard and deep on the subject, but had never before considered that it had a name. Or that the name "collaboration" applied to what they were doing.
- Many expressed surprise, wonder, and gratitude at the notion. Most have given dozens of interviews, and yet remarked that they had never before discussed this facet of what they did, because they had never been asked about it. And yet, what they were doing was indeed collaborating, and in the most profound sense. Mankind got where it has gotten through collaboration. A recent fashion for applauding all of society's mavericks, whatever their goals or motivations, has left collaboration, this most human of activities, in low account. Perhaps the tide will change in the coming years.

Personal Note

Working closely with the original casts of *A Chorus Line* and *The Fantasticks* on two of my previous books, I became fascinated with the dynamics within the teams who created those long-running milestones. One thing the two projects had in common: the original directors, Michael Bennett and Word Baker, and other members of the creative team remained in collaboration with the productions long after they had opened. And both began flagging in their long runs once those directors died, and the sustaining collaboration dissolved at last.

Collaborating was something that was part of their lives, like a marriage. I tried to bring that awareness to my work with the essayists on this project. The lessons I learned from one, I tried to apply to the next. The questions got better, and enriched the kind of answers I got. Editing the words of these award-winning artists became a balancing act as well. When should I trust their instincts—and when should I trust my own? I tried to apply the lessons of collaboration as I discovered them, and thereby learned firsthand how sound they were.

Such lessons couldn't help but spill over into the rest of my life and my relationships with co-workers, my two sons, and the rest of my family.

Perhaps nowhere were the lessons better learned and applied than in my relationship with my wife, teacher and journalist Catherine Ryan, with whom I had collaborated on some writing projects years ago, but not since we began working together to raise our boys.

Catherine transcribed virtually all the interviews and initiated discussions that helped me think through the arcs and themes that run through the book. We visited the country that composer Stephen Flaherty felicitously calls, "a place that you couldn't find on your own."

This is what collaboration is all about. And this book is nothing but true-life stories of how these precepts work in real life for some of the most talented people alive.

— ROBERT VIAGAS

Part I

PEN TO PAPER

CHAPTER 1

Wendy Wasserstein
Playwright

Wendy Wasserstein won the Pulitzer Prize and Tony Award in 1989 for *The Heidi Chronicles*. Her 1993 play *The Sisters Rosensweig* was also nominated for a Tony as Best Play and won the Outer Critics Circle Award. Born in Brooklyn in 1950, she was educated at Calhoun, Mount Holyoke, and the Yale School of Drama, and made her Off-Broadway debut at age 23 with *Any Woman Can't* at Playwrights Horizons, which also hosted her first musical, *Mont Pelier Pa-Zazz* in 1975. Her first commercial success was *Uncommon Women and Others* in 1977. *Isn't It Romantic* (1979) ran nearly two years Off-Broadway in a revised 1983 production.

The Heidi Chronicles bowed at Playwrights Horizons and moved to Broadway, where it stayed for 621 performances. *The Sisters Rosensweig* played 556 performances. Her 1997 drama *An American Daughter* had a limited run on Broadway in 1997 under the auspices of Lincoln Center Theater, which also produced her 2000 drama *Old Money* and her 2005 drama *Third* at the Mitzi Newhouse stage. A musical adaptation of her children's book *Pamela's First Musical* has a score by Cy Coleman and David Zippel. She passed away in January 2006, after completing final edits on this essay.

Generosity

A play comes alive only through collaboration. Plays are written to be performed, usually by multiple voices. And then, of course, there is the director and the others who work with you to get a play on.

Some solo artists perform their own plays, though even *they* don't usually direct them. So even a solo show becomes a collaboration. When you are writing a play, you must always remember that you are working in a collaborative art form, which is different from any other kind.

The first step in the collaboration comes when you choose who will be the first to see your play. For me, the first person who sees it is the typist, so I always say to the typist, "What do you think?" And of course the typist says, "It's *great*." And it could be *awful*. But I only hire a typist who I know will say it's great. I find that a good way

to start. I tend to show it to them first because it gets scarier when you show it to the director. I don't show it to a director until I think it's pretty good.

Next, I show my plays to friends or colleagues whom I've come to trust. I've worked with André Bishop at Lincoln Center Theater for a long time. I've given my plays to Ann Cattano who's the dramaturg at Lincoln Center. I ask them, "Tell me if you think this is crazy."

I show my plays to somebody like director Daniel Sullivan, who has a wonderful sense of storytelling. There's a reason why the plays he directs win so many awards. He asks you the questions that help you tell your story and to effectively make your play what was in your mind.

Director Gerald Gutierrez used to do something called "The Weekend Method." We'd go away for a weekend and I'd read the play out loud and he'd ask line-by-line questions. We did that with *Isn't it Romantic*. Dan Sullivan doesn't read the play out loud with you but he will sit with you and go through it line by line.

Readings are very helpful but you have to be careful about what you take away from them. You have to hold on to your voice because so much of development—certainly in the movie business—is all about people giving you notes and expecting you to change things. I've been involved in things where people said, "Take the black character and make him white"—crazy things. You have to know what to accept and what to reject.

I recently had the experience of writing a one-act play called *Third*, of which André Bishop said, "This is really great. Why don't you make it full-length?" So you have to really think about what you were intending.

Most of the plays I write don't evolve from an outline; they evolve from character. As a result, the plays tend to be three hours long at a first preview and need to be cut. In terms of cutting the play I've always been very much helped by the director. A playwright's closest collaboration is with the director. The director, in turn, collaborates with the actors. I'm always there but I like being a playwright because I like *listening*. The one time I directed one of my own plays was a reading of *Uncommon Women* at the Second Stage. I found myself saying things like, "You should cry here," which is not the right way to collaborate with an actor. So I have a great deal of respect for the chemistry between actors and directors. Directors like Gerry Guttierez, Dan Sullivan, and Nick Hytner understand the development of an actor's "journey," and know it is something that has to be handled very well and very protectively.

I think when you are directing a new play the worst thing you can do is to try to make it your play and not the playwright's. I know of playwrights who've gotten notes like, "Why don't you set it in Ohio?" or, "Make the woman a man," or crazy things like that. A note like that can send you off on a two-month wild goose chase after which your play is a mess. If a director asks for a change, it has to be something that the playwright thinks will work for their play.

I once had a play in which the director told the actors to wink whenever something was funny. I went to see this play and it looked like they all had astigmatism. I wanted to send them all to an optician.

When I wrote *The Heidi Chronicles* I put a note on the front page that said, "This could be performed on seven folding chairs." I was concerned that because it took place over a span of thirty years and had eight characters and the first scene took place at a high school dance, no one would want to do it, figuring it would be too expensive. But Dan Sullivan looked at it and said, "You can't just have a 32-year-old playing a 16-year-old. You've got to explain it somehow or the audience will think: what *is* this?" And I could see that he was right.

He was the one who steered me to playwright Herb Gardner's wife, Barbara, who is a formidable lecturer. That's where I got the idea of making Heidi a lecturer. I did all kinds of research on women artists because I had an idea that she was a feminist historian. As it turned out, the lectures Heidi gives about women artists became the crux of the play. *The Heidi Chronicles* changed substantially for the better thanks to my collaboration with Dan Sullivan.

Gerry Gutierrez once told me that André Bishop's genius was in his ability to withhold. When he is looking for you to do something he won't say what he thinks the answer is. He lets the artist find it themselves, and then comments on it. He has his judgement but he withholds it until you discover it yourself. I do think that's right.

That's why it's imperative that you only work with people you respect and trust—and then really trust them. One of the big mistakes people make is not believing that the other people they are working with have solutions. You can't do everything yourself. In a collaboration, other people have to be able to pour in their creativity, too.

In *The Heidi Chronicles* there's a scene that takes place outside the Chicago Art Institute in the rain. Dan Sullivan said to me, "How do you think we are going to do that?" And I said, "I have absolutely no idea. You and Tom Lynch, the designer, can work that out."

Learning how to rely on your collaborators really frees you. Because you know you can imagine unencumbered while the set designer will figure out a way to create the world of your play, and the costume designer will know exactly how your characters will dress, etc. But you have to know exactly whom to give a problem to. Cy Coleman once said that if you ask a choreographer, they'll always solve it with a dance.

And, of course, you have to trust your actors to find their characters. And the actor, in turn, has to trust the playwright's material and not say, "I can't say this."

SPECIAL BONDS

Though the director does most of the collaborating with actors, there are times when you, as a writer, develop a special bond with a particular performer. It can begin at the first reading of your play. Sometimes the voice of the actor who reads the play merges with the voice of the character that you're creating. That happened to me with Joan Allen and Heidi in *The Heidi Chronicles*, and it happened to me with Madeline Kahn and Dr. Gorgeous in *The Sisters Rosensweig*. Then, when you go back to rewrite your play, that voice is in your mind.

Actors notice very different things than playwrights. When we were doing *The Heidi Chronicles*, I had a habit of putting my hand over my mouth and twirling my hair when I was sitting in the rehearsal room. Then I noticed Joan Allen putting her hand over *her* mouth and twirling *her* hair. I don't notice behavior or study it in the same way. I can remember what somebody said or how somebody talks, but I don't retain details of behavior like that. Actors do; it's part of their craft. It's a different point of observation and a different way of adding dimension to a character. Between us both, we collaborated in our different ways on creating Heidi.

In *The Heidi Chronicles*, Heidi's best friend is named Susan. My friend Caroline Aaron played Susan in California. Caroline is a wonderful actress and a great comedienne. But one time we were talking about the play and she said, "I really feel that we want to see Susan in the next scene." I said, "Caroline, this is the *Heidi Chronicles*, not the *Susan Chronicles*. No one wants to see Susan in the next scene. She's gone, finished, bye." And Caroline said, "Oh. You know, I thought the play was about *me*." And I think somewhere that actors do have to have that ability to say, "This play is about *me*," which is fantastic. One of an actor's jobs as a collaborator is to think of their character that way. Caroline Aaron's job was to keep her eye on Susan, and she fulfilled it beautifully. My job is to keep my eye on the play and see that the whole story of the play is fully told.

One of the best collaborations I ever had with an actor was with Madeline Kahn on *The Sisters Rosensweig*, for which she won a Tony Award. She gave a great performance as Dr. Gorgeous Teitelbaum. She once suggested a great change in one of her lines. Her sister, Pfeni, is dating a bisexual director. Dr. Gorgeous said to her something like, "Honey I know you can't judge a book by its cover, but maybe it's not the best idea to be dating a bisexual." Madeline said to me, "I want to say something like, 'Honey I shouldn't be judging a book but this might not be the best idea.'" She wanted to turn a straight line into a comedy line, and was groping for the right joke. So I went home and I wrote, "Honey I know you shouldn't judge a book by its cover, but you're in the wrong library altogether." It always gets a laugh, and that's really because of Madeline. I would sit up late at night trying to write funnier things because I knew Madeline would be saying them.

Madeline Kahn changed my life—and, in some ways, Dr. Gorgeous changed hers. Madeline turned 50 when she was doing this play. She turned to me one day and said, "I'm so happy. I'm turning 50 and I'm getting to do this wonderful part." Very sadly, Madeline died in 1999. It was a great loss to the theatre, because Madeline always found the dignity of the character in her comedy.

I'm the youngest of three sisters and that play was a lot about my oldest sister, Sandra, whom Jane Alexander played on Broadway. Sandy died in 1997. In spring 2004 we did a benefit of that play for the National Breast Cancer Foundation with Blair Brown in the Sandra role. I found that it was like spending the evening with Sandra. That's the great thing about plays: through that collaboration, characters and stories can come alive again.

Stars

Collaborating with "stars" is a separate issue. During my life in the theatre I have seen the negative influence of television and movie stars infiltrating the theatre. They feel they can come in and try to dictate what they will do and say. Under terms of the Dramatists Guild contract, an actor can't change your language. No one can do that without your consent. That's very different from the case in Hollywood.

The really great ones don't *demand* changes. If you are dealing with Madeline Kahn or Meryl Streep, these are people who really love the theatre and they know when and how to approach you. When I did *The Heidi Chronicles*, I'll never forget Joan Allen asking, "Do you mind if I say 'a' instead of 'the'?" in one scene.

A movie star who is going to drop the script on the floor and say, "I won't say this," is not the kind of person I want to work with. That's not why I'm writing plays.

Dealing with big stars is another reason you need a really strong director. Stars can be difficult people, but you have them for a reason. They are stars because they are talented and sometimes they know very much what will work for them. But it's important not to lose sight of the fact that your job as a playwright is to make sure the play works.

Writing Musicals

I worked with Cy Coleman and David Zippel on a musical based on my children's book, *Pamela's First Musical*. Collaborating on the book of a musical is very different from writing a play. As I always tell students, it's because it's a *musi*cal and not a *book-sical*. Ultimately, it's not about you, the book writer. Abe Burrows, co-librettist of *Guys and Dolls*, came to Yale when I was a student there and gave a lecture at the Drama School. He said the thing about a musical is you've got to have a tree to hang the bananas on. The book of a musical is the tree and the songs are the bananas. I think that's really true.

Martin Sherman, who co-wrote the book to *The Boy From Oz*, told me that writing musicals is more fun to rehearse than a straight play because the actors sing and dance, which I love. When I went to Cy Coleman's house, he'd sit at the piano and start writing songs based on a story I imagined, and that was pretty great. One of the songs is about collaboration. It's called "It Started With a Dream," and that's really how all collaborations begin.

With a play, you do all the writing yourself. With a musical, there are other writers who have their own ways of telling the story and revealing the character. But, as with directors and actors, you have to give away a part of the storytelling. Or merge your way of storytelling with theirs. That's real collaboration. The songs can not repeat the book; the songs must be the emotional highlights of the book. When Kristin Chenoweth sings "Popular" in *Wicked*, you can't have a whole scene about "Oh, I'm popular." As book writer, you have to make sure she leads up to that, then it's in the hands of the songwriters.

The Audience

I write comedies. If you write comedy you're totally collaborating with the audience because if you think it's funny and no one else does, you are laughing alone in the theatre. I sit in the back and listen to the reactions, which help me to decide where to cut. I never sit through opening night or a critics' night. I'm next door drinking. But I do sit there—certainly during previews I come all the time. I listen for them listening. In comedies, you listen for the laughs, but it isn't just the laughs. You can tell, when the audience is moving around, that the play hasn't grabbed them. And that's where you cut.

There was one preview of *The Heidi Chronicles* at the old Playwrights Horizons, which had fewer than three hundred seats. I was in the back row and Heidi started giving her speech, "I feel stranded," which is the pivotal speech of the play. At that moment, a woman in the audience literally took out a nail file and started filing her nails. I was this close to turning to her and saying, "*You* are what's wrong with the American theatre!" But I didn't. I just thought, "God. Oh God." I was so mortified and angry.

An audience needs to do its part. The audience needs to collaborate, too, and it can do it two ways. *Focus* is one thing. The other is *generosity*. People should come with the hope and belief that the play will be good.

Audiences can be surprising collaborators. *An American Daughter*, which is about a woman in government who is harrassed by the media, may be the most political play I've written, and it also got the most erratic audience response. There are people who loved that play. One of its really interesting fans was Martha Stewart, and long before her trial. Martha came up to me on the opening night in 1997 and said, "You've got it."

My all-time best story about somebody responding to one of my plays takes place at Mount Sinai Hospital where I had had minor surgery. I'm in the recovery room. I'm just waking up out of anesthesia, and this woman doctor—big curls, big thick glasses—comes up to me and says, "You're Wendy Wasserstein!"

I'm moaning.

She says, "Oh I have to thank you!"

I'm rasping, "Water!"

She continues, "You know I saw the *Heidi Chronicles* and it was so depressing that I got married right away!"

What could I say? I said, "Can I have some juice please?"

With *The Sisters Rosensweig* I met *endless* Rosensweig sisters. They all came to the theatre and would come up to me afterwards and say, "We're the Rosensweigs! You wrote about us!"

The most important people I meet are young women who want to become playwrights, and say, "I saw your plays when I was in high school." I love writing about women. The body of my work has been very much about putting women on stage. When I started writing plays I knew that women go to plays and I wanted to see the people who were in the audience reflected on the stage.

LEARNING FROM COLLABORATION

Strangely enough, I think the collaborative skills I learned as a playwright helped me get through the birth of my daughter, Lucy Jane, who was born prematurely at just twenty-seven weeks, and spent the first ten weeks of her life in a neonatal intensive care unit.

Hospitals, in many ways, are like theatres. You go inside, the lights go down, and you focus. Crazy people start running in and out and bells go off. But in order for there to be a success, there needed to be a collaboration of me, my premature daughter, her doctor, and her nurses. And I believe, just as in the theatre, that the people I choose to collaborate with work to the best of their ability. They know things I don't know and I know things they don't know. And if we all work together and believe it will work out, then at least we've got a good shot at doing something good.

That's what you do when you put on a play. You cannot put on a play in a state of negativity. You must enter the theatre in a state of optimism. You must learn to respect your collaborators. And, even if it's a ridiculous false hope, you must believe that it will work out.

I very much brought that into the situation with my daughter, which was certainly the most intense life-and-death situation I've ever been in.

Throughout my life I've always had the ability to *watch*. I had that ability to sit through all those endless previews, and I had the ability to detach; to watch something, even if it's mine, and to view it honestly. All of us in the theatre—whether you are a set designer, a writer, a director—learn to have a discerning eye. To discern how you can make something better. The trick to collaboration is in some ways you become less egotistical. It's like the old Mayflower doughnut slogan: Keep your eye on the doughnut and not on the hole.

In the Dark

Theatre is about people who like to go into a room in the dark and put on a play. If you listen to people in theatre they don't talk about it as "the business"—"Are you in the business?" They say, "Are you in *theatre*?"

There is a fundamental character to theatre that is a *collaborative* character. I love the note sessions after a preview. Sitting in four rows are the actors, the designer, the director—who is probably giving the notes—and the playwright. And if you look at each of them closely, you can tell exactly what all these people do by the way they dress and the way they carry themselves. You can recognize the casualness of the actor's attire. Your eye goes to the actor's face whereas the playwright's sort of recedes. I always think of a playwright in the dark. We each do our own little thing in this tiny world. But we do it together.

CHAPTER 2

EDWARD ALBEE
PLAYWRIGHT

Edward Albee's plays include *The Zoo Story* (1958), *The American Dream* (1960), *Who's Afraid of Virginia Woolf?* (1961–62, Tony Award), *Tiny Alice* (1964), *A Delicate Balance* (1966, Pulitzer Prize and 1996, Tony Award), *All Over* (1971), *Seascape* (1974, Pulitzer Prize), *The Lady From Dubuque* (1977–78), *The Man Who Had Three Arms* (1981), *Finding the Sun* (1982), *Marriage Play* (1986–87), *Three Tall Women* (1991, Pulitzer Prize), *Fragments* (1993), *The Lorca Play* (1995), *The Play About the Baby* (1997), *The Goat, or Who Is Sylvia?* (2002, Tony Award), and *Occupant* (2002). He is a member of the Dramatists Guild Council and president of the Edward F. Albee Foundation. Mr. Albee was awarded the Gold Medal in Drama from the American Academy and Institute of Arts and Letters in 1980, and in 1996 he received both the Kennedy Center Honors and the National Medal of Arts.

Creation and Interpretation

On the first day of rehearsal of *Who's Afraid of Virginia Woolf?* I went to the rehearsal room and there were seventy-five people sitting there. This was for a four-character play. There were producers and actors and designers and, of course, everybody's assistants. I said to the producer, Richard Barr, why are all these people here?

And he said to me, "Don't get a swelled head about this Edward, but remember one thing: all of these people are sitting here in this room *because you wrote a play.*"

Hearing that is a great piece of encouragement for you as a playwright. But it puts a lot of responsibility on you not to fuck up. It places a tremendous amount of power in your hands, but also the requirement of responsibility. They go together.

I dislike the term "collaboration." No one collaborates with me on a play because I am not writing the play with them. The process of working with directors and with actors after I've written the text may be termed "collaboration" by them. But they aren't creating anything. When they try to "create," it's destructive creation, usually, unless the play is terrible. Let us call it "having my play done properly" rather than "collaboration."

There are two parts to doing a play: "creation" and "interpretation." I prefer those terms. Play writing—"creation"—is something I do, alone. "Interpretation," on the other hand, is something I do with others. Or, more correctly, something others do with me.

The process of interpreting is essential, it is exciting and it is wonderful—just as long as we know that it's not a creative act. I know this makes directors and actors very unhappy to think that they are not creating. But really they are not. They're interpreting.

"Everything I Intended"

Only work with a director who is planning to direct the play you've written. You should start by having long discussions with the director so you know that you both have the same target. Avoid directors who try to move the play too far from the author's intentions, directors who consider themselves the creators. Avoid concept directors and directors who feel "the text is a springboard for my genius." I've had to work with people like that. If they think they can write a more interesting play than I have, then they should write it.

What should a director bring to one of my plays? Everything I intended. He reaches that through reading the text, having conversations with me, and generally knowing my work.

There are many ways of interpreting, of course. That's the most important thing about collaboration. I don't want to sound like I have such a specific vision of my text on stage that interpretation is impossible. There are many ways of getting at my result. There's more than one way to skin a cat.

Whenever I am directing a play of mine, I tell my actors the first day of rehearsal that I expect them to speak my words in the order that I wrote them and not leave any out. I tell them, do the text properly and I want you to do anything you like as long as you end up with exactly what I intended. They are often both puzzled and grateful.

Sometimes, no matter how hard you try, someone will indeed try to use your play as a springboard. There was a London production of *Who's Afraid of Virginia Woolf?* in which I chose the director and I chose the actors. The problem was the set.

They had the walls careening in from act to act, and they also had ivy all over the fucking place, including indoors, which I thought was ridiculous. That was a case where the director thought that he had sole approval of the set, so he went ahead and approved it and they started building it. When I got there he learned differently, but it was too late to fix it. People should read their contracts.

Many authors, particularly in musicals, have ceded their power to directors and designers and everybody else. They do that because producers are leaning on playwrights to give up that control, and producers are doing that because people like theatre owners are making it tougher and tougher to get their work financed.

But all playwrights should know that the Dramatists Guild basic minimum contract gives us sole control of our work. Unfortunately there's no way to stop playwrights from ceding their rights if they so choose. A lot of young playwrights are not willing to take the chance of getting their show canceled. They're not willing to resist some producer saying, "I love your show but unless you agree to this we won't put it on." You've got to stand up and say, "OK, then don't put it on." Most of the time the producer will back down.

Young playwrights are also pressured to have the plays "workshopped"—that awful term. Workshops are often just places where a play get all its rough edges sanded down so it won't offend or injure or affect anybody. That's so dangerous. The people who are pushing that process are the people who are putting the money in the plays. They want something safe. Be very, very wary if you get involved with anybody in the theatre who refers to what you've done as a playwright as "product."

My most fruitful collaboration was with Richard Barr and Clinton Wilder Off-Broadway in the 1960s. Those were two first-rate producers who respected text. Now I'm working with Liz McCann. She has exactly the same attitude about where the manifest importance of theatre is. She agrees with that attitude, so we work together happily.

THE PROPER ACTORS

Some people say actors love to be loved. That's a calumny on actors. Really good actors don't go on stage to be loved. The ones that do go out there to be loved usually turn out to be in musicals, and I don't write musicals. That's not what good actors are about. They are about performing their craft, and the thrill of engagement between a good text and a responsive audience.

Any director and most playwrights will tell you that if you get the right actors, ninety percent of the job is done. When I'm watching a play, I like to see the actor *become* the character. There are a few actors I've worked with again and again who have that ability. Jessica Tandy and Peggy Ashcroft, for example, had three things that are so wonderful: understatement, intelligence, and sensitivity. Whenever they were on stage I never saw acting; I saw *being*. I get so tired of seeing *acting* on stage.

I like when actors ask me questions that go beyond the text. And I always have an ear open to learn: is that scene long enough? Is that phrase really felicitous to the character's mind? I will make subtle changes if I can help the actor become the character. But I refuse to make any changes because the actor can't handle something. If the actor can't handle something they shouldn't have the job.

THE AUDIENCE'S RESPONSIBILITY

I find audience feedback sessions very useful. On *The Goat, or Who Is Sylvia?* we had them once a week. Those sessions help me get a sense of whether the audience is participating in the play we all think we put in front of them. I'm not interested in their prejudices and, "We don't want to see plays that are disturbing" kind of comments. I don't give a shit about that kind of response. But I want to be sure that they're getting—whether they like it or not—what we are putting in front of them. That's important.

The audience has a responsibility to come to the theatre alert and sober and, most important, willing to have whatever experience is presented in front of them that works dramatically whether they approve of it or not.

I'm quite pleased when I am watching a performance of a play—especially previews—and I see a couple of people walk out. If you, as a playwright, can't offend some people, then you are not doing your job properly.

CHAPTER 3

CY COLEMAN
COMPOSER

Cy Coleman's scores distinguished Broadway musicals for four decades, the most recent being the multi-award-winning musical *The Life*, with collaborators Ira Gasman and David Newman, which he also co-wrote and co-produced; plus *The Will Rogers Follies* (winner of six Tony Awards, including Best Musical and Best Score, and the Grammy Award for Best Musical Show Album); and *City Of Angels* (winner of six Tony Awards, including Best Musical and Best Score). His first complete Broadway musical score was *Wildcat*, which starred Lucille Ball and introduced one of his most popular songs "Hey Look Me Over." In 1962 *Little Me* won Coleman the first of his twelve Tony nominations and introduced "I've Got Your Number" and "Real Live Girl." The smash hit *Sweet Charity* followed with the show-stoppers "Big Spender" and "If My Friends Could See Me Now." In 1986, *Sweet Charity* returned to Broadway, earning four Tony Awards, including Best Reproduction of a Play/Musical. A 2005 revival of *Sweet Charity* was again nominated for Best Reproduction of a Musical. The 1970s introduced three more Cy Coleman musicals to Broadway: *Seesaw*, *On The Twentieth Century*, and *I Love My Wife*, the latter of which won him a Drama Desk Award. *On The Twentieth Century*

won both a Drama Desk and Tony Award for Best Musical Score. In 1980 Coleman made his debut as a producer with the musical *Barnum*, for which he also wrote the score. He also collaborated with A. E. Hotchner on the Broadway show, *Welcome To The Club*. Coleman began his career performing at the piano in Steinway, Town, and Carnegie halls between the ages of six and nine. He played clubs in New York in the 1950s and composed many pop standards, including "Witchcraft" and "The Best Is Yet to Come." He won three Emmy Awards for writing Shirley MacLaine's TV specials *If They Could See Me Now* and *Gypsy In My Soul*, and scored the films *Father Goose*, *Power*, *Garbo Talks*, and *Sweet Charity*, for which he also earned an Oscar nomination. Coleman was honored with thirteen Grammy nominations, a star-studded tribute at Avery Fisher Hall, and the Irvin Feld Humanitarian Award from the National Conference of Christians and Jews. He was inducted into the Songwriters Hall of Fame, and was a recipient of their Johnny Mercer Award. An elected member of the ASCAP Board of Directors, Coleman also served as its Vice President. He was president of Notable Music Co., Inc. This essay was one of his final projects before his death in November 2004.

Fighting Honestly

I'd describe collaboration as breathing new life into somebody and getting new life from them. You get a whole new way of seeing things and hearing things, and you learn a different way of working. There's always something new that comes out of collaboration, and I've always found that to be exciting especially since I try to stay flexible.

I've had a lot of great collaborations with a lot of great people, and on each one, the chemistry was a little different.

EARLY CAREER

I started playing the piano at an early age, before I was 5 years old. My early background was in classical music with the later addition of jazz.

When I was still a student at Music and Arts High School in New York, I was sent to a music publisher who put me together with a lyric writer named Joseph Allen

McCarthy. His father was a famous writer for the theatre who wrote the shows *Rio Rita* and *Irene*. His son was following in his footsteps and the publisher thought we'd make a good team, even though he was eight or ten years older than I.

Joe was friendly with a very big cabaret singer named Mabel Mercer who used some of our songs like "Why Try to Change Me Now?" and "I'm Gonna Laugh You Right Out of My Life."

We even got a song in my first Broadway show, a revue called *John Murray Anderson's Almanac*. The song was "Tin Pan Alley" and it came at the end of Act I. A lot of great people came out of that show: Bock and Harnick, who'd later write *Fiddler on the Roof*; Adler and Ross, who would do *Pajama Game* and *Damn Yankees*. It was an amazing show.

But the songs came very slowly because Joe was a very slow worker. He would sweat every "the," "and," and "but." In those days we didn't use tape recorders, which meant I had to sit at the piano and play the melody over and over again while he went through the labor pains of writing the lyric. Complicating the procedure was the fact that Joe developed something of a drinking problem and would sometimes become morose and work became more and more difficult. As a result, our collaboration didn't last.

He did leave me with something valuable. What I got from Joe McCarthy was an absolute obsession with the song. Joe was so ferociously into songs and their construction and that is what he instilled in me. Writing songs became more than a passion to me. It was almost a religion.

Because of my background in classical and jazz, I have a big palette to choose from and I like to use all of it. Joe showed me how satisfying it was to use all those muscles and as a result, I've never been afraid of collaboration with a wide variety of people.

However, I have my own way of writing a song that doesn't change. I don't just play phrases. In fact, I don't write at all until I get a "message" in my head. Where does this message come from? Who knows? It comes out of another place. But when it calls, I answer.

If I have a lyric to set, I'll read it over, then read the scene. That's important because I'm not just setting the words of the song, I'm setting the music of the entire scene. I look at every song from a dramatic viewpoint.

CAROLYN LEIGH

I worked at the Brill Building, which was the headquarters of Tin Pan Alley. I used to hang out at the Turf Restaurant nearby, which is where I met my next big collaborator, Carolyn Leigh. We were talking at the Turf one day and I told her I'd broken up with Joe. She said, "Why don't we write something?" It was a nice offer because she'd just had a big hit with the song "Young At Heart."

We went back to the Brill Building, found a piano in one of the offices, and began to write a song called "A Moment of Madness." George Paxton, an old bandleader who had a publishing office up there, heard us playing it and said, "I want that song!"

Paxton gave us a nice advance and the next day we went to see Sammy Davis, Jr. with it. Sammy liked the song and agreed to put it on his next album. It all happened so fast, it was like one of those old movies. And Carolyn and I were off.

We had a huge hit with the song "Witchcraft" and we were getting recorded regularly by the likes of Patti Paige. I was also getting a lot of high-paying concert work in clubs, which drove Carolyn crazy because she saw it as taking time away from our songwriting. I even had my own club for a while but it was too much work and not enough money. Carolyn could be very difficult. She was very possessive of my time and would have hysterical fits when I'd take concert gigs. She'd call frantically. "You're at it again. You're playing the clubs."

We fought a lot but regardless of how we fought, there still was an element of respect.

One day she came to me with nothing but a title: "Witchcraft." Promising title. The first thing I went for was the exotic. I wrote a very lush melody with all kinds of mystery to it. She liked it and I liked it. We tried to work out a lyric but we weren't having much luck. One day I was at the piano and started plunking out a little melody that came to me. She asked me to repeat it. I did. She looked at me and said, "That's 'Witchcraft.'"

But it was just a phrase at that point. So we began writing the lyric and the melody hand-in-hand.

Usually, we'd work together for a while, then I would go home and she would go home and we would each go in our own directions. Then we would get together and try out what we had done. So we'd make a little more progress each day. It was a true collaboration in every sense of the word.

After we'd had a few hits, Carolyn and I were hired to write our first complete Broadway score, *Wildcat*, starring Lucille Ball who had just finished up her landmark TV show *I Love Lucy* and was looking to try something different.

Now here was a problem: how to write for a woman who had five good notes. And not just any woman, but the biggest star in the world at the time. What is she going to sing when she steps out on that stage for the first time? She had to land big or else we were all dead. Carolyn and I managed to write a great deal of the show without having that opening number. And I was stymied because everything that I was writing was sounding like warmed-over Ethel Merman.

Carolyn could see I was stuck and, because she knew me so well, she figured out a way to take the pressure off. She said, "Cy, let's get the specter of this big star out of our eyes. What if it wasn't Lucille Ball? What if you had to write the opening song for somebody who had just an ordinary amount of talent?"

I said, "Well, then I would write this." And I wrote the opening melody line right then and there to "Hey, Look Me Over." But we didn't shout eureka! We didn't want to use it at first. We had an image of ourselves as sophisticates and we thought, "This is our first Broadway show. We can't have our introductory song be something as simple and straightforward as that." So we left this half-melody and tried to move on.

Then one morning she called and said, "You know that funny little melody you left with me? I have a really funny lyric. You are going to break up." She sang,

Hey look me over, lend me an ear.
Fresh out of clover, mortgaged up to here.

I though it was cute but I still didn't want to use it. I mean, we were the team that had written "Witchcraft"!

Then we went to our publisher. That's another part of the collaboration. We played him a lot of songs. Most of them he didn't like. But when we played "Hey, Look Me Over," he said, "That's it! That's it. That's wonderful. That's a hit song."

So we finished the song. When we first met Lucille Ball, she turned out to be more nervous than any of us. She knew what her singing capabilities were and she was worried. But when we played "Hey, Look Me Over," she bolted upright and said, "I can sing that!" We hit a bull's eye with that. And that was how that collaboration worked.

Collaborations blow hot and cold. Sometimes you work together smoothly; often you rub each other the wrong way. However it's going, if something interesting is still coming out of the collaboration, then it's worth the trouble.

I have the greatest respect in the world for lyricists but very often I find that lyricists become so interested in minutiae they can lose sight of the overall story. They're after that little rhyme, that little turn of phrase. The composer often has a broader view because he's building themes that weave throughout the whole show. Carolyn would fight for a rhyme, as if to say, "The hell with the rest of the show, I'm not going to lose that rhyme!"

LITTLE ME

Little Me proved to be a hard time, and my collaboration with Carolyn Leigh began to fray. The star, Sid Caesar, was going through bad times in terms of his health and his habits. Director Bob Fosse and he were not getting along, and book writer Neil Simon and Fosse were barely getting along. Carolyn Leigh did not get along with any of them. It was one big fight all the time. The score was great but it was despite the atmosphere, not because of it.

During tryouts at the Erlanger Theatre in Philadelphia we had a song called "Don't Cry" at the end of Act I that was dying. It was a good song, a funny song, performed well. The whole show was roaring along like a locomotive until we got to that number. Then the applause died down and we couldn't figure out why.

The creative team had a very contentious meeting in the back of the theatre after one performance. There was a couple sitting with us, and each of us thought the couple was with somebody else. We let each other have it for hours. Carolyn even said, "I suppose I should be writing with somebody else but I'm stuck with you." We hashed out everything we thought was wrong with the show.

We were standing under the marquee at the end of this thing and the couple walked over to us and said, "We want to thank you for the most exciting and enlightening evening in the theatre that we've ever had" and then they walked into the dark. We all looked at each other and said, "I thought they were with you!"

Then Bob Fosse cut one of Carolyn's lyrics without getting permission. When Carolyn heard that, she ran out of the theatre. You have to picture her: a huge woman who was tall and weighed a lot. This woman ran four long blocks to City Hall, commandeered a traffic cop and hauled him back to the theatre right at intermission. She pointed at Fosse and said, "I want you to arrest him!" She also wanted the cop to arrest the producer, Cy Feuer, and the book writer, Neil Simon. She decided to hold off on me.

The cop explained that he didn't have the power to enforce Dramatists Guild rules but then asked if he could stay and watch the second act.

We'd get into these intense arguments but we never let it affect the work. It wasn't a love/hate relationship because it wasn't love in the "love" sense. I don't know if that's what she expected. I don't think so. She was married and divorced more than once. But it just got too hard. So, after *Little Me*, we went our separate ways.

We got back together briefly to write two songs for a movie called *Blame It on Rio*. She called me one night to say she was having chest pains. I told her to call the doctor and evidently he just told her to take two aspirin because it was the weekend. I can't imagine what he was thinking. When a woman that size has chest pains, you should take them seriously. She died the next morning. I was really broken up about it.

I wound up writing the two songs with Sheldon Harnick, which presented a very different kind of collaboration. Sheldon and I talked about doing a show together but we could never get on the same wavelength about what we wanted to write. I like edgy things even if it's a melodrama. Sheldon liked them soft and sweet. But we wrote some nice songs together. We did the movie *Heartbreak Kid* for Elaine May, and *Blame It on Rio*. But to write something as demanding as the score for a Broadway musical, a composer and lyricist really have to be on the same wavelength. So I moved on.

DOROTHY FIELDS

I met my next collaborator, Dorothy Fields, at a songwriters' party at Sheldon Harnick's house. She was the daughter of Lew Fields, of the vaudeville team Weber and Fields, and considerably older than I. She had amazing Broadway credits going back to the 1920s. I told her I was a great fan of hers and asked if she would consider writing something with me.

"Thank God you asked," she said. "Maybe people are intimidated but my phone doesn't ring at all."

I was amazed and I knew this was a great chance for me. We started working together the next day. She had an apartment on Central Park West. In deference to her age, I went over there to work. Sometime when we were running out of juice, my mind would start to stray. I would go into her bathroom, not to go to the bathroom, but for the view out the window: a great panorama of Central Park. It was just the place to cool out and clear my mind. I got to a point where I would be going to the bathroom a lot but I always came back with an idea. It became a joke with us. Whenever we'd run dry, Dorothy would say, "Cy, it's time to go to the bathroom."

Dorothy's working habits were quite different than mine. I worked nightclubs, she worked in movies, and that turned out to be significant. She had her own fastidious way of working. Once we agreed on an idea for a song, she would get up at 5 in the morning, set up her card table, get a cup of coffee, and write intensely starting at 6 a.m. Harold Arlen called her "Speedy" because she wrote so fast. She would finish up at 8 a.m. while I was still in the middle of a gorgeous dream. She'd call me up at that ungodly hour and want to sing me what she'd written. I tried to convince her that I couldn't listen to anything at 8 in the morning, but she kept calling. So finally I shut my phone off. She was so absolutely hurt by it that we made a bargain. She promised to wait until 9:30 a.m., and I promised not to shut my phone off.

Later, I'd go over to her place for a work session and we'd rewrite until 4 or 5 in the afternoon.

Sometimes Dorothy would drink. She got that from her Hollywood group who would do their work in the early part of the day, then sit around the pool and drink. I found that Dorothy was two different people: when she was drinking and when she was not. I learned that after 4 or 5 p.m. it was a good time to take off from Central Park West.

That's how our collaboration worked. We wrote *Sweet Charity* and *Seesaw* that way. It may seem odd, but every collaboration is unique.

Dorothy was a brilliant and attractive woman but she suffered the tragedy of losing her husband and her beloved brother in very close succession and it was just too big a blow to her.

Being an older women, she found she sometimes needed a "walker" to escort her around town. One time she called me up and said, "Cy, why don't we go," and I stopped her. I said, "Dorothy, I have a very good life. A very active life. Our relationship is a professional relationship. I am not an escort."

She understood, and it didn't hurt our collaboration. It's important in any collaboration to set the boundaries, and not to cross them.

SWEET CHARITY

The first musical I wrote with Dorothy Fields was *Sweet Charity*, which was based on the Fellini film *Nights of Cabiria* but it was really the conception of Bob Fosse. The book was originally by Fosse, writing under the pseudonym Burt Lewis. Neil Simon didn't come to the project until later.

One of the things Fosse and I fought about on *Little Me* had been the way he would add accents to the music that I didn't intend and the way he would open up the songs for dance breaks in places that I didn't like. Every time I would ask him, "Why is there a dance there?" he would say, "Why not?" And the argument would start.

When we started work on *Sweet Charity* I decided that I would write a song that was full of accents—but accents where I wanted them to be. I decided they'd be written into the music in such a way that they were locked in and couldn't be changed.

So I started by writing a vamp that was all accents. I wanted it raunchy and yet funny. Anyone who hears it will recognize it as the opening vamp to "Big Spender," but it began as my way of trying to out-Fosse Fosse. Out of that vamp came "Big Spender" and that vamp proved to be the essence of the entire score.

Sometimes collaboration can be a friendly rivalry. Sometimes you do your best work when you have a rivalry with someone you respect.

Bob, Dorothy, and I talked a lot about what the essence of the story was. What do you write a score from? You write it from the essence. You winnow it all down to a pulp. Then you boil it until you find out what the emotional essence is and you write your score out of there.

What are the main elements of the lives of the dance hall girls in *Sweet Charity*? Desperation, boredom, longing—all the things that go with having to do something you don't want to do and then having to repeat them again and again. Those girls are there every night doing the same come-on every night for a ten-cent ticket. In a way, it's even more humiliating than working as a hooker. At least they get some money for the degradation. But for ten cents these girls would compete for a ticket to dance and be pawed over by some guy they may never see again. Some did some hooking on the side but that's another story.

Dorothy and I put that essence into the music and Fosse took it and that's what he interpreted on the stage. He's the one who put the bar across the stage and created the wonderful moment when the music builds up and all of the girls look straight ahead and sing all Dorothy's lively words with blank dead faces. That's "Big Spender."

"If My Friends Could See Me Now" was an easy song to write. Here is a girl whose life is so pitiful that if she picks up a candy wrapper she's in ecstasy. She has no self-esteem. So when an Italian movie star picks her up and brings her back to his apartment, it's the biggest moment in her life. It's not hard to build a number on that.

We found that moment in Neil Simon's book. It's better when the songwriters find them than when the book writer indicates them, because you're working on a moment that simply inspired you. You have to have an eye for those moments. They always make the best songs.

But some numbers you have to fight for. One of them was "Where Am I Going?" in *Sweet Charity*. That song originated with me. Charity Hope Valentine is a girl who walks around lousing up her life, always going with the wrong guys and always making the same mistakes. To give her any sense of humanity, she had to have a moment where she looks at herself in the mirror and says, "What am I doing? Where am I going?" I felt very strongly that we needed that song.

Dorothy didn't like the title but she got used to it. Our leading lady, Gwen Verdon, wanted to cut the number because she said she was already dancing too much and was too tired. I think the true reason was that she didn't like the idea that Barbra Streisand had already recorded it before the show opened, and people might make comparisons.

The song stayed in, so I won. But Gwen didn't always let it go at that. She used to cut it sometimes. She would just decide not to do it that day. What were we going to do? Fire Gwen Verdon? Sometimes when you're collaborating with a star, you're at her mercy.

She once got a letter from a man who said "Where Am I Going?" was his favorite song in the world and the day he came to see the show, she cut it. He said it was a wasted afternoon. Well, Gwen sat down and figured out how many songs were in the show and divided it into the price of a ticket. She sent the guy a check for the cost of that one song.

Sometimes you have to be tough with your collaborator. They may not want to hear something but it's your job to make sure they do hear it. During tryouts we took *Sweet Charity* from Philadelphia to Detroit. Fosse had a number called "Give Me a Rain Check" that was dying. It was a gospel number that was supposed to open Act II. It felt terribly old-hat. He did ten versions of that number and not one of them worked. Fosse could be very, very stubborn and he was determined to do "Give Me a Rain Check."

Fosse had to make a trip back to New York for a few days, during which Dorothy and I wrote a new song called "The Rhythm of Life." It was inspired by Bach with a lot of interweaving polyphonic musical lines and was quite a challenge for Dorothy. She worked at it like a jigsaw puzzle and put the lyric together one phrase at a time.

I rehearsed the entire cast on it and had it ready when Fosse returned. Fosse refused to hear it. He was going to make "Give Me a Rain Check" work. I was furious. Finally I left him a note, and I told him, "I've given up. You're going to die with 'Rain Check.' You've died every time you put on 'Rain Check' and you are going to die some more with it. Have a good time. I'm through."

The next day I walked into the theatre and he had already choreographed half of "The Rhythm of Life."

The two biggest mistakes that people make in collaboration are either being too insistent about having your own way, or not being insistent enough. It's not easy to determine that. You have to judge circumstances and then determine what to fight for and when to let go. You have to rely on instinct and experience. If you truly believe you're right, go with it, fight for it. Fight honestly and be aware if the other guy is fighting honestly. By honestly, I mean fight to make the show better and not just to boost your own ego.

Once you've fought, it's important to know when you've won, and when you've lost. If you've won, don't gloat. Just keep working. If you've lost, figure how to work your way around it and try to maintain the working relationship. Don't put the collaboration in jeopardy or else the whole project will be in jeopardy.

MICHAEL STEWART

Dorothy Fields passed away after our second musical together, *Seesaw*. I next teamed up with Michael Stewart as lyricist. Michael was a fascinating guy. He started off as a lyricist but he couldn't get work, so he started writing scripts and librettos and was very successful. He was part of the group that wrote for Sid Caesar's "Your Show of Shows." He then teamed up with Jerry Herman, and they wrote *Hello, Dolly!* and *Mack & Mabel* together. But all along, Michael really wanted to write lyrics. He loved to write them and he was very good at it.

Michael was very nervous and very feisty, like a bantam rooster. He was always ready to fight but a very theatre-wise guy. He always knew exactly what he was talking about. He came to me with a little French play, *Viens Chez Moi, J'Habite Chez une Copine*, that had been done Off-Off-Champs-Elysées. It was a little farce about two suburban couples who wanted to join the swingers' scene but couldn't quite bring it off. The French troupe had this little sex farce going on but every so often one of the characters would walk over to the side of the stage and mime to a song that would be played on the theatre's sound system. It would always have something to do with the story, however remotely or abstractly. When the song was over, they would go on with the show.

In turning it into the Broadway musical *I Love My Wife*, we decided to do more or less the same thing but have the actors actually perform the song, accompanied by a small band whose members would also double as supporting characters. It used a revue format but it wasn't really a revue. It was a book musical. It was like *Little Me* in that way. I like that form because you get a lot of freedom and you get chances to do a lot of funny things. It was very different from most of the other shows around at that time and I liked it that way. It may be a hybrid but a hybrid is what I am. Beethoven, jazz, Broadway, TV—it all mixes up into who I am. That's why I don't mind going to different places. It excites me. The most important thing that I can bring to a project aside from my talent is my enthusiasm. I like to feel enthusiasm in my collaborators. If someone is really dead, I'm not going to work with them.

I admired the fact that Michael didn't worry about writing like everybody else. He was fearless and smart, and I knew that he knew he could make that unusual format work. I trusted him and wound up with a show that ran nearly two years.

BARNUM

Mark Bramble came to me with an idea for a musical about P. T. Barnum. I looked it over and turned it down. The circus part was interesting but there was no story. Barnum got married and started a circus. That was it.

Michael Stewart brought it back to me and asked me to think about it again. I thought if we told whatever story we had and did it in a circus environment using the circus conventions, then we might have something. I could see it would give me a chance to play around with circus music and there's a lot of life in there. We had a style, so I agreed to do it.

Michael pushed people in a good way. He pushed himself and he pushed me. When I worked with him, he always had something to get me started. He had done his homework. He always had a full lyric or a half a lyric or something to ignite me. It's too bad he died so young.

I remember bumping into Jerry Herman, with whom Michael had done *Hello, Dolly!* Jerry said that if Michael were still alive he'd have three more shows on the boards. I said, along with your three there'd be two more for me. He was that kind of guy.

As the composer, of course my closest collaboration is with the lyricist, followed by the book writer and the director. I also collaborate with actors, too. Every actor has his own set of tricks. I try to find out what the actor can do well and I make sure to write to those strengths. When Jim Dale was learning the score to *Barnum* he came up to my apartment and I asked him if there was something he could do really well. I suspected he had something like that because he was giving me hints. They all do. They hope you can pick up those hints, and they get less and less subtle until you do.

Jim said, "I can recite very quickly and clearly." You can hear that on the *Harry Potter* tapes he later did. So I called Michael Stewart and told him Jim wanted a fast patter song. And he came right back with "Quite a lotta/Roman terra cotta...."

That's collaboration. The whole thing is collaboration. If you can't collaborate you can't do musicals.

BETTY COMDEN AND ADOLPH GREEN

I worked with Betty Comden and Adolph Green on *On the Twentieth Century* and *The Will Rogers Follies*. They had hits going back to *On the Town* and *Singin' in the Rain*, so they were from a slightly older generation. Their composers of choice were Leonard Bernstein and Jule Styne, but then they turned to me. They were charming and fun and wonderful to work with, although they sometimes vacillated on whether they wanted to do a given project or not—even when they proposed it in the first place.

I didn't want to do *On the Twentieth Century* at first. I knew there was a certain perception that the show should have a 1920s score. I didn't mind doing a period piece but it was not a period that I wanted to do. I felt it was too boxlike and confining musically. We talked about doing a lot of different crazy projects. For a while, we talked about doing a Tarzan musical. We kept coming back to *On the Twentieth Century*.

One day we were talking and I was remembering how much I liked Rossini when I was 5 or 6 years old. My piano teacher was Constance Talerico and she had me do a lot of songs from the comic operas of Rossini. I really learned to love it.

Suddenly I thought, that's it! Comic opera! Comic opera is about people whose personalities are magnified, are bigger than life. Well, that's just what the characters in *On the Twentieth Century* are. So if we wrote them, not as 1920s characters but as comic opera characters, I wasn't in a box anymore. In a sense, my music teacher collaborated with me at that moment. Later, Betty and Adolph said it came to all of us. In a collaboration you find you lose a lot of your ideas to somebody else very quickly. You say something and then a week later it will come out of somebody else as something totally new and fresh. You try not to be bitter. If you think it's a good idea, just be happy it landed. That's just the way it works in a collaboration.

On the Twentieth Century was written very fast. I was really getting to explore my love for Rossini—with a little Gilbert and Sullivan thrown in. It was my thing and I just went for it. I was just pouring out music. I wrote so fast that they were afraid we'd lose things, so they kept a tape recorder handy. Whenever I would sit down at the piano, Betty and Adolph would dive for their tape recorder. I loved working like that.

When we were trying out in Boston, I had an idea for the overture. It would sound like a locomotive starting up, building up to full steam, then ending as it comes into the station. I brought a fire extinguisher into the pit so we could have the sound of whooshing steam as part of the orchestration. I was pretty pleased with the idea but Betty and Adolph were afraid it would overshadow and kill our opening number. Being a good collaborator, I said, "OK, I'll try to think of something else." But I couldn't get that idea out of my head.

One day Hal Prince took us all out to eat and he turned to me and said, "Cy, we're in Boston for almost three weeks. Where's the overture?"

I told him I'd had an idea, but Betty and Adolph didn't like it. He asked to hear the idea, and once I explained it, Hal said, "That's fantastic!" Betty and Adolph finally agreed.

David Zippel

With *City of Angels*, I wanted to do a show that really smacked of jazz.

I went to Larry Gelbart to write the book and Larry immediately understood the concept. I picked out a property from the era I wanted: *The Maltese Falcon*. It was totally arbitrary. Larry said, "Why don't we do an original?" I said, "Hey, I love originals! Let's do that!"

He immediately ran into trouble because he was trying to write a straight detective story and I was going to have all the fun of writing my jazz. When he complained, I said, "Let's find a way to make it fun for you, too." That's when he came up with the idea of doing a double story: one story involves a hard-boiled film noir detective, the other involves the guy who is writing the story of the hard-boiled detective. They were alter egos, Stone and Stein.

We found a lyricist who began working on the project, but he wanted to use *Guys and Dolls*–type humor. That's not what we were doing. He wasn't getting it. So we paid him off and began looking for another lyricist.

In the meantime, a young guy named David Zippel, who had several songs with my publishing company, Notable Music, heard we had dropped our lyricist. He called me and said, "I would like to get a shot at this." I tried to talk him out of it, telling him it wasn't really his era and we didn't want to get ourselves in another situation where we had to hand out another payoff.

He said, "I'll tell you what. I'll make a deal with you. I'll write two or three things and if you like them, put me on. If you don't like them, I'll walk."

I called Larry and said I thought Zippel was talented. Larry agreed and it all worked out great. I didn't have to teach him anything. I did things my way, and he got used to that.

Working with David was fine. I could see that he was a talent. I led the way a lot because I knew this music and I wanted to make sure it was going to swing. There are certain phrases that do not swing. Lyricists always want to add an extra syllable to make a rhyme and there are times when you cater to that. Sometimes that extra syllable stops the flow. David had to take my word on that because I'm the guy who knew how to swing. I understood the soul and spirit of the music. He respected that and wrote witty and wonderful lyrics around that. So it worked very well. That, in turn, earned my respect.

That's why I've been able to work with people of all ages. Respect doesn't come with age, necessarily. Respect is earned by achievement.

CHAPTER 4

TERRENCE MCNALLY
LIBRETTIST AND PLAYWRIGHT

Terrence McNally won his fourth Tony Award for the book of the musical *Ragtime*, music and lyrics by Stephen Flaherty and Lynn Ahrens, with whom he also collaborated on the Off-Broadway musical *A Man of No Importance*. McNally won the Tony in 1996 for his play *Master Class*, in which Zoe Caldwell created the role of Maria Callas; the 1995 Tony, Drama Desk, and Outer Critics Circle Awards for Best Play as well as the New York Drama Critics Circle Award for Best American Play for *Love! Valour! Compassion!*; and the 1993 Tony for his book of the musical *Kiss of the Spider Woman* (music and lyrics by John Kander and Fred Ebb). He also served as the book writer for the Broadway musicals *The Full Monty* and *Chita Rivera: The Dancer's Life*. His other plays include *Corpus Christi*; *A Perfect Ganesh*; *Lips Together, Teeth Apart*; *The Lisbon Traviata*, and *It's Only a Play*, all of which began at the Manhattan Theatre Club, plus *The Stendahl Syndrome* and

Dedication or The Stuff of Dreams. Earlier stage works include *Bad Habits*, *Frankie and Johnny in the Claire de Lune*, *The Ritz*, *Where Has Tommy Flowers Gone?*, *And Things That Go Bump in the Night*, *Next*, and the book for the musical *The Rink* (music and lyrics by John Kander and Fred Ebb). For the Central Park opera trilogy presented at the New York City Opera in the fall of 1999, he wrote the libretto for *The Food of Love*, with music by Robert Beaser. The San Francisco Opera presented *Dead Man Walking* with McNally's libretto and music by Jake Heggie. He recently wrote the book for *The Visit*, with a score by Kander and Ebb. McNally has written a number of TV scripts, including "Andre's Mother" for which he won an Emmy Award. He has received two Guggenheim Fellowships, a Rockefeller Grant, a Lucille Lortel Award, and a citation from the American Academy of Arts and Letters. He has been a member of the Dramatists Guild since 1970.

A Blueprint for the House

I find it ironic when people win awards for being the best
playwright or the best this or the best that. Because, really,
every time someone gets an honor in the theatre everybody
involved in the production should be up on the podium.
Theatre is totally collaboration.

I'm a playwright and I have a very healthy ego, but this is a
collaborative art from the get-go. The only thing I do is the
draft of the play. But that's just the
beginning of putting a play on. The
collaboration begins the minute you
turn your script in.

Most people think writing a book
for a musical is like writing a play,
but leaving blanks saying, "She sings
a song expressing her great love for
him." Or, "He sings that he's no
longer emotionally attached to her."
No.

Collaborating on a play is quite
different. My plays are original and
I am the sole author. Everything you

hear was my idea. But when you're working on a musical you must collaborate with the other writers and, as a team, do what's right for "our musical." I'd never talk that way about a play. A play is a very personal extension of who I am. It's a story that never existed until I wrote it, so that's very different.

Nevertheless, it infuriates me when people think that a playwright is "slumming" when he does a musical—that it's playwriting "lite." They should only try writing a book for a musical. I take it very seriously. The five musicals I've done all have very strong emotional resonance. I care about them very deeply.

A librettist has two jobs: to provide structure and inspiration. Handing the first draft of a libretto to your collaborators is like saying, "Here's a blueprint for the house. I suggest this room be painted blue and maybe this room should be baroque." And then the composer and lyricist start decorating it.

The librettist will start by writing a complete scene—usually it's much longer than a scene would be for a play—then will turn it over to the composer and lyricist. They probe through it to find a phrase or a suggestion or an idea that can be turned into a song. Fred Ebb called it "cannibalizing the playwright's libretto."

You try to give them suggestions. But sometimes a line or a phrase or something completely unexpected will trigger a whole other thought. It may have nothing to do with anything already in the scene, but it inspires your collaborator. Then it's your job to reshape the scene around that.

The book writer has to provide a very strong bedrock. If scenes do not go to the heart of the dramatic story, the resulting songs usually will be weak and they'll eventually get cut. If the songwriters can't find any musical idea in the scene at all, then there's probably something wrong with the scene. It may be fine for a play, but not right for a musical.

In modern musicals the songs have to amplify something about the story. In the old shows the songs were just pure entertainment, whether they made sense to the story or not. I saw a revival of *Can-Can* recently. The libretto seemed very flimsy. Great Cole Porter songs, of course, but if you didn't have a great personality like Patti LuPone singing them, I don't think you could sit still. They hardly justify taking up time dramatically. And the story is so silly.

Musicals have changed incredibly. Even by the time I started going to the theatre, *Can-Can* was already old fashioned. The Rodgers and Hammerstein shows like *South Pacific*, *The King and I*, and *Carousel* are still models of serious, intelligent dramaturgy, and they invariably move you. But Porter was never a part of that. He was kind of a relic even then. Porter would write his scores in Paris. The producers would cable him: "Merman wants a ballad for the second act," and he'd write her something like "Down in the Depths on the Ninetieth Floor." And then Porter would come over for opening night.

It doesn't work that way anymore.

I'm always realistic when I go into writing a musical. I love good book scenes and well-rounded characters, but musicals are called *musi*cals for a reason. People go to musicals to hear the music, not the book. Yes, the libretto of a musical is very important. But what you take home is "I Could Have Danced All Night" or "Trouble" or "Some Enchanted Evening."

Which is not to say that a book writer is dispensable. If you don't do your job well, the songwriters' work is in vain. But you are there to serve the music and lyrics, not the other way around. You're fine as long as you accept that what *they* do is, in the end, more important than what *you* do. Understand and accepting that is the essence of being a good book writer and collaborator.

Let's put it in football terms. The librettist is like the center on the team. Yes, the quarterback and halfback are going to do the long dramatic passes and the runs down the field and get their pictures in *Sports Illustrated.* But if the center hadn't defended the quarterback and the halfback, they couldn't have made those long passes and runs.

There aren't any really famous book writers. You are not acknowledged the way you are when you write your own play. It's not the same ego trip. No one says, "Let's go see this show. It's got a book by Terrence McNally!"

Nevertheless, it's a great job because you know Ahrens and Flaherty and Kander and Ebb couldn't have written their great songs if the scenes hadn't been there. So I'm very proud of what I do.

BEING ON THE SAME PAGE

To write a musical, find a book or a movie or an idea or a historical character you love. Part of collaboration is choosing, not only the right project but the right people for the project. Find a composer and lyricist who are reading from the same page as you. Choose your collaborators every bit as carefully as you would choose your spouse.

If you love the world of *Hairspray* and *The Producers*, why would you seek out someone who writes very much in the style of Sondheim? That would be a terrible choice. If you wanted to tell dark interior stories, why would you go to Jerry Herman? Pick the right collaborator for the style of the project.

If I heard that person X was incredibly difficult and treated book writers badly I would not even entertain working with that person. Most of the horror stories you hear about monsters are true. It's immature to think anyone will ever say, "So-and-so was a monster until they worked with Terrence McNally. Terrence turned them into a pussycat!"

I learned long ago that you can't change monsters into pussycats.

You have to be crazy about your collaborator's talent and really enjoy hanging out with them. A lot of theatre is just hanging out with people. Life's too short to waste on people you don't adore.

I adore my collaborators Kander and Ebb (*Kiss of the Spider Woman* and *The Visit*), Ahrens and Flaherty (*Ragtime* and *A Man of No Importance*), and David Yazbek (*The Full Monty*). We are friends. We have lunches and dinners and do things together. And I love working with them.

Everybody in the room has to be "right" to tell that particular story. It can be hard, though. When you hear a really famous name, sometimes you're tempted to work with that person simply because you are dazzled. But that's absolutely the wrong way to choose a collaborator.

Producer Garth Drabinsky did something very unusual on *Ragtime*. I had already written a twenty-page treatment of E. L. Doctorow's novel and we needed to pick a songwriting team—but who? Garth asked five composers to submit songs on spec. Then we listened to tapes of their songs without knowing who had written what. We all listened to them separately. Afterward I remember telling Garth, "Whoever is responsible for tape three is the only one who hears *Ragtime* the way I heard it. Those are the people who were born to do this show."

When I found out it was Lynn Ahrens and Stephen Flaherty, I was delighted. I had seen *Once on This Island* and thought it was a terrific show. Some of the tapes were by people much better known than Lynn and Stephen at that point in their careers. But of the four songs they submitted on that tape, three of them were still in the show that opened on Broadway two years later, which says something about how right they were for it and how we were in sync.

I didn't start writing musicals until I was over 40 and I was wise enough to get involved with good projects.

Your first collaboration is with the creator of the source material. My first collaborator on *Ragtime* was E. L. Doctorow. On *Man of No Importance* and *The Full Monty*, it was with the creators of those screenplays.

By collaborating, I mean honoring the voice of those writers. Doctorow was every bit a collaborator of mine on *Ragtime*, even though I never worked directly with him. With *The Visit*, I collaborated, in a sense, with Friedrich Durrenmatt, even though he's no longer living. Or Manuel Puig on *Kiss of the Spider Woman*—I didn't meet him until the show was up and running. But it was my job to honor their sensibility.

I certainly did not want Puig or Doctorow to go around badmouthing the musicals we had made of their work. Doctorow was very critical of the screen version of *Ragtime*. I didn't want to have that happen with our musical. I respected the tone, the essence of his book. It's an extraordinary novel. Every chapter could be put on stage. Shaping it into a musical, obviously, eighty percent of the book had to vanish. I tried to keep the essential twenty percent. As it turned out, he was very pleased, which pleased me. His main criticism was that he wished every scene from the book could have been in the show. I would have liked that, too, but if we had listened to him, *Ragtime* would have been a full week of five-hour performances.

It's very important that I honor even as light a piece as *The Full Monty*, which began as a film set in the north of England. I made the condition that the action be moved to Buffalo, New York, because I wasn't comfortable writing in the original dialect. Despite the change of locale, I think I stayed true to those characters and to the heart of the piece.

You have to be well suited to the material. For instance, I never could have written *My Fair Lady*. If I'd been offered a chance to make a musical of *Pygmalion* I would have said there's no way these characters sing. If I'd been greedy for the job, just for the chance to work with Lerner and Loewe, I would still have been wrong, because in my heart I would have thought it was not a good idea for a musical. I've certainly turned down nine or ten projects because there was not enough for me to bring to them as a playwright. You have to treat a musical libretto with the same love, attention to detail, patience, and scrupulousness that you apply to a play of your own.

The next step to collaborating on a musical is working with the composing team. Some librettists like to sit in the same room and throw out ideas to each other, and write that way. With all due respect, that's not the way I work. Kander and Ebb, for instance, worked that way with each other, but the three of us almost never sat in a room together and wrote. They did their work when I wasn't there. I did my work when they weren't there. We may have gotten together to talk about what a song could be about. But we didn't all sit in a room and write the show that way. No.

I don't want my collaborators sitting in there when I'm at the word processor. I just get in the subway and go up to see them, or they come here. Sometimes we work in adjacent rooms and we come together to show each other what we've come up with. I bought a piano so the composer can't say, "We can't work at your place." Lynn Ahrens used to live around the corner from me, so that was handy when we were working on *Ragtime*.

Collaborating with Directors

On a play, I begin the collaborative process by giving the script to a director whom I think will direct it well. If a director has too many reservations about it, or doesn't get what I'm trying to do, obviously I go to another director.

A director can make very good suggestions and that's fine. That's collaborating. But when a director starts demanding rewrites, that's not collaborating anymore. That's bullying.

I tend to work with directors who are intelligent. I learn from them. I've worked with most of the top directors in the American theatre. When they say something—"What if...? Could we try this?"—I'm very attentive.

A director is a bad collaborator when they start throwing scripts down and threatening to quit. There is really only one thing to do in a situation like that: you say, "Fine. Go."

Even if you never get to that point, there's still a lot of give and take in any production. Sometimes a director will ask you to do something you may think is ridiculous or wrong, but if you respect your collaborator, you give them the benefit of the doubt. In rehearsal you try it both ways and see which is better. Trial and error. I find that when something is right, everybody just knows.

That's why I say you must choose your collaborators as carefully as you choose a spouse. You need to choose people you will feel comfortable being married to, emotionally and professionally, for perhaps years at a time. Most musicals take a while to get off the ground. They need readings and workshops. In the old days, Ethel Merman could say that if you could have a show ready by Labor Day she'd go into rehearsal. *Gypsy* was written in a matter of months.

I wish we could go back to that because I think good theatre comes out of white-hot deadline pressure and emotion. I think things get workshopped to death now.

As for dramaturgs, what work of art is perfect? Start with Shakespeare. A dramaturg would rip apart Shakespeare. "Why doesn't Gertrude react to what Hamlet says? Gertrude vanishes for a whole hour of the play!" Imagine a dramaturg with Eugene O'Neill. "It's so repetitive!" What makes O'Neill work is you have to sit there for three and a half hours. He didn't write two-hour plays. I don't think that an O'Neill play would even get a reading these days.

I'm really in favor of getting a work up on its feet in front of people who love the theatre.

PRODUCERS

There's a paucity of great producers now. Most Broadway shows have more people producing the show than are in the cast. I like the old days where it was Robert Whitehead, Kermit Bloomgarden, or David Merrick. When you went to a show, you knew it represented the taste of one person.

Garth Drabinsky, who produced *Kiss of the Spider Woman* and *Ragtime*, was a very hands-on producer. I found his passion for the projects kind of wonderful. But Robert Whitehead was also a wonderful producer and he did not work that way.

Garth wanted a giant stereopticon hung over the *Ragtime* stage to give the impression that you were watching the show through it, seeing something from that period. I didn't like it, but Garth insisted. In the end I thought, well, I didn't write that, but it's not the end of the world if the show begins that way. I found out later that it cost $30,000 a week to rig. It was overtime every week. If I'd known what it cost, I would have argued even more.

On the other hand, Robert Whitehead wanted to play a recording of Maria Callas singing "Vissi d'arte" as the audience filed out of the theatre after *Master Class*. I told him that was the corniest thing I'd ever heard. Did he have the right to do it anyway? Probably, because I did not write what happens after the curtain fell. As a producer, I suppose, he could have insisted. But I won that one. Maria Callas did not sing.

I've not had big fights with people. Sometimes my point of view has not prevailed, but I don't consider that a defeat. I've been convinced that their way was better. Or, equally, when my suggestion that we go a certain way prevails, I've simply persuaded people. There's nothing wrong about persuading. Or being persuaded. It sounds so combative to say, "You're going to lose." It's such a collaborative thing that it's hard to put it in those terms.

Sometimes—rarely—you find yourself at an impasse. Your collaborator is adamant. They either refuse to even consider making a change you want, or insist on making a change you don't want. At some point you say, "I am withdrawing from this project" or, "I think you should withdraw."

I don't think you can write scene three of a show if you are not in agreement about scene two. It all comes home to roost if you are not happy with something. We worked a long time on the opening of *Ragtime* and the first number of *A Man of No Importance* and got the show started right. If we hadn't gotten it right we couldn't have gotten to scene two.

Theatre finally has to be one point of view. Many people will tell you the final word should come from the director, but I think it should come from the authors.

I think there were two times in the entire experience of *Ragtime* where I did not get my way in something, or where I saw things a little differently. We had healthy discussions, and finally someone else prevailed. I don't know if it's the heart of collaborating, but you have to be gracious. You have to put your ego to one side.

ACTORS

Sometimes good actors can be wonderful collaborators, especially at a reading. You know right away that the scene is too long or it's not clear or it's not funny.

By the time a play opens an actor knows his character better than the author does. And each actor inhabits his character in a different way. Playwrights learn to respect really good actors. If one says, "I don't need this line," you listen.

All theatre is collaborative, not just musicals. Shakespeare obviously had great actors in the Globe troupe. Chekhov's writing isn't judged any more when *Three Sisters* is done, and there have been plenty of terrible productions of *Three Sisters*. If one of those had been the first production, the play would have vanished.

You walk into *The Producers* with a memory of the movie that we all loved. How is it going measure up to that? It's the responsibility of choosing the right actors. One of the big mistakes people make in the theatre is rushing. A play has to be done right the first time. If you have to wait a little longer to get the right actor, my advice is: wait.

I've written several plays that featured Nathan Lane, notably *Love! Valour! Compassion!* and *The Lisbon Traviata*. Collaborating with Nathan goes like this: "When do you want to have lunch?" We eat. We talk about everything in the world, but not about the play. Zoe Caldwell and I never discussed Maria Callas when we were working on *Master Class*. Why? They just get it. They hear the music I imagined. Our rehearsal talk was, "Where do you want to have dinner?" If you are sitting there with an actress explaining every line, she's probably not the right one to do it.

I had a very unhappy collaboration with Geraldine Page, arguably one of the great American actresses of her time. We were working on a light comedy I had written called *It's Only a Play*, and we were not a good team. She tortured me and I suppose she felt that I tortured her. It was not pleasant. I was much younger then, and when they said Geraldine Page wanted to do my play, I thought, "Oh my God!" But I quickly learned that just because someone is famous and great doesn't mean you will automatically have chemistry with them. And collaboration is all about chemistry.

You have to cast actors who get your sensibility. I wrote many plays for one of my dearest friends, James Coco. He understood my rhythms and my point of view.

In addition to the right actor, you also want a set designer who gets that point of view. Some plays want a really realistic set. Some want something much more poetic. Once I saw a friend's work and the set was so realistic it killed the play. The play clearly was imaginative and didn't want real walls and moons and windows and doors. I couldn't believe how it could be so misunderstood by the designer. But if you choose the right director, you usually get the right designer, too. Good directors choose good designers.

WORKING IN THE DARK

And, finally, the audience is a great collaborator. If a scene is meant to be comic and they are not laughing, it doesn't matter if everyone thought it was hilarious back in the rehearsal room. The audience is telling you it's not funny and something's got to be done.

You can feel an audience get restless when a scene goes on too long. You don't need the *New York Times* critic to tell you it's too long or tedious. People are shifting, shuffling, coughing, and fanning. On the other hand, there's nothing more silent than an audience engrossed in drama or more wonderfully unified than an audience enjoying a comedy. People don't complain about how hot a theatre is when they are enjoying a play. It was pretty hot at the recent Broadway *Long Day's Journey* revival, but nobody was fanning. You could hear a pin drop. That's what I strive for.

CHAPTER 5

Lynn Ahrens and Stephen Flaherty
Lyricist and Composer

Lynn Ahrens and Stephen Flaherty have been writing musicals together since 1982. Broadway: *Ragtime* (Tony, Drama Desk, and Outer Critics Circle awards, two Grammy nominations); *Once on This Island* (Olivier Award, two Tony nominations); *Seussical* (Grammy nomination); *My Favorite Year*; *Chita Rivera: The Dancer's Life*. Off-Broadway: *A Man of No Importance*, *Dessa Rose*, *Lucky Stiff* (Helen Hayes Award). Film: *Anastasia* (two Academy Award nominations, two Golden Globe nominations). Concert: With Voices Raised (Boston Pops). Separately, Flaherty wrote incidental music for *Proposals* and *The Ragtime Symphonic Suite*. Ahrens wrote lyrics for *A Christmas Carol* produced annually at Madison Square Garden for more than a decade, and later adapted for TV. Other television: Emmy Award, four Emmy nominations for songs to *Schoolhouse Rock*.

A Place You Couldn't Find On Your Own

FLAHERTY: Lynn and I met in the fall of 1982. At the time I was writing both music and lyrics. Lynn, who had written some music, had begun focusing on primarily on lyrics. The first time we became aware of one another's work was in the BMI Musical Theatre Workshop.

AHRENS: I was always impressed by Stephen's work, both his music and his lyrics. But I thought, "He doesn't need anybody. He's fine on his own." One day I was standing out on the sidewalk talking to a few people. Stephen hurried by and sort of waved but then yelled over his shoulder, "Hey Lynn, do you want to try writing a song together?" I was flabbergasted because he was this very self-contained, shy entity. For him to make that gesture was very flattering.

We wrote a song about two people placing ads in the *Village Voice* personals. I had worked with a number of wonderful composers, but when I sat down at a piano with Stephen Flaherty something special happened. He took this silly little lyric that I'd written and put his hands on the keys very thoughtfully and started to give the words their voice. He had a special connection with the words. I remember thinking, "This is it. Now I get it. I've found that collaborator."

There is a wonderful synergy between us: because he has written lyrics, he has a knowledge and sensitivity to words. And because I've written music, I know what he will be looking for and what he will respond to. We inform each other in that way.

FLAHERTY: We became each other's editor. I was taking what she was giving to me, responding to it, molding it, and adding my own ideas, and then throwing it back to her. And vice versa.

When we first met we worked in very different ways. I was used to locking myself away and scoring everything out, which was more the way classical composers work. Lynn worked in a much more improvisational manner. It really was interesting to shake things up and find a new way to approach my own writing. That new energy is something you try to find in a collaborator. You want somebody who is both complementary and yet leads you down paths you might not have taken on your own. I don't know if that's something that can be taught. A lot of it is mysterious. A lot of it is alchemy.

AHRENS: It would be like a class in how to get married. I don't think it would work.

FLAHERTY: What makes a good collaboration is like what makes a good marriage. Working as a team is about...

AHRENS: It's personality, it's ego, it's...

FLAHERTY: ...shared artistic interests...

AHRENS: ...shared artistic interests. And a shared sense of humor. In our case bodily time clocks factor in as well because I'm a morning person and he's a night person—at least, he used to be.

FLAHERTY: At the time we met, I was earning my living as a working musician. I was playing in pit orchestras or playing around town and I'd get home after midnight. So I got used to giving my biggest shot of energy late in the day. It became a challenge just finding a time and place to work together.

AHRENS: I work on my own starting first thing in the morning and I get a lot done. Then we get together for a work session around 11 a.m. I tend to pass out around 4 p.m. So 11 to 4 p.m. is a good time for us. And then he goes and works on his own.

FLAHERTY: I recently discovered that writing in the morning is actually a very good time for me since I seem to have an easier access to more subconscious ideas then. During sleep my ideas seem to gestate and evolve. It's then my job to gather those ideas each morning as they make themselves known.

BECOMING THE CHARACTER

FLAHERTY: Writing for the theatre is about shedding your own personality and your own skin and becoming the character. You need to find a way to become less self-conscious and stop yourself from thinking, "I'm sitting in a room at a keyboard." You have to get right with the emotion, right with the character, and right with the dramatic situation.

AHRENS: That applies to collaboration in a larger sense. Somebody said something to me a long time ago and it stuck in my head: check your ego at the door. Writing is not about showing off. It's about trying to subsume yourself within a character and let that character speak truly and emotionally.

That also applies to how you work with your partner, with your director, with all the people with whom you have to collaborate. It's really easy if you come in with the attitude that what is important is the *show*.

For instance, sometimes you fall in love with a particular piece of writing: "This is the greatest lyric I've ever written! I can never be more brilliant than this!" But eventually you have to assess it in terms of how it fits in the whole piece. If it doesn't work for one reason or another—and we've had that experience a number of times—you just throw it out. You have to have the humility and trust to turn to your collaborators and say, "How do we solve this moment?" You must always keep your eye on the most important thing, which is the show and not your own pride.

WORKING WITH A STRONG DIRECTOR

AHRENS: The director should be the center of command on a show. Everybody should go to the director. The director should be the conduit for the business side as well as for the artistic side. Even if the producer has a problem with something we've written, we generally feel he or she should filter it to us through the director. It's our job to assess it and try to solve it and improve it. And if we can't, we have to tell the director that we can't. If a director isn't the focal point, the whole operation turns into a Tower of Babel. We've had that situation. It gets very complicated and very bad. The creative team needs to be a cohesive unit with the director as the leader.

FLAHERTY: A good director is a good sounding board. That was certainly the case with Frank Galati on *Ragtime*. We wrote the show in big sections, maybe twenty minutes at a time, and there were times when we'd write ourselves up a cliff, wondering how to get to the next dramatic beat. We would meet Galati at regular intervals and play through these chunks. Sometimes just getting the right sentence from Frank created a link that allowed us to find our way into the next section.

AHRENS: However, we've never had the experience where the director had the absolute final word, per se, on our writing. There was never a "This is how its going to be. I am laying down the law. We're doing it this way." I don't think I would ever want that experience. However, we keep a tremendously open mind to what the director is seeing. And we like the director to keep a tremendously open mind to what we are writing and what we have already written, and try their best to interpret what seems to work. If something doesn't work we are grateful for any suggestions as to how to make it work. And we're especially grateful when they have an idea that we hadn't even thought of.

For instance, on *A Man of No Importance*, were writing a song for the main character, Alfie Byrne, in Act Two. We just could quite manage to figure out this one moment. Director Joe Mantello said, "I keep seeing him in Confession. We don't have a confessional scene and it's so integral to that whole Roman Catholic world. I think there is something to be found in there."

So we wrote two or three confession songs and we ended up with the song that's in the show, "Confession," which walks a fine line between emotion, fantasy, and comedy. It's a lovely moment. We knew he was right. We just kept going until we found what felt right to us as well.

FLAHERTY: Being an Irish Catholic myself, I was so excited about writing something about Confession because I knew I had a lot of personal experience in that area. The first song that we wrote for that moment was basically an out-and-out comedy number. It was very funny. I personally think there is a lot of humor in Confession, in the situation. But Joe Mantello felt that there were other emotional layers and a dramatic point that could, and probably should, be made at that moment, and we weren't hitting it. I saw that he was right. So we wrote song number two, which was a very dark, almost brooding, Irish purging about Confession. It turned out, that wasn't correct tonally either, because there were elements in our first impulse that were correct. So we started again and wound up with a number that does have a lot of humor in it, but also a lot of humanity. It's much more character-oriented and combines the best of the first two songs. It also provides a great pay-off in Act Two.

AHRENS: That's the give and take of collaboration. Plays and musicals stem from writers' minds and hearts—the book writer, the composer, and the lyricist. Everybody else who comes in on the process forms a second layer of collaboration, and that includes the director, even great directors like Mantello or Galati or Graciela Daniele. They enhance, interpret, and help further the creation—the physical production—of the show. It would be weird to have somebody say, "No you can't to do that," because it's our work to start with, our voice.

FLAHERTY: Theatre is really different from film in that respect. A film director, if he's a known quantity, always gets the final cut. Theatre, on the other hand, is truly a collaboration between director, the writers, and the designers.

AHRENS: In our first Broadway musical, *Once on This Island*, we had written the show in a rather presentational way. It was all there, very well structured...

FLAHERTY: ...Very *Story Theatre*...

AHRENS: Very *Story Theatre*. And the director, Graciela Daniele said she wanted to try an experiment. She took a little girl and put her in the center of a circle and had the show's characters tell the show to the little girl. Suddenly it wasn't us telling the grownup audience. It was the characters telling a little girl, which made the whole show more like a fairy tale or a bedtime story. Not a word of what we wrote was changed by doing that, but that little touch transformed what we had written.

FLAHERTY: The theme of the show was storytelling, why we tell stories, the importance of storytelling and the idea of passing stories from one generation to another.

AHRENS: So, in one stroke, Graciela's collaborative notion made the show into the thing it really wanted to be all along. The best collaborators are always thinking, "What does this show want to be? How can we all, as one team, best come up with that?" Graciela always says, "I am here to interpret."

FLAHERTY: Which is not to say that we didn't change anything on *Once on This Island*.

AHRENS: We had a beautiful song called "When Daniel Marries Me," but we had to cut it.

FLAHERTY: I would say it was a group decision.

AHRENS: It's always a group decision, but it starts as somebody's idea.

FLAHERTY: It's a beautiful song and it was hard to give up, especially for our leading lady, LaChanze. She was absolutely brilliant in the role and it was her eleven o'clock number. But it became clear at that point in the show that the audience was well ahead of her character.

AHRENS: I could see the audience twitching and looking at their watches and their *Playbills* during that song because everyone already figured out that Daniel *wasn't* going to marry her. They could see what was coming next. So, as lovely and as good as the work in it was, it had to go. Sometimes I cut too quickly. Stephen sees the integrity of each moment and I tend to see the broader shape of the show.

FLAHERTY: I think that's a good thing.

AHRENS: It *is* a good thing. I think that's part of our personalities and why we work so well together.

FLAHERTY: We have a pretty good idea of when an idea can be developed further—and when it can't. It's bad for a collaboration when someone passes final judgement on something before it's fully fledged, and cutting it before you've seen how far it can be developed. The flip side of that coin is when you know something is no good, but someone insists, "First, let's see how it plays in front of an audience."

AHRENS: You get to a point where you just know something's not going to work. Then you put it in front of an audience and, sure enough, it doesn't work. In the meantime, you've lost your rehearsal time to fix it or you have to fix it at the expense of other things that need to be fixed even more. Some collaborators are touchy. Some get cranky. You have to negotiate a lot of personalities. We've had banging on tables. None of that is helpful.

FLAHERTY: A lot of it depends on how you present the idea. That's an important lesson I learned from my early workshop days. How you make a point is as important as the point. If you have a good criticism but present it in a lacerating way, it can cause that person to turn off and shut down.

AHRENS: But it's crucial that you be open and honest. You just have to learn kindness and respect if you really want your ideas to get across. Also, you need to pick what are the most important points to make.

Here is my technique when one of my shows is in rehearsals. I bring a yellow pad and take lots and lots of notes every day. But I don't say a thing the first day. The next day I sit there again, and this time, I cross out the ones that the director and actors have solved on their own. The third day, more and more get addressed and crossed out. Maybe a new one will crop up but basically you whittle down your initial list. If any are still on the list at the end of the week, then I'll go to the director and say, "I've had a thought...."

Some people think they have to say everything that pops into their head. If you are the big-mouth writer who keeps being unhappy with every little thing, that's pretty much guaranteed to get you thrown out of the room. You have to let people do the work.

WORKING WITH A LIBRETTIST

FLAHERTY: There is another collaboration that must be mentioned: the book writer. It's an exciting thing to bring a third person into our collaboration. It's another viewpoint.

AHRENS: It starts with a meeting. You all need to sit down in the same room and figure out how you are going to tell your story—and to make sure you're all telling the same story. Stephen and I will be telling it in music and lyrics; the librettist will be telling it in words. Generally we start by deciding what the beginning is going to be, what's the end of Act One going to be. How do we start Act Two and how do we end Act Two? You set up these goal posts for yourself. Some times the librettist may come up with a scene first, sometimes we come up with a song first. But we generally sit in the same room plotting out the bold strokes of how the thing will lay out and certainly where those key moments have to be. And then we evolve from there.

On *Ragtime* librettist Terrence McNally joined us for weeks of very intensive sitting together and talking: Where does this go? What happens here? How do we get from here to here? That show was really hard to write because there were three main stories and you had to keep a lot of balls up in the air. But we just kept having meetings and kept trying things. Terrence is very giving. He'll be very relaxed about letting us take a scene he's written and making a portion of it into a song, using only a line or two of his text as the lead-in. Sometimes Stephen would come up with a musical notion which would then inspire Terrence to write something else. We were all working back and forth. As the lyricist, I consider myself the "bridge" between the bookwriter and the composer. I try to make us all join seamlessly into one voice—the voice of the character.

FLAHERTY: A lot of people don't understand a very important thing about writing music for the theatre: the composer's job is not just writing the melodies and harmonies. A composer has to be a dramatist first. My language happens to be music. I try to find ways to use music to bring dramatic ideas together. For example, the song "Journey On" in *Ragtime* builds on a small transition in E. L. Doctorow's original novel. The character of Father is sailing out from New York harbor and sees an immigrant ship coming in, which contains Tateh, who will become one of the other principals of the evening. Making it into a duet dramatized both their different takes on life, but also linked the two characters in a way that paid off powerfully later in the show, when one man winds up with the other one's wife. If you can create ways for the characters to be singing their ideas simultaneously, the audience is then able to feel the emotional link between them.

WHEN ONE OCTAVE ISN'T ENOUGH

AHRENS: We write certain songs in advance, which are needed to tell the story. But once casting has taken place, we also write some songs with the particular actor's voice in mind.

55

In the novel of *Ragtime*, the character of Sarah has no dialogue; there is nothing to reveal her but her actions. I remember seeing Audra McDonald, who played Sarah in the first reading of *Ragtime* (and later on Broadway), just sitting there while everybody else was singing, and we realized we hadn't given her any material. We thought, "Here we have Audra McDonald in the room. We better give her something to sing or we're stupid!" We hadn't fully paid attention to the character of Sarah before. We wrote "Your Daddy's Son" in one day and she learned it on the same day and it was presented to our producer on the same day. It was thrilling. We had learned her voice so well and knew where she could go with it, that we could write a song that was right for the character of Sarah, but tailored to the skills of the actress playing the role.

I've heard of composers who don't like changing keys—

FLAHERTY: —"It's A-flat, dammit, and that's where it's going to stay!"—

AHRENS: —but I don't understand that attitude. It's self-destructive. The actors are your friends and also tools of the production and they are going to make your work shine if they shine. We're always looking for their "money" notes, the ones they do especially well. We also try to be aware of what they *can't* do well, and write in a way that protects them so that they'll look good even if they can't sing all that well or hold long notes or whatever the problem may be.

FLAHERTY: Audra is a Juilliard-trained mezzo soprano. I don't think I would have written the kind of song "Your Daddy's Son" is without knowing that Audra was going to be singing it. Knowing her voice allowed me to write music with larger vocal gestures that was more operatic in scope. Vocally, that song is one note short of two octaves, which, for a theatre song, is quite a wide range.

AHRENS: She sounds great, of course, but it does makes it tough to cast that role. Not that we haven't had other great Sarahs, but it's been hard to find them.

FLAHERTY: Still, it was really terrific to work with someone who had the vocal instrument to fully explore the emotional landscape of that song. I would have been hard-pressed to write that kind of dramatic moment with a smaller range. They're not the kind of emotions that one octave could contain.

AHRENS: We've worked with many actors over the years. And you learn that actors are human beings. They are wonderful. They can be needy. Some of them are brilliant and will come to you and say, "I have a thought about this character, and its not because I want another song." Other times you have to deal with an actor who really does just want another big song, whether or not it's right for the show. You learn to negotiate those shoals and bumps. Hopefully, while you're keeping your focus on what's best for the show, you can also accommodate their needs, so they become collaborators in a different kind of way.

FLAHERTY: Of course, when you are writing for a star you are dealing with other issues too. For instance, you have to deal with audience expectations. If your star is one of the all-time greatest dancers in the American theatre, you'd better write them a big dance number somewhere. But it becomes a balancing act. I've seen many musicals where the big dance break in Act Two derails the drama because it doesn't come organically out of the dramatic scene or the needs of the show at that moment.

AHRENS: If the producer has brought them in to sell tickets, well, dealing with that is part of your collaboration with the producers. Obviously they have needs and deserve to be heard. We try to make sure it's the right star and that we can tailor the musical material to make that actor look good. We've never been told that we had to write a particular song for a particular star, but we have been asked very nicely! If the idea seems worthwhile, we'll always explore it. If it really seems bad, we have to go back and say so. But we usually try to offer an alternative idea.

That's what collaboration is. It's being open and honest to other people's ideas and hoping they'll be the same way to you. Collaboration is being able to voice your concerns and sometimes, very occasionally, plant your feet. You have to pick and choose your battles. If it's something that you really think is going to harm the show or is something that's distasteful or awful, then you stand your ground. But oftentimes, if you think about it and try to solve the problem creatively, you can find a solution that you do like.

I really do feel that producers have to be able to express themselves to the creative team. They have a huge stake in a show so they have the right to express their concerns, their problems, their confusions, their fears. But they shouldn't dictate the solutions to us.

FLAHERTY: That's not their job.

AHRENS: Our job is to come up with solutions and make the show work for everyone involved. And you can't forget that, ultimately, the show has to work for the audience as well. It's a performance medium, after all.

The Last Collaborator

FLAHERTY: Graciela Daniele has a famous saying: "The audience is the last collaborator."

AHRENS: Our very first show together was a children's show for TheatreWorks USA. It was an incredible learning experience. Sometimes a thousand children would be sitting there watching our show. And they let us know, in the first five minutes, exactly how they felt about what they were seeing. If kids are bored, they stand up, they yell, they run up the aisles, they throw food, they go to the bathroom, they talk to each other. But if they like it, they pay attention, they are silent, they sit forward and they are rapt. Thanks to that experience, we learned how to read an audience and use their reaction to help us figure out where to cut, where to clarify.

Adults are exactly the same way. Oh, they may have learned not to throw food and run up the aisles. But what's happening in their heads is exactly the same thing.

The whole point of writing is the fun of taking things that are emotional and meaningful to you and finding a way to connect with a room full of strangers. If they are not getting it, if it's going too fast, if it's too loud, not clear, boring, not landing in the right way—

FLAHERTY: —or not truthful—

AHRENS: —you can sense it. At the first preview of *Once on This Island*, I was sitting in the back in Playwrights Horizons and you could hear a pin drop. It was silent practically from beginning to end. I started to get this horrible sinking feeling. I thought they were just sitting there hating it. But at the end they leaped to their feet and screamed. And I suddenly thought, "Oh I get it. They were paying attention." They were listening hard. They absorbed the accents. They absorbed the culture. They got it and they were completely rapt to the very end. It was very thrilling to experience that.

FLAHERTY: Another thing I've learned from the audience is about applause. Applause is about emotional and psychological release. I think one of the reasons that *Once on This Island* really works and gets that huge burst of applause at the very end comes partly from the way the show is constructed. In the last twenty minutes there isn't a single applause break. It goes from one musical moment to another to another. We don't allow the audience to blow off steam.

I was invited to a dress run-through of the *Follies* concert with the New York Philharmonic. They were going to record it live in performance. At the dress run-through they needed to get very clean beginnings and endings and also an extra take available if something didn't go right in the live performance. We were a large group of people watching this. It was tremendously emotional not only because of the material but also the stars who were performing the material. We were not allowed to clap. By the end of Act One, I was a basket case. I was just drenched. And that's when I first realized: that's what applause is for. You have to expel the energy. Knowing that, you can guide the audience emotionally and dramatically through the terrain that you need to cover.

AHRENS: You don't want them clapping after every number because then they get exhausted.

FLAHERTY: Or its breaks their absorption in the story. Giving them just enough breaks for applause is an important way that we, as theatre writers, collaborate with the audience.

A Common Language

FLAHERTY: If you want to be a good collaborator in the theatre, find out as much as you can about everybody else's job. If you are a composer, study painting, study playwriting. Learn to sing, even if you can't sing. Take an acting class. Try to understand what everybody's processes are. Listen to every kind of music. Take as many classes in the corresponding disciplines.

The important thing in a successful collaboration to find a common language. Composers count in beats of music. Dancers count in counts of eight. Directors count in seconds and minutes. Film directors count frames. Open your mind. It enriches your own life as well.

AHRENS: Stephen and I have been working together for more than twenty years. We've had our disagreements, we've had our annoyances, we've had our fights. But the bottom line is we've been respectful and open with one another.

The essence of collaboration is being kind, being respectful, and being open. If you can't do that, or you find you're not getting that, end it. It's like any relationship: if it doesn't feel right say thank you so much, and move on. If it does feel right, cling to it, and try to develop it.

FLAHERTY: The interesting thing about working over time as a team is that the team develops and changes and goes through ups and downs. As an individual, your own personal interests are changing and developing and something that might be right for one collaborator at a given time isn't necessarily right for the other collaborator at that same time. For example, Lynn found *Dessa Rose*, the novel, in 1993. I wasn't ready to write that show then. The novel was a very difficult read. I couldn't see in it what Lynn saw.

AHRENS: So I bided my time.

FLAHERTY: Lynn didn't force the issue, but she had a vision of what the piece could be. So I said to her, "Is there some way you can let me into your head?" Lynn took some time off and she wrote virtually a complete act, almost like an opera libretto.

AHRENS: Which I had never done.

FLAHERTY: It wasn't our way of working. Usually we work together in the same room or back and forth. This was a totally different kind of piece. I needed to understand it clearly and emotionally. Once I saw Lynn's libretto, I got it. After ten years, I felt it was absolutely the right piece to be working on. After that, the music came very quickly and very fluidly.

A young writer once asked me, "How do you deal with it if your collaborator says, 'I hate that melody'?"

I replied, "First of all, you don't say, 'I hate that melody.' Even if you do hate the melody, you can't speak to your collaborator like that." You both have to respect one another's ideas and learn how to give criticism in a supportive way.

I think our most exciting collaborations come when I have a strong idea, and when Lynn has a strong idea. They are not necessarily the same idea. The interaction of those ideas creates—not exactly a hybrid—but an exciting, unexpected piece that involves words and music and character that I don't think that either one of us would have come up with on our own. I think that's what makes a good collaboration. That's the exciting thing. The dynamic of two people working together leads you to a place that you couldn't find on your own.

Part II

CAPTAINS

CHAPTER 6

GERALD SCHOENFELD
THEATRE OWNER

Gerald Schoenfeld is chairman of the Shubert Organization, which has been in the forefront of the American theatre since the start of the 20th Century, operating theatres in New York, Boston, Philadelphia, and Washington, D.C. The firm's notable productions and co-productions include *Cats*, *Sunday in the Park with George*, *Dreamgirls*, *The Grapes of Wrath*, *Little Shop of Horrors*, *The Heidi Chronicles*, *Jerome Robbins' Broadway*, *The Life and Adventures of Nicholas Nickleby*, *Song and Dance*, *Lettice and Lovage*, *Dancin'*, *Amadeus*, *The Gin Game*, *An Inspector Calls*, *Chess*, *Passion*, *Indiscretions*, *Closer*, *Amy's View*, *The Blue Room*, *The Ride Down Mt. Morgan*, *Dirty Blonde*, and *Dance of Death*. The Shubert Organization pioneered the reclamation of Times Square and is dedicated to the revitalization of the American theatre. In 2005, Broadway's former Plymouth Theatre was renamed the Gerald Schoenfeld Theatre in his honor.

The Theatres Remain

The Shubert Organization owns or manages sixteen and one-half Broadway theatres, more than any other company. We are very aware of our responsibilities as stewards of these buildings, many of which are approaching their hundredth year of operation. We think of ourselves as much more than landlords. We also co-produce many of the attractions that appear at our theatres. And we try to be very involved in all the shows we host, whether we co-produce them or not.

In both the area of managing theatres and the area of producing, the Shubert Organization is confronting some serious challenges. Nevertheless, we collaborate with the people of Broadway in various ways.

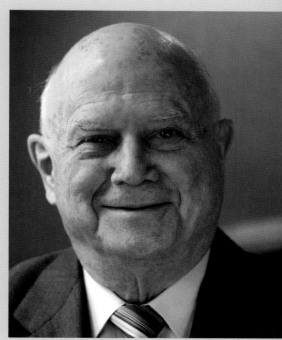

I have no reservations about giving producers my views of their show that we intend to book, or that we are interested in. First of all, I have to make sure all the business aspects of the production are in place. I don't want to be left hanging there with an empty theatre, being told that they didn't raise the money, or that they suddenly could not get some key cast member, or that they decided to make structural changes in the script. So we collaborate to that extent. We compel them to act like responsible businesspeople—or they don't get a theatre.

We like to know the creative team for shows coming into our theatres, and managers and the press agent, and the cast and the advertising agency, and we may give comments about some of those elements. But, unless we are co-producing, it's basically not our show. Our role is advisory. We're not a part of the decision-making process. We cannot veto any of those things. We can just give our opinions, and I think our opinions are worthwhile because we've been at it for quite a while.

We certainly do want to know who the creative people are. We want to know who is going to be the producer, and who is going to be running the show. And it's gotten harder to track that. More and more, you see shows produced by consortiums. In my opinion, consortiums of fifteen people are not productive. You can't run a show by committee. That doesn't mean we won't work with partners. We do have partners and they are very participatory. But they are few. If there are very many in others' productions, we like to see that they have a lead producer who is knowledgeable about the business.

There are two kinds of experience you need to succeed: the creative kind and the business kind. Many people in the business today are new, and lack one or both kinds of experience. We look carefully at potential general managers of a show to see if they have the right combination of the two.

It's the responsibility of the general manager of the show to protect the theatre building as well as the show. A properly run show can make a lot of money. But an improperly run show has the capacity to cost both the producer and the theatre owner a lot of money by incurring expenses that shorten the run, such as profligate promotion and advertising. Or by engaging in activities which may subject the theatre to risk because the show doesn't have enough advance sales to pay its costs. Theatres must be properly maintained, repaired, and updated to meet building and safety codes. We're pretty vigilant about protecting the physical venue in that regard.

We have to do it. Producers come and go. I came and someday I will go. But the theatres remain. A long time ago this was called a "combination business." Broadway was dominated by great theatre owners who produced shows for their own theatres, which they tended carefully. Daniel Frohman is perhaps the best example. Some of these owner-managers were playwrights as well, and wrote many hits for their playhouses. We now own some of the best-known of these, and they retain the names of the people who built them: the Belasco Theatre for

David Belasco, the Broadhurst for George H. Broadhurst, the Cort for John Cort, etc.

You can't replace these theatres. Economically, they cannot be replaced without some help from government.

And I'm not talking about handouts. New York government collaboration on support or assistance for Broadway's theatres is almost non-existent. Most Broadway theatres are between eighty and one hundred years of age. The only new theatres that have been built are the result of some form of subsidy, whether by zoning incentives to the developer, or low interest loans (with respect to renovation of the New Amsterdam Theatre), or federal urban development grants that resulted in the Gershwin, the Minskoff and the Marquis. All of these were the products of subsidy.

Yet the older venues are expected to continue to exist with no help at all. As it was explained to me by Mayor Edward Koch, "Why should we help you? You can't move!"

Producers also refuse to pay a penny more in rent for a newly renovated theatre than for an old, unrenovated theatre.

These venues were built for another period, built for a different state of the art, built for people of different shapes and sizes. And they are expected not only to continue to function, but also to be maintained, despite their age, and regardless of cost. We try to keep them booked and beautiful, but government is one area where collaboration ought to exist, but doesn't. The burden of maintaining these theatres is on the theatre owner, and there is no form of assistance of any kind.

Sometime we will agree to allow the reconfiguration of one of our theatres. We did it for *Candide* at the Broadway Theatre in the 1970s, and for *Cats* at the Winter Garden in the 1980s. Those shows paid for that. Any time a producer wants the stage trapped or special things installed, there is a fee. Not only must the work be done, but the theatre must be restored to its original state afterward.

Producers agree to that. On the other hand, if we put in new rigging, we put in new light trusses, put in enhanced bathroom facilities, new seats, new carpets, etc., producers don't want to see that reflected in the rent at all. Now, if I told you that I would refurbish your apartment, you would expect to pay a higher rent. Not so on Broadway.

Also, we are expected to pay for upkeep of our landmarked theatres. The marquee of the Lyceum Theatre is landmarked, Its wavy design is very expensive to maintain, But we cannot change it because it is landmarked, and we get no money from the city to care for it.

The Rules Are Changing

The producer should be the ultimate boss of a show. He's not necessarily the creative boss, but the producer ought to run the show. Unfortunately, respect for the producer by the other people in the show has been substantially diminished because of a lack of assertiveness on the part of the producer. It's a gravitational shift.

Nothing is more complicated than a musical. For a musical to succeed there has to be someone in charge. People have to know whose word is final, or else there is chaos. A producer must have respect for the director, respect for the cast and respect for the designers. But a producer must make it clear that he or she is the boss.

The rules of collaboration have changed over the past four decades, because few collaborative teams are still in existence—especially among the newer people. You don't have Rodgers and Hammerstein or Rodgers and Hart or Lerner and Loewe or Bock and Harnick and so on. There once were playwriting teams as well, like Hecht and MacArthur, Lindsay and Crouse, and Lawrence and Lee. All gone, or nearly.

Today you mostly have a separate music writer and a separate lyricist and a separate book writer. After a show, they move on to collaborate with others. So you don't get the same kind of continuity, or, for that matter, the same number of shows. Collaboration is a discipline, and few young people coming up today are learning how to do it.

The producer used to be very actively involved in working with the writers, both in finding or initiating a project, and then making sure it evolved into the kind of work they wished to produce. They collaborated to the extent that they would discuss ideas with their writers, and visa versa. Nowadays the conceptual process takes different routes. For instance, writers often independently create a work, then bring it to a producer and expect the producer to involve a director. Or the writer may initially work with a director and then bring it to a producer.

Rise of the Director

The most notable development in collaboration today is the abdication of the traditional prerogatives of producers and writers to those of the director.

Contracts still provide for approval by the producer, and still protect the creations of the writers. But in practice everyone defers to the director, especially on musicals. Many aspects of musicals that used to be less significant have become extremely significant, such as the production design, such as the casting, such as the decisions about rewriting and new material going in. Because all these elements need to be coordinated, the director becomes the final arbiter and the master collaborator. At one time, it was the producer, whose power came from writing the checks. But today a unified artistic vision has become all-important. The center of power moved from the writers and producers to the director.

Also today, with the risks being as high as they are, producers have to organize staged readings or workshops, then regional theatre productions, etc. All that requires casting and a lot of other elements that ordinarily would not have been organized until later in the process. Because a lot of the younger producers and writers aren't familiar with the performing talent out there, they turn to a director who has worked with a lot of different people. As a result, all the actors and designers owe their jobs to the director, not the producer or the writers. And another element of control falls into the director's hands.

I'm not sure this is a good development. I would be happy to abdicate creativity to Jerome Robbins or Michael Bennett or a small number of their colleagues. But I would feel frustrated if I did that with most others. I don't want to single anyone out. The trend is much bigger than one or two people.

I had a chance to observe Jerome Robbins up close for three years when we did *Jerome Robbins' Broadway*, and everyone who worked with him were of one mind: he was the meanest, most difficult person they ever worked with—but he was a genius. Tough. He didn't care whether they liked him or not.

Michael Bennett was much easier to get along with, but he was very tough, too, in his own way. An actor came to me once to complain that Michael had promised him a part in *A Chorus Line*, and then reneged. I asked Michael if he had made that promise, and Michael said, "Yes, I did, but I don't care whether I did or I didn't. The actor wasn't right for the show, and I was wrong."

There are those who don't take kindly to suggestions from the Shubert Organization. When I do offer suggestions I'm not necessarily seeking to put my personal imprimatur on a show. But I am interested in having my views heard and discussed. If I don't get that kind of satisfaction from somebody who has not reached a level where I'm comfortable abdicating, I certainly will speak up.

Why is it that authors and producers have abdicated their decision-making power? I'm not a historian, but I have witnessed a fair sweep of Broadway history. Let's look at that history. This development is tied to the emergence of the director/choreographer, which started really with people like Jerry Robbins. We had a period of time where there was a number of excellent director/choreographers who delivered many hits. The choreographer started off as a member of the dance chorus, and then that person became the dance captain, then became the assistant choreographer, and then the choreographer. Then the natural extension of that was to become a director/choreographer so all stage movement was directed to a purpose.

All this makes directors stronger bosses, but not necessarily better collaborators. I once asked Jerome Robbins, "Why did you leave Broadway after *Fiddler on the Roof*?" He said, "No collaborators." He liked to do everything, and would have done everything on a show, if he could have.

Bob Fosse is another one who loved to do it all. Direct, choreograph, write the script—all aspects of creativity, except one. He needed a producer to put up the money to do it.

The role of the dance in a musical has changed. The role of the choreographer is now different. The choreographer's job is to tell the story through dance. There are few today who are able to do that in a way that communicates to a broad public. You also had pure Broadway choreographers who didn't tell stories, but their signature steps were such that they created brilliant pieces of dancing, novelty dancing, acrobatic dancing. They were unique.

A number of musicals today have less dancing in them than was common many years ago. That's especially true of some of the musicals from England, *Cats* excepted.

The trouble is, today we have very few top-drawer director/choreographers. There are only a few names you can go to. And those names have the power to dictate terms.

The director now regards himself or herself as somebody whose work is separate yet integral to the work. They believe their contribution is copyrightable. Not only do they expect financial participation in the work over time, but creative participation. They want to say you cannot separate their work from the material, and cannot present the material without their staging. That's something new.

I'm not saying this was a plot of any kind. I think it just evolved. It's a result of the complexity of the musical work. Collaborating on a musical was easier in the past, when there were fewer collaborators and the financial stakes were not so high. Now it is much more difficult and requires a commanding general.

A star director may come onto a project and immediately tell the creators, "We're going to start making changes. I know the Dramatists' Guild says you control the script, but if I'm going to direct, we need to make some changes. If you don't trust my judgment, let me know and you can get another director."

So what do the writers say? "OK, we trust your judgment."

This would be wonderful thing if, as a result of that shift, we had hit after hit after hit. But we don't necessarily see that.

Producers have been conditioned to rely on directors, too. Agents for directors have begun asking for a share of authors' royalties, and some authors have acquiesced.

I've never made an analysis of how many successes each director has had with musicals. I've never tallied up Hal Prince's credits against Morton DaCosta's or Joshua Logan's. But directors of musicals are not as consistently successful as they used to be.

And it comes at a time, ironically, when producers and authors are increasingly allowing their work to be dominated and controlled by directors. If a director says, "I don't think this song is working, I want a rewrite," the author can legally and contractually say, "I am not rewriting that song, I don't agree with you." But I don't think that happens very often.

BE ON THE GROUNDS

I'd like to end with a few words of advice for aspiring producers: be on the grounds of your show as much as you can, especially at show time. Let everybody get to know your face. Be prepared to do anything you're asked to do.

If you find someone in the business you really respect, try to have them become your mentor because only then will you have people pay attention to you.

One last thing: if you don't love what you're doing and it starts to seem like work to you, find something else to do.

CHAPTER 7

ROCCO LANDESMAN
PRODUCER

Rocco Landesman has been the President of Jujamcyn Theaters since 1987, and a partner in Dodger Theatricals. He has served as lead producer or associate producer on many Broadway shows, including *The Producers*, which won more Tony Awards (twelve) than any show in history. Broadway productions include *Angels in America*; *Gem of the Ocean*; *Caroline, Or Change*; *Sixteen Wounded*; *Into the Woods*; *Big River*; *City of Angels*; *Urinetown*; *42nd Street*; *Proof*; *The Music Man*; *The Civil War*; *Death of a Salesman*; *Footloose*; *High Society*; *Titanic*; *A Funny Thing Happened on the Way to the Forum*; *Seven Guitars*; *Moon Over Buffalo*; *Smokey Joe's Café*; *The Who's Tommy*; *Guys and Dolls*; *The Secret Garden*; *The Piano Lesson*; *The Young Man From Atlanta*; and *Pump Boys and Dinettes*. Prior to becoming a producer, he taught dramatic literature and criticism at the Yale School of Drama. He has written articles and reviews for many publications, including the *New York Times* and the *Wall Street Journal*. He serves on the boards of the Municipal Art Society, The Actors' Fund, and the Times Square Business Improvement District. He also serves as pitcher on the three-time champions of the Broadway Show League, the softball team from *The Producers*.

The Potential for Greatness

The producer is in charge of the show. Ultimately he has the authority to hire and fire. He controls the money, so he controls everything that happens with the production.

Producers on Broadway serve two not always distinct functions. A producer can *originate a project*, which means he thinks it up and then goes out and hires the different component elements to put it together. He'll choose and hire the book writer, the lyricist, the composer and the director. This kind of project is put together at the initiative of the producer, and this was largely the way business was done years ago. It is the most creative kind of producing.

A producer can also *adopt a project* that is already in development by the writers. With the advent of workshops and readings, as well as a dearth of creative producers, this has become much more prevalent in recent years.

Over the *River* and Through the *Woods*

My first Broadway project, *Big River*, was developed the first way. My then-wife Heidi and I had this idea to do a musical based on *Huckleberry Finn*, with music by Roger Miller, who was my favorite composer. We approached Bill Hauptman, who was a classmate of mine at the Yale Drama School, to write a book. We went to Des McAnuff, whom Heidi had worked with at the Public Theater, to direct. Robert Brustein, who was the dean of the Yale School of Drama when I was there and had since moved up to American Repertory Theatre in Cambridge, Massachusetts, agreed to give it a first production at ART.

My second production was developed the second way: the producer presents a show that has been created by someone else and already exists. The show was *Into the Woods*, by James Lapine and Stephen Sondheim. They had done a lot of the creative work on it before the producers got there.

Then the job of the producer now becomes one of shepherding it through the process until its opening on Broadway. That's less of a creative process, more of a presenting process. It's a wonderful show, but it's much less satisfying for a producer because you are not there at the birth of the project. You are really an enabler for someone else's dream.

Most producing these days is in the latter category. It's rare, as Margo Lion recently did with *Hairspray*, that a producer thinks of a project in her head and then does all the work to put it together. With *The Producers*, we went to a reading and fell in love with it. Our participation was to say, "You guys have done great work. This should be on Broadway. Will you anoint us to be the producers of it?" That is a less important process than the origination of a show but those are the two kinds of things that producers do.

In both cases, the producer is responsible for the functioning of the show. The producer will hire a general manager and set up an office and organize all the physical mechanics that enable the show to run. A theatre has to be booked. People have to be paid. Sets have to be built. A marketing campaign has to be organized. Ultimately, then, the producer is responsible for everything involved with the show except the actual performance on stage. And he's ultimately responsible for that too with his choice of a director.

David Merrick's Influence

I've always been fascinated by David Merrick's career. He was from St. Louis, too. In fact, my office on 44th Street used to be Merrick's office. At that time it was painted red. I'm not quite that flamboyant. It's natural that I would take him as a role model in some ways, though I hope not in other ways. He was notoriously imperious and capricious and autocratic. For me, firing someone is a last resort. For David Merrick, it was option one: "Fire 'em now, ask questions later."

In today's theatre world Merrick would have a tougher time because it is much more of a collaborative enterprise now. You have to gain the confidence of some very important directors and writers and you have to collaborate with them. If you try to exercise autocratic authority through your ability to hire and fire, that won't play well anymore. It's just a different time.

A lot of it has to do with the fact that genuine creative talent—the few star directors, composers, lyricists and playwrights—are so few now that producers compete to work with them. These days, a lot of creative talent gets deflected into movies and television. The ones who are left have real leverage by virtue of their talent. The producer can't simply wheel and deal, hire and fire these important artists with impunity.

In Merrick's day, if you fired a book writer, there were a dozen other good book writers lining up to work on that show. That's not true today. The next one may not be nearly as good as the one you have. And if the one you have is the best, it better be your job to find out how to work with that person. Your job becomes developing a way for that person to be happy and satisfied with the collaboration. It's a different world than when those giants walked the earth.

SHIFTING THE BALANCE

There has been a shift of the balance of power in recent years from the producer to the director. With so few star directors, the best ones can pretty much get their way about everything. The producer becomes someone who can suggest or cajole or try to persuade rather than wield direct authority over a production.

My relationship with Susan Stroman on *The Producers* was one of advisor, but certainly not someone in real authority. She was the director of the show before I got there, and she and Mel Brooks could have anointed another producer if they so chose. As these important directors tend to exercise more and more control in a kind of auteur fashion, the producer's job becomes more and more that of a handmaiden. That can work very well with someone like Stro, who has total command and expertise in her area. It can be more problematic if the director starts going off the track.

But even though we trusted Stro, there were times when we wanted some scenes shortened, fewer stagehands to move scenery and some tightening in the show, and we couldn't always get what we wanted. To be fair, she couldn't always get what *she* wanted.

THAT'S OUR HITLER

There's a very funny scene in *The Producers* where Franz Liebkind shows one of the auditioning would-be Hitlers how to sing a German song "properly"—very show-biz. At the end of the number our leading character, Max Bialystock, famously shouts, "That's our Hitler!" In today's Broadway it's not the producer that would choose the leading actor, but the director. A good producer will make his opinion known. He might even pound the table a little bit if he feels strongly. But ultimately it's the director who must live, on a day-to-day basis, with the decision. So it is natural that the director have final authority on casting.

In this business you have to be willing to lose quite a few arguments and not take it personally or harbor ill feelings about it. You make your best case, but you've got to be gracious if you don't get your way. Life goes on and you still have to maintain a strong relationship with the director. In a case where the director is in a very strong position with the creative team and with the show, you keep trying to persuade. You may get relentless about it to the point that when the director sees you coming, you may not be the most welcome sight in the world. But you just have to keep at it.

Also, your argument has to have logic. In order to be able to persuade, you have to have a good point. In the case of the cuts in *The Producers*, the creative team ultimately agreed, but the stars didn't. In this case, Nathan Lane and Matthew Broderick also had a tremendous amount of clout. They just didn't want most of the cuts we were suggesting and they got their way. I remember complaining about it to Mel Brooks, who said, "There is a certain deference due a couple of guys who are selling that many tickets for you."

Nathan and Matthew were essential to the success of the show and were, by the way, great. They earned a certain amount of authority.

UNIONS

There are many ways to cope with the ever-rising costs and demands of theatrical unions. One of the most constructive was the relatively recent creation of the position of technical supervisor. The technical supervisor's job is to organize scheduling and resources to make sure that the union employees' time is put to the most productive use possible and that you are getting work done for the lowest possible cost. If you're not careful, a big show can cost one million dollars just to load in the set from the trucks! A technical supervisor is there to make sure this process is efficient. It's the kind of collaboration that really shows up in the bottom line.

Temperament

It's hard to imagine the kind of stress people work under during the final weeks before the opening of a big, expensive show. Keeping an even temper is probably the most important thing on all sides. One of the great things about Susan Stroman is that she is the opposite of an hysteric. She is always contained, rational, approachable, easy to deal with—never volatile.

If you have a director who is temperamental, who will say to you, "I don't have to do it this way! I don't need this!" and walks off with some frequency, it gets to be stressful and exhausting after a while. Nothing is gained by anybody from that sort of behavior.

James Lapine, who directed *Into the Woods*, is another director with a very even temperament who is a pleasure to work with. Every discussion is low key and respectful. There is a genuine dynamic of speaking and listening that goes back and forth. When you have that, the work tends to be better because there's a real dialogue that goes on.

But it's safe to say that not everybody who's brilliantly creative is also low-key and even-tempered. This is a business of tremendous egos. A good producer is sensitive to, let's not say their egos, let's say their "creative credentials." These often go with a certain kind of elevated temperament.

You never want to be in a situation where someone is pulling a power play and saying, "I'm in charge! You'll do it my way!" Whether it's the producer or the director who says it, if you reach that point, something has gone seriously wrong.

People under pressure tend to be more volatile and shorter-tempered. I try to be aware of that and adjust accordingly so that I keep an even keel. It's one of the things a producer has to do. The best managers in sports are the ones that stay very cool under pressure. Look at the New York Yankees manager Joe Torre, and all his success. You can never tell by looking at him what the score is or what kind of situation he's in—except maybe when he's chewing gum. And I don't chew.

I don't remember ever yelling at any member of a creative team on any show that I've done. There are times where you might want to take a time out and come back and have the discussions later. But I'm not a yeller and I really don't like dealing with people who throw tantrums and yell. I just don't think it's a productive way to work.

Are there times when I want to strangle a director? Perhaps. But I have developed a technique for dealing with that. I deal with it "tomorrow." The biggest mistake made by people under pressure is getting too caught up in the moment, and their urgency to make a certain change or to have their way *right then*. Of course part of the pressure is the pressure of time. First preview is bearing down on you and you have to get the show up.

But sometimes if you just take a day and let things settle down, people calm down. The producer's impulse to rush up to the director right after he or she has given notes to the cast and insist on your point right there is very counterproductive. You can make your point, but it's sometimes better to give it a little time. Let cooler heads prevail. When the dynamic is calmer the problem often works itself out.

And I mean that literally. I shift my focus for a few hours. I have other outlets. I have pressure valves. I tend not to punch holes in the walls. I listen to country music, which I love and which I always find relaxing. I focus on my life outside the office with my wife Debbie and my three boys. I'll go to see a baseball game. I'll stop thinking about the issues of the theatre for a while—and I will let my antagonist do the same thing. Experience has taught me that when we see each other the next day, chances are we'll both be in a better frame of mind.

Sometimes the biggest contribution that a producer can make is to not say anything. You waste a lot of time and create a lot of needless friction by rushing up to the creative team with a fistful of notes that you are insisting on being put in and acted on right away. Instead, just pull back and let the creative team, which is already on the case and which is probably already aware of the problems, deal with them themselves. You hired them to do a job. Let them do it

MEDIATING CONFLICT

Not everyone lives by these rules, however. Sometimes it's up to the producer to either mediate a conflict between an actor and a director or sometimes to take a side. We recently did a production where there was a strong conflict between the director and an actor. The actor asked for a meeting, and I don't know if he thought we would fire the director. But I said, basically, "This director is not going anywhere. Work it out."

Sometimes the producer has to take a side like that. Sometimes the producer has to simply bring everybody in the room and say, "Let's resolve our differences. Let's air the issues and take a course of action."

As mentioned earlier, in this business you have to be willing to lose certain arguments. The hardest thing to realize in any business is that it's not always important to be *right*. It's important to be *effective*. In a collaboration, everyone has to be going together in a common direction. It's like a basketball team: if you have a star who's in his own game and the other four players are standing around, it's not going to work even if he's a better player and his opinion is right. You still have to work as a team.

The hardest thing to do in any enterprise is to give up on your point of view when you know you are right. But sometimes it's necessary. You have to tell yourself, "I'm right about this. I really think that we're going off in the wrong direction. But if that's the decision of the group, of the director of the team, I'm going to play that to the best of my ability."

That's what you do if you are mature and responsible. You've got to apply your ego to the project as a whole, not just your own point of view.

WHERE IT HAPPENS

Collaboration takes place almost anywhere. It can happen over a drink, at lunch, backstage, very often the conversations in the theatre itself during rehearsals or after rehearsals or after previews. Sometimes the conversation happens in my office. It can be anywhere.

The only bad place is in public, within hearing or observation of someone outside the production—or even some people inside the production. If issues are being thrashed out, you want that discussion to be as private and protected as possible. It's important that your collaborators have great confidence in your discretion, that what's said between you stays between you and isn't going to get used as fodder in some kind of public campaign. That's the quickest way to lose the confidence of a collaborator.

And I'm not just talking about the press. People need to be open and frank with you without worrying that it will get back to other people in the cast, or a p.r. person, or another producer. Certain conversations have to be protected and private.

THE AUDIENCE'S JOB

You have to be very mindful of the audience during previews. After all, that's why we have previews: to gauge the reaction of the audience and make changes accordingly. This is especially important in comedy where the audience actually becomes an integral part of the dynamic of the show. It's our job to make them laugh. Director Jerry Zaks is the greatest master I have ever seen at understanding what's happening in the dynamic between a show and the audience. He does it by listening to the audience, and not just for the quantity of laughter. He's listening for all kinds of responses.

I recently did a drama called *Sixteen Wounded*, about a Jew and a Palestinian trying to come to terms. In previews I could feel that the audience wasn't really responsive to the show. They were respectful of it, they were seriously engaged by it, but not really moved by it or really excited by it. I liked the script, but I could sense from the audience that it just wasn't landing. A producer must go and feel what's happening in the audience especially during previews. It's an important part of putting a show together.

PASSION

A producer has to be a believer in what he's producing. He has to be passionate about the show itself. I believe this with all of my heart.

The worst kind of producing is to produce for someone else's taste. To say, "I don't particularly care for this piece of fluff but it's going to be commercially successful," is a terrible way to go about your business. Once you do that, you have really lost your bearings. That's the road to disaster and usually the road to a big flop. The worst thing you can do is to aim low and miss.

The best producing happens when you are a believer in your own show. You have to be ready to throw your heart and soul in it, and be prepared to give your all to the people you will be collaborating with. You have to believe that the show you're doing has the potential for greatness.

CHAPTER 8

HAROLD PRINCE
DIRECTOR AND PRODUCER

Harold Prince directed the premiere productions of *She Loves Me*, *Cabaret*, *Company*, *Follies*, *Candide*, *Pacific Overtures*, *A Little Night Music*, *Sweeney Todd*, *Evita*, *The Phantom of the Opera*, and *Parade*. Among the plays he has directed are *Hollywood Arms*, *The Visit*, *The Great God Brown*, *End of the World*, *Play Memory*, and his own play, *Grandchild of Kings*. Mr. Prince also directed *Bounce*, which was seen at the Goodman Theatre in Chicago and the Kennedy Center in Washington, D.C. His opera productions have been seen at Lyric Opera of Chicago, the Metropolitan Opera, San Francisco Opera, Houston Grand Opera, Dallas Opera, Vienna Staatsoper, and the Theatre Colon in Buenos Aires. Before becoming a director, Mr. Prince produced the Broadway premieres of *The Pajama Game*, *Damn Yankees*, *West Side Story*, *Fiddler on the Roof*, *Fiorello!*, and *A Funny Thing Happened on the Way to the Forum*. He served as a trustee for the New York Public Library and on the National Council of the Arts of the NEA. He is the recipient of a National Medal of Arts for a career spanning more than 40 years, in which "he changed the nature of the American musical." The recipient of twenty-one Tony Awards, he was a 1994 Kennedy Center Honoree.

The Perfect Collaboration

I am not a solitary worker. I like to work in company with other people.

I originally wanted to be a playwright but I know now that I wouldn't have enjoyed it as much as what I have pursued my whole life: directing and producing. What you get from collaboration is a lot of fun and a lot of excitement—and, I guess, some pain. I guess? I *know*. I suffer the same as anybody else when a show I love gets bum reviews, or when I realize I've made a mistake.

I was a producer for many years. But I stopped and became exclusively a director because that is where I am happiest. The director today is at the center of a circle of creative people. It's that circle of collaboration that I love most.

But I did produce for years, and successfully, and enjoyed it. I tried it again a couple of years ago and found I no longer enjoyed it. A producer's primary obligation in today's Broadway is to raise capital from affluent, often corporate, investors, and to "brand" his "product." It all saps the most important element in producing which is creative.

When I began producing in the 1950s, the commercial theatre in New York was a collaborative journey that involved a creative producer, director, author or authors, and designers. In those days there were no sound or lighting designers. I know it sounds like I'm a thousand years old but it's actually not that long ago.

In those days, lighting was handled by the electrician, as supervised by the director. Lights were always all the way up for the comedy scenes. I remember George Abbott calling out to the electrician, "Lights up. Lights down. Let's have less light on this song and then bump up to the old cue when the song is over." When the number was over and the audience could see the lighting restored to normal, you'd get a hand. That was pretty much it for lighting design.

There's far more sophistication today. But the primary difference between the collaboration then and the collaboration today is that the producer was a towering force and *had* to be. The buck stopped with him. I know there are those who would say it now stops with the director. I agree that today it tends to stop more with the director—unless the producer gets unhappy and fires the director, and that's certainly in his (or her!) power.

Here's how collaboration used to work: the creative producer read a book or a play that he felt would make a good musical. He would then choose the writers and the director he felt would best tell the story. Already those were *creative* decisions.

Then, as in my case, the producer also chose the set and costume designers. George Abbott never cared much for designers. Jerome Robbins did, but I was certainly in on his decisions. By the time we got around to *West Side Story* we added Jean Rosenthal who had been a dance lighting designer and had done lighting for all Jerry's dances. Her arrival on *West Side Story* opened a whole new element of creativity in the musical game for me: telling a story with light.

Years later, we added sound design. There was no such thing when I started producing. It was all acoustic. You went into a theatre and got used to the sound of the actors' natural voices in that space. For the first few minutes you might have some difficulty understanding, even if it was a play, what (for example) the Lunts were saying—and they were the king and queen of pronunciation and projection. But you still sat forward. And soon you began to hear the show. The main point is you were investing more than you do now.

In musicals, orchestrations were designed to serve the voice, which was not being amplified. There was less brass and more strings. Most voices in those days were thinner than they are now. Except, of course, for Ethel Merman.

As the power of the producer has decreased, the sheer number of producers on each show has increased—another trend that's neutralizing creative producing. It's not uncommon today to see more producer names above the title of a play than there are people on the stage. I can't even imagine how so many people collaborate to make any decision, except perhaps on which quotes to use in the ads.

Something Missing

I've done both plays and musicals on Broadway, but I have tended to focus on musicals largely because when I do a drama, frankly, I miss the collaboration.

Musicals and plays are very different animals, and so are the people who create them. Tony Kushner may have decided to do a musical, and I am very impressed that he tried something as ambitious as *Caroline, Or Change*. But most playwrights aren't fully comfortable with the kind of give and take that a musical requires. Most playwrights abhor the musical theatre book writer's process. They regard the picking and fussing and changing in a musical collaboration as incursions on their creative effort. They don't like collaboration because they don't want to abrogate their authority. There are exceptions, however. Brilliant ones. Alfred Uhry for one, and Terrence McNally for another.

The intricacy of musical theatre collaboration is clearly greater than that of nonmusical theatre. When I direct a play the playwright expects to sit at my elbow and participate in every decision. And the actors tend to look past the director to ask a question of the playwright. These are working habits that are not comfortable for me. Whenever I've done a musical with a playwright who has not done a musical before, I warn him that things will be very different. Frequently some of the book writer's best dialogue is appropriated by the lyricist. That can come as a surprise!

And because scenery in musicals is far more complex and usually there is much more of it than in a straight play, the book writer and the composers need to accommodate certain adjustments to suit the needs of the designers. For example, it takes time to make set and costume changes.

Probably ego has hurt us more than anything in the world. Our history is filled with stories of authors who've been barred from theatres when in rehearsal, or even previews. That events have been allowed to go that far is absurd.

George Abbott

Playwrights aren't the only ones who have trouble opening themselves up to the collaborative process. I've seen some pretty peculiar instances of young, extremely talented artists refusing to accept guidance or make compromises, and walking away from collaboration into ignominy never to be heard from again.

My ideal collaboration consists of me, one or two veterans, and inexperienced but talented artists. We have so much to share. It's a recipe I learned from George Abbott. He gave careers to more giant talents than anyone in the history of the theatre—Leonard Bernstein, Jerome Robbins, Kander and Ebb, Bock and Harnick, Jerome Weidman, Comden and Green, Garson Kanin—the list is endless.

He [Abbott] was able to work with them and mentor them and remain unthreatened because he was so secure in his own talent. He didn't have to prove anything to anybody. And the element of who gets credit for what never troubled him because *it never entered his mind.*

Working with new, young talent isn't just a noble altruistic move. When veterans work with newcomers, everybody wins. The newcomers get the benefit of the veterans' experience, and the veterans get the exposure to contemporary thinking.

George Abbott would not have come up with *On the Town* on his own. Comden and Green gave him an absolutely buoyant, chirpy story, and Bernstein wrote magnificent ballet music for Jerome Robbins to stage. However, it was Abbott who put them in a room together and made those unique proportions work in popular musical theatre terms.

Young writers today are suffering from the lack of opportunity to put their work in front of an audience, to fall on their faces, then to dust themselves off and do another piece the next year. We learned that way.

And we learned on Broadway.

Coincidentally, most of us were rejected the first time at bat and succeeded on the second. Today's production costs often prevent a second chance.

The opportunities to work with experienced talented, patient, knowledgeable artists have grown fewer and fewer.

GHOSTS

The best collaborations start with an idea. Your collaborators expand on it, and sometimes what you wind up with is something you never anticipated.

For example, when I was directing *Follies*, I hoped to set the opening of the show in a moody and mystical place. Stephen Sondheim wrote an overture to be staged, introducing our company arriving in an empty space, a theatre that would be torn down the next day, but abstractly is half torn down already. They are confused and disoriented. You recognize them as old Follies people returning for a reunion. I proposed that we should place dummies on the stage in period Follies costumes, and as the evening continued, we'd change the costumes. Our actors would play the show as if the dummies weren't there.

Michael Bennett, who became co-director and choreographer, suggested, instead, that we hire live showgirls, that they wear Florence Klotz's exquisite costumes, and that we move them, almost imperceptibly, across the stage during the evening. If you didn't keep your eye on them, you would be surprised to see that they traveled from one side of the stage to the other. We flew to Vegas to cast those models—among them, a German girl who opened the show, center stage. She was over six feet tall, but with Klotz's costume, she measured six feet, eight inches. When the curtain rose, you saw her in a black and white sequins costume. Throughout the night, mysterious people appeared in black and white, gliding so slowly. It was as if you had gone to a museum and the art was suddenly animating. Ghosts from the past.

To support all of this, the librettist, James Goldman, adjusted the tone of the entire production's dialogue from real to eerie abstract.

Years later, Sondheim and I gave a seminar at Marymount College for teacher Pat Hoag-Simon. The question of who got what idea kept coming up and we couldn't remember. I think that must be good. In a true collaboration you shouldn't have to remember.

ENERGY

I have a lot of respect for actors and all the artists who ply different elements of this trade. I enjoy the energy that comes off them. Positive energy. I find it difficult to work with people who are reluctant and unbending. It's frustrating and can be paralyzing.

The trick is accompanying your own vision with an open mind. You must listen to everyone. And I mean *everyone*. The lady who follows you up the aisle at the preview may have something more useful to say than your collaborator. But listening does not mean accepting. It just means listening.

My collaborators Sondheim, Kander and Ebb, Bock and Harnick, Lloyd Webber, are true theatre artists. In that respect I've been extremely lucky and I do not recall an instance of those relationships stymieing me. Quite the contrary. They surprise me and take me places I never imagined.

EMPTY SPACE

The audience for live theatre has changed. The money in our country is in different hands. The top price of a theatre ticket is now one hundred and ten dollars. Not so damned long ago it was five dollars and some cents. Theatre was available to a larger and more varied audience. Very likely, more discerning, more adventurous, more political. I blame the change on today's entrepreneurs. There is a generally accepted and misguided notion that audiences dictate what you put on a stage. I learned early on that audiences can be very grateful when you take them on a journey they didn't anticipate—somewhere they've never been. I suppose I can thank *West Side Story* for that.

When it first opened we had to struggle for audiences. But gradually, people began to appreciate it. But it wasn't until the film came out that they finally "got it." Now, of course, it's probably revived as much as any other American musical in our history.

Cabaret was another dangerous, controversial show when I produced and directed it in 1966. People asked what the hell we were doing with Nazis on stage. *Cabaret*, too, is part of our history, and people have come to think it makes a sure-fire revival.

Today's productions often emulate film, television, and mass media, forgetting that theatre has something special—*different*—to offer that often cannot be duplicated on film or on television.

My favorite theatre still happens in a black box—an empty space. Given the sumptuousness of *Phantom Of The Opera*, it may be difficult to recognize that it essentially is told in a black enamel box. There are glorious curtains, beautiful props, elegant costumes, but the rest is black. Each member of the audience imagines details where there are empty spaces—wallpaper, additional furniture, that sort of thing.

Of course, audiences go to theatre to be entertained. It is defining "entertainment" that matters. Few people equate a good time with controversy, with being emotionally disturbed by what's happening on stage. But those, too, are the components of entertainment. Personally, crying is a lot more entertaining for me than laughing. Laugh is cheap. I laugh fifty times a day.

POSTERITY

The director may have a great deal of power over a production—but in the long run, does he really? It's the material that lasts. Who remembers the director? In her interview with Sondheim and me at Marymount College, Pat Hoag-Simon threw out a question, "I read somewhere that you, Steve, don't give a damn whether you have a reputation after you're gone, and you, Hal, do. Is that true?"

I replied that it's easy for Steve to say that, because he *will* be remembered. And it's harder for me, because I probably won't. At least not for long.

I guess I love the possibility of having my work extend beyond my lifespan.

CHAPTER 9

Susan Stroman

Director and Choreographer

Susan Stroman is one of the top director-choreographers working on Broadway today. She's been nominated for eleven Tony Awards and won five, most notably for her blockbuster collaboration with Mel Brooks on *The Producers*, which won more Tony Awards (fourteen) than any show in Broadway history. The 2005 film version was nominated for four Golden Globe Awards. Other projects as choreographer and/or director include *Contact, Crazy for You, Big, The Frogs, Steel Pier, A Christmas Carol, Thou Shalt Not, And the World Goes 'Round,* and award-winning revivals of *The Music Man, Oklahoma!,* and *Show Boat.*

Having the Last Word

On a Broadway musical, the director has to have the last word. That's not to say that a director should be a tyrant or be on a power trip. But for a show to succeed, the whole team of collaborators has to be working on the same show. For that to happen someone has to be in charge, to keep the bigger picture in focus. That's the job of the director.

Within that structure, amazing things can happen. It's a big step for any theatre artist to hand that kind of power to a director. But if an artist isn't sure of a director, isn't ready to go on a journey under a director's leadership, he or she should take their materials elsewhere.

In return, the director has a responsibility to keep her ears and eyes open—and keep her mind open. One of the biggest lessons to be learned about collaborating, especially on a musical, is never to be afraid to propose any idea, even if the idea sounds crazy at first. Someone else may take that idea and shake it up and turn into something else, hopefully something better and, finally, something *right*. A good director will create a climate in which every idea that is thrown on the table will be respected and, somehow, a piece of each idea will be applied to the project. The director is there to give the ideas shape and direction. But ultimately the director has to have the final decision.

LEARNING PROCESS

Every actor comes to rehearsal with a different way of approaching a role—a unique "process." A director has to respect that process and help the actor use that process to evolve the best performance. During the first week of rehearsals almost all a director's energy goes toward learning each actor's process, and understanding the speed at which each actor works. As you can imagine, that's a challenge, especially when you are working with a big group. That's why the first couple of weeks of rehearsals are generally the most exhausting.

The same thing applies to the team of producers, writers and designers. Every person has their quirks. Learn them, and a director will know where their ideas best belong. You hope that anybody who has gotten this far in their professional career has achieved a certain level of professionalism. But everybody works at a different pace. Once a director understands the pace at which each person works, she can schedule accordingly. Some people write faster than others, just as some actors learn faster than others.

No small part of the success of a complicated musical comes from being firm, but having realistic expectations of your collaborators.

DIPLOMACY

I've been very lucky that my career has been a series of steppingstones. With each show I've done, whether it's been a financial success or not, I've been able to learn something, then apply it to the next "stone." I've been very fortunate that the people I collaborated with were generous in sharing their knowledge and skills, starting with my late husband, Mike Ockrent, with whom I collaborated on several shows, notably *Crazy for You*.

He taught me that diplomacy is the real key to getting the best work out of people. You always have to keep your door open and your phone connected any hour of the day or night, and be available to everyone on your team.

That's not to say that you never get angry or frustrated. But there is a right way and a wrong way to communicate that. You don't want to make the person feel like an incompetent; you want them to do their job right. For example, you should never say things like, "You are so far off the track that it's going to take three people to pull you back on!" That may feel momentarily satisfying to say, but it doesn't help the show.

You just just say, "That doesn't work," then give examples of why it's doesn't. Whenever I have to approach somebody because they are off track on a particular "moment" in the show, I try to spark them with some alternate ideas to help get them back on.

Being in a collaboration is a very grown-up situation, and everyone needs to be able to open his ears and eyes to other ways and other possibilities. I've come out of many production meetings where, even if I didn't totally agree with a particular point, that disagreement forced me to think of a new idea. Disagreements shouldn't shut you down; they should inspire you to another track. The lesson here is: there's no such thing as a wrong idea. You may not wind up using that idea in the final show for one reason or another, but voicing it may prompt your collaborators to think of something different and better. There is never just one way to do something. You have to be sure that the particular way you choose fits with the entire journey of the piece.

I've heard nightmare stories about how certain directors have alienated their companies, where there's been near-mutiny between the cast and the director. It's usually caused by a lack of communication or a disrespect for the different departments. You really can't be disrespectful when you're working on a musical. A musical is the hardest thing to create in the theatre because there are so many different departments. In addition to the writers and actors, a director has to deal with sets, sound, costumes and lighting, plus, often, fight directors, child wranglers, dogs, etc. You have to respect every one of those departments. Respect is a key word. And they have to respect the director.

If you want to collaborate fully, you have to arm yourself with information about every part of the business. The more you know about the demands of each person's job, the better able you are to supervise that job, and give direction on that job. For instance, enlightening yourself about what it costs to produce a show will make you think twice about going overboard with an unnecessary production element. It forces you to be resourceful about coming up with more clever ideas.

I don't think young people considering careers in theatre fully understand what it takes to be a good collaborator. It really takes a village to put up a musical, with every department making its contribution. I've been very lucky to have had some very strong collaborations, but every collaboration is different.

WORKING WITH KANDER AND EBB

The model for a great collaboration is the one between John Kander and Fred Ebb, the songwriting team behind *Cabaret* and *Chicago*. I've worked with them on *And the World Goes 'Round* which was an Off-Broadway revue of their work; *Flora the Red Menace* in an Off-Broadway revival; and of course *Steel Pier*, their Broadway musical about dance marathons. I love working with them.

They benefit from having a diversity of experience and perspective. One always has a harder-edge take on something than the other. Its not unlike their song "City Lights," where they talk about hating the country and loving the city. Fred Ebb loves the city and can't stand the country. But John Kander loves the country and can't stand the city. So they always have the essence of the city and the country with them. They're two sides of the same coin.

They are constantly thinking, constantly at work, constantly talking with one another. They taught me that in a successful collaboration, you must say whatever you are thinking because someone else will take the idea and run with it. We've begun each of our projects by having a big meeting in the kitchen of Fred Ebb's apartment. We start with an outline of the piece and then talk about the direction we are taking it. Then we get down to tossing out ideas about where we should put a ballad, or where there should be an up-tempo number.

Then I begin assigning tasks or what I call "missions." Knowing the pace at which they work, I can tell the songwriters, "By the end of this month, I need to have this song done." Or telling the book writer, "The middle section of the first act needs to be done by the first of July."

I give everyone specific duties to tackle, and point them in the right direction.

WORKING WITH MEL BROOKS

The collaboration with Mel Brooks on *The Producers* was unique because of the way he feeds off the ideas and creativity of everyone who shares the room with him. He is a life force and he loves being inspired by other people who are life forces, too.

Mel is not one of those writers who goes off into a small room by himself and locks the door. He likes to work face-to-face. In his early career he wrote for TV's "Your Show of Shows," which used a circle of top comics like Neil Simon and Woody Allen as the writing staff. That's the way they collaborated then, and the way he still likes to collaborate.

Sitting there with him, you can see him *become* the characters he's writing. A lot of the scenes in *The Producers* came about because Mel would become Carmen Ghia or he would become Roger DeBris. He'd even become Ulla at times. Mel places the comedy inside himself. He thinks nothing of jumping around the room as scenes and music and lyrics pour out of him.

At the same time, Mel was a very strong collaborator because when I would tell him a line or a lyric was good, but not good *enough*, he would accept that. He always had something more, something different, because he is a very creative man. He wouldn't stop until it *was* good enough. Whatever his public persona may be, when we were collaborating in that room, he would put all personal ego aside in his goal to get the best possible show. That's the key to a successful collaboration.

WORKING WITH STEPHEN SONDHEIM AND NATHAN LANE

The idea for *The Frogs* (with a score by Stephen Sondheim, and book by Nathan Lane, who also starred) came from Nathan. He had taken part in a studio recording of the score, which was originally written back in the early 1970s for a production at the Yale School of Drama. Burt Shevelove adapted the book from a classical comedy by Aristophanes, but it was more like an extended sketch than a musical. Nathan came to me with the idea to open it up as a full-length musical.

I said to Nathan, "I can be a part of this only if Sondheim is willing to write more music and fully realize this. The worst he can say is no, so why don't we go see him?"

We called and made an appointment and went to his house. I told him that we wanted to do a full-length version of *The Frogs*, and if we did this it would mean him going back into it and writing seven more songs.

His first question was, "Why? Why do you want to do it?" I thought that was interesting. He was less concerned about us rewriting a show of his that wasn't completely realized, and more concerned about the fundamental dramatic reason we wanted to do *The Frogs*.

I told him that when I read the Aristophanes *Frogs* I realized that they were having the same problems in 405 BC that we are having today. It is about Dionysos, the god of drama and the god of wine, coming down to earth after a catastrophe and realizing that we need a leader who can speak to the people because our leaders can't seem to put words together to ease the hearts of the people. Dionysos goes to Hades to bring back a great dramatist of the past to speak to the people. In the time of Aristophanes he went and brought back Euripides. In the musical, he wants to bring back George Bernard Shaw.

It all seemed so pertinent and so important. Aristophanes was the great satirist of his time. He was able to break the fourth wall and talk to the audience about both issues of the day, and issues of all time. I thought, Nathan is very outspoken, very political and very funny. Who can do that better than Nathan Lane?

When I explained that to Sondheim he said, "I'm on board."

It's about art making a difference to politics, which is something that Sondheim has been preaching his whole life. He gets quite frustrated that people don't seem to listen.

Sondheim works very differently from Mel Brooks. Sondheim loves to have meetings about what a song or a scene should be, but then he goes away and works on it by himself. Whereas Mel would love to finish the whole song, write it down and sing it for you, and nobody leaves the room until everything is over.

On the other hand, Sondheim and Nathan Lane have a very similar way of working. They both have great instincts and visceral reactions to individual moments in the show. You always know exactly where you stand and exactly what they think. That's not always true of collaborators. I quickly learned to be alert to their instincts and be prepared to act upon their reactions.

There's no right or wrong about these different styles. You have to learn about your collaborator and work whatever way they are inspired most.

Our collaboration on *The Frogs* started with many meetings about what kinds of songs were needed to flesh it out. We went back to the basic story, and made an outline, then built from there. Nathan would write big sections with long paragraphs on what a song might possibly be. Sondheim took those and fashioned them into new songs.

Here's how one of those worked. There is a wonderful scene where Dionysos talks about his wife Ariadne. There is a myth that when she died it was so upsetting to Dionysos that he took a crown and threw it into the sky. You can see that image today in the constellation Corona Borealis. We decided that was a lovely moment and would make a lovely song. Nathan wrote out a page of dialogue in which Dionysos tells about this tragedy in his life and about how it was transformed into a myth.

Sondheim took Nathan's Ariadne speech and turned it into the most beautiful ballad about Ariadne. It's hard to express how moving it was to take a song through that process with talents like Nathan and Sondheim, and then to sit and listen to a song you'd help instigate—a song that has a little bit of you in it, and now will be out there, forever.

Bad Timing

I've never been on the verge of quitting because someone was not collaborating properly. But there are many other kinds of strains on a collaboration.

Probably the hardest case was *Thou Shalt Not*, the 2001 musical I did with

Harry Connick, Jr., based on *Thérèse Raquin*. We opened eight days after September 11. No one knew if New York as going to be hit by terrorists again. No one really knew what was going on. The theatre district was very frightened. And there we were, doing a very dark story of adultery and murder. Not only was I dealing with a very dark show but I was dealing with a very dark time in the United States, a very dark time in New York. During those weeks, I don't think anyone wanted to see anyone do anything wrong on the stage. People wanted something lighthearted. It may have been a great time for *The Producers* but it was not a great time for *Thou Shalt Not*.

I think some members of the team were not as strong as they normally would have been. I can't blame them. Everybody dealt with September 11 in a different way. If someone couldn't rise to the occasion to get a musical on its feet, it was completely understandable. I did all I could do to rally the troops, but in the end I just had to back off. I do feel that someday, perhaps seven or eight years from now, I might try *Thou Shalt Not* again.

Sometimes things that are happening in the wider world have a great impact on a show's success—or failure—in a way that is entirely beyond the control of the production team. *Thou Shalt Not* was a good example of a show whose timing was off.

COORDINATING THE DESIGN TEAM

A director's job goes far beyond coordinating the book, music and lyrics of a musical. You also must coordinate the design team. I've seen many shows in which music, lyrics and book did a wonderful job but the design team took the show down because no one was paying attention. The costumes, sets and lighting component upstaged what was wonderful about the music and lyrics.

Conversely, the design team can sometimes give you the key to an entire show. For example, in *Contact*, I merely told costume designer William Ivey Long that I envisioned a girl in a yellow dress. Nothing more than that. It was William who came back to me with the absolute right color yellow and the absolute right style. He chose the idea of a classy dress—classy yet sexy. And he chose a more of a cautious yellow—the yellow you might find in a traffic light to make you proceed with caution rather than a bright sunny yellow or a mustard yellow.

He was exactly right. That dress became an iconic element in that show, and took its place in theatre history.

Another example comes from *The Producers*. I told set designer Robin Wagner that I wanted to make sure the set was in no way cartoonish. I needed the comedy to be played on a naturalistic set. When we get into Max Bialystock's office, it has to look like a real office. And the exterior of the Shubert Theatre in the opening scene has to look like a real theatre. I believe that playing comedy in a natural-looking environment makes the comedy stronger. At the same time, I told Robin that we would have a couple of fantasy moments, and *that* is when we would have fun.

When Leo Bloom is sitting in his dull office dreaming about becoming a producer, you need to really see how dull his life is. That's why it's such a great surprise when we go into his imagination and the showgirls suddenly start popping out of the file cabinets in the "I Want To Be a Producer" number. Robin was delighted to follow that logic. When the girls appear and the cabinets disappear, we go into a beautiful open space. Robin then followed Mel's lyric about seeing, "my name, Leo Bloom, in lights" and the whole stage lights up. The most successful designers follow the lyrics and the dialogue to come up with many of their ideas.

Robin Wagner and William Ivey Long are great collaborators. They not only listen to me as the director, they listen to the lyrics, they listen to the script, they listen to the type of music that is in the show. They understand that the more you know about everybody else's department the better off your own department is going to be, and the better your whole show is going to be.

TELLING THE SAME STORY

One of the biggest mistakes you can make as a director is failing to communicate. You have to make sure from the beginning that everybody is on the same page. What is the idea that you want to present? Do you want to present an entertainment? Do you want to present some serious morality tale? Do you want to present something that pulls at the heartstrings? Something that teaches a lesson? There are different types of theatre for different people and the director has to make sure that the whole team knows exactly what the point is and why they are working on the project. That goes not only for the writers, but for the technical side, and the visual side. Everybody has to be telling the same story.

You may joke that you're doing it to make money. But I've learned that the point can never be purely about money. "We're doing this to have a show that runs sixteen years and makes us all rich." I never want to hear that brought up, ever. It always has to be about why we are doing this *for the audience.*

Ultimately the audience is the last part of the collaboration process. When previews begin, you have to listen to the audience. You have to see if there is something in the show that makes them restless or uncomfortable. You have to see if it makes them laugh or if it makes them cry.

Even beyond audible sounds, I can feel the *breath* of an audience. It tells me if we are on the right track or not. I can hear in that breath if they are or aren't coming along on our story, and I know that I need to make changes. For me, the previews are about listening to the ultimate collaborators—the audience.

CHAPTER 10

GEORGE C. WOLFE
DIRECTOR AND EXECUTIVE

George C. Wolfe was producer at the Public Theater in New York for more than a decade, during which time he also personally staged more than a dozen productions Off-Broadway, on Broadway, and in London. These include *Caroline, Or Change*; *Topdog/Underdog*; *Elaine Stritch: At Liberty* (also London's Old Vic Theatre); *Bring in 'Da Noise, Bring in 'Da Funk* (Tony Award); *The Tempest*; *On the Town*; *Twilight: Los Angeles, 1992*; *The Wild Party*; *Jelly's Last Jam*; *Angels in America: Millennium Approaches* (Tony Award); and *Angels in America: Perestroika* (Tony Award). Other directing credits include *Harlem Song*, at the Apollo Theatre; *Spunk*; *The Caucasian Chalk Circle*; *Blade to the Heat*; *Macbeth*; *Radiant Baby*; and *Amistad* (Chicago's Lyric Opera). For television, Wolfe has directed *Lackawanna Blues*, *Fires in the Mirror*, and *The Colored Museum*. Writing credits include *The Colored Museum*, *Spunk*, and the books for *Jelly's Last Jam* and *The Wild Party*. Other awards include Drama Desk, Outer Critics Circle, AUDELCO, Drama-Logue, and Obie Awards; the Paul Robeson Award; the SSDC's Calloway Award; the Ilka Award from H.O.L.A.; and the "Caring Spirit" award from APICHA. He was named a "Living Landmark" by the New York Landmarks Conservancy.

The Solution Can Come from Anybody

As a child, I was always obsessed with theatre. I was creating theatre even before I knew the word for it. There's a part of my personality that's very, very public. I like throwing parties. I like building communities. I like ordering worlds.

I learned my first great lesson about collaboration when I was directing an original musical in college. The opening number wasn't working. The cast was on a break, the composer and I were standing around talking, trying to solve the problem. So, we're talking and the cast is hanging around the piano making all this noise. So I yell out, "Quiet guys, we're trying to work." But they kept on singing and laughing. I asked them to be quiet again. The noise continued. Just as I was about to yell, I finally heard what all the noise was—they had musically solved the opening number.

It was a huge moment for me. I realized in a true collaboration, the solution can come from anybody. The solution can come from an actor. It can come from the stage manager. By shutting them out, I was shutting out a possible solution, an impulse. That taught me: when you are the director, you have to be *available* to the room, as much as you have to be in charge of the room.

TAPPING POTENTIAL: *JELLY'S LAST JAM*

I first worked with Savion Glover (as young Jelly) on *Jelly's Last Jam*. Working with him and Gregory Hines (as Jelly and choreographer), I learned, so much.

For one thing, it taught me how sophisticated tap can be, and suggested its dramatic potential. Tap had always been an expression of exuberance. But deep down, it's really an unending series of mathematical equations; as much a cerebral art form as a physical dance art form. When dancers would leave those rehearsals, their *minds*, as well as their feet would be hurting.

As both director and librettist on that show, I played around with Gregory using tap to express energy, rage, isolation and powerlessness.

Another important rule of collaboration is you have to allow yourself to truly be affected by the people you are working with, if in fact you and the show are going to grow. You have to make yourself available to that which you don't know. But people often get very scared of learning new things.

Gregory and I had legendary battles on *Jelly*. He would always fight with me about the dramatic content of the piece, the darker aspects of the character. He was incredibly smart about energy and momentum in numbers. He knew how to dazzle. But I was concerned about things being too slick. In our collision we were in essence learning each other's truth, secrets, and strengths.

It was also during this show that Savion and I developed a close friendship and trust. We decided we wanted to work together again. This led to one of the great collaborative experiences of my career.

THE MIND LIKES TO COLLABORATE: *BRING IN 'DA NOISE, BRING IN 'DA FUNK*

After I was hired as producer of the Public Theater, I invited Savion to come down and create a show here. Once he finished the national tour of *Jelly's Last Jam* in 1995, we started to explore some ideas. I had an abstract notion that rhythm is reflective of history and history creates rhythm. I asked Savion, what kind of show he wanted to make. He said, "I want to bring in the noise. I want to bring in the funk." I said, "OK, that's our title." And so we started working.

We assembled a team of people, most of whom we had worked with before. Daryl

Waters and Ann Duquesnay had been a part of *Jelly*. Daryl brought in Zane Mark. Reg E. Gaines had done some work at the Public Theater with the Community Affairs department. Shelby Jiggetts was in the literary department at the Public, and then later, Jules Fisher, Peggy Eisenhauer, Ricardo Hernandez and Paul Tazewell joined the team; all of whom I'd worked with before.

I've never had a collaboration before or since like I had on *Bring in 'Da Noise, Bring in 'Da Funk*. The room was like a factory. A raw idea would be thrown out, and everybody would get to work.

I would dream numbers. I dreamed that one of the drummers was playing the bottom of Savion's feet. I came in and drew a structure with a lot of bars that would allow Savion and the dancers to lift themselves up, so that the drummers could reach their feet. Looking at it, it looked so mechanical. So I thought, maybe this was the way to explore the industrialization of America; how the Black migration from the south to come work in the Chicago factories resulted in altering the rhythm of this country. A structure was quickly built, and Savion set out to create these urbanized rhythms, and the number "Industrialization" was born.

We did lots of research at the Schomberg Center for Research in Black Culture, in Harlem. We found this article about how many Black people had been lynched in 1916. That gave way to the jubilant, but ultimately harrowing number called "The 1916, 50 Negroes Lynching Blues."

There is this wonderful blues lyric, "219 took my baby away, 219 took my baby away, 404 going to bring him back someday." These were trains. There is so much incredible, brilliant stuff stored in blues lyrics, and we tried to model the structure of our show on that—a succinct condensation of history in rhythm.

All over the world in the 1920s there were these huge, exuberant cultural explosions. But beneath the surface, fascism was taking root. Hitler was on the rise. Membership in the Klan was mounting. The '20s always fascinated me because while the whole world was dancing, these other forces were on the march. I went to Savion and said, "Can you create a tap Charleston that feels like the world is about to end?"

While that was happening, Reg E. Gaines was off writing a poem about the Harlem Renaissance. The dramaturgical team was off collecting names of slave ships. I gave them to Ann Duquesnay and Zane Mark and they went off into a room and wrote the song "Slave Ships."

It was an astonishing, intense, accelerated time. Everybody had an incredible level of trust going on, so each day, the work just *revealed* itself. Everything that was built came to fruition. After just three weeks of work, we had forty-five minutes worth of great material. By the time the show opened at the Public Theater, there was only one number that we started with that wound up getting thrown out.

In the morning I'd work on *Noise/Funk* and at night I was rehearsing *The Tempest* for its move to Broadway. On my days off, I was flying down to Texas, because my mother was dying. The adrenaline of the collaboration helped me get through it all. I was pouring all of my belief and sense of possibilities into *Noise/Funk* because I was, on a deep primal level, rendered numb by the fact that my mother was going to die.

The Tempest opened at the Public Theater in November. Then, in December, my mother died. And then, in winter 1996, the day before tech started for *Noise/Funk* moving to Broadway, my house burned. Then we opened on Broadway in April, and won four Tony Awards in June.

It was one of those intense times where, if you feel safe in a collaboration, extraordinary things can happen.

BOUNDARIES AND VOCABULARY: *ANGELS IN AMERICA*

My collaboration with Tony Kushner on the two parts of *Angels in America* evolved a great deal from Part One (*Millennium Approaches*) to Part Two (*Perestroika*).

With *Millennium Approaches*, I was given in essence "sacred text" which everybody had already decided was flawless, perfect, and amazing. Somebody called me up and said, "Everybody knows that the play is brilliant so if it gets screwed up, it's your fault."

Perestroika was the opposite. Tony gave me a draft that was very long, and which he was still rewriting, as we went into rehearsal.

We were also working under very unusual conditions. The actors were performing Part One by night, and rehearsing Part Two by day, plus with the script constantly changing, it created an incredible schizophrenia within the cast.

But this severe pressure only strengthened my collaboration with the actors and Tony. Tony and I have a unique dynamic between us. We were both at New York University at the same time, but, I was in the playwriting program, and he was in the directing program. So we understand each other's craft. He's a very intense collaborator, and so am I.

In Part One of *Angels* we learned each other's vocabulary and learned each other's boundaries. Learning your collaborator's boundaries is very important. So that by the time Part Two came along—we'd learned to trust one another. I felt on Part One, I was doing a job. On Part Two I felt like I was on a journey with him.

Now collaboration does not mean *surrender*. One of my earliest professional collaborations in New York, I agreed to a lot of things, because of wanting to get along, not because of what I knew to be right for the piece. I ended up getting clobbered by the critics, the show ended up getting clobbered. The energy of willing cooperation is crucial, but don't surrender what you believe just because you want to be a cheerleader and because you want everybody to love you. That's not why you're in the room.

Collaboration consists of going forth with your strongest passion and your strongest idea and meeting someone, or any number of people, with their strongest idea. And then, something new emerges, something hopefully better. Something that incorporates all of what all of you are thinking. Maybe it's your idea with somebody else's influence in it. Maybe it's somebody else's idea with your energy in it. It's bringing your craft and bringing your intelligence and bringing your sense of play into a room and allowing everyone else to do the same.

A CHORUS OF DIFFERENT VOICES: CAROLINE, OR CHANGE

The lessons of boundaries and having a shared vocabulary were very helpful when Tony and I were working on *Caroline, Or Change*. I first read it when it was just a libretto, before there was any music attached to it. I've been there every single step of the way. I got to watch as composer Jeanine Tesori joined the project and began to pour herself into it, and began to bring in songs that she had musicalized from Tony's libretto.

It was a very successful and very close collaboration. As I stated earlier, Tony and I are very intense, but so is Jeanine. I think it is very easy for Tony to intimidate people because he is so smart and so passionate, and also because he argues well. When he feels something, he so completely and totally feels it; a lot of people become overwhelmed by that. But Jeanine is very strong too, and very clear. She's totally available to the collaboration, and at the same time, she also has her very strong opinions, and is a deeply gifted artist.

The worst kind of collaboration can happen when you feel like you are pulling somebody along. It's one thing when somebody is in the process of learning. It's another thing when they aren't bringing enough skill into the room. That's really, really hard.

The best is when you're in a room with people who have incredible amounts of skill, intelligence, and passion. Then, it's exciting. Another thing that's exciting is when you combine many different voices into one voice. Jeanine not only brought her knowledge of composing, but also her knowledge of being a mother, which neither Tony nor I have. Tony being Southern and Jewish, and therefore being a part of a community—that apart from the larger community brought his point of view. By virtue of my being Black and Southern, I bring a similar, but also very different point of view.

At times these different visions complemented each other—and other times they collided. But often, when things collide, as is the case in all aspects of collaboration, something else richer and more textured emerges. Also with the cast we got into some very intense conversations about race, history, JFK, the power dynamics and the very complicated and complex relationship between Blacks and Jews in the South and in the North.

These conversations frequently got awkward because there was so much trust and commitment in the room; people were saying what they really believed and not some sanitized version, so as to avoid the tension. As a result, I think that texture, that edge, that sense of messy truth is in the production; as is the heart, compassion and desire to know and to live inside of other people's experience, which was at the base of these conversations as well.

Some people mourn the fact that American mass culture used to speak with a single voice, but no longer does. I don't think that's a weakness. I think it's a glorious strength. Also, when you repress any energy that's in a rehearsal room, it ends up playing itself out in some destructive way, backstage. You've got to let the energy come out.

WORKING ON THE SAME SHOW

One of the biggest problems in a collaboration is when the collaborative team isn't working on the same show. That's so common. Somebody thinks, "We're doing a zany musical comedy," while somebody else thinks, "We're doing a dark and probing vision of America," while somebody else thinks that they are working on a star turn. That's deadly. It's the director's responsibility to keep people communicating, so they stay focused on the same agenda, the same show.

SPEAKING IN TONGUES

There are two schools of directing. You either stand there and demand that everybody come to you, or you go to where your collaborators are. The first kind of director is a bully, usually resulting from the fact that directors feel uncomfortable around people who speak a different artistic language.

The second kind of director woos their collaborators, cajoles them, charms them, seduces them, and challenges them to go on a journey. Then, when they get there, they feel much more empowered because they feel it's their creation. Of course, you've guided them and you've asked the questions and you've challenged them in a way it ends up fulfilling the original vision that you had. But if it all works right, you get something that's even richer than you envisioned.

To do that, however, a director has to learn to speak many artistic languages. I may not understand as much about music as my composer, but I have to be able to discuss the music *dramaturgically*. I have to be able to tell a collaborator where I feel the storytelling of their music, of their book, or their acting, or their dance isn't clear. A director can't just say, "I don't like that" or, "It's not good." A director has to be able to explain where their storytelling is not working, and why. Otherwise, you are not going to help them, nor are you going to get what you want.

Getting the Elephant To Tap

I have a saying when I direct: "If the elephant doesn't want to tap dance, then don't make it." If you work on something and work on something and it's not revealing itself, or finding its groove, that's a signal something's off in the material. Or, something is off in the way you are approaching it—so, it's time to fix it, or find another way of doing it.

One day we put a new number in *Caroline, Or Change*. The cast picked it up and worked it in quickly, which is always a good sign. When things take a lot of effort, sometimes that effort is needed, but sometimes it's a sign that your actors don't feel comfortable with it. If you're a good collaborator, you won't ignore that.

You have to be opinionated but not rigid. You have to be forceful, but not willful. Those are difficult balances to maintain when you are working on a big show—or, for that matter, any show. You have to protect yourself from your own rigidity.

I Want To Be a Producer

I feel my eleven years as a producer at the Public Theater have made me a better citizen in the world.

Producing requires tremendous ego-energy with very little personal ego satisfaction. It's probably akin to parenting, in the sense that you put out all this energy so other people can grow.

And that's a part of collaboration, too: making sure the other guy gets his due. This job has afforded me a chance to put in to practical application my sense that we all have a responsibility that when we get ours to make sure that other people get theirs. I put my name and my face out there to try to get the money so other artists can have a forum.

And when I see artists empowered, and people like Suzan-Lori Parks and Jeffrey Wright, Nilo Cruz, and Liev Schreiber's careers blossom, I feel very proud and very full. There's a side of me that loves being in charge, and creating community, and going on intense journeys with people, and that side of me is a director. But there's a side of me that likes to empower people to create beautiful things and that part of me is a producer.

CHAPTER 11

JAY BINDER
CASTING DIRECTOR

Through his firm, Jay Binder Casting, Binder has cast more than fifty Broadway productions, including *The Lion King, Movin' Out, Chicago,* the 2005 revival of *Who's Afraid of Virginia Woolf?, Once Upon a Mattress, The King and I, Damn Yankees, Beauty and the Beast, Laughter on the 23rd Floor, Lost in Yonkers, Rumors,* and *Jerome Robbins Broadway.* Film and television credits have included *Dreamgirls, Chicago, I'll Fly Away,* and East Coast Casting director for Warner Bros. Television. His firm has earned seven Artios Awards, the highest standard in casting.

Discreet Maitre D'—or Pushy Waiter?

Why do you hire a casting director? Several reasons. One is to save the director time. Casting directors see everyone who's out there. We know their strengths and weaknesses and unique qualities. If a director tells us what sort of actor he's looking for, we can send him three or five who we know are very close to what they want, rather than that director having to see dozens who may or may not be right.

They hire us, not only for what we know, but also for our taste and our opinion. And that extends beyond just gender/age/physical type. We study the play's text, talk to the director, and try to understand the character's heart.

Matching the right actor to the role may be the decision that determines whether a show is going to be a hit or a flop. It's a huge determining factor in any show. We also try to match the chemistry of the actor with the chemistry of the director. Despite all that, a director can disagree with my opinion. There are directors I can name who have turned down an actor I thought was perfect for a part. When I've asked why I've sometimes gotten, "Because I'm the director."

"Because I'm the director" is not an acceptable answer. If I am asking the question, it's to learn something. If I bring you an actor and you don't like that actor, you need to explain to me why. I have no interest in a director that just wants me to bring in an actor at 3:10 p.m. and another at 3:20 p.m. and another at 3:30 p.m. I'm not your guy, because I have too much to say. I need to be able to sit down and talk about what is wanted and what is needed for the given show and the given part.

That's the thing I love about the City Center Encores! series. They make me an intrinsic part of the artistic vision from the very beginning. Casting is the most important element of Encores! shows like *Chicago* and *Do Re Mi* and *Wonderful Town*, and it has to be done on a very tight deadline. In a situation like that, a casting director can really contribute to making a show a success or not.

STRUCTURING THE AUDITION

I'll give you an example: casting the role of Robert Baker in the Encores! *Wonderful Town*. It is the male part with the most lines, but is he the leading man? No. He's the romantic interest of Ruth Sherwood. There's a big difference. You can not put a heroic leading man in that part. You have to find an actor who will be believable as Ruth Sherwood's love interest, but who will not compete with the two leads, who are the two Sherwood sisters. What kind of charming character actor can fit that very delicate niche? Gregg Edelman, a gifted artist. When they moved *Wonderful Town* from Encores! to Broadway, we lost Laura Benanti, who played the younger sister, Eileen. It was so daunting to recast that role, because Laura had had such success in that part. We saw every ingénue in town. At the very last minute I remembered an actress named Jennifer Westfeldt, who had sung and gone to Yale and then did film work. She's a gorgeous girl, and the role of Eileen is the girl that every man is supposed to drop dead over. When she first came in, she had on a sloppy shirt, a bad skirt and clunky shoes. Clearly she was a wonderful actress and obviously technically capable of executing the role, but she wasn't showing us that she could be Eileen. Being politically correct is one of the biggest wastes of time in the world.

I called her up and said, "Jennifer, I want to see bosoms, I want to see your waist, I want to see your hips, I want to see your legs." And she understood.

The next time she walked in, she was breathtaking. She could stop traffic, which is exactly the effect that character must have. She wasn't just an actress, she was *Eileen*.

Here's another example: the 1999 revival of *You're a Good Man, Charlie Brown* had fifteen producers, which was more producers than it had actors. We were down to two actors for the role of Snoopy: Roger Bart and Actor B. Both were very good, but I preferred Bart. The creative team and the producers were split on which actor to go with. I said to the director, as funny as Actor B is, Snoopy is more than just funny. Snoopy is the most intelligent person on the stage. In order for the play to work, that innate irony and intelligence and world-weariness have got to come across.

I decided that the problem was the structure of the audition. Both actors had to sing "Suppertime" and do the Red Baron speech, and that was it. The truth is, anybody could be good doing those two isolated things. I looked at the whole play, and the kind of credibility that character had to project, and I knew I was right. But how to demonstrate it to the creative team? Snoopy's part in the script consists of a series of little vignettes, short philosophical speeches, like comic strips, interspersed with scenes of the other characters. I pulled out eight or ten of Snoopy's vignettes and put them together, so it became vignette, vignette, and vignette.

I asked that both actors be called back again and had them both—not sing anything, but do these vignettes, one after another. And it was suddenly clear to everyone that it was indeed Roger Bart's part.

From the Beginning

The casting director comes in on a musical usually at the very beginning. Unfortunately I'm not old enough to have worked in an era when, after you decided to do a show, you would open it out of out of town and refine it in three or four cities before opening on Broadway.

Today, musicals get produced by reading, reading, reading, reading, workshop, workshop, regional production, regional production, another reading, and then, maybe, Broadway. I don't think all those readings necessarily help because until you are performing it in front of a paying audience you never get a real reaction.

On a big show, I'm often involved from that first reading. My agency is sometimes casting seven shows at the same time. We have an audition space right in our office and we do our own pre-auditions of actors all the time, so we know whom we are sending to the actual auditions for the director.

I have close relationships with many of the top agents. I'll sometimes send them a breakdown of a show I'm casting, which outlines what they need, and they send me their ideas for people. If they suggest somebody I don't know, I see them.

I once was doing pre-screens for a revival of *Bye Bye Birdie*, and director Jerry Zaks asked to sit in. He seemed to be having a great time, but I was getting paranoid because I'm a perfectionist. He was seeing a lot of people he would normally have been spared.

Is every director going to like every actor I bring in? No. But I always want that director to see there is a reason I sent that particular actor. I don't want to waste anybody's time. I may get, "Let's see someone else." But very rarely do I get, "He's completely wrong for the show." I try very hard to send in actors who I think are right for the role.

Most American directors use "audition" as a noun, which means they sit here and you act there. But "audition" should be a verb. People like Jerry Zaks, Graciela Daniele and Walter Bobbie are not shy. They will get up and work with the actor to get a sense of what they'll be like at rehearsals. So, my part of the collaboration is to look at the play as a whole. Some directors have a tendency to audition in minutia or just audition whatever song or scene is in front of them, in that room, in that time and space. But if you are a real pro, you try to see the whole picture. You have to know dramaturgically why this character functions the way it does, and what their place is in the play.

I also believe there are all sorts of directors. I worked for Jerome Robbins on his last show, *Jerome Robbins' Broadway*. Jerry always wanted to see a bazillion dancers. But when it came to actors, even principles, he wanted see my four best people, and get out of the room. Directors come to me because they know I won't send them anyone unless they are carefully chosen. Because there is the trust. Many have no patience, and don't like to have their time wasted. Which is fine. When I first started working at this level, I had to learn hard and fast, or else I was out. So I learned very quickly.

But, still, many directors don't feel satisfied. They think there may still be someone else out there. They like to see the whole wide world. I have to respect that process. I may not agree with it, but I have to respect it and work with it, because they are also hiring me for my service. And bringing in as many actors as they want to see is part of the service. Casting for Broadway is more difficult than ever because there are very few actual bankable stars who work on Broadway. The trend now is for the star to come in for eighteen weeks, in and out, so they can pursue other projects, too. That's how you get stars like Liam Neeson or Vanessa Redgrave between movies. It becomes very difficult to do a commercial play without a limited engagement.

There are certain times in casting when you have to admit you just don't have the right person. I'm the first one to raise my hand and say, "Don't settle." Producer Manny Azenberg said something to me when we were casting *Lost in Yonkers* that I have tried to live by: if an actor is not empathetic, no matter what he is playing, don't cast him. I know what he means by that. You have to want to spend a whole night with somebody, whether they are playing the hero or the villain. And look at that cast: Kevin Spacey, Mercedes Ruehl, Irene Worth. We refused to compromise and got one of the greatest casts ever.

The author of that play was Neil Simon and he has a saying that is God's truth: when you are casting, the actors pick us, we don't pick them. What he means is, when an actor walks into an audition and "owns" it, there's nothing to talk about. We all go, "Yeah."

THE GENERALS

One of the best collaborators I ever had the great fortune to work with was the late Mike Ockrent. Every production needs a leader, and he was a general. I used to say if I were trapped on a desert island; the one person I would have wanted there with me was Mike because he would have gotten all of us off the friggin' island. He knew how to command an army. Susan Stroman worked at his side and was trained by him and by other great directors. So Stroman is a superb collaborator. She understands how to gather a group of artists and get them to work together. And while she may disagree with your idea, she creates the atmosphere in which you are encouraged to collaborate. Which is not to say there weren't moments when she wanted to belt me and I wanted to belt her. But that's also the joy of collaboration: two strong people with strong opinions.

I started working on Broadway with Neil Simon and Gene Saks who were great collaborators because the way they functioned was very clear. Neil would write a play. Gene would direct the play. Gene has an ability to present what Neil wrote at its best so that Neil would know where the changes needed to be made.

Jerome Robbins was a very different kind of collaborator. His vision was the vision that had to be on the stage, period. But he had the ability to make you think and challenge you and dare you and intimidate you to do your very best. That also is a form of collaboration. Unfortunately, generals like Ockrent and Robbins and Stroman and Saks and Jack O'Brien and Jerry Zaks are few and far between. The greatest joy is working with someone who trusts you completely, and whom you trust completely in return. As a casting director I have worked with Walter Bobbie now for a decade. Walter and I speak the same language. It is the most joyous collaboration I could possibly have because I can say to him, "You are out of your fucking mind!" And he can say, "So are you!" I don't have to be on my best behavior. He doesn't have to be on his best behavior. From that kind of honesty comes the greatest collaborations.

Graciela Daniele is high on my list. I think she is a breathtaking collaborator. She surrounds herself with a group of artists she trusts and allows everyone to contribute. Sure, she rejects some ideas and perfects others, but that's another joyous part of collaboration. I've also seen directors grow into their ability to collaborate. My decade-long collaboration with Kathleen Marshall is joyous. Kathleen can come in with one idea and ultimately be open enough to learn something and I'm open enough to learn something as well—and, again, that's about trust.

I was Julie Taymor's casting director on the original Broadway production of *The Lion King*. On one level that collaboration was blissful because Julie would allow me to do something that was unheard of: to actually get up with her and the actors and work with them. What was difficult for Julie was to come to realize the way a musical had to be put together in order to function properly eight times a week over a long run. Practicality never should rule, but it should also be in the back of your mind that a show is a machine that is going to have to function with human beings as the gears.

Twyla Tharp, who put together *Movin' Out*, was a very different sort of practical artist. She had a great collaboration with her dancers, which everyone sees. But what people don't see is the great collaboration she had with her brilliant producer, Manny Azenberg and the Nederlander Organization.

Twyla comes from the dance world. *Movin' Out* is a ballet company, and things were fine-tuned to run with the dancers' needs in mind. Which helped the show more than you know. Because of the story, the show was designed for dancers who were not kids anymore. From the very beginning Twyla worked out how many different sets of leads she would need, how many alternates she'd need to keep from overworking the dancers, to keep them fresh. Manny and the Nederlanders were generous about the number of swings and the vacation time, so we were never denied the ability to maintain the show at the highest level. The financial consideration was considerable, but the producers found ways to make it work and still earn a profit. They knew you always pay more in the end when you try to cut corners. If it weren't for the strength of the collaboration between savvy Twyla Tharp and intelligently generous Manny Azenberg, we wouldn't have had the show we had.

Sometimes there is just a mismatch between director and Casting. One experience was with a director so arrogant he refused to even greet the actors. He just sat back and rolled his head at them. Sometimes he didn't even look at them. How dare he? You should have the decency to treat actors with some respect, say hello and thank you. Look at them. It's only human courtesy. How dare someone treat another human being without respect, whether you think they are talented or not. Harold Prince, I am told, always takes the time to be polite. Jerry Robbins was polite to every single human being who walked though the door. After they left he may have screamed at me. But that was his right. I'm a great believer in honest, truthful communication. If you don't like something, it's your job to say something. Not everyone welcomes this.

I would rather be in the room with Paul Gemignani than any other musical director working on Broadway today. If someone proposes something that will cause him to do less than the best, he won't hesitate to say, "Not in my fucking lifetime, pal." You always know exactly where he stands. I love that.

Cy Coleman was a man from the old school, too. If he didn't like something, he put it all out there. Suddenly you were in a wonderful impassioned argument about creativity. You were communicating.

Too much is at stake to be silent.

PICKING BATTLES

Most people try to avoid battles, which is generally a good instinct. But sometimes you can't. I strongly opposed the casting of the young lady who got the leading role of Peggy Sawyer in the recent *42nd Street* revival. She was proficient at everything: she sang acceptably, she tapped well, she was pretty. But she was cold as ice. As a result, the audience had no empathy for Peggy Sawyer. Everyone in the audition room saw it and knew it, except the director. Basically I came very close to a fistfight. But in the end, they hired her.

You have to pick your battles. If you believe in something strongly, you have to fight. You can't just sit back and let it happen. But if you lose, you lose. But I fought my battle. And I lost. My big mouth has gotten me fired from shows. I was fired from *Chicago* when it moved from Encores! to Broadway because I badmouthed another production from the same producers. I wanted to audition an actor for a role in the revival of *Once Upon a Mattress*. He was in a production of *Applause* at the Paper Mill Playhouse that the same producers wanted to take to Broadway. When the actor's agent told me he wasn't available because the show was moving to Broadway, I told him, "That show isn't moving out of the parking lot." That got back to the producers. But I was right, the show didn't move.

I would have been fired from the 2004 revival of *Fiddler on the Roof* in a day. I would have turned to the director and said, "Are you out of your mind?" It was a lovely production, but being Jewish and having such love for Jerome Robbins's original production, I wouldn't have lasted a minute. It didn't have to be exactly the same production as Jerry's, but it did have to come from the same heart.

FATHER FIGURE

Working in the era of Broadway since the 1980s, I really pine for what this industry used to be. Back in the 1940s and 1950s, it was smaller but there was cama-

115

raderie of collaboration that we lack today. The nature of the business has changed. If you were in trouble out of town with a show, Joshua Logan or Abe Burrows or George S. Kaufman or George Abbott or Noël Coward or one of your other friends would instantly be there for you, and lend you their expertise. I'm sure there were disagreements. There are famous stories about Josh Logan and Maxwell Anderson having violent disagreements about *Anne of a Thousand Days*. But it wasn't about the money. It was about a close group of theatre professionals.

Even as some of these giants were breaking ground and creating new forms in the musical theatre, veterans always made sure to hire and work with promising newcomers. They passed their knowledge along. Example: you had a father figure in George Abbott who hired newcomers like Jerry Ross, Richard Adler, Hal Prince, Hugh Martin, Kander and Ebb, Burt Shevelove, Larry Gelbart and Stephen Sondheim. He wasn't afraid to work with young talent and give them a chance.

So we don't have the mentoring process that leads to collaboration the way we once did, and we don't have the reliable hit makers like Abbott, Kaufman, Robbins, or even a Bennett, Champion, or Fosse. Yes, these men had a lot of flops, too. So did Logan and Moss Hart. But they all came from the same background and they spoke the same language and they helped each other to the best of their ability.

I did a workshop of *Sweet Charity* with a very gifted young English director and a very gifted young choreographer, who were supposed to work with Cy Coleman and Neil Simon. But there was no collaboration between these four men. Part of the problem was the age difference, part was a cultural difference. They had no common points by which they could actually communicate.

Another reason for the decline in collaboration is the growing sophistication of electronic communication. You don't have to be in the same room any more. In the old days there was no such thing as a fax or email. You had to be in a room to collaborate. I've worked on shows, like *Aida* or *Beauty and the Beast*, where a lyric would be faxed from the lyricist to the composer and that was the collaboration. The technology seems like it makes things easier, but in the end it's actually a stumbling block. To write a show you need to be face to face to thrash things out. That's how great musicals come about. Collaboration is sometimes a matter of putting all the pieces of the puzzle together to create the right team.

Seeking Equality

One of the great frustrations of the casting director is not being treated as an equal, no matter how well we may do our job. We are second-class citizens. We are servants. I have to change my entire life around somebody else's schedule. There are very few times when anyone will change their schedule for me. And most directors never call you with the good things. They only call you when they want to fire someone. When someone calls me to tell me something good and thank me, I'm surprised and floored. Usually the phone rings and I answer it, "Who's fired?" But I really only enjoy working with people who want to collaborate. I want to be part of a family, part of a team. Collaboration to me is the ability to sit in a room with a group of professionals and be honest. Being honest is the most difficult thing in the world to be. I am not always successful at it. You can't worry about people's feelings. You have to establish enough groundwork that everybody is in the room respects each other.

I love what I do and I love to be in a room with people who are as smart as I am. I want to learn something every time I enter that room.

One last thought. About seventeen years ago, Gene Feist, the founder of the Roundabout Theatre Company, fired me. He then sent a letter defining my job as a discreet maitre d', not a pushy waiter. Somewhere between the two, lies the perfect casting director. I am still learning.

CHAPTER 12

PAUL GEMIGNANI
MUSICAL DIRECTOR AND CONDUCTOR

Paul Gemignani's Broadway credits feature original productions of *Follies*; *Pacific Overtures*; *Candide*; *A Little Night Music*; *Sweeney Todd*; *Evita*; *Dreamgirls*; *Merrily We Roll Along*; *Into the Woods*; *On the Twentieth Century*; *Sunday in the Park With George*; *Jerome Robbins' Broadway*; *Crazy for You*; *Passion*; *High Society*; and revivals of *Kiss Me, Kate*; *Assassins*; *Pacific Overtures*; and *The Frogs*. TV: *Follies Live at the Philharmonic*, *A Little Night Music* (PBS' Live at Lincoln Center), *A Cele-*bration of the American Musical (Great Performances, 1998), *Into the Woods* (Showtime), *Sunday in the Park with George* (PBS), *Passion* (American Playhouse). Awards: Tony Award for Lifetime Achievement (2001), Special Drama Desk Award (1989), Los Angeles Drama Critics Award (1994); Grammy nominations include *Passion, Crazy for You,* and *Kiss Me, Kate*. Honorary Doctor of Musical Arts, Manhattan School of Music.

Unison and Harmony

I'm called "Musical Director" and not simply "Conductor" for a reason. Conducting is the artistic side of what I do, but there is a whole administrative side that nobody sees, but which is equally important.

I coordinate all the music between the orchestrator, the composer, the dance arranger and the musicians, to make sure everybody is on the same page. I work out a timetable so that there is sheet music on the music stands in time for the first orchestra read, and the orchestrator is not at home trying to get the last nine numbers finished. I also work with the sound designer, the singers, even the set designer sometimes.

When you work on a musical you are in collaboration with everybody.

History

I love music. I love the ideas in the musical theatre. It's so creative.

Before I had the leader's job I was a cellist and a drummer. I played classical music in college and, later, to make a living, I played drums in a nightclub and sometimes in the opera. I always knew that I wanted to conduct. My mother had taken me to see *Gypsy* when I was a kid, but I grew up on the West Coast and hadn't seen any other musicals. In 1967 I was on tour with a singer and we came through New York. My friend, the actor Ed Winter, was in *Cabaret* at the time. I went to see him in the musicals and thought, Wow! This is something I could get interested in.

I wound up playing in the pit orchestras of several shows of that period: *Follies, Cabaret, Zorba.* I got my first conducting job on the national tour of *Zorba*. John Kander, the composer, has always been wonderful to me. John came to see it, and orchestrator Don Walker sent him away from the orchestra rehearsal in Philadelphia saying, "Let the kid alone. Let him get the orchestra on its feet, and then you can give him notes."

I came back to New York to play the drums in the pit of the original *Follies* on Broadway. Hal Hastings, the musical director of *Follies*, urged me to take the job but I told him I was happy working on the road. Remember, I'm a West Coast boy so a lot of things about New York meant nothing to me at the time. He told me, "You must do this. It will be good for your career. Hal Prince is the director and he's someone you must work with. Plus there's Stephen Sondheim and Michael Bennett!"

I knew Prince because he had produced most of the shows I had worked on, but I hadn't worked directly with him. I literally had to ask who Sondheim and Bennett were. When Hal Hastings was ready to leave the show, he twisted my arm and I agreed to replace him, and the rest is history. I never went back to the drums again.

Joy about Playing

It's the musical director's responsibility to hire, schedule, rehearse, and conduct the orchestra. It starts when the orchestrator, the composer and I sit down and talk about what instruments are going to be needed in the orchestra. Then I go out and I pick the best people. If I'm going to ask them to be my artistic partner, I've got to have some relationship with them.

I look for the same things in all the musicians I hire: not just excellent playing but a real joy about playing. I don't want some tired, worn-out person who doesn't like to do it any more. Playing in a Broadway pit is really hard work. There are a lot of demands on you. It doesn't matter how old you are or how young you are, those demands are still there. And they don't get any easier when you become 50 than they were when you were 20. I look for people, whatever their ages, who have that spirit left, who care about music and still have fun playing music no matter what it is.

One of the best orchestras I ever conducted was for the 1999 *Kiss Me, Kate* revival. The musicians were practically singing along with the singers. There was two reasons for that. One: Don Sebesky is a great orchestrator, so the musicians had interesting parts to play. Two: the spirit of the musicians. They actually cared about what they were playing. You have no idea how much something so subtle can add to the energy of a show.

I also deal with casting. Casting is very collaborative. Director Susan Stroman may say she needs eight dancers. I say I need six singers. You don't hire dancers who can't sing. That's not what the musical theatre is about, at least not anymore. It's about doing three things: acting, singing, and dancing. Making sure that the performers can sing is part of the musical director's job. Then you are responsible for teaching all the music in the show and, in my case, you wind up writing a lot of the vocal arrangements.

Some shows have a separate arranger, like Peter Howard on *Crazy for You*. Then we share. He might have an idea and we'll do that. I'll have an idea and we'll do that. It never stops being collaborative. Just because it said "dance music by Peter Howard" in *Crazy for You* doesn't mean that's all he did. He did a lot more than that. It's one of the few businesses that I know that are so collaborative.

The collaboration between Stephen Sondheim, Hal Prince, and Hugh Wheeler may have been the best I ever saw. If I learned anything about collaboration it was from those three guys on *Sweeney Todd*.

When *Merrily We Roll Along* wasn't working in previews, instead of getting hysterical, Steve and Hal dug in and try to make it work. They tried to figure out why it didn't work and tried to fix it. Instead of saying, "Screw this. It's not going to work," they just kept at it. That's a great lesson.

Talking Back to the Architect

My job is fulfilling the intentions of the composer. I don't tell the composers how to do their job. After all, I didn't write the piece.

But let's be realistic. If I think something can be better, I will bring it up with the composer. I ask all questions—with respect. Sometimes there are also practical problems the composer couldn't have anticipated. Composers usually don't know the actors in the show as well as I do because they don't work with the cast and the musicians every day. So if I think that Bernadette Peters would be better if one line in a song was a little different, because it's not in the best part of her voice, I might say to the composer, "If that line was a fourth lower or if you could rewrite that line, that whole song would soar."

Sometimes the composer will take my advice. Sometimes not. He'll say, "That's the way I want it." Fine, I lost the point. But I don't really consider it losing. I consider it a suggestion on which my employer has passed. When I'm there, I'm basically working for the composer.

Let's take my spring 2004 project, *Assassins*, as an example. There was not a lot of dance music in *Assassins*. Not a lot of extra music was written at all. But when the director or the choreographer felt that more music was needed, to underscore a scene for instance, it was my job to put the music in. I didn't compose my own music, naturally. I took themes from Stephen Sondheim's score. Many shows have a separate dance arranger, but there was so little dance in *Assassins*, I supplied whatever little music was needed that wasn't there already.

Another of my 2004 shows, *The Frogs*, not only had a choreographer/director in Susan Stroman. It had a fantastic dance arranger/incidental musical person named Glenn Kelly. Together with the composer, also Sondheim, we formed a little creative team within the creative team, focused on the music.

But I don't limit myself to the musical end. In my view we are all making the same show. If I see something in the book that needs looking at, I have no qualms about saying, "Hey what about that joke in scene three?" The same way that the book writer could come to me and say, "Why are those people singing that?" It's a totally collaborative art form. That's the only way I have ever worked.

It's interesting how much detail you get from the composer and the orchestrator. Steve Sondheim puts more down on a piece of paper than most people do. Jule Styne did the same thing. It was so clear that you could give it to a first-year orchestrating student and they could have a pretty good idea of what the composer wanted. As opposed to some of the more pop-oriented composers who just write a melody line and chord changes and its up to you to fill in the accompanying figures.

We get some parts copied out by hand, and some that are computer printouts. Michael Starobin, who did *Assassins*, sends his totally from a computer. Jonathan Tunick would never use a computer. He likes to hand-write everything. It *looks* like he printed it out, that's how neat it is.

William Finn writes on legal pads, which is fine. Music is music. I don't care how it gets there. So that means Michael Starobin has to come up with accompaniment figures. It's still collaborative. You still have to go back and ask the composer if the result is what he had in mind. You have to be multi-faceted. You have to be able to fill in the gaps—and when to back off if you find there are no gaps.

Whether I'm working with David Shire (*Big*) or Sondheim, I am always perfectly honest with them. If I see something that isn't going to work—if an actor can't sing a passage as written—I will ask if I can change the key, and most of the time they'll say fine. Sometimes they'll take that person over to the piano to check, and get the person to prove me right or wrong.

Steve is one of the best collaborators I have ever worked with in my life. He literally hands me the music or faxes a new song and we try to do it just the way he wants it. He may come and see it and make an adjustment, but they both like feedback.

Cy Coleman liked things to be done exactly the way he wrote them. I did *On the Twentieth Century* with him. He was more in love with what he wrote than others, but that doesn't mean that he wasn't open-minded.

Here's an example: the song "Life Is Like a Train" from *On the Twentieth Century*. We didn't have singers who could handle the range of what Cy Coleman wrote, so I manipulated the music a little bit and showed it to him. The original had a very high note, and I pointed out that the only way to do it was to have an actor go into falsetto, and that would take the volume down. He wanted to try to make it work the way he had written it, so he worked with the singers, trying to get them up to that note, but he couldn't get it. So he looked at what I did, and said, "Fine." That's how we collaborate.

With Steve Sondheim and I, unless it's something major, I don't even ask him; I just do it. If he hears it and doesn't like it, he'll tell me. In the musical theatre it's not like opera. You fit the piece to the singer. Just because George Hearn can sing "Epiphany" from *Sweeney Todd* in a certain key doesn't mean anybody else can. So why force them to and not sound as good? So you find the key where that person sounds good, and you put the song there.

If I had to pick a song to illustrate how I collaborate with a composer, I'd pick "Sunday" from Sondheim's *Sunday in the Park With George*. When "Sunday" came in there was just a melody line—there was no harmony in it. We had some actors for whom singing was not their first love, and were a little insecure about their singing. Part of my job is to help them sound great. So I came up with the idea of a harmony line.

Now, my theory is "less is more." If a song doesn't need harmony I'm the last one to put it in. In fact, I will take it out sometimes because I think a given song may be more powerful without it. But for "Sunday" I wanted to add a line. If you listen to "Sunday" you'll hear a unison note to the word "Sunday," and then there's the harmony note. I called Steve on the phone and asked if I could add the harmony, to give the passage more weight.

He said, "I don't want it harmonized."

I said, "I'm not overharmonizing. One note. I'm harmonizing a third. It won't get larger. I'll add more people as we go along and what will happen is it will sound like the harmony is growing but the harmony won't grow." And that's what happened. I respected his music and he trusted my judgement.

On shows like *Crazy for You* and *Kiss Me, Kate*, Gershwin and Porter aren't here to answer questions or approve changes. So I research their music as if they were alive. I read a lot about them. I find out what their attitude was. I ask questions to people who may have been around. I listen to all of their music that I can get before I start a project. So I have an idea of their era and what they were writing.

Cole Porter was a lyricist too, obviously. So I made sure that any vocal arrangements weren't gratuitous. Lyrics were his passion and he wanted them heard. You try and find what their passion is. I think Gershwin thought about lyrics, too, but I don't think he thought about them like Porter did. Gershwin's music is just more "there." Without a live composer the only thing you can do is research.

THE TOP OF YOUR GAME

What kills a collaboration is thinking that you are always right, and not being open to other people's suggestions. Even if you thought you wrote the best lyric in your life, there's always another way of doing it. Will it be right? Will it be better than what you wrote the first time? I don't know—but there are five people here making this decision so you are obliged to try everything. If you are writing the lyrics for a show, you can't dig your feet in. Because then the creativity comes to a screeching halt.

That's why picking a creative team for a show is one of the most important decisions a producer can make. When Roger Berlind put together the creative team for the 1999 *Kiss Me, Kate* revival, he did a great job. You had Michael Blakemore, Kathleen Marshall, and David Chase—a brilliant lineup right there. He matched those people up in his head. Some of us had never worked together before, but we ended up having a great time.

The same is true of Susan Stroman. If she asks for a fanfare to be played I feel comfortable replying, "You don't really want a fanfare there, do you? Listen to it." And I'll have the orchestra play it.

I'll ask again, "Are you sure you want a fanfare there?"

She'll listen to it. And sometimes she'll say, "You know? You're right." And sometimes she'll say, "*I want a fanfare.*"

And we do it and it becomes part of the show. It's that kind of feedback. As long as it's done with respect and caring for the end results, you don't get a lot of flak.

However, if it becomes apparent that you're just throwing your weight around, then feedback doesn't mean anything. Word flies until everybody finds out.

But if it's apparent that you actually care about the quality of the performance, then the doors open up. Anybody can say, "That's not a good idea," without worrying about hurt feelings. It's been said to me. I've said that to people. But you're like family by that time. If you are working that intensely eight hours a day for what amounts to about six weeks, you are family.

Unless I can have that kind of freedom, I can't do my job and I am just miserable.

It's important that you get along with the others on the creative team, and it's really important that you love the project, especially if you are putting something new. Conducting a show where you're not really fond of the score is a big mistake. In this business you have to be at the top of your game all the time. You can't have an "off" day like in an office. It's a pressure kind of a job. You have to constantly come up with great ideas about how to do it. And there's no way you can be at the top of your game if you don't like what you're conducting.

The same is true of the musicians I am conducting. They have to be working with me every minute because there's no way I can enforce discipline during a show. This little white stick I wave makes no noise. If the musicians are not good and happy with what they are doing then I'm the one who will look like an idiot.

I'm pretty loose in terms of discipline. I don't care about what the musicians wear, as long as it's dark because I don't want it distracting from what's on the stage. The union allows musicians to take a certain number of days off as long as they send in a qualified sub. I don't care if they sub the exact amount of time that the union says. What I care about is what you do when you are here and to make sure that the sub you pick is every bit as good as you are. That is where I will be strict.

I have final say on who gets into the pit. Nobody gets in before I hear them play. If they are not fine, then I throw them out. Some musicians send over subs who don't play as well as they do because they are afraid I'll want to keep the sub instead of them. That's a dumb thing to do. You hire the best person you can find even if you think they play better than you. That's the smart thing to do. It shows respect for me, for the show, and for the music. And I repay that kind of respect.

DYNAMICS

A musical director sometimes has to fight to make sure the audience can hear the orchestra. For a long time now, the trend has been to hide the pit under the stage, or even backstage so you can put in more rows of seats, and then mike them. It winds up sounding like you are listening to the cast album already.

There's a psychological price to be paid for that, too. The musicians may be totally into the show, but if you destroy their natural sound, they start to feel like they are superfluous. A live musical is supposed to have live musicians. It's not supposed to be musicians in a pit which is covered over so their music has to be piped in.

In *Jerome Robbins' Broadway* I remember telling set designer Robin Wagner that the stage could not be so close to me. I told him the dynamics of the music would be lost if he put us in a hole.

It also creates an impossible problem for the sound designer. His job then is to try to pretend we are not covered over, and there's no way he can do that. In the dance shows like *Kiss Me, Kate*, the dance numbers would never have been so lively and engaging if the orchestra had been covered over.

That said, the hardest thing for an audience to do nowadays is *listen* because their hearing has been destroyed by hearing everything loud. Television is loud. You go into movies and, I don't care where you sit, they blow your eardrums out. People come to the theatre and they listen to Kevin Spacey speaking without a microphone in *The Iceman Cometh* and they think they can't hear. What does that do to music? You have to fight to play dynamics—the differences in volume that help tell the story.

Don't tell me you can't hear because it's not loud enough! Listen! This part may be soft; but it will get louder at some point. You have to listen. That's the job of the audience. It's what the word "audience" means: those who listen. I think it helps when people can see the musicians. They accept that the music is coming from real people and not a loudspeaker. Recorded music has given people permission to treat music like something in the background that can safely be ignored without being rude. That's just not the case in the live theatre.

Listening is the audience's part of the collaboration. But nobody instructs the audience in how to listen. Everybody in this business is sublimely trained to do their job—except the audience.

A lot of show people will say they listen to the audience and make changes based on the reaction of the audience. But I don't agree. Ninety percent of the time I pay no attention to it at all.

Audiences are never the same—which is one of the things that is great about them. Eight shows a week, some laughs are guaranteed and some aren't. Some silences are guaranteed and some aren't. It changes depending on what the makeup of the audience is that night. I love audiences and I love live theatre but I don't let them dictate what I do. There's an old director's precept that says don't go to the audience with the material. Bring the audience to you. You rehearse a piece, you know how good it is. You do the piece and you bring them up to you. Don't go after them.

The only exception I can think of is when we're trying something specific, like the timing of a sight gag to get a laugh. But in a show like *Assassins*, I would never listen to the audience. Some people laugh when they're uncomfortable. Or they don't laugh at all. Or they are quiet. Sometimes they get up and walk out. Is that because a show like *Assassins* is ineffective—or because it's too effective? How can you use any of that to change the show? You're not clairvoyant. You can't tell why they react as they do. And everyone's different.

WORKING FOR THE PHONE COMPANY

I see a lot of young people come through the door who don't appreciate what it means to be working on Broadway. There are many, many people out there with lots of talent who are working for the phone company. You have to want to work in the theatre so badly that you develop the patience and the endurance to keep at it. Some people make it quickly and some people never make it. That's just the game.

If you're an actor and you don't get a job at an audition, it doesn't mean you're no good. It just means that according to three people's opinion you are not right for that show. Three other people would think that you are perfect and you would get the show. If you really have a passion about the theatre, keep after it and don't settle. Don't say, "I guess I'm no good," and go work for the phone company. You only get one time around, and if you don't follow your passion you are going to be sorry for the rest of your life.

PETER LAWRENCE
STAGE MANAGER

Peter Lawrence has originated eighteen Broadway productions as production stage manager, including major revivals of *Gypsy* and *Man of La Mancha*. He was production supervisor for the Broadway production of *The Graduate*. He was executive producer for *Miss Saigon* and *Les Misérables* (Broadway and national tour) and was the production supervisor for the Broadway revival of *Annie Get Your Gun* and *Sunset Boulevard*. Lawrence directed the U.S. national tours of *Social Security*, *Broadway Bound*, *Rumors*, *Lost in Yonkers*, and *Sunset Boulevard* and the Asian tour of *Miss Saigon*. He has taught in the drama departments of Transylvania College and the University of Hawaii.

When I first began stage managing in 1973, I was always told that if you could sweep a stage and tell time, you could be a stage manager. And Off-Broadway, you didn't need to be able to tell time.

I started out to be a lawyer—it's the family business. But in college it became clear to me that the only profession I've ever loved and the only place I've ever felt completely at home is the theatre. I've been an actor, a lighting designer, a drama critic, a box office treasurer, a theatrical photographer, and I hold an MFA in directing. I actually moved to New York, from Hawaii, in 1972 to be a drama critic. Once when I was broke in New York, I lied to a producer of dinner theatres and said that I was a stage manager. I found I had an aptitude for stage managing and worked my way through stock, touring, Off-Broadway and finally to Broadway in 1977. I have only been an assistant stage manager once in my career, and so I'm entirely self-taught.

In the world of commercial Broadway

production today, with musicals costing upwards of $15 million and plays costing upwards of $3 million, the requirements for stage managing have become a bit more stringent than they were when I began. Stage managers today are responsible for the safe, efficient and artistically stable running of shows which not only cost a good deal than they did thirty years ago, but also run longer and require more maintenance.

In rehearsal, the stage manager must be sure the director and choreographer is allotting his/her time well and that the atmosphere of the rehearsal hall is both safe and productive. We must forecast what eventual scenic timings will be, make recommendations on understudy assignments, keep an up-to-date staging book with script changes, advise all technical departments on changes in the show, schedule production meetings, make the daily rehearsal calls, keep an eye on the budget, and plan out the technical/dress rehearsal schedule. In my view, stage management is the only department required to understand the totality of a production—artistic, technical, and financial.

The nature of the collaboration with the various departments and individuals in legitimate theatre actually depends upon the personalities involved. Some directors and choreographers feel quite comfortable with set and lighting issues, some are more conversant with costumes and hair designs. Some have prejudices against individuals or crafts; some unite a production, while some try to divide a production. The job of the stage manager is to facilitate, to interpret those areas of the production with which members of the artistic team are less knowledgeable and to keep all members of the production team on the same path with the same information.

For instance, Mike Nichols, with whom I've done five productions, is very comfortable directing actors, working with costume and hair designs, but is less comfortable with moving scenery and lighting issues. I pay careful attention to decisions made about scenery and lighting and try to help Mr. Nichols understand the issues involved in both, while I pay virtually no attention to costume and hair on his shows. Mr. Nichols is excellent at casting plays and also uses the actors' time very well. He is less conversant with musicals and so on our next show, which is a musical, I intend to be quite active in letting Mr. Nichols know the effects, in both time and money, of certain scenic and lighting decisions. I will also be quite vocal regarding understudies and swings, since musicals are so different from plays in the coverage needed.

I love working with Mr. Nichols because he is not only an artist of the very first rank, but a man of spiritual generosity and intellectual depth. I always learn from him and he always unites a company of actors.

Terry Johnson, who directed and adapted *The Graduate*, is English. He had directed the show in London and the Broadway production used essentially the same set and costumes. This was Mr. Johnson's first American production. I was of use to him in pointing out British-isms that had crept into his script, and how best to use American actors because of the differences in training and attitude from their British counterparts. It is also difficult for British directors to understand the union rules in the U.S. And so on *The Graduate*, I functioned more as a directorial assistant than as a technical stage manager.

My collaboration with Mr. Johnson was also a good one because he came to rely on me for the differences between London and New York—artistically, technically, and procedurally.

Colleen Dewhurst (on *An Almost Perfect Person* and *The Dance of Death*) and later Glenn Close (on *Sunset Boulevard*) taught me that every member of the production must try to unite the audience, to lead them through the same narrative line, to think the same thoughts. Ms. Dewhurst used to say that if she had done that job on four performances a week, she was happy. This uniting of the audience is why cameras, especially flash pictures, and cell phones are so destructive to a performance—they fragment an audience. Ms. Close was/is meticulous about getting all her emotional ducks in a row, to be sure her moment-to-moment reality is airtight, to be sure her story had no holes. And if an understudy or replacement is working opposite her, the characterization may vary, but not the details of the story. Both Ms. Dewhurst and Ms. Close are prodigious in their concentration.

Bernadette Peters (on *The Goodbye Girl*, *Annie Get Your Gun*, and *Gypsy*) taught me that a great star makes discipline problems disappear just by example—if she can perform ill or exhausted, so can everyone else. Twice during *Annie Get Your Gun* she became ill during a performance, ran offstage to be sick, and then continued the performance. She has performed with vocal infections, nausea, sprained limbs, and personal tragedy. There have been fewer actors or stagehands out of a Bernadette Peters show than any other shows I've worked on.

George Hearn (on *An Almost Perfect Person* and on *Sunset Boulevard*) taught me that the theatre is about fairness and love. George is Irish, sings in restaurants and has as fearless an emotional life as any man I've ever known. He once tried to attack a producer in a regional production I did with him because George felt the producer was disrespecting the work of the director.

Zoe Caldwell (on my first Broadway show, *An Almost Perfect Person*, and its tryouts) taught me about loyalty. After a year of regional tryouts, the show was optioned for Broadway. I had never done a Broadway show, even as an assistant. Ms. Caldwell said she would not do the show unless I was the stage manager. And

I was hired. She felt I had earned the right to do the show on Broadway during the regional tryouts. I owe her my career. In a different way, Artie Siccardi on at least a dozen Broadway shows has taught me the same valuable lesson. He is intensely loyal to those who do a good job for him, and conversely, never forgets being let down. I made it my job never to let down Artie Siccardi, and when I've asked his advice, I've always taken it. I've modified Artie's iron-clad rules of loyalty to fit my own career, but I would be foolish not to honor them.

Jules Fisher and Peggy Eisenhauer (on *Death and the Maiden* and the 2003 revival of *Gypsy*) taught me how to be fearless in pursuit of your vision. They are notorious (if you're a producer) or visionary (if you're an artist) because they constantly invent new technology, demand new standards for lighting. Time and budget are less of a concern to these two great artists than realizing an idea. And who has worked longer or is more highly thought of than these two?

Manny Azenberg (in my five years as his Production Manager) taught me that a budget is a flexible document. The numbers must fit the production and not the other way around. I did five Neil Simon comedies with Manny as well as a half-dozen other Broadway and Off-Broadway shows. Manny will fight to keep a budget down, but will always support his artists—no matter what the cost. Manny believes in serving the production. Robert Fox (the producer of *Gypsy*) taught me about both graciousness and nerve. As the budget for *Gypsy* worked its way higher, Robert and his partner Ron Kastner would always ask "why" of director Sam Mendes, but would never say "no." Robert also believes in serving the production and artists who work on it.

But it is Mike Nichols who gave me a method for approaching the artistic side of the work and how to stay interested over the long haul. Mike believes in owner-ship of the work—that is, that everyone associated with the production creates a piece of it. The actors must believe they have created their characters and staging, the designers must believe the same about the environment and clothes. But also the press agents, stagehands, management, musicians—everyone—must believe they have contributed to the whole. This means everyone on the production will fight for its survival. And when new cast or management members join the production, they must be made to feel that they've made a worthwhile change in the show. Stage managers are very important to Mike; he has always made me feel that the way a show is set up to run, the backstage atmosphere, the parties, the fairness are all crit-ical to the long-term success of a show. And most importantly, Mike has always given me a great deal of freedom in noting the actors and in directing cast replace-ments. He told me once, "Before you can give an actor a note, you must first figure out what they think they are doing." This respect for actors and for everyone on a production is his hallmark and why everyone (including me) wants to work for Mike Nichols.

Each production is entirely different. Each requires different staffing in stage management. Some shows work better with mostly male stage managers, some with mostly female. Age, gender, sexual orientation, background, foreign language, experience in different venues, training and demeanor all figure in my selection of a stage management team. Everyone in a production must feel comfortable speaking with some member of the stage management team about any problem, personal or professional. The team must be cast to serve this need.

I think stage managers must try to see where potential communication problems exist on a production and then bridge those gaps. It is our job to make each area of the production understand what the other areas are doing, and why they are doing them. This way, pockets of antagonism don't form; an atmosphere of mistrust and blame is not allowed to gather. Everyone is working towards the same definable goal. Often, the director or the producer can identify this goal and push the top creative staff towards it. But it is up to the stage manager to bring everyone to this goal.

It is also the job of the stage manager to be sure that the first preview performance happens safely and on the date scheduled. I always think that it is the director who gets a show to opening night, but it is the stage manager who gets it to the first preview.

After the press opening on Broadway or at the first stop on a national tour, the stage manager's job switches 180 degrees from an organizational/technical function to an artistic one. The director leaves the production on opening night and is infrequently seen after that. The stage manager becomes the director's surrogate, maintaining his/her vision for the show, keeping the running times of each scene at approximately what it was on opening night, noting the actors and calling brush-up rehearsals, and rehearsing the understudies. Often, the stage manager does the recasting when original cast members leave the production. The stage manager literally runs the onstage and backstage show. (The company manager runs the front-of-house and financial portion of the show.)

It is imperative for the stage manager to stay in touch with the director, choreographer and designers of the show regarding the artistic condition of the performances and to recommend that one of them attend performances and conduct rehearsals when necessary. Since the resolution of personality conflicts falls to the stage manager, it is quite important that these problems are handled fairly and even-handedly and that the resolution is known to the producer and general or company manager of the show. In other words, the stage manager cannot run a fiefdom. He/she is responsible to many parties and must honor the areas of primary responsibility these creative, financial and managerial people hold. The worst mistake a stage manager can make is to be uncommunicative—it is far better to risk boring people with too much information than to leave them uninformed.

A word needs to be said about fun. The theatre is the opposite of drudgery. It depends upon high spirits and the sense of improvisation pouring across the footlights. Keeping it light backstage, making sure the actors never feel like they're in jail, being careful that the stagehands feel respected and included, and never allowing a party to be thrown without everyone involved in the show being invited—all contribute to the health of a long-running show. I'm a great believer in throwing parties at the theatre—complete with entertainment, food, and drink. Jim Woolley, with whom I've done thirteen productions, decorates the entire backstage and dressing room areas for virtually every holiday. Everyone loves coming to work when Jim is on a show—they feel that backstage is personal and caring. And beyond the sheer fun of these events, I believe a light atmosphere keeps a company together longer.

My advice to anyone reading this piece, no matter how young or old you are, no matter what your level of experience in the theatre may be, is to work with as many professionals who love the theatre as you possibly can. The theatre is a very rewarding place, sometimes not financially, but nearly always emotionally and intellectually. At the very top of the commercial theatre are professionals who love the buildings in which they work, the material they bring to life, the history they call upon each time they work and the people with whom they work. Everyone contributes to the whole; everyone tells the story.

Part III

THEIR HOUR
UPON THE STAGE

CHAPTER 14

CHITA RIVERA
LEADING LADY

Chita Rivera has won two Tony Awards (*Kiss of the Spider Woman*, *The Rink*) and received seven additional Tony nominations. In December 2002, she received a Kennedy Center Honor in Washington, D.C. Her career was the subject of the 2005 Broadway musical, *Chita Rivera: The Dancer's Life*, in which she starred. Her electric performance as Anita in the Broadway premiere of *West Side Story* (1957) brought her stardom, which was repeated in London. She created the role of Velma Kelly in the original Broadway production of *Chicago* opposite Gwen Verdon (1975) and appears in the film version. Recent starring roles include the new Kander/Ebb/McNally musical *The Visit* and *The House of Bernarda Alba*; the London/Las Vegas/Toronto productions of *Chicago: The Musical*; and *Chita & All That Jazz*. Career highlights: starring roles in *Bye Bye Birdie* (originating the role of Rosie), *Bajour* and *Jerry's Girls* (original Broadway casts), the 2003 revival of *Nine*; plus *Guys and Dolls*, *Can-Can*, *Seventh Heaven*, *Mr. Wonderful*. Tours: *Born Yesterday*, *The Rose Tattoo*, *Call Me Madam*, *Threepenny Opera*, *Sweet Charity* (and film version), *Kiss Me, Kate*. Her most treasured production is her daughter, singer/dancer/choreographer Lisa Mordente.

Playing

In order to collaborate you have to learn about yourself.

The chorus line is an excellent place to do that, because it's the place you also learn about others. A chorus line must be a unit— but within that unit you must learn how also to be the person next to you, and how to work with the person at the end of the line. You all have to do things that are at times are identical, at times different, but linked and interwoven. To make that happen, you not only have to know your job, you also have to understand how others are doing their jobs.

People see the Rockettes and they go, "Oh my God, how fabulous." It's because the Rockettes are completely aware of each other. There's power in numbers, but there's even more power in being aware of each other. I wish the entire world did that in everything, not just in theatre.

In the original cast of *Can-Can*, I was one of eight girls in the chorus who had to do cartwheels, one between the other. If you didn't know exactly where the person was next to you, respect their space and be in control of your own giving and taking, there would have been collisions all over the place. Working in the chorus teaches you that you can't just walk around in your little fishbowl and expect to get anything back at all—or even do what you yourself have to do—unless you are very much aware of the next person. That serves you well, whether you're working in the chorus, or working downstage in the spotlight as the star. Paradoxically, it's almost selfish, because you get so much from everybody else.

Some people think they are too good for a chorus. That's so wrong. That's the best training you can have to begin to learn how to collaborate.

Breathing

Actually, I don't think the word "collaborate" accurately describes what we do. I think of it as creating and living and even *breathing* together. When you see a Jerome Robbins collaborating with a Leonard Bernstein on *West Side Story*, or Fred Ebb and John Kander collaborating with each other on *Chicago* or *Kiss of the Spider Woman*, what you really see is a merging of creative spirits. If you want to create theatre, you cannot be an island unto yourself.

Maybe, instead of "collaborating" we should call it "learning." I think what moved me from chorus part to leading lady is the fact that I never stopped learning from others. I kept listening and observing and figuring out how what I do can fit better with what everybody else is doing. It's a gradual progression and a natural one. And, if you do it right, you find that you are learning and teaching at exactly the same time.

The more I think about it, the less I think the word "collaboration" is the right one. It's such a funny word. It means "laboring together," but "labor" is such a harsh word. And what happens is deeper than that. It should be a warmer word than that. It's really *living* something together. Collaboration is living and sharing.

When I worked with Bob Fosse and Gwen Verdon on the original *Chicago*, we had so many times where, creatively, one plus one would somehow equal three. There was a number near the end of the show, titled "Hot Honey Rag," which Gwen and I called "Two Dancing as One," because that is what Bob asked us to do. Gwen and I had to be identical. To do that, we had to be inside each other's heads every time. And when we did it right, the audience got so much more than the effect of either of us dancing alone. It was something beyond that. What is the right word?

TRAINING

I was trained as a ballerina. In Washington, D.C., I worked with a fabulous teacher called Doris Jones. George Balanchine sent some scouts, and Louis Johnson and I were selected to come to the School of American Ballet on scholarships. That's where I learned the principles of collaboration. That training is with me still, and has kept my head above water all my life.

Dancers are very obedient. We do as we are told. But if the creators are the kind of people that I have been fortunate enough to work with, they will be very critical of their own work. They have an "eye" for what's not just right. And they will listen to you.

You go into a rehearsal hall. You've got your script and you've got your music from the collaborating team. Then the director gives you something to do. No matter what it is, no matter how challenging or offbeat, you try it. You do what you're given. I'm a firm believer in doing what the creative team asks of you first.

If I do exactly what I've been asked to do and it still looks odd on my body or it doesn't look right to the creator's eye, then the creator will change it. If it feels uncomfortable, I'll ask if we can do it another way, or sometimes I will suggest another way. Most truly great choreographers will be able to create many different variations on a theme. So they'll have you try it this way and that way in order to get to a way that works for everybody—and works for the show.

Some people think things have to be one way only. *There's nothing that's just one way.* Your idea is not the only idea that's out there. It's only one of millions and millions of ideas.

If everyone is lucky, it may turn out that the idea you use is a step beyond what the directors or choreographers had originally conceived. That's what those rehearsal halls are all about. It's throwing into a huge pot everyone's ingredients and coming up with a great stew that everybody loves and understands. Creativity is a gift that God gives you. You use it to work things out in a way that, hopefully, satisfies the audience. Instead of "collaboration," let's call it *creating together*.

BECOMING A LEADING LADY

Bye Bye Birdie was the first show on which I had top billing, though just a tiny bit more than Dick Van Dyke's. I had gone from bottom of the chorus to the top of the marquee in just seven years. That show was all about collaboration. Our captain was Gower Champion, who had made his name in movies as a dance partner with his wife, Marge. He would later stage *Hello, Dolly!* and *42nd Street*, but this was his first major Broadway show as both director and choreographer. There were a lot of firsts on that show. It was the first score for Charles Strouse and Lee Adams. Even Paul Lynde hadn't done a lot of shows at that point, so we were all sort of in the same pot.

I can't say there was a certain moment where I learned how to be a leading lady. I've been "Chita" my whole life. As you get older you learn lessons. You get more mature. You know how to hold a stage better. These are things that happen automatically. I didn't wear sneakers and jeans and then suddenly change into leading lady clothes. I just did my job and tried to keep the company together by being a good example. It's as simple as that. I always just try to appreciate who I am working with, appreciate the piece that I am in, and appreciate the audience that I am trying to please. I try to do my very best and give back every single time I do a show.

If you want to see a living example of how to do it all right, there's Brian Stokes Mitchell. We worked together on *Kiss of the Spider Woman*. He's the crème de la crème. He's an example of how to keep a company happy and keep it constantly creative. He has the ability of give and take. He is a constant vessel of love and creativity. He allows his own creativity to come out. He is very open to everybody and therefore he allows everyone else to be creative. That comes from love, really, and respect: respect for his business, respect for his co-workers and respect for the piece he is doing. You know that old expression "what goes around comes around"? Stokes lives that.

Part of collaborating is understanding what your collaborator's limits are. In the taunting scene of *West Side Story* I played Anita and I was trying to deliver a message to Tony. The other boys in the gang start insulting me and throwing me around and making racial remarks to me. My father was born in Puerto Rico, so it was very difficult. Jerome Robbins never made me rehearse the taunting scene more than once a day because he saw that it was taking so much out of all of us. That, too, was collaborating.

Not everyone has that kind of sensitivity. A lot of times, ego gets in the way. When people refuse to collaborate, what they're really doing is refusing to think of the piece as a whole. Sometimes that can be very hard. In the original production of *Chicago*, Bob Fosse had to let go an actor who was absolutely brilliant. He played my agent and had an amazing Kander and Ebb number called "Ten Percent." But Fosse's "eye" told him that the part—not the actor—was pushing the play off-balance. So he made the decision, and it broke his heart, and all of our hearts, to see the actor go. Now, Kander and Ebb could have said, "We like that song, and we're going to keep it." And there could have been a big fight. But they trusted Fosse, and they let it go. Sometimes collaboration means that, too. They did it for the sake of the play as a whole.

WATCHING KANDER AND EBB

I worked with Kander and Ebb on three shows: *Chicago*, *The Rink*, and *Kiss of the Spider Woman*, so I've had a chance to observe them closely. They are amazing collaborators—not just with each other, but with everyone. They know exactly what Liza Minnelli is about, they know exactly what I'm about.

I once spent the night at Freddy Ebb's house. I'll never forget sitting there, listening to these two amazing men in the next room, creating wonderful things for me to sing and to say and to dance. I couldn't believe how it was pouring out of the two of them. They'd go back over and over something and then say, "No, that doesn't seem right." Then Freddy would yell out lyrics that were just amazing. And John would say, "What about this music?" And they'd change it and they fix it. They have a gift for it, a gift from God.

PLAYING WITH MY DAUGHTER

Something horrible happens as you get older: you develop a fear of trying things, and a fear of looking foolish.

When my daughter, Lisa Mordente, was little we used to sit in the middle of the bed and play for hours. She was brought up on Danny Kaye movies and Jerry Lewis movies and Chaplin's and all the great clowns because I believe that humor is a vital thing, especially these days. She would say, "Mommy, do Jerry Lewis!" And I would act the fool for her, and she would roll all over the bed laughing. And then I'd say, "Now it's your turn!" And we would play that way. I suppose we were collaborating. We were collaborating on how to laugh and be free and enjoy each other. And I could see her getting better and better at imitating these people.

Perhaps that's a better word than "collaborating." In the theatre, we play. That's why we call them "plays" right? We're playing together. That's a sweet and gentle way of saying it. Except its very real. It's grown-up play. And it's how we stay in touch with the child within us.

Working with Dick Van Dyke on *Birdie* was play. He was absolutely hilarious. We would laugh so hard that we couldn't stop. Gower would say to Dick and myself, "All right, you two...!" But we improvised a lot of funny stage business that way.

When I was working with Gower on "The Shriners' Ballet" he would encourage me to do things that were absolutely silly and fun, and he would say, "Keep it!" And I would say, "Are you kidding?" And he would say, "Yeah, that's really funny."

Liza Minnelli loves to play like that, too. She subbed for Gwen in *Chicago*, and played my daughter in *The Rink*. First of all, we like each other. It's not hard to be free with someone that you like and you truly respect. It's like a reflection, almost. It means you understand. And if you understand, then it means there is something in you that is comparable to what is in the other person. That was a wonderful time for us creatively. We had a mother-daughter fight in a song called "Don't 'Aw Ma' Me," and we got off on laughing with each other. I would get such pleasure out of seeing her do that, and vice versa. A lot of that wound up in the staging, too. And we kept pushing each other every night.

If you're planning a career in the theatre, you have to keep certain principles in front of you always: You must watch. You must listen. You must share. You must breathe together with others. You must respect your work. You must respect the creativity in the air around you. And you must relearn how to play.

CHAPTER 15

BRIAN STOKES MITCHELL
LEADING ACTOR

Brian Stokes Mitchell is one of Broadway's most popular leading men. He's been nominated for the Tony Award four times (for his performances in *Ragtime*, *Man of La Mancha*, *King Hedley II*, and *Kiss Me, Kate*) and won once (for *Kate*). His early theatre adventures landed him in Los Angeles where he started a long television and screen career: from *Roots: The Next Generations* and seven years on *Trapper John, M.D.*, to the more recent *Double Platinum* with Diana Ross, *Ruby's Bucket of Blood* with Angela Bassett, *Call Me Clause* with Whoopi Goldberg, the animated film *Prince of Egypt*, and recurring roles on *Frasier* and *Crossing Jordan*. He has performed at the White House and Carnegie Hall and made numerous appearances at the Kennedy Center,

including the title role of *Sweeney Todd* at the Sondheim Celebration. He has appeared on more than a dozen record albums. His Broadway credits include *Mail* (Theatre World Award); David Merrick's *Oh, Kay!*; *Jelly's Last Jam*; *Kiss of the Spider Woman*; *Ragtime* (Tony nomination); *Kiss Me, Kate* (Tony, Drama Desk, and Outer Critics Circle awards); August Wilson's *King Hedley II* (Tony nomination) and *Man of La Mancha* (Tony nomination). He has also appeared in the New York City Center Encores! *Do Re Mi*, *Carnival*, and *Kismet*. In 2002 he authored the preface to the new edition of the book *At This Theatre*. His solo album *Brian Stokes Mitchell* was released in 2006 on Playbill Records.

An Actor Watches

The lead in a musical has a special collaboration with the rest of the cast. The most visible part of a lead's work is onstage, and is seen by the audience. He may have the most lines and the biggest songs, and his character's actions drive the story.

But an important part of the lead's collaboration takes place backstage, and subtly. The lead owes a special kind of respect to his fellow actors and, indeed, the entire company. This isn't mere tradition or formality; my experience is that it's crucial to the success of the show.

I learned this lesson from Chita Rivera, who played the Spider Woman when I appeared opposite her in *Kiss of the Spider Woman*. First, she made everybody feel welcomed. She made

everybody feel valued. She made everybody feel like his or her artistic contribution was as valuable as the next person's. She made it a fun place to work. I remember watching her and thinking, if I am ever lucky enough to be the head of a company that's how I am going to do it.

The day I met her I was rehearsing on the stage. She came out from the wings and gave me a big hug and said, "I am so glad you are here."

It wasn't just the words; it was feeling coming from her. She is an incredibly collaborative artist. It probably comes from her gypsy roots. She was raised as a gypsy, which quickly teaches you how to collaborate with other dancers, and with the choreographer. Her attitude is never, "I'm the star." Her attitude is, "Let's make the show work."

At the end of each week, she would serve champagne in her dressing room and she would invite people just to sit down and talk. And her guests were not just the other leads, or even just other actors, but people from every part of the production. I gradually came to realize that she knew the names of every person on the crew and in the orchestra. She made it a priority to know those names.

It's so simple to make people happy: know who they are and appreciate what they do. It makes them feel as an important part of the team as everybody else—and they are. Everybody works harder when they feel appreciated and they feel that what they do is valued. That's a very important thing when you are relying on those people.

And one of the keys to Chita's stardom is that she makes the audience feel the same way. She communicates a feeling: "I'm glad you are here. Let me give you a gift." That's her heart you can feel radiating from the stage.

LONG-FORM ART

Next to the director, actors have the most collaborative job in theatre because we have to interface with so many different people. We interface with the producer. We interface with the director. We interface with the crew. And certainly we must work hand-in-hand with the costume designer and the prop people.

I call theatre a "long-form" art because you are collaborating with the company and the audience over a period of weeks, months and sometimes even years, if you are fortunate that way. The company—the stage crew, the orchestra, the other actors, the house crew—become your backstage family. One of the advantages of work in a long-form art is that you have time to try things different ways. I might have one idea of how something should be done, and director may have another idea, but you have the time to try it both ways and see which actually works the best.

Perhaps neither will work, and together you'll find a third way that works best of all.

Sometimes you get stuck with things, like a set you don't like, or a costume, though that's more changeable than a set. So your collaboration becomes either trying to get it changed, or figuring a way to work with it or around it.

That's why I always say, try everything you are asked to try. You may find something useful, if not for one audience, then for another. And, ultimately, the actor controls what happens on the stage. If you want to flap your arms and squawk like a chicken one night, nobody is going to be able to stop you. Not that you should do that, of course. But ultimately you are going to be able to give the performance you want. So I say try whatever the director or anyone else you respect asks you to try.

With directors, there's always the Machiavellian question: is it better to rule through fear or rule through love? Machiavelli decided it was better to rule through fear. Some directors agree. I don't. However, Frank Galati and Graciela Daniele, who were director and choreographer on *Ragtime*, definitely rule with love. I've found that when a piece is created in a cauldron of love, that's what you get back.

It was especially true of *Ragtime*, which is ultimately about triumphing through love. The same was the case with *Kiss of the Spider Woman*, and indeed almost all really great art and theatre. If you can start a company with that vibe already, it makes the rest of the job easy.

A Family of Actors

The actors on a show are like a family within a family. You're in the crucible together. You see everybody in their absolutely best light—and their absolutely worst light. I've seen people give their best under impossible conditions countless times. And you share triumphs like a family.

When you're in a show that wins the Tony Award, you can feel the shared vibe: "We did this together!"

But even the Tony for Best Actor in a Musical that I won on *Kiss Me, Kate* was not won by me alone. It was won by a team of people that included the costume designer, the set designer, the director and the producer, among others. I made a contribution to that effort, and it was recognized. And I was the lucky guy who got to hold it in my hands and take it home. But that couldn't have happened without the team.

The thing I love about theatre is—unlike film and television—there are no edits, no cuts. An editor can't digitally remove your mistake. It's you on that stage facing the audience, and if something's goes wrong, it's up to you to fix it. The only help you have comes from those people on the stage with you. If you go up on a line, you need to be able to trust that actor next to you to get you out of the situation. And she or he has to be able to trust you the same way.

Where that can go wrong is when you have someone who is a very selfish performer. Such people are all about "me, me, me, me." Well, all I can say is, if they think they are perfect, they better *be* perfect. That actor better never forget a line or make a mistake. If they have failed other actors too many times, or made other people feel small, then you can't blame those people if they step back and fold their arms and wait for the crash. Collaboration is imperative. It can mean survival.

In live theatre, sometimes circumstances require you to ad-lib. If you feel comfortable on stage, keep a sense of humor and look to your fellow performers for help, you can get through it and even make something great out of it.

One night in *Kiss Me, Kate*, I was alone on stage with my solo, "Where Is the Life That Late I Led?" and I completely went up on the lyrics. Usually I'm good at making up lyrics if they go wrong, but the lyrics in that song were too quick and intricate. Finally, I had to stop the show. I looked down at conductor Paul Gemignani in the pit, and I said, "Maestro, can you help me out here?"

The audience loves to be in a moment like that.

Paul mugged looking down at his rostrum for a cue, but of course there was no score there because he always memorizes the score. He looked up at me and shrugged his shoulders in a way the audience could see.

The audience laughed and loved that. Even though he wasn't able to help me out with the lyric, we had so much fun improvising that moment. And the audience picked up on it. A lesser conductor might have panicked, but Gemignani and I were so hooked into each other, and into the fun of the show, that it became a memorably fun moment for the audience.

Costars

When you're a leading man, collaborating with your costar is key to the success of any show. I've been very lucky in that I have had the privilege of working with some of the great ladies of the theatre.

I have appeared four times with Marin Mazzie: in *Ragtime* and subsequently in *Kiss Me, Kate*, *Man of La Mancha*, and *Kismet*. But of all the people in *Ragtime*, she was the one I knew the least, because we were on stage at opposite times, for the most part. Neither of us went out to parties so we never really got to know each other off stage. Our one scene on stage was about not understanding each other.

So when we were both cast as the leads in *Kiss Me, Kate*, we went out and had a lunch together—to get acquainted! We started by discussing some of the tensions we'd experience backstage at *Ragtime*, such as when part of the cast was asked to stay with the tryout production in Toronto while others moved on to the U.S. premiere in Los Angeles before Broadway. As great as *Ragtime* was, we decided that *Kiss Me, Kate* would be different—smoother, with less tension. At that lunch we did a pinkie shake and resolved, "We're going to make this the most fun we've ever have ever had on stage." And we did.

I've taken that resolve to every production since then. And that's another thing I learned from Chita Rivera. The producer and director may initially set the tone of the show, but once the show is up and running, you rarely see them. It basically just the company that is left: the actors, the stage management and the crew. Then, I think the stars of the show set the tone. That's what Chita did on *Kiss of the Spider Woman*. I try to carry on that same tradition, and pass it along to the other people I work with.

The biggest enemy of fruitful collaboration is ego. It's very useful to have an ego for one part of the show: wanting to do your best for the audience. But it also can get in the way because it can become a power struggle between the people creating the show. That's not what art is about. Art is about something bigger and greater. Drama is about humans collaborating with each other in the world for better or for worse. Living is collaboration. That's what we are trying to show: stories of collaboration or non-collaboration.

There is a lot of fear involved in making a show. There is so much insecurity. People worry that they don't "have it" any more. But there is a solution to that. If everybody is looking out for the good of the *show*, then everybody will look good.

There are a few rules I've learned for creating harmony backstage. Always take the high road. Don't gossip maliciously about somebody's performance. Only make positive contributions to the show, even if you hate what the other actor is doing and you know you could do the job ten times better. That's not your job right now. It's the other actor's job. Your job is to support the show and be true to your character. If you have the opportunity to do that role later on, then you can do it your way.

A great attitude will also help you get hired again. If you are a team player, you make the show look good. If the show looks good, the director looks good. And the casting director looks good. And the producer looks good. And these are the people who do the hiring.

Energy Loop

The last character that comes into the show is the audience. And it's the last group you collaborate with as an actor. The audience will tell you pretty quickly if you are brilliant—or the opposite.

One of the most fun things about live theatre is that it's never the same thing twice. What keeps it fresh for you as an actor is that you are always collaborating with a different audience. Every audience gives you something a little different. Some actors thrive on that. Some actors will give you the same performance no matter what, but some actors will adjust theirs according to the audience.

Going to the theatre is not like going to a movie, where, no matter what the audience feels like, the performance is going to be exactly the same every time. The theatre is three-dimensional because it's alive and the actors on stage are alive and the audience is alive and everybody is interacting with each other. In a really good show an energy loop forms from the stage to the audience and back again.

Of course, sometimes the audience doesn't hold up its end of the collaboration. If an audience is bad, and the actor tries to go along with that, the actor may end up not being very good either. When that happens, an actor should fall back on his technique, do the show right, and hope that the audience eventually comes around.

But the ultimate judge of what works is the audience, not the critics. Theatre is always changing, which is one of the reasons I think theatre criticism is a little silly. It's a judgment on one performance, and we may never give that performance again.

The six-week rehearsal period is a safe womb for actors, But it's also a time where you can lose perspective, especially if the play is funny or light. After you've heard a punchline or seen an actor's funny little physical bit thirty times, it's not funny any more. You start to lose your perspective on whether the show is any good or not. I believe that is what accounts for shows that open up and people in the audience say, "My God, how could they let that happen? What were they thinking?"

It takes a really skilled team of producers and directors to keep an open eye to that, but even they don't really know whether it communicates to the audience until that final collaborator arrives. You don't know that until you hear the laughter or you see the tears or sense the silence in the audience. When people are coughing all over the audience it's a good sign you are not holding their attention. Even when it's cold season, if there is something riveting going on the stage, the audience will sit absolutely silent, and you know you have them.

I've learned to play with each night's audience, because each audience is different. One audience may be just fidgety. One audience may be depressed. One audience may be jocular. One audience may be surly. One audience may be cold and cranky. Another audience is playful. You try to learn how to play to each kind, within the parameters of your character.

And, of course, you change each night as well. You might do a brilliant performance one night and the next night you just fall flat. Sometimes it's the actor; sometimes it's the audience. The chemistry changes slightly with each performance.

Figuring that out and being able to work with that is part of the alchemy of theatre.

I've thought a lot about this when I've been an audience member myself. Sometimes I nearly have to cover my mouth because I just want to jump up and sing along. A lot of audience members do just that. I know that happened a lot during *Man of La Mancha.*

Sometimes I go into an analytical mode, especially if a performance is particularly brilliant—or if it's particularly not brilliant, I'll analyze why it's working so well or why it isn't working. Sometimes I'll look at members of the audience and feel what's going on around me. It's hard to get lost in a performance the way a regular audience would. Occasionally if there's a really wonderful performance and I'm in the right mindset I'll get lost in the performance. It's very useful when you are able to do that, because that's what your audience is doing.

The more you can put yourself in their heads, the better off you are. A skilled actor also is able to do that from the stage. But sitting in the audience yourself can help remind you why you are there. It reminds you that people are paying one hundred and ten dollars a ticket, not to see your back but to see your front, and to have an emotional or intellectual experience. It's very important to keep that in mind.

There are things the audience can do, too.

I call cell phones and cellophane the killer "cells" of the theatre. They both drive me crazy. Partly, because they are both controllable. You can turn off your cell phone and choose not to unwrap your wrapper during the show.

Usually what happens is you don't hear them during the first act because they make the announcement and everyone is really conscientious But then people go out during intermission talk on their cell phones and when they come back they forget to turn them off. Act Two is when cell phones start to ring.

During *Kiss Me, Kate*, there was a line, "He who knows how to tame a shrew now let him speak. 'Tis charity to show." I would address the line to the audience and afterward open my arms, as if to invite anybody to pipe up with an answer—which, of course, no one has. It's written as a comedic moment. One night I did that, and waited, and in the silence a cell phone went off.

It got a laugh, and I ad-libbed something like, "If it's my agent kindly tell him I'm *in the middle of a show.*" And that got a great laugh from the audience, because after all, it is a show about an actor. But, inside, I was angry. No matter what you are doing on stage a cell phone always takes you out of the show.

I tried to make it a collaborative moment with the audience. Getting the laugh and the applause gave the audience a chance to think, "Oh yeah we hate cell phones, too!" It's one of those happy accidents that the universe throws in your lap at the right exact moment.

I remember going to a musical called *Triumph of Love*. It didn't have a long run, which was too bad, because F. Murray Abraham was particularly great in it. He had a line in the show: "You're late again." The night I saw it, three people came back late from intermission just before he said it, and they were sitting right in the middle of the front row. So just as they were pushing their way in, and everyone was getting up in the row to let them pass, he came out with the line, "You're late again," as he passively stared at the latecomers making their entrance. It brought down the house.

There's an interesting collaboration too. In a sense, F. Murray Abraham was on stage with me during *Kiss Me, Kate*. That's one of the neat things about being an actor: when you are performing, all of the people you ever performed with or who inspired you are, in a sense, on stage with you. Frank Galati was on stage with me during *Kiss Me, Kate*. Chita Rivera was on stage with me during *Kiss Me, Kate*. Director Michael Blakemore was constantly on stage with me during *Kiss Me, Kate*.

You collaborate with people who aren't even there. My acting teachers, my singing teachers, my dance teachers, my wife who was not in *Kiss Me, Kate* with me but whom I would use as a sounding board. You are constantly collaborating with people that aren't even seen. It really is a kind of magical thing that happens on stage. There are more people on stage with you than you even know.

CHAPTER 16

Kathleen Chalfant

Actress

Kathleen Chalfant's stage career has featured major productions on Broadway, Off-Broadway, and in London's West End: *Wit* (Drama Desk, Outer Critics Circle, Obie, Drama League, Lucille Lortel, Los Angeles Ovation awards), *Angels in America* (Tony and Drama Desk nominations), *M. Butterfly*, *Racing Demon*. New York City Center Encores!: *Bloomer Girl*, *The Vagina Monologues*, *Sister Mary Ignatius Explains It All for You*, *Henry V*, *Nine Armenians* (Drama Desk nomination), *Twelve Dreams*, *Endgame* (Obie Award for Sustained Excellence in Performance). Film: *Murder and Murder, Five Corners, Side Streets, A Price Below Rubies*. Television: *The Laramie Project, A Death in the Family* (American Masterpiece Theatre), *Law & Order, Spin City*, the Steven King miniseries *Storm of the Century, Voices from the White House*, Laurie Solt in *The Guardian*. She is the recipient of the 2003 Obie and Outer Critics Circle Awards for her performance in *Talking Heads*.

Playing Both Parts

For actors, there are primary collaborations and secondary collaborations.

Primary collaborations are with the director, with fellow actors and, finally, with the audience.

Secondary collaborations are the ones with costume and hair designers and, to a lesser extent, the set and lighting designers. You may laugh, but these definitely are collaborations too—and intimate ones. I'm particularly sensitive to that because my daughter is a set designer, and we talk about it all the time.

STARTING OUT

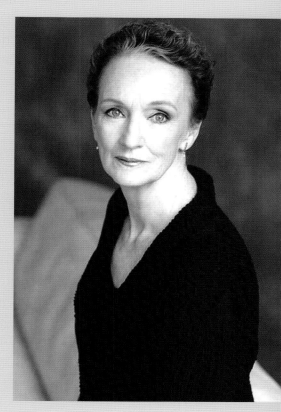

I never went to acting school. Like a lot of people I first acted in school plays. I still remember myself wrapped in a blue sheet as the Virgin Mary for a Christmas play. When I was in high school I spent a lot of time in the drama department. My senior year was like working in rep. I ran lights in a production of *Annie Get Your Gun*. Then, in a production of *Huckleberry Finn*, I played the woman who exposes Huck as a boy by throwing a ball into his lap. And then I played the title role in *Hedda Gabler*. Quite a year.

We had a wonderful drama teacher, Donald Springer, who encouraged collaboration and the feeling of an ensemble. There weren't any stars in that company. You had to be prepared to play any part and do any job. It was a very important lesson.

Playing Both Parts

One of the first things you learn as an actor is to avoid a phenomenon called "playing both parts." If you are acting with someone else and they don't seem to be doing what you think they are supposed to be doing, your impulse is to behave as though they *are* doing what they are supposed to be doing. It's never successful. Theatre is live; it happens in the moment. You always have to respond to what you are getting, and not what you think you should be getting, even if it's unexpected and challenging and hard. Because then there are two people involved in the making of the work of art, and not just one in her own little bubble.

The most transcendent moment for an actor on the stage is when the collaboration between you and the person you are acting with seems seamless and inevitable. There is nothing better than that.

I don't remember learning about collaboration specifically. I just remember the fact of it. I only know what I know: collaboration is the basis of all work in the theatre. It's an understanding that each part of the enterprise is essential. Most successful productions are those that are infused with a sense of mutual respect; when the people on the stage understand that the running crew of the show is as essential to it as they are.

Directing from the Inside

Collaboration doesn't mean that the collaborators don't have to have clear ideas of their own. Collaboration means working together to find out how everyone's clear notions are compatible. Some notions complement each other, some trump others in the end.

What Shakespeare says is true: "The play's the thing." The thing you are trying to do is put on the play. The job is to communicate what the writer has written to the audience, which is the final part of the collaboration.

Who decides which ideas get used and which don't? In the end, it's the director. The director has the larger view of the entire project. There are two things you should never try to do as an actor. The first, as I said earlier, is to try to play both parts. The other thing you shouldn't try is to direct yourself from inside the production.

It's always disastrous for an actor to try to direct the play from inside—to try to be both in the play and to imagine the effect of it on the audience. An important part of the collaboration between the actor and the director is the actor trusting the director's eye. When actors don't trust directors, chaos ensues because then everybody makes their own adjustments to try to fix whatever they think is going wrong. And that will never work because you can't tell from inside the play what it looks like from outside.

Nor should you. As an actor, your job is different—to communicate, not to see. It's the director's job to see and ultimately the audience's job to see.

ANGELS IN AMERICA

I was involved with Tony Kushner's *Angels in America* for six years, from the first readings in 1988, until 1994 when it was on Broadway. During that time there were vast changes in the script, and the characters continually grew. We actors felt we were important to Tony. Through us he could see his characters take shape. We talked a lot in the company about things that worked and things that didn't. And Tony listened. He didn't always use what we said, but we could tell he was listening to us.

The script evolved as we worked on it, but it wasn't written like *A Chorus Line*. Those certainly weren't our life stories. Nevertheless we played our part in shaping that show. The way Tony writes, you often get new material very late in the process. So, part of the collaboration was to be prepared to make changes right up to opening night. It was exciting—frightening, but exciting.

Some actors like that sort of excitement more than others do, and there are some circumstances in which it is more welcome than others. When you are doing a workshop in a rehearsal room in Los Angeles for ten people on the staff of the Mark Taper Forum, changes are welcome. When you are going to open on Broadway and the *New York Times* is coming and you get ten new pages the day before it happens—well, not every actor is up for that. But what are we in it for, if not to push ourselves and participate in great works?

Sometimes collaborations break down as the pressure rises. But not always. The best directors are the ones who conduct the rehearsals so that when the first audience comes, it seems natural. You are just inviting new collaborators into the process. Some directors do that very well. The most seamless one in my experience was Richard Eyre directing *Racing Demon* at Lincoln Center. There was no sense of rising tension. One day it was time for the audience to come. And they came. And that was all.

George C. Wolfe is a great director. He is a great general. I always thought that if there was a war and you wanted to follow the person who would get you through it, you should follow George. George is a fierce defender of his artistic collaborators. He defends them against the outside world in all kinds of ways. He makes you feel safe, as though you are in his world, and you go in his direction.

He and Tony Kushner have a wonderful collaboration, which would be very interesting to investigate. George, because he's also a writer, has very close collaborations with writers. He also has a great gift for finding the particular thing that each actor needs to hear; that will make them the best that they can be. The day the press came to *Angels in America* on Broadway, George went around and talked to every member of the company separately. I don't know what he said to anybody else, but he came up to me and said, "Kathy I want you to be sure to be *clear*."

I take great pride in being clear. I might not do anything else, but clear is my thing. The effect of George saying that was to square whatever clarity I had. I was the first person you see in the show, and I came out and hit the stage as though there was a black line drawn around me. Meanwhile, I was thinking, "What does he mean, saying that to me? That's what I do!" And then I realized: It made me take care to do what I do as well as I could do it. It made me so mad that I was over being afraid of anything else that was going on. And it worked. It was a *brilliant* tactic.

I don't know what he said to everybody else, but all I can tell you is, that was one hell of a performance.

WIT

In *Wit* I played Vivian Bearing, a scholar of the poetry of John Donne, who discovers she has incurable cancer. In the time before she dies she discovers the deepest meanings of the poems she's known and taught all her life.

Unlike my experience working so closely with the playwright on *Angels in America*, I rarely saw the author of *Wit*, Margaret Edson. Maggie is a teacher in Atlanta, and was never with us when we were doing the Off-Broadway production. Maggie had done all the developmental work at South Coast Rep in California where the play had already been presented, very successfully, starring Megan Cole as Vivian. It won lots of prizes, but then no one would do it anyplace else because it was about a 50-year-old bald woman with cancer who taught John Donne.

Maggie then gave the play to Derek Anson Jones who had been her best friend since they were in high school together. Derek gave the play to me. Whatever collaboration Maggie did was with Derek. The whole time we worked on it, there were only two line changes. In that situation, you are collaborating only with the text. Derek was speaking both for himself and for Maggie.

One thing that became a big issue when we moved to New York was whether or not the actor playing Vivian Bearing would have to be bald. We spent a lot of time trying to find an alternative solution with the costume designer Ilona Somogyi. But no bald cap, no matter how carefully done, would solve that problem. In New Haven we did it in a short run in a small theatre, but it quickly became clear that, despite my personal terror of being bald all the time for what we hoped would be a long New York run, there just wasn't any substitute for me shaving my head.

And this has a bearing on collaboration. Besides the fact that a bald cap made Vivian look as though not only had she had radiation treatment but she'd been a burn victim, it also took almost two and a half hours of preparation. That meant the other eight people in the company would get no time from the hair and costume person. That seemed absolutely outrageous to me because they actually had many harder things to do about changing costumes than I did. As a collaborator, I had to swallow my fear and just start shaving my head,

DIRECTOR DAVID ESBJORNSON

The director with whom I have worked the most is David Esbjornson. We've done maybe fifteen projects together. David is one of the best collaborative directors I know. When we work together there's no barrier. If I disagree with something he's said, I am very clear about disagreeing. But more often than not I come back the next day and discover that he's been right. The important thing is the process of the discussion.

For example, he may have a suggestion for what a particular line means. Meanwhile, I may have understood it quite differently and have been playing it with that understanding. We have a spirited discussion about which of these interpretations is right, and often I discover that David's view is the correct view. But the fierceness and clarity of the discussion will have been important in clarifying that section for the both of us.

FIAT AND FEAR

I was an understudy in the original company of *M. Butterfly* and the director was a man who simply did not collaborate. He was the kind of director who worked by fiat and fear. He divided the company on the first day—entirely arbitrarily as far as I could determine—between those people who were "on the bus" and those people who were "off the bus" as far as his affections and regard were concerned.

He fired somebody on the first day. From then on the company was permeated with a sense of unease. A few more people fell off the bus in the course of the rehearsals and the out-of-town tryouts in Washington.

As a directorial technique, terrorizing people is simply not successful and never worth it. The thing that is produced is always essentially bloodless. I haven't had to work with many directors like that. I've been very lucky.

Dealing with Stars

The most successful star-driven shows are the ones in which the star takes responsibility for the ensemble and makes the ensemble feel like a family.

Theatre is egalitarian, in a way, because everybody has to show up at the same time, and trip over the same cables backstage, and live in the same tiny dressing rooms. They have to stand in the wings together, being frightened, human-sized, all doing the same thing. So the most successful stars respect the other members of the ensemble, and in some way look after them.

Working with Designers

An actor's collaboration with the costume designer is the most intimate of the collaborations, especially for women, because it's all about how you look. You always have to negotiate, especially character actors, between how you want to look or how you imagine you might look and what is necessary for the piece of work you are doing.

One of the most successful and seamless of these collaborations for me was *The Last Letter*, adapted and directed by Frederick Wiseman at Theatre for a New Audience, Off-Broadway. I played a woman who was imprisoned by the Nazis for three months in a ghetto in the Ukraine during World War II. I had long discussions with costume designer Miranda Hoffman about the dress because the character had only this one dress. The question was how she should look because she'd been a doctor and obviously had traveled abroad. We had to decide how fashionable this dress would be and how universal it would be because an elderly woman in a black dress with a yellow star is a kind of universal icon.

We found a wonderful solution which both fulfilled the iconic nature of the image and gave me what I needed as a character, which was a sense of what this woman's life had been before the Nazis came.

Another great designer to discuss is Paul Huntley, who won a special Tony Award in 2003 for his career as a hair designer and wigmaker. Paul is a genius. And it's always collaborative with Paul. He understands that it's supposed to be your hair and it's supposed to be part of you, so you can never tell they are wigs from inside or out. Paul has an encyclopedic historical knowledge and a great ability to synthesize what you have to say about the character and express it through their hair.

In *The Last Letter*, the character had a white wig, but it wasn't just pulled back and stuck in a bun. It was immensely detailed so there was, even in the wig, a sense of the character's past—who she had been and what she had lost.

A Communal Event

The whole point of the enterprise is communication with the audience. We're there to communicate what the writer has written and it doesn't work unless there is collaboration between the audience and the actor. The actor must view the audience as a collaborator, not as the enemy.

All you can ask of the audience is that they go along with the play, make themselves available to it, realize that it's a communal activity, and not do anything that makes it difficult for the actors to concentrate or for the people next to them to hear the play. So lose the cell phone, don't crinkle the cellophane or rattle the ice. It's a communal event in which some either beautiful or funny or important or transcendent or silly thing is going to be communicated, and everyone needs to do everything possible to make that communication happen.

What's More Important

I have worked all my life in a form that requires collaboration to succeed, a form in which it is more important to be effective than to be right. I try to live my entire life that way. I've been married for thirty-nine years, so there must be some collaboration going on there. I have two children who both speak to me still. And I have two grandchildren, Amelia and William, who seem relatively fond of me—so far.

Collaboration in life means that—at least on your best days—you listen to what other people have to contribute. You try to figure out whether your need to be right—to win an argument—is more important than seeing the project succeed. If I've learned a lesson, that's the lesson.

CHAPTER 17

DICK LATESSA
CHARACTER ACTOR

Dick Latessa received a 2003 Tony, Drama Desk, and Outer Critics Circle awards for his performance in the musical *Hairspray*. Other Broadway appearances include *Cabaret* (Helen Hayes Award), *Proposals*, *A Funny Thing Happened on the Way to the Forum*, *Damn Yankees*, *The Will Rogers Follies*, *Rumors*, *Broadway Bound*, *Rags*, *Brighton Beach Memoirs*, *The Education of H*Y*M*A*N K*A*P*L*A*N*, *Passione*, *I Oughta Be in Pictures*, *Chapter Two*, *Follies*, *Awake and Sing*. Off-Broadway: *Chaucer in Rome*, *Over the River and Through the Woods*, *Philemon* (Obie Award), *Juno*, *Diamonds*, *Sophistry*, *Fit to Be Tied*, *Man in His Underwear*. New York City Center Encores!: *Promises, Promises*; *DuBarry Was a Lady*; *Li'l Abner*. Regional: Kennedy Center, Huntington, Long Wharf. Film: *Stigmata*, *Substance of Fire*. Television: *Thicker Than Blood*, *Law & Order*, *True Blue*, *Working It Out*, *Philemon* (PBS), *Izzie and Moe*, *Soul Man*, *The Sopranos*. Films: *The Event*, *Great New Wonderful*, *Alfie* with Jude Law, *The Last New Yorker*.

The Art of the Second Banana

I'm a very willing collaborator. That's because I went into the business not knowing anything about it, so I asked everyone to help me. In return I tried to give them what they needed. Without realizing it, I had stumbled on the formula for collaboration.

I didn't start in the theatre until I was in my late twenties. I had a pretty good natural voice and I always could dance, but I'm from a working-class Italian family in Cleveland, Ohio, and the words "You're talented" just didn't exist. We didn't have larger-than-life dreams. We had small dreams.

I was working in the circulation department at the *Cleveland Press*. I was single and people were always trying to marry me off. One day, a co-worker invited me to meet a girlfriend of his wife's. They took me to the Karamu Theatre in Cleveland to see Rodgers and Hammerstein's *Pipe Dream.* As I sat there watching, I thought, "Hell, I sing as well as that guy does."

They say fools rush in where angels fear to tread. Well, that's me. I went backstage afterward and sought out the musical director of the place, an older Jewish man from Germany named Benno Frank. He said, "Do you sink?" I said yes. He said, "You come back here next veek and sink for me. Next, ve're doing *The Kink and I.*"

I went the next week and sang for him. I got the role of Lun Tha, the young lover of Tuptim. It was perfect: two beautiful songs and ten lines. But I was terrified. I knew nothing about acting. I had no theatre background whatsoever. I just tried to do my best with the talent I had. They must have liked me because I subsequently did three musicals and three plays during the next two seasons. In one of those I met my future wife. She said the words I never heard from my family: "You're talented, you should go to New York."

I told my mother I was taking a leave of absence to go to New York and study theatre. She thought I was crazy, as they all did. But that's fine. I *was* crazy at the time. It was so exciting to come to New York—and frightening. I thought, "I won't last six weeks." Instead, I've stayed some forty-odd years now.

So I didn't look for theatre. Theatre found me.

BEING READY WHEN YOUR CHANCE COMES

The first show I did on Broadway, *The Education of H*Y*M*A*N K*A*P*L*A*N* was directed by George Abbott. There are kids today who don't even know who he was. He was great as a director.

He would give somebody a line and listen to how it landed with the audience. The next day he would come in and say, "That line is not going to be yours." And he'd give it to someone else. He'd keep going like that until he found the person who knew how to deliver the line. Often, that person was me. Sometimes I would apologize to the person who lost the line, but what are you going to do? It wasn't my decision. We all get hurt. The director isn't trying to hurt you; he's just doing what's best for the show. You've got to accept that as an actor even if it busts your balls a little bit. If somebody gets your speech, you think, "I lost that one. Maybe I'll get something the next time."

The important thing is, you've got to be ready when your chance comes. You have to be able to deliver it. If you can't deliver it, it ain't going to stay with you. You know it's going to go to someone else.

I've seen understudies go on and just be adequate—just get through the role. And I think, they blew their chance. If they went on and they were good, they might get that role eventually. Maybe not in the New York company. Maybe in the touring company. But it can happen.

I see a lot of kids who don't worry as much about the acting as their singing and dancing, especially musical people. And that's a disaster. You've got to act *better* than you can sing or dance. I've always felt I was an actor who could sing. Dancing I don't do, unless it's under duress. But I get the parts because I can act.

The Education of H*Y*M*A*N K*A*P*L*A*N had a great cast. Tom Bosley was the lead, but we also had Hal Linden, Nathaniel Frye, and a lot of other talented people. The show was about an English class for immigrants, and we had several scenes in a classroom that had desks angled to the audience so the audience could see all of us, more or less. Most of the cast was very giving but we had one person who was very self-serving. One night she took me by the shoulders and moved me so she could be seen better during a performance. I got offstage and said, "Don't you ever *ever* do that again." I couldn't believe somebody would have that much audacity.

If something is bothering you, you can ask that person if you can try something to improve the problem, but this was just a "move out of my way" situation. I hate that crap in the theatre. Do you know where people like that end up? At the bottom. Like she did. She never went anywhere.

BASICS OF ACTING

When you come on stage, you've got to come on with *something*—something that you bring to your character and something you can offer the other actors on stage with you. That's your collaboration with your fellow actors. Acting isn't something you do alone; it's a give-and-take with other actors, and with the audience.

The disaster is an actor who doesn't listen. Listening is half of acting. I've done shows with some people who are wonderful listeners. They're very still and you can see them absorbing it all. That's one of the basics of acting. On the other hand, you can see, by certain facial gestures and head movements, when people aren't listening at all. They're only interested in what they're doing, rather than interacting with what's happening around them.

I say: Listen. Learn. Watch. Watch the good people. Watch what they do. Listen to what they tell you.

THE WILL ROGERS FOLLIES

Betty Comden, Adolph Green and Cy Coleman wrote some wonderful stuff for me in *The Will Rogers Follies*, in which I played Clem Rogers, father of Will, who was played by Keith Carradine. They wrote me a great song in Act One, "It's a Boy!"

Originally, one of the plot lines was about the problems Will Rogers had with his dad, who never liked what he did. Clem considered Will nothing but a vaudeville performer, which he thought was way beneath his son. But, as they did rewrites, the story began to change and become more about Will's relationship with his wife. So the father's story became less important, which was very upsetting to me.

It was also upsetting when they cut our duet "Fathers and Sons." The lyrics were so good and clever, and they kept rewriting them to make them better and funnier and clearer. But the lyrics weren't the problem. The song was over-choreographed to death. It was staged with us going up and down these stairs, so the staging became more important than what the lyric was about. It became a song about walking up and down steps. That song would have worked with the two of us just sitting there on those steps, singing to each other rather. But Tommy Tune likes to keep things always in motion.

I have to admit that I thought of getting out of that show after that. I wasn't too happy. But I thought, Dick, you made a commitment, you have a contract. Work through it. It's not the last show you are going to do. Sometimes in life you just have to grin and bear it. Sometimes you have to compromise, in the best sense of the word. You don't get everything you want, but you get some of what you want.

A collaborator shows respect to the people he's working with. I'm not a prima donna. If I were a prima donna I wouldn't have worked as much. But I like to be treated with a little consideration.

You can't carry resentment on stage. You hurt your show, and you wind up screwing yourself. There are other ways to get through it. Talk it out with your friends. My wife and I don't live together any more but I always talk to her on the phone. Sometimes I just vent. Or I'll run around the house and yell at myself. I let off steam. That's acting in a way, too.

Overall *The Will Rogers Follies* was a good experience for me: great show, wonderful actors, Comden and Green, Peter Stone. And don't forget Cy Coleman, the best. What more could you as an actor want? The first day of rehearsal when I saw them all, I thought I was in musical heaven.

HAIRSPRAY

I got the role of a lifetime playing Wilbur Turnblad opposite Harvey Fierstein in *Hairspray*. We did five different readings of *Hairspray* over twenty months before we went into rehearsal, and it was one of those shows where you knew from the start that you were working on something special.

Every time director Jack O'Brien gave a speech to the cast, it was like getting a two-year education at NYU. At the first invited preview of the Seattle tryout, the audience went bananas. The next morning, Jack spoke to the cast, which consisted mostly of youngsters. "Kids," he said, "We experienced something last night that's very rare. We who have been in the business a long time know that you don't experience that very often—if ever. We have something here that is very important and very special. So you must treat it with great integrity. Be gentle with it. Trust yourself in it."

Part of what he was saying was, this is not an easy business. Every other day it's going to kick your ass and deflate your ego. You've got to learn how to live through those bad times and make it through to the good times. And when you've got a good show, enjoy the thing. Be a dependable person who comes in and does a great show every night.

That's what Bernadette Peters does. You're never going to see her lay back in a performance. That's why people love her. That's also why I get hired. I give the same performance every night. I always tell myself how lucky I am to have the job. You have to gear your whole life to doing that show at night. You have to take care of yourself so you can deliver what you are hired to do.

If I have any regret, it's the fact that they, once again, cut one of my songs, which I loved. Called "Positivity," it was a number for me and Marissa Jaret Winokur, who played my daughter, Tracy. It was a wonderful comedy song written specifically with me in mind. It was a song about an uncle who was gay and would go out in drag. One day the cops picked him up and threw him in jail—where he found the love of his life. The song was my way of telling Tracy how to survive: to stick with her dream and everything will work out, perhaps in an unexpected way. It also showed the connection between me and my daughter, which you never see in the show as much as you do with Harvey and the daughter.

But some of the people on the producing side had problems with the lyrics. They thought they were too risqué. Scott Wittman and Marc Shaiman kept rewriting it until I didn't know one verse from the next. And finally they cut it. Frankly I was crushed. I tried to get over being miserable about them cutting that song, and, after a couple of months I was over it. I talked through it with my friends and my wife. They knew I was pissed but I couldn't bring that into rehearsal.

We are all insecure. Hell, I'm certainly insecure. When they cut the song, I said, "Marc, I'm so sorry they cut that song. If it was my fault that they cut it I really apologize. Maybe I wasn't doing it well."

He said, "No. That's not it."

I wish that they had sat me down and said, "Here's the reason that song is being cut. It's a great song, but we've we need to cut some time out of the first act and the song is redundant."

In the preceding scene, I tell my daughter, "You go for it!" The song was a repetition of that, but it had a funny touch to it.

If they had told me that was the reason the song was cut, it would have probably been a little easier on me. But no one did. I figured this out myself after watching what other changes they were making to the show. It wasn't my fault. I sang the heck out of the song. It was funny and everybody loved it, but it was redundant and they needed to move ahead with the play. I could have accepted that. I *did* accept it, but I had to figure it out myself.

You have to learn to take those things philosophically. You have to accept that you're not going to win every battle. The important thing is not you, the important thing is *the show*. I'll sing it for an audition sometime.

Besides, I still had "Timeless To Me" which is one of the greatest numbers ever. What was I going to do, walk away from a number like that and a show like that? Never. Not in a million years.

"Timeless To Me" worked from the first day. When Harvey and I got up and sang that in front of an audience, they went bananas. And that's the way it's been ever since. Every night it stopped that show. It reflected the amazing chemistry that Harvey and I had together.

Harvey played my wife, Edna. I love him dearly and we got along wonderfully, but, after a while playing an old couple, we began to act like an old couple. We'd bicker, but there was always love there, underneath. Sometimes he did things that made you want to choke him. I'm sure there were nights when he wanted to choke me, too.

The two of us worked really well together, in part because I know how to work with a star, which Harvey was and is. There is a special skill to being a supporting performer. I had a very distinct persona in that show. I didn't fade into the scenery. If I had, "Timeless to Me" would never have worked. Even the critic from the *Times* said it was really my number. But in the end, I was not the star, Harvey was.

How to Work with a Star

The star is the person you hope is going to sell the tickets. My job is to help that star be a star. I don't go in there thinking I'm going to grab everything I can. I'm going to help that person be the best they can be.

With a few exceptions like the musical *Philemon* and Neil Simon's play *I Ought To Be in Pictures*, I'm generally cast as the second banana. I've carried shows. I am capable of it. I don't have any doubts about myself. But when you are working with somebody else and you are playing opposite a person like Elaine Stritch or Harvey Fierstein, your role changes. There's an art to being a really good second banana.

One of the reasons I get hired is because I'm able to let them have the spotlight but at the same time I never let my character fade into the background. I hold my own.

I try to enhance what the star is doing, while at the same time bringing something unique to my role. In *Hairspray*, I would show Harvey affection. I'd touch him. Hold him. Everybody said that the minute I walked on stage, they could tell that Harvey and I were in love. It provided the emotional foundation of the show. Edna and Tracy could go out and do all the great things they did because the audience knew they felt that no matter what the world threw at them, they were loved at home. That was my contribution.

The star is like the bricks in a wall, and the supporting player is like the concrete. Nobody calls it a concrete wall, they call it a brick wall. People admire the bricks, not the concrete. But the job of the concrete is to hold the bricks together and support them.

I was not out there to compete with Harvey. I was out there to enhance Harvey's performance and consequently my own. If you are doing that for that star, you are going to come off great. That's collaborating. Collaborating is doing the job you have to do within the limitations of your role and that show. It's hard to learn, but very important.

I've worked with some good people. Considering my background and my education I feel blessed to have gotten to where I am. Winning the Tony Award for Best Featured Actor in a Musical for *Hairspray* was the culmination of my career. It was Everyman's award.

Giving and Taking

I sit with the script and do a lot of homework. I try not to come into the rehearsal hall not knowing anything and wasting everybody's valuable time. Some actors don't think twice about wasting time. Teresa Stratas was very demanding on *Rags*, but you can forgive anything because of that voice.

I can think of one other well-known star who was a nightmare about that. I did a reading with her and she tried to make it all about her, her, her. I tried to rationalize it. We're all a little selfish. She's really talented and she makes things work. I admire her. But she's also extremely selfish.

The director said, "Let's just read through this script for timing. OK, start!" And immediately she started asking, "Why is this line like this? Can I do it like that?" All of the attention of the director had to come to her. The rest of us had to just sit there and wait. She just sucked all the oxygen out of the air.

There are some people in theatre who are giving, and some who are not. A lot of people don't want to work together as equals. The attitude seems to be that chorus is chorus and principals are principals. But I never believed in that separation. Being giving means treating people as equals, on stage and off.

If a principal actor is not giving, they're playing by themselves. They step on your lines. To this day I have people step on my lines. I look at people who do that as being very insecure.

In a situation like that, you should meet with the director separately with your questions. When do you speak up? When you can sense that something's not working. When you feel that your scene is not moving the show forward. That's the most important thing. Things have to move forward. If you've got a good instrument you can *feel* when something is not working.

When that happens, you might talk to the actors you're working with and say, "How do you feel about this?" Then you go to the director—*not* the playwright. It's the director's job to go to the writer, if he so chooses. I would never take it on myself to go to someone like Neil Simon and say, "Neil, about this scene..." I would never pass Gene Saks or Herb Ross or any of these guys who direct for Neil.

But maybe Neil Simon isn't the best example, because Neil is so smart. He can see when a scene is laying an egg. And the next day it's gone. Totally rewritten. He's the rewriter of the world. He's not married to anything. All that rewriting shouldn't be a problem for an actor—at least not when the rewrite makes thing better. And Neil's is always better. When you're in a creative process you always have be very mobile. If you're not mobile, you're rigid. Then you're not in a creative process anymore. And you're only going to hurt yourself.

Most directors have a plan of how they want a scene to work and how they want people to move. They may give you more or less freedom to move within the scene where you feel it's organically right for you to move. They may work with that. But you know they've done their homework. You know they know that scene. And there are others who say, "I don't know, what we should do here? What do you think?" I don't always mind that. I like to be given a little free rein as an actor to bring my own creativity to it. I try to understand what the director has in his mind, and then express that in my own way. That's how I collaborate with a director.

PAIN IN THE ASS

If there is one word of advice I'd give about being a good collaborator, it's this: don't be a pain in the ass. It's very important that you, as an actor, not get too full of yourself and start to think you're God's gift to the American theatre.

Maybe you are—but if you're a pain in ass to the director and other actors, you ain't going to be God's gift very long. Because there's always somebody to replace you.

I work a lot because I get along with people. I am not a pain in the ass. In situations where I've had problems working with someone, I've just thought, "I won't work with this person again." I don't raise hell at the time. I just put them on my short list.

When I see people being a pain in the ass, I think, why are they doing it? Why are they wasting their time and ours? And there are so many pains in the ass out there. I saw it a lot when I was in *Hairspray*. Complainers. The minimum salary on Broadway was at that time $1350 a week. From my Depression mentality, $1350 for someone in their early twenties is still a hell of a lot of money. These kids, they're in a smash hit show like *Hairspray*. Granted, it gets to be a job after a year, but if you want to buy an apartment, do the show! I can't tell you how many of these kids miss performances. They do the matinee, but don't show up for the night show. At one point we had nine, ten out each week.

Attendance got so bad that director Jack O'Brien came in and spoke to them. He's a brilliant speaker and his speeches to the cast were like little works of art. "Look," he said, "nobody asked you to get into this business. You came into this business because you wanted to. You have to decide: What do you want out of it? And what kind of performer are you going to be in this business? A dependable one? Or one who shows up for one performance but not the next? Do you want to stay in the business?"

Attendance suddenly went right up.

If you take a job, do the job. Or quit the job. Don't come in and out and moan and complain. *Hairspray* was my twentieth Broadway show. I have never heard an audience reaction at curtain call like *Hairspray* gets. You don't bring negativity like that into a show like *Hairspray*.

Being Politic

If you're in a show, you've committed yourself. You've got to be politic with those around you. My agent said, "Dick, you are the most politic person I've ever seen. You know how to work around things."

If you have a problem with somebody, you don't blow your stack. You just think to yourself, "This guy's driving me crazy, but I'm going to get through it by keeping my eye on what *I* want."

If you can't take it anymore, you don't go after that other guy, especially when he's the director. You just say, "I cannot give you what you want. I would like to bow out of this situation."

On Broadway that happens, but rarely. A lot of times, you *can't* bow out. So you have got to allow yourself, without driving yourself crazy, to work within what you've been hired to do. How? Just accept people's shortcomings. Period.

You can sit down and have discussions. You tell them what you're having a problem with, and say, "This comes from my gut." You try to compromise. "How about if I try something else?"

Most directors will sit and listen to you. You were hired because you have the talent for that specific role. You have to sit and talk to the person you are collaborating with.

Lessons from Backstage

There's a whole etiquette to working and living backstage. A happy backstage makes a better show. My overall thought is, be social. Some principals never associate with the chorus or the ensemble. I don't buy that. Playing on Broadway is not just a job, and the people you meet backstage are not just assembly line workers.

There are some key people that it pays to get along with. Number one: the Stage Manager. He's the guy that runs the show when the director and the other creators move on. I also try to get to know the stage crew and the guys in the orchestra pit. They're working just as hard for the show as anyone else.

Here are some backstage tips:

THE COSTUME DESIGNER I can't imagine, unless you're doing a one-man show, that you aren't constantly collaborating. That's what collaborating is all about: working with other talented people in all their various respective fields.

One of the best is costume designer William Ivey Long. I trust him implicitly. If William gives me a costume to wear, I never argue because that is a man who knows his business. He knows what he wants the show to look like. If he wants me to wear a certain costume, he has a damn good reason. I will alert him if the costume is too tight, of course, but I never question the look of the costume as a whole. They know what they want that show to look like. I never say, "I don't want to wear that suit, it doesn't look good on me." Because it's not really Dick Latessa up there wearing the suit; it's the character. When you collaborate, you have to trust the talent of your collaborator.

THE PRODUCTION STAGE MANAGER It's important to maintain a good working relationship with the stage manager. Be on time. Don't be late. You would be surprised how many people are late, or neglect to sign in when they arrive at the theatre. Every night you hear the PSM on the loudspeaker backstage: "Is so-and-so here?" You can tell he's annoyed. He shouldn't have to worry about that.

If you are going to be legitimately late or sick, call the stage manager. Call him early in the day so he can let the understudy know, especially if it's the understudy's first performance, so they can check costumes.

PSMs are with you long after the director has moved on. They have to keep the show as clean as they can, so when they bring you a note, you do it. The stage manager is the point of communication between yourself and everything else in the show.

NEW KID An important part of this business that nobody talks much about is the art of bringing a new person into a long-running show. The person tries to fit into the performances that already exist, but, especially when it's a primary or secondary role, the whole show adjusts a little bit to the new person.

Backstage is like a family. It's usually hard when someone leaves, especially when it's one of the original cast members. I always try to make an effort to welcome the new person. I introduce myself. I tell them to relax and have a good time. I tell them not to take everything too seriously. If the show's good, it will take care of itself. As long as you do your job, you'll be very happy.

I remember once a friend of mine was understudying a pretty good role and she thought she'd naturally move up when the person left. Instead, they picked someone from outside the show, and she was very unhappy. She was ready to quit.

I said, "Look, you don't have another job and you've got two kids to support. You can't quit this show. OK, you're miserable. I understand how you feel. We've all been in that boat, where you wanted something and you didn't get it. Somebody else got it. You have to suffer through it. You can't walk away from a job that is paying you a decent wage. You have to push your ego out of the way. Eventually the pain will subside. It does subside in all of us. You will get over it."

She stayed, and she and the new actress became the best of friends. And she thanked me many times for the advice.

LONG RUN If you're in the middle of a long run of a show and you notice somebody's performance gets broader, you don't tell that person. First, it's not your job. You go to the stage manager and tell *them* if it's hurting the flow of the scene. Second, a lot of your fellow actors won't see that you're doing it for the good of the show. They will listen to the stage manager or the director before they'll listen to you.

CHAPTER 18

CYNTHIA ONRUBIA
DANCER AND DANCE CAPTAIN

Cynthia Onrubia is an accomplished Broadway "gypsy," dancing in many shows on Broadway and on tour. She has also served as dance captain, assistant choreographer, and choreographer. Her Broadway credits include: *A Chorus Line* (at age 15), *Bob Fosse's Dancin'* (and national tour), the original companies of *Got Tu Go Disco*, *Cats* (created Victoria), *Song and Dance* (and national tour), *Jerome Robbins' Broadway* (and national tour), *Metro*, *The Goodbye Girl*, *Damn Yankees*, *Victor/Victoria*, *Cabaret* (and national tour), *Cabaret* (Australia, for which she won a Sir Robert Helpmann Award for Best Choreography), *Little Me*, *Dame Edna* (and national tour, for which she received a 2001 National Broadway Theater Award nomination for Best Choreogra-

phy); and *Chicago* (American Choreography Award). Other credits: *Fourtune* (Off-Broadway); *Carousel* (Kennedy Center); Michael Bennett's workshop *Scandal*; *Pal Joey* (Boston); *Chita & All That Jazz*; *The Best Little Whorehouse In Texas* with Ann-Margret; New York City Center Encores! *Promises, Promises*; *Li'l Abner*; *Ziegfield Follies of 1936*; *Wonderful Town*; 1998 and 2002 Kennedy Center Honors. Television: *Today Is Ours*, *Wonderama*, *City Arts*, *Broadway Beat*, *Dining Out With Dancers*, *All My Children*, *One Life To Live*, *Search for Tomorrow*. Film: *The Jade Man*, *Night Passage*, *Everyone Says I Love You*, *Cradle Will Rock*, *Center Stage*, *Chicago*, *Analyze That*, *Big Fish*, *Connie and Carla*.

The Other Person's Head

One of the most important things I've learned in my career is that, in collaborating, you always have to have your own ideas, but you also have to get inside the other person's head. It's being on the same page, but also standing on your own.

When I first was cast as an understudy in *A Chorus Line*, Baayork Lee, the original Connie and the show's original dance captain, came into rehearsal. I thought we were going to go through numbers but instead she brought two chairs on stage and she sat down with me and said, "OK, tell me about [the character of] Maggie."

She was more concerned about my story and about how I was going to build the character than she was about the dancing. I loved when she did that. In the end, steps are cheap. If you are going to be a dancer on Broadway today, you need to think about the character.

I've always thought that dancing goes beyond technique. The job also goes beyond the steps, even beyond just the musical numbers. I've always been interested in making sure the dances jibe with the scenes. The 1988 musical *Jerome Robbins' Broadway* was very important for me because working with Jerry advanced my understanding and ability directorially. Jerry always said, "My work comes from the book"—meaning each show's libretto—and I'm a big believer in that.

BOB FOSSE

My first contact with Bob Fosse came when I auditioned for his musical *Dancin'*. I was doing *A Chorus Line*, but I don't think I was even sixteen yet. He saw me audition, but didn't pick me, so I stayed in *A Chorus Line* for another year.

When they started casting the national tour of *Dancin'*, I had turned seventeen and had started dating. I went back to audition for him again, and we did the same combination. I guess it was just the way I looked in his eyes. Fosse was standing quite close to where I was dancing. After we finished the combination, he put his arm around me and he said, "You've grown up a lot."

And I thought about that for a minute as I walked to the side of the room. I realized he wasn't talking about the way I was dancing. I wasn't dancing any better than I had when I first auditioned. It's that I had discovered my sexuality. He saw something inside me that was crucial for his kind of dancing—something that went beyond technique, that went beyond something I could "act." It was something in me. I was now ready to be a Fosse dancer. That's how I "came of age" on Broadway.

And Bob's nickname for me became "Little Mighty Mouse."

When we originally rehearsed for the first national tour I did most of the work with Christopher Chadman and Kathryn Doby, a.k.a. "Mother Doby." (Kathryn was Bob's assistant on everything he ever did and the dancers called her that.) Bob would come in from time to time to work on something that was of special concern to him. Once he made eight of us rehearse "Sing, Sing, Sing" all day. He was looking for a particular feeling. It was an electric shock in the body and then a melt, which all of us could do—but he wanted us all to do it exactly the same because we were in this amoeba-like clump and he wanted a very specific kind of jolt when the shock came. He was determined, and he worked on that step until he got exactly what he wanted. He applied that to everything.

Then there was the flip side to all that hard work. When you were performing, he would sometimes pop into the theatre appear in the wings, stage right. You'd be dancing, and Bobby would be down in his crouch and you could hear him saying, "Go, baby, go!" He'd be egging you on and urging you on. How exciting was that, to be a dancer and have Bob Fosse right there in the wings just making you want to do it better?

He understood how to make dancers be their best. It was his collaborative gift.

Memorizing Steps

Every dancer memorizes steps differently because everyone's mind works differently. Some are very visual. Some do it with music. Some need to do it with counts. Some people like to feel it. To me it always goes back to music and counts. But you don't start telling a story with your dance until you get past the counts and start to put your acting into it.

Some choreographers like their steps very exact. They like every finger—every pinky—to be in a precise place at a precise time. The head must be turned at an exact angle, the foot must be pointed in just such a way. Some are very, very strict about that and others are not.

I was very fortunate to work with Michael Bennett and Bob Fosse. They want you to put your own personality into your dancing, and I've tried to do the same on projects I have choreographed. To me, steps aren't just steps. They always have to come from somewhere. What's the number about? On Broadway, our job is to tell a story.

Graciela Daniele and Rob Marshall are the same way. You always have to look at the script. It's especially great collaborating when you have the author in the room and can ask them questions that will go beneath and behind the script.

Sometimes the choreographer will see a place in the story where a dance number might help further the story. If the writers and the director agree, they can offer ideas of what the dance could be about and how it could develop. The composer can write some new music, or develop themes that are already in the scene. If you are all on the same page, it's great, because that's good collaborating.

Some directors always want to be in the room with the choreographer. But that can also be a little stifling at times. At a certain point, the director needs to back off and let the choreographer create. Then, when the choreographer has something, the others can add their comments and suggestions. It's great when everybody is hands-on, but artists also need their private time.

So what do choreographers talk about with their assistants and their dancers behind those closed doors? "What if...?" I love the question, "What if...?" First instincts are usually correct, but you always want to explore the possibilities of where a number could go.

MICHAEL BENNETT

Michael Bennett's collaborative style wasn't so much about the steps. He was a dancer, and he would make each dancer do what they needed to do in order to progress. He was very good to me. I remember a company call on *A Chorus Line* at which he made me do the jazz combination by myself. For a long time, I thought, he just wanted to show off the baby, the youngest one. I didn't realize until years later why he really did it. He wanted to show me I could hold my own.

But if you didn't progress, he had no time for you. I remember another company call on *A Chorus Line* where five people were let go. Some of them had been with the company more than a year. He told one of the people, "You aren't the character anymore." I was shocked, but I learned a lot from that.

DANCE ARRANGER

There is one collaboration that rarely gets discussed, but which is absolutely essential to creating a musical with dance: the choreographer's collaboration with the dance arranger. The choreographer experiments with different meters and steps and their rhythmic emphasis as he's creating. As he's doing it, the dance arranger takes themes and other bits of music created by the composer and makes up variations on it to fit the steps. The steps and the flow of the music are created at the same time.

A dance arranger can change the whole feeling of a number by taking an existing piece of music from the score, and slowing it down, or playing it in a minor key, or jazzing it—whatever mood fits the steps the choreographer is inventing. A lot of times dancers are also very closely involved with this kind of collaboration, because in the pressure of the moment, the choreographer will use steps that those dancers at that moment can actually do. So really all three are working together, the choreographer standing with the dancers, and the dance arranger sitting at the piano matching the flavor and the spirit of the dances, and quickly scratching notes onto staff paper.

Every great dance you ever saw on Broadway was created that way, and in the moment that it's happening, it's some of the most thrilling collaboration you've ever seen.

JEROME ROBBINS

During the course of pre-production for *Jerome Robbins' Broadway* as Mr. Robbins got to know me, I always called him "Mr. Robbins." After a time he said, "Call me Jerry." But I kept calling him "Mr. Robbins." After a few months he again said, "Call me Jerry," and I replied, "I have to earn it." That sure got a smile out of him.

Jerome Robbins' Broadway was a retrospective of great dance numbers from shows like *West Side Story, Fiddler on the Roof,* and *Peter Pan.* It proved to be a very interesting collaborative process for me because there weren't a lot of charts listing the steps for the numbers that he wanted to do. We had to reconstruct numbers from memory—usually Jerry's memory, but he'd done so much and so many years had passed that we found ourselves hunting for archival film or even consulting the original dancers.

One of my assignments was watching the movie version of *Gypsy,* which contained Jerry's original choreography for "All I Need Is the Girl" (which we called "Tulsa," because that was the name of the character doing the dance). I wrote down all the steps, but it was hard and I realized why. It's because I wasn't learning it in a studio. Your mind can always remember better when you are on your feet. Your body—your muscles—have a kind of memory, too. If you are just watching something you might be able to remember it, but it's not in your body because you haven't transposed it into your blood.

Dancers are basically computers. There are dancers who will remember all the steps when they are doing a show, but when they leave or the show closes, those steps disappear from the brain. My peers and my "babies"—the dancers I've taught or hired—all call me "the computer brain" because I remember everything I've ever done. I used to do big industrial shows like the annual *Milliken Show* for the Milliken corporation. There was the adult ensemble, the "Beautiful Milliken Girls and the Gorgeous Milliken Men," and there was the children's ensemble called the "Milli-kiddies." I can still remember all the steps I had to do as a "Milli-kiddie."

I had a chance to draw on that skill when Jerome Robbins was recreating the numbers from *The King and I,* which he also choreographed. Jerry was having trouble remembering some of the steps. I had done *King and I* in 1972 at Jones Beach Theatre. I was Princess Ying, the littlest of the king's children. I'd watch the dances from the wings every performance. I found that I remembered that choreography really well, even though I hadn't seen or done it since I was ten. Jerry took me into a studio and said, "Show me," and I remembered the whole thing. When I was a little girl I just wanted to be a sponge and learn everything in the show. I didn't know that I was going to end up teaching it back to Jerome Robbins years later.

MISTAKES

Great dancers really respect the choreographer. They will do basically anything they are asked. This obedience is so ingrained in dancers that it's a shock when someone violates the unspoken code. I was in a room where a number was being taught and a dancer said—not to the choreographer, but out loud—"That's terrible!" I was simply mortified. I couldn't believe it. And I thought, "How disrespectful! Even if you are thinking that, keep your mouth shut."

In return, choreographers respect experience and reputation. Once they know your strengths and weaknesses, they will actually try to create something expressly for you. A choreographer has to protect his or her work, but they know that the dancers are the ones who are going to be up on stage every night and you always want them to like what they are doing.

GILLIAN LYNNE

I originated the role of Victoria, the white cat, in the Broadway production of *Cats*. In rehearsal, director Trevor Nunn wanted to change the character's name and make it more elaborate like all the others. I asked him please to keep it "Victoria," because that was the other name my mother was considering giving me when I was born. I told him I loved the purity of it, and he agreed to leave it "Victoria."

We opened in 1982 and I left the show in 1984. In 1993, choreographer Gillian Lynne asked me to come back and supervise. By then I was dance captain for the Broadway revival of *Damn Yankees*. I went back into the Winter Garden and I felt like I never left. It was a huge cast and a lot of people going in and out, and I remember telling my husband that if I took the job, I'd probably never get a day off. But I wanted to do it because I had been away from the show long enough that it would be fresh again. I still had all the memories and I still remembered all the steps. And, being an original cast member, I knew I had something unique to offer: I could recreate the training Gillian gave us when she was putting it on the stage for the first time, and pass along stories and lore from those earliest days. Gillian is very hands-on, and she would come to many of the rehearsals. But I figured that since I was a dancer just like them, I could communicate some of the magic of that first *Cats* to the fifth or sixth generation *Cats*.

DANCE CAPTAIN

A dance captain is in charge of learning the entire show, teaching it to the dancers, and then keeping the show sharp throughout the run. You chart everything about who goes where and when—basically, traffic patterns—and write it down in a book, called the "bible."

Some dance captains need to write down specific steps as well. I never needed to do that because once they are planted in my brain, they stay there. There are certain times when the choreographer will return to a production and change things to keep the show fresh, or, if a new star is coming into a show, you have to restructure it for them, of course. That's when you start to write down the various versions of the choreography.

Every choreographer collaborates differently. If they are still dancing, they usually love to get up and teach the staging themselves, walking you through the whole thing. Very hands-on.

Sometimes they'll have their assistants teach the steps while they are creating the number in their heads. As dance captain, there have been times when I am asked in a room with the choreographer and he teaches it to me ahead of everybody else so I can the help in teaching. Some choreographers trust the dance captain to the point where they will run auditions for replacements on long-running shows, though I always call the choreographer to get approval before I offer a contract.

When something is going wrong with a performance, I'll "give a note." Sometimes it's literally a written note, sometimes it's a verbal reminder to the dancer. This is a sensitive area. You can give the same note to twenty-five different people twenty-five different ways. You have to deal with the individual's personality and be aware of how they are going to interpret the note. There are some people that will take the note, and it's done. There are some people, where it takes three shows—if you are giving them a note on a step or something—to fix it.

I remember the first time I got a director's note. I was still in my teens and I was understudying in the Broadway production of *A Chorus Line*. I was rehearsing as Diana, the Puerto Rican girl who sings "What I Did for Love," and we were doing the "alternative" scene where I talk about how I sometimes feel depressed. The dance captain came up to me and said, "Your speaking is fine but can you be a little more expressive in your face? Because it's not reading."

I thought about trying to grimace a little more, but it didn't feel right. I didn't want to overact. The show is supposed to be all about honesty. Then I realized what the problem was. Because I was so young, I didn't have a lot of lines on my face yet. My skin was still so smooth. With no frown lines that could be seen from the audience, I needed be more expressive without overdoing it. I thought I was doing enough but obviously it was not registering at the back of the house. It was a useful lesson, and I never forgot that note.

I hate when dancers fool around and stop taking the show seriously. It's such an honor and a privilege to be working on Broadway. They struggle and pray, "Please let me get this show!" But sometimes, once they get it, and the show is a hit and goes on for a long time, they forget. It becomes just a job. Can you imagine?

I remember seeing it during *Jerome Robbins' Broadway*. They'd be doing the wedding scene from *Fiddler on the Roof*, and I'd see people eyeing each other when they were supposed to be standing still and watching the ceremony. Whenever I would see people fooling around, I'd nail them and say, "Please don't do that anymore."

They might stop for a few performances, but then it would start up again and I would have to go back up to them and say, "You know what? This needs to stop. It's pulling the audience's focus."

I saw it illustrated during the wedding sequence from *Fiddler on the Roof* that Jerome Robbins recreated for that show. There's a certain attitude he wanted, a sense of dignity but also a sense of joy in the physical release of dance for these characters, and he was very insistent that it be done exactly that way. Sometime he was insistent in the extreme. A lot of the dancers were intimidated by the way he spoke to them. Some people think it's very bad when a director gives them a note saying that something in their performance needs correcting. Jerry would say, "You're doing this wrong," and the dancer would be devastated. But that's not how he meant it. What he meant was, "Please try to do it a different way."

I've learned over the years that different people hear and interpret things very differently. It's important to word things very carefully and diplomatically, but firmly. Getting what you want from a dancer is psychological as well as technical. It takes a special kind of intelligence to be aware of that and act on it. It's really about tact. I try to give notes nicely and with respect to the other person. But I'll give a note forty times if I have to, if the problem isn't getting fixed. That's the responsibility of the dance captain to the choreographer.

As a dance captain sometimes I feel a desire to change the choreography slightly to suit the talents of a particular dancer, especially a talented replacement. Sometimes I'll approach the choreographer and say, "This new person has got a great jump, so where there's a kick, do you mind if I put in a jump instead. Usually, the choreographer trusts me enough to say, "Go ahead."

It's great creating for people. As a choreographer, I love learning what people's strengths are. I'll be teaching them something and they'll do something instinctively and they'll say, "Oh, I made a mistake." And I'll say, "No, but you did that naturally. Let's try it again." You have to pick whichever move makes them look better and which is right for the song or for the piece.

Sometimes what they consider a mistake is actually something organic that they did naturally. It's like the way somebody interprets a song. It's the way they feel it. It's honest. If you can find a way to use something like that in a show—without changing the meaning of the dance or the show—it always pays to try.

Bernadette Peters

I like to observe stars and see the many different ways they collaborate (or not) with their fellow actors.

Bernadette Peters, for example, is a great team player. I had two chances to see her up close. I was a dancer on her shows *Song and Dance* and *The Goodbye Girl*. She's so easy to work with and she's also a generous actress on stage. She's not selfish at all. She always gives to her fellow actors. She gives you space to breathe. She listens on stage. She goes with the flow and she'll give it right back.

I watched her work with Martin Short on *The Goodbye Girl*. Marty is so hilarious and spontaneous, so Bernadette had to be that spontaneous, too, to keep up. The rhythm of their scenes would change every night. Marty would always try to crack her up and she had to hold her own. There were times when you could see that she was on the verge of losing it, but she would exert amazing control. You could see her thinking, "No. I'm going to think of something else, something serious, so I won't break." She's really good on stage that way.

On the Andrew Lloyd Webber musical *Song and Dance*, she was the entire first act (the *Song* part) and we, the dancers would come on in the second act. The first act is a solo musical with twenty-three songs, and Bernadette did all the parts. I don't know how she did it. We'd be warming up and we'd hear her singing these songs, and we'd get emotional. To be out there by herself on the stage I think was a journey for her. She ended up winning the Tony Award for it, and deservedly so.

Long Runs

Long runs represent special challenges and opportunities for a dancer. Steady employment is one of the great opportunities, of course, but I try always to get better. If you don't feel really good about the way you danced last night, you analyze what went wrong, and how you could boost it the next night. There's nothing like feeling satisfied with your performance. At the end of each performance you want to go home and feel like you did the best show you could. But that gets harder, the longer a show runs. One technique I use: I put an idol in the house. I sometimes imagine, say, Chita Rivera is in the audience and I dance as well as I can, just for her. You have to challenge yourself like that, because if you get in a rut, it always shows.

Also, if you have lines, you have to be vigilant to make sure your performance doesn't get too broad. That's harder with the dances, because the conductor controls the tempo of the music. But, as an actor, if you get a good laugh with a line, you want to get a bigger laugh the next night, so you make it just a little bit broader. Over time, a whole scene can go to hell. As Neil Simon says, "Just say the line." Don't over-interpret it. Just speak.

Sometimes people just get lazy later in a run, and the dance captain has to work hard to keep the energy level up. But sometimes shows, or parts of shows, actually improve over time. In *Victor/Victoria* there's a number called "Le Jazz Hot." In the men's section we had choreographed a double pirouette at one point. Later in the run we got some replacements who were *fantastic*. I noticed that we had time to do a triple turn in the same spot instead of just a double. So I asked the new people if they wanted to try it, and they did, and it was a killer. In that case, the audience was actually getting a better show later on.

One thing that audiences take for granted is choruses dancing in precise and clean unison. Dancers have to be strict with themselves. They have to think as a group, and feel as a group. Anybody can learn steps, but it takes something special to be able to move together as a group like that. You have to feel it in your body.

AUDIENCE

Those of us who have been performing for many years sometimes forget what it's like to be an ordinary audience. When we watch a show, we're thinking, "Is this number serving the piece? Is this performer serving the piece?" I think like a choreographer when I'm watching a show.

But audiences watch all sorts of things. They may be admiring one dancer's legs, or looking at the set, or who knows what. For *Dame Edna: The Royal Tour*, Barry Humphries asked me to hire tall, leggy, gorgeous women, so I brought in the beauties.

Most people don't know about great dancing, and you can't blame them for that. Some of the hardest choreography is meant to look effortless. Some of the easiest is meant to look difficult. If either effect is achieved, then we're doing our job. But I do hope that people notice more than just our legs. I hope that people think, "Gosh she has great technique. She's so passionate when she dances." Even if they don't know the fine points of technique, I hope they at least get the impression of the joy of great dancing.

I think you always want the audience to feel what you are feeling. And I think that comes from being honest as an actor. If a performer on stage is not being true, it shows. If you are thinking about what you are going to make for dinner while you are dancing, then you are going to be a boring dancer. You must always keep in your mind the material and the story you are supposed to be telling. You must always relate to your partner if you are dancing with another girl or another guy. If you are not really looking in their eyes, then you are not being honest.

Part IV

COMPLETION

CHAPTER 19

ROBIN WAGNER

SET DESIGNER

Robin Wagner's Broadway designs include *The Boy From Oz*; *The Producers*; *Flower Drum Song*; *Kiss Me, Kate*; *Saturday Night Fever*; *Side Show*; *Angels in America*; *Victor/Victoria*; *Jelly's Last Jam*; *Crazy for You*; *City of Angels*; *Jerome Robbins' Broadway*; *Chess*; *42nd Street*; *Dreamgirls*; *On the Twentieth Century*; *A Chorus Line*; *Jesus Christ Superstar*; *Lenny*; *Promises, Promises*; *The Great White Hope*; and *Hair*. Ballet and opera include the Metropolitan, Swedish Royal, Vienna State, Royal Opera Covent Garden, and New York City Ballet. Honors include Tonys, Drama Desks, Outer Critics Circles, and others. He is a trustee of the New York Shakespeare Festival and a member of the Theatre Hall of Fame.

Many Gifts Put Together

The playwright, the songwriters, and the director are the ones who imagine the world of a musical theatre piece. It's the set designer's job to make that world concrete, to provide a place where the characters will live and play out their stories.

Collaboration is the ultimate necessity in any kind of theatre. I believe that it begins with the text and then is reborn with the director and then you can go and have fun.

I learned how to collaborate during the time I was an assistant to Oliver Smith. You have to learn the way the designers think and the way the director thinks. Directors usually have a very strong line of thinking, whether it's visual or not. They force you always to consider: What is the play about? What's the scene about?

What's the "obligatory moment" when the whole thing has to come together visually, like in the "Springtime for Hitler" scene in *The Producers*?

When I begin on a project, I won't do anything until I've read the script and talked to everybody involved. I will read a script half a dozen times on my own, then sit down in a room with the rest of the creative team and read through the script together, from page one. We talk about everything that's visual in the piece. We ask questions about the intention of every moment.

That process was especially fun on *The Producers* when we had Mel Brooks there with us to answer questions. Mel would never stop. He was involved with the design process a lot more than most writers. He told us what kind of posters he wanted on the walls of Max Bialystock's office. He'd say, "The actors have got to be able to go outside. The actors have to have a place to hide. The whole stage has to be covered with scripts...." He was describing everything exactly as he envisioned it, and all I had to do was write it down and make it happen.

The first step of the collaboration is to get from the director the style of the show. The director has to decide whether or not it's going to be realistic or naturalistic or high style or whatever. That will also determine how the actors will act and how the costumes, the lighting, and the scenery will work. You have to be sure that the behavior of the actors will work on this particular set. If you have a dark, dull set, it's going to work against a frothy comedy. If you have a flat suburban living room and the characters start speaking in verse, they're going to look ridiculous.

Most directors know what they want. They have a specific vision. That's one of the reasons they get chosen to direct a particular piece. They are able to envision how the piece is going to come to life for an audience, and how it is best served by the actors. The director, in turn, enlists designers to help determine just what that reality looks like.

Often, directors will bring me onto a project at a very early point, sometimes when the very initial script is being developed, especially if it's a musical. I attend the first five or six creative sessions, sometimes long before they're ready to discuss how the show is going to look. At that point there's no visual context. It's only what is the play about, how best to serve the play, how to bring it to life. That's the very first part of what a director does.

Only after those kinds of meetings do I begin designing. I start by making quarter-inch white models out of paper so you can easily tear them up, cut them up and change them. I learned that from Oliver Smith. He never committed to anything until the drawings were accepted, then he would start to build the half-inch scale that would serve as the model for the building of the actual set. The preliminary design lets people see what it will look like, but also lets them feel free to make changes. I always think less is more. I'm always sitting here with scissors saying, "We don't really need that."

As a designer, it's very important not to be married to your first idea. You have to keep an open mind. It gives the director an opportunity to really get involved in the visual. The director is the one who has to keep the whole project integrated, to make sure all the elements have the same vibe and are part of the same vision.

Some directors are more visual than others. Michael Bennett would spend hours talking about exactly the kind of look he wanted, and all three of us, the costume designer, the lighting designer and myself, would try to work together to make it look like a single vision.

Michael always worked with a team that included his designers. We would be part of his projects from the beginning. I was at the first recording session for the project that became *A Chorus Line*. Everyone sat in a circle and told their life stories into the early hours of the morning. There was no music yet, just an idea. But already he had me thinking of what kind of set I could do for such a project. His team was at work from the start.

TEAMWORK

Most directors who work a lot come to rely on a certain team of designers. Not only is there trust, but you speak a common artistic language. After a while, it becomes shorthand. Many producers do the same.

I first worked with Michael in 1968 on *Promises, Promises*, which was produced by David Merrick, based on the film *The Apartment*. It had a book by Neil Simon and music by Burt Bacharach and Hal David.

Merrick brought Robert Moore, the director of *Boys in the Band*, and, as choreographer, Michael Bennett, on one of his earliest Broadway projects. Fashion designer Donald Brooks was brought in to do the costumes. That was Merrick's way of doing things. That was his way of participating in the creation of the work.

Just as Merrick was very good at putting teams together, he also was ruthless at tearing them apart—usually publicly—when they weren't working. He was not an easy man to work with, but he was a very keen theatre person and really understood how to make a show work. He was one of the last of the big producers who had the power to direct the director.

I learned that expression from Joseph Papp. Early in his career he directed a lot, but after a while he devoted himself to producing and running the Public Theater and the New York Shakespeare Festival. I once asked him why he had stopped directing.

"What do you mean I'm not directing?" he said. "I direct the directors!"

And it was true. That's one of the major things that the artistic director of an institutional theatre has to do. They go in and help the directors, where needed. That's all a part of their unique collaboration.

William Ivey Long and Theoni Aldredge are the two costume designers I've worked with the most. William always says his job is easier because the set designer picks the colors, but the truth of it is that he really chooses the colors. I go to him with palettes and say, "William, can you live with this?"

He's an incredibly flexible collaborator. You could tell him the only color he could use was gray, and he would come up with something. I know this is true because that's exactly what we did on *Double Feature*, a double-bill of ballets by Susan Stroman at New York City Ballet in early 2004. The stories were inspired by black-and-white movies, and Stroman decreed that entire design would be in black, white and gray. My only discussion with William was whether it would be a green-gray, a blue-gray or a brown-gray. That was a challenge because it's hard to get subtle variations in black and white and still have the audience feel it's looking at black and white.

That's an example of a situation where the director sets out an unusual parameter and you work within it. Stroman has always done that. She's very strong, visually. Sometimes things have to be in a certain color because it's logical. Usually it's pretty subtle. I used that a lot in *The Producers*. There are the colors of Max's office, the colors of the accountant office, the colors of Broadway, the colors of the courtroom and the color of the prison.

To find the correct colors, I work very closely with the costume designer, who has to dress people in a way that conforms to those colors or contrasts with those colors, depending on the situation. It's a kind of a marriage. William Ivey Long would send me fabrics and I'd send him paint samples. Then the lighting designers come down and we show them samples and colors and they figure out the kind of lighting that will give those colors their full effect.

Sound designers present a special problem for set designers because they have needs that often infringe on the set. They need to put their speakers in certain places, which can block sight lines or even intrude onto the performing space. But you work with them to make them as unobtrusive as possible. Because, in the end, if you can't hear the show, it doesn't matter what it looks like.

Good sound design has become more and more important and, with the decline of purely acoustic theatre, the audience's desire to have a CD-like sound has become a major issue. And our job is to combine the needs of sound, lighting, costumes and sets so it all seems to have been created in one piece. And that's why the director is so central.

Gower Champion always had strong visual ideas on all the shows I did with him, from *Hello, Dolly!* to *42nd Street*. Example: the 1974 musical *Mack & Mabel*. He had twenty-eight girls and he wanted them all to come down a giant slide onto the stage. Making that work was a challenge, but it's the kind of challenge I relish. When you were working with Gower, the first job of the designer was to get into his head and see what he envisioned.

It was the same when we did *42nd Street* in 1980. He had an idea for a number "Sunny Side to Every Situation" where you could see all actresses in their dressing rooms at once. I asked if we could stack the dressing rooms. He said sure. So we stacked them and put them behind a scrim and the girls turned the lights on and off to create various visual and musical patters. It was such a striking idea, they used it again in the 2000 revival. It's a great help to a designer when a director has clear, strong, and dramatically interesting ideas like that.

Michael Bennett had his own visual strengths, though they were quite different. He would start from the beginning of the show and conceive staging and movement for each moment as it came up. Whenever he would hit a place where he didn't have an inspiration of his own, he would say, "Let's make this a costume moment" or, "We'll make this a scenic moment or a lighting moment." He knew he had many different tools besides the script and the actors. He didn't regard design elements as problems, but as solutions to problems. And he let us have our moment to shine. He considered us part of the show, not just a background to the show.

In the early workshops for *Dreamgirls* we needed to think of a way to move from one scene to another and one time to another. We came up with the idea of using towers of lights. Originally they would just stand there as part of the set, but one night I got a call at two or three in the morning. It was Michael and he had an idea: "Can the towers turn?"

I immediately said, "Yes, of course!"—not having any idea how to do it. The next morning I was on the phone to the shops, trying to figure out a way to make these lighting towers turn. And of course, we did. He, in turn, created choreography for sets and lights. Think about that.

They gave you the sense that you were watching something about showbiz, with all those lights, but also the sense of going somewhere. It also created excitement in the audience because every time they turned, the lights flashed in the audience's eyes—flash!—and when you looked again the towers were in different positions, and you knew you were in a different place. Sometimes we'd add a simple element like a sheer scrim or some Mylar drops. Then, from behind the Mylar, the three Dreams would emerge in different costumes. It enabled us to make scene changes in a split second.

But he was always trying do that: make transformations that would remove you from one moment into a new moment and transform everything into a new place.

Tharon Musser was the lighting designer on that show. We had worked together on *A Chorus Line* for Bennett, and on *Mack & Mabel* for Gower Champion. We definitely became part of Bennett's team after *Chorus Line*, along with costume designer Theoni Aldredge. Whenever he had a decision to make, he'd call together his "family" and we'd all go to dinner and drink a lot of wine. Then he would tell us what we were going to be doing next.

When we started work on *Ballroom*, he called us up to his apartment on Central Park South and showed us these three videotapes. One was Quentin Crisp's *The Naked Civil Servant*. Another was *Queen of the Stardust Ballroom*, which had been a TV movie. He said, "What do you think we are doing next?" We all assumed it would be *Naked Civil Servant*, but he said, "No, we're doing *Queen of the Stardust Ballroom*."

It's about a middle-aged widow who thinks her life is over, but who gets a second life when she takes up ballroom dancing. All the characters are middle-aged or older. I asked Michael why he chose that one, because I actually didn't like it very much.

Bennett said, "Because no matter what I do next, everyone wants to see *A Chorus Line 2* and I'm not going to do that. Secondly, I have thirty friends, all dancers, who are over the age of forty and who will never work on Broadway again unless I do this show. Thirdly, I am paying for it myself so no one is going to lose any money on it except me." He could do that because by then he was making pretty good dough off *A Chorus Line*.

We did *Ballroom* and, I'm sorry to report, it failed. But all those things he said came true. All those dancers were dancing again and they were as happy as kids. It was just wonderful. Not only was the choreography brilliant, but it was Michael's way to say thanks to people he'd worked with all those years. He loved to work again and again with people he knew and liked. They were part of an extended family. He created the workshop space at 890 Broadway out of his profits from *A Chorus Line* and filled it with artists knew and respected. That was true collaboration.

INSECURITY

The way he took those stories and put them together as *A Chorus Line* was the ultimate act of collaboration. Some people who gave him their life stories never even got to do their own material. It was mixed around and given to others. He included the entire design team from the beginning. If you had an idea, he wanted it. Every good director I've ever worked with has been that way. If you have an idea that is strong or visual, even if it influences the script, they want it and it becomes part of the collaboration.

One of the worst mistakes a director can make is to create an ambience where the contributions are really not welcome. That usually happens only with a director who is insecure or who has not done big shows. They are very fearful that their vision of the show will be tampered with in some way. Secure directors don't have a problem. If you have a strong idea, they want it. And they give you strong ideas. If you are not capable of executing their version of how it should look, then you are the one who is not collaborating. When people are insecure, that's when you don't get the full benefit of collaboration.

I taught a workshop for directors at Columbia University's graduate program for about eight years. I discovered that young directors tend to be very hesitant about expressing—or even having—visual ideas. Those things grow as they get older and stronger. Young directors look to the designer to do it all, and—this is coming from a designer—that is a mistake. What happens is, you get a set that is so strong or costumes that are so striking that are so overwhelming that they control the show.

That's not such an issue in opera. In Vienna, for instance, the designers have all the muscle. In theatre, we depend on the director to keep all the elements in balance. Producers have great control over that, too, because they are paying for it.

Directors have gotten more and more power over the years. I saw it happening back in the days of *Hello, Dolly!* and *110 in the Shade*, but it's much more now. I assisted Oliver Smith on both those shows, and he used to control a lot of big musicals because the directors often came from another sphere or were primarily directors of straight plays. But on *Dolly!*, director/choreographer Gower Champion was the boss.

The look of the show became very, very important during that period. Take the circular ramp that Dolly used to come out beyond the orchestra and talk directly to the audience in the Harmonia Gardens scene. That was not a new thing. It had been done all through the 1890s. We got a lot of credit for adding this exciting element to the show, but that was born from research, which most designers do. If you are working in a period, you want to get as much of the natural ambience as you can. Oliver was wonderful at recreating periods, as he did in *My Fair Lady* and *Camelot*. He really would get the sense of something, and I learned a great deal from him.

Promises, Promises had a unique set design. Everybody wanted to make it modern— "right now," which was a premium in 1968 when we were working on it. So for research I walked down Sixth Avenue in Manhattan and took a look at whatever was brand-new. I did the entire show with great glass panels for the corporate scenes, and the look of brownstones for the apartment scenes. I used actual details from a brownstone on the Upper West Side, where it might have been. At the time we felt that composer Burt Bacharach was the latest thing in music, so we tried to have the set reflect that. David Merrick loved it and I believe it influenced a lot of other shows. You suddenly started to see plastic and mirrors. It looked very "today" for the time.

I developed a very different look for *A Chorus Line*. It has the most minimal sets of any big musical, but it wasn't that way originally. The show was developed over the course of two workshops, and so were the sets. In the second workshop we began with comparatively realistic scenery for every scene. One of the things that Michael wanted to do was to explore what kind of sets you could have. We'd build a prop, but then explore why we really needed it, and *if* we really needed it. That led us to apply the same principle to the sets. We decided to see how little we could do the show with. Finally, it came down to the reality: we could actually do the show with nothing but a white line. We didn't start with that; we ended with that.

Michael always liked a black box space: demanding the ultimate imagination on the part of the dancer to create an ambience. He was able to demand that with the dancers. He could get things out of them. He could make the audience visualize so well, that no set was needed. Each number in that show creates something visual: the steep and very narrow stairway in "At the Ballet," or running seven blocks in "I Could Do That" or an improv classroom in "Nothing." You could see that sled and large ice cream cone as she was singing about it. Ultimately, what did you need to built a sled or a classroom for? The original plan was to have a huge Ziegfeld finale with the cast coming down a flight of stairs. But the story wasn't about stairs, it was about those dancers and stairs would distract from that.

When we were doing the workshop in the Newman space at the Public Theater, we marked off the stage with these four-by-eight mirrors. We'd used the same ones previously in rehearsals for *Seesaw* and *Promises, Promises*. They were on wheels so they could be moved around easily, and Michael decided to use them in this show that takes place at an audition. He started choreographing their movement. So you see, he was choreographing scenery from the very beginning. It was part of what we were exploring together. He would always say, "You make the instruments and I will play them." He demanded maximum flexibility with any object on the stage so it could appear all at once, and then disappear in a second so he could have a clean stage on which to choreograph.

The other element on that stage, which few people think about, are the *periaktoi*, an ancient Greek device consisting of three-sided columns across the back of the stage. On one side I put a mirror, so it could suggest a rehearsal hall. You could then rotate the *periaktoi* to the second side, which was black, so the mirrors could disappear.

I didn't decide what to put on the third side until we were at the point of choreographing the finale and the curtain calls. Theoni did sketches for these amazing golden costumes for "One," and I told her I'd put something on the third side that would appear only in the finale, and would back up her costumes. We made a few sketches and came up with the stylized sun. So the periaktoi went back and forth throughout the play, black, mirror, black, mirror.... But then, at the finale, they would rotate and, surprise!, reveal that rising sun.

Tharon Musser did something similar with the lighting. During the "internal" numbers—when you heard the actors' thoughts—they were lit from the back and the sides. But when they were talking to the director or it was one of the "show business" numbers, the lighting was straight out front. As a result, you always knew where the character's reality was—when you were in his head, and when you were watching the story. Coordinated by Michael Bennett, all these things mixed together in a way that could only have been arrived at as a product of collaboration.

Michael always used that word when he did interviews—"everything begins with collaboration." I always try to teach my students that as well.

It's crucial on Broadway, but with opera it's often a problem. I work at Covent Garden or the Metropolitan Opera, and I may see the director from time to time, but nobody else. They may build the set in July and it won't get on the stage until December. They depend on the designers for individual visions for their version of, for example, *The Barber of Seville*. So there's not much collaboration. Where, in the theatre, it is quite different.

SOMETHING FROM NOTHING

When I taught a director-designer workshop, I would give the students projects and then set them a challenge: How little scenery could you do this play with? What's the absolute minimum? That's the beginning of the imagination for the director.

I worked with actor Kevin Kline on a production of *Hamlet* that he was directing for the New York Shakespeare Festival. Joe Papp said, "What do you need to do this play?" I thought about it and I said, you need a skull, you need some rapiers and, if you're going to do it naturalistically, you need some poison—and not much else.

That production turned out to be very spare. We didn't even have a grave because there was no trap in that particular theatre. Instead, we carried out a pile of earth in a wheelbarrow with a skull sitting on the top and a shovel sitting on the side. That became the gravedigger scene. You can do most plays, even a big Broadway musical, with practically nothing, as *A Chorus Line* and *Dreamgirls* demonstrate.

Now, it's true that on Broadway most audiences expect to see more elaborate scenery. But you don't have to give it to them. We found with *Dreamgirls* that they would imagine it. I used to get letters saying things like, "My favorite set was the Miami nightclub." Well, there was no Miami nightclub. In that scene everything folded around itself and suddenly the three girls were there. It just *felt* like a nightclub.

The imagination of the audience fills in everything. If you are able to suggest the scenery, the audience's imagination takes over from there and does much more than you could ever afford to do with wood and canvas. That's their collaboration with me.

It can be fun to do the opposite, too. In *The Producers*, we were adapting a beloved film, so the sets needed to recreate little clips of the scenes from the film. But we didn't put just anything on the stage. If you look closely, you see every single object in the room has something to do with what's happening in the scene, from the posters on the walls of Max's office, to the cages of pigeons on Franz's roof.

Take the "I Want To Be a Producer" scene, which starts in the accounting office. The accountants are all slaves of the system and they're sitting there looking miserable, next to their sad-looking filing cabinets. But then, thanks to Leo Bloom's imagination about what it would be like to be a producer, the file cabinets burst open and out come all these magical chorus girls. We worked with the girls themselves to make the cabinets as small as they could be, and still contain these six-foot women. That was a great deal of fun. And remember that when Leo goes off into his fantasy of being a producer, there is no set whatsoever. All you see is Leo and the chorus girls. Later in the song we bring in his name in lights, but that's it. The rest of that moment is played in a black box.

For Susan Stroman and I, the girls popping out of the filing cabinets was the continuation of an idea we had when we worked together on *Crazy for You*. In the opening scene, a limousine arrived in front of our leading man and all these girls came piling out. So when we started talking about doing a dull office in *The Producers* it was very clear we needed to do something wonderful to get the girls on stage. The moment was born from that earlier moment in the first show.

When you work with a director multiple times, as Susan Stroman and I have, the ideas begin to flow more easily because they are coming from an inventory of ideas you've shared in analogous situations.

LOSING MICHAEL BENNETT

Losing Michael Bennett to AIDS was a calamity on many levels. For one, it came right in the middle of our collaboration on the musical *Chess*. Only four of us knew he was sick and we were all counting on *Chess* to be his great farewell. He had a magnificent vision for the piece. He saw it as a kind of rock concert, but one that would explore the power of the media.

The show was to have been played in front of a bank of sixty-four television screens, the number of squares on a chess board. They were linked so they could show 64 different images, or even combine to make one giant image. The TVs would set the various scenes, and sometime have people on them who would talk to the characters and the audience.

Michael was incredibly interested in media. He felt very strongly that media influences the politics of the world in much stronger way than we are aware of. If the media say something is so, people believe it and political attitudes start to change. Michael was frightened by that. He thought it was a very powerful force that was out of control.

But then Michael got too sick to continue and Bernard Jacobs of the Shubert Organization brought in British director Trevor Nunn to take over. Since so much money had already been spent, Jacobs asked the design team to stay on, and Theoni and I agreed.

Once again, the stage was to have been nearly bare in Michael's production. But, while Trevor tried to stay true to some of Michael's ideas, he's a realist at heart. So the show changed drastically. Now, every scene had to have chairs and tables.

I never felt I was one of Trevor Nunn's "team," like John Napier and David Hersey. I loved the piece and wanted to stay involved with it. But the collaboration was not the same.

ACTORS IN MIND

I'm always conscious of the fact that actors need to live and work comfortably and safely on my sets. Accidents are just the worst thing that can happen on the stage.

Michael Bennett was incredibly demanding. He expected his performers to be able to do anything. We did some numbers in Boston in *Dreamgirls* that would have raised the hair on the back of your head because they were so dangerous. In one, the dancers would get off one platform onto a twirling tower, off the twirling tower onto another platform and then go up in the air. It was scary, and people complained that it was just too much. Finally Michael listened to them, and killed it.

I try to be very safety-conscious, especially with things like staircases, raked surfaces and raised platforms. I make sure to have railings and safety harnesses wherever possible.

But sometimes it's not possible, so I have to do whatever I can. In *The Boy From Oz*, they wanted Hugh Jackman to dance on a piano—no railings, no harness. So I made a piano with a faked-out top that was twenty-four inches wide instead of just twelve, and had little moldings along the edges. Hugh is an amazing athlete, but I wanted to give him that little extra edge of safety.

The Boy From Oz was also about show business. I seem to do a lot of show business musicals, like *42nd Street* and *The Producers* and *Dreamgirls*. Maybe it's because I love show business. Broadway shows are a lot about themselves in many ways. Once you realize that fact, you can tap it in your work, like vein of gold.

Actors are usually pretty game for anything, so when one expresses a concern, I don't take it lightly. I consult the director, of course, but I always respond in some way. If a door is sticky, we fix it. If a surface is slippery, we can sand it, or use a different kind of paint or put rubber on it so it's safer. That's a very important part of any set designer's collaboration with the actors.

One of the biggest challenges was in a 2003 show called *Never Gonna Dance*, which had a number where the leads, Noah Racey and Nancy Lemenager, were supposed to be dancing on the top of a building under construction, jumping from I-beam to I-beam.

They created that whole dance in a workshop on narrow, eighteen-inch-high boxes. Once the patterns of the dance were set, we recreated the spacing things that they had been working on, but making them into I-beams that were the same distance apart, but of course much higher off the ground. When they first started working on the number out in the shop we had big rubber mattresses in case anybody slipped. As they got used to the set in technical rehearsals, we took the mattresses away. Thank God, no one ever had an accident. Those two kids were brilliant. They came to me with that dance already set. All I had to do was get them to the top of the building.

Many actors have trouble visualizing the set from a half-inch-scale model. They don't really *see* it until they leave the rehearsal studio and step onto the stage. But whenever an actor expresses an interest, I try to respond. A great example is *Kiss Me, Kate*. When they were rehearsing, Brian Stokes Mitchell came into my studio and asked how the set would work in a given scene. So I was happy to take him on a "tour" of the model. He's one of those actors who really wants to know everything. He's absolutely brilliant—a total theatre man.

On that production, director Michael Blakemore wanted everything that was backstage to have an utterly real, naturalistic feeling. Real brick, real steel. It's a play within a play, set in the 1940s, and he wanted to see real period scenery built of pine and canvas. In the dressing room the door needed to be able slam shut or smash against a wall and have it sound like a real wall. And the acrobatic number where Michael Berresse swung himself up three tiers of dressing rooms on a series of catwalks and railings—you know that had to be built as solid as a rock.

MANY GIFTS

Collaboration is a fascinating thing. Nobody talks about it as a separate discipline, but it's the best thing for a young person to learn. It's like many gifts put together. As a group you can come up with something that no one of you could have thought of.

Dreamgirls is full of striking images. People always ask whose idea was this or that. But really, you couldn't say. Something could be born from a single comment. Someone else would respond with a second comment. Then a third person would reply with a suggestion that would solve a problem or add something wonderful. Had the first two comments not been made the third comment would never have been arrived at. So many great things are born from these moments of collaboration, these chains of inspirations.

CHAPTER 20

WILLIAM IVEY LONG
COSTUME DESIGNER

William Ivey Long has designed costumes for many Broadway and Off-Broadway productions, notably *The Producers* (Tony, Drama Desk, Outer Critics Circle Awards), *Hairspray* (Tony, Drama Desk, Outer Critics Circle Awards), *Crazy for You* (Tony, Outer Critics Circle Awards), *Contact* (Hewes Award), *Nine* (Tony, Drama Desk, Maharam Awards), *Chicago*, *Guys and Dolls* (Drama Desk Award), *Assassins* (Obie Award), *Lend Me a Tenor* (Drama Desk, Outer Critics Circle Awards), *Thou Shalt Not, Six Degrees of Separation, Big, The Frogs, Music Man, A Christmas Carol, Steel Pier, Twentieth Century, Little Shop of Horrors, The Boy From Oz, Cabaret, Never Gonna Dance, 45 Seconds From Broadway, Annie Get Your Gun, Sweet Charity, The Man Who Came to Dinner, Swing!, The Mystery of Irma Vep, 1776,* and *Smokey Joe's Café.* He also designed costumes for the film version of *The Producers.*

Doorknobs and Pocketbooks

I feel there are a lot of jobs on Broadway that are a mystery to the general public. What does a producer produce? Why would a musical with all singing and all dancing need a book? And other such unsolved mysteries as these. But everyone knows just exactly what a costume designer designs.

The costume designer is, in fact, the one person—after the director and the choreographer—who deals with the actual corporeal body of the performer. Neither the set nor the lighting designer deal with the actual live human being, at least not up close.

Working with actors—and often up to thirty-six of them, presents a whole lot of variables. Such variety is indeed the spice that keeps me interested and going.

The primary delight I receive in this business is in helping an actor become someone else. The entire process—from reading the script, meeting with the director, choreographer, and the other designers, developing the designs, working with the costume shops, choosing fabrics—is all about helping the actor create the character, guiding the arc of their experience in the world of the story that is being told on stage.

In our initial meeting, I try to develop a trust and a bond of support between myself and the actor. We discuss the play and the general direction the director has told me to go. I ask how the rehearsals are going, what specifics in movement and action the actor requires—"How high do you lift your arms?" is my favorite first question (dance gussets in the sleeves usually solve any problems). So you see, I try to stay connected with what is going on in the process of making the play come alive in the rehearsal process. Usually the director encourages me to attend rehearsals to see for myself. But sometimes not. Sometimes the rehearsals are closed, or limited-access only. In those cases, I ask the actors even more questions during the fittings.

The fitting room is a sacred place. The inhabitants are the actor, myself as designer, the costume fitter, and sometimes the actor's assistant or mine. I personally have taken a self-imposed Hippocratic oath to protect all the secrets of that room. I'm often asked questions by Peeping Toms of the press, but I never tell. Even the photographs we take during these sessions are locked away. Sometimes I photograph the process, cropping off the actor's head. Sometimes I don't even take a photograph, because of some sensitivity. The photographs help me remember just how a garment fitted on the actor, the cut of the bodice on the hip, etc. But if the actor is nervous about the camera, we just have to remember it all. A quick pencil sketch sometimes does the trick.

I have a rule: "smiles after a fitting!" No actor is allowed to leave a fitting, first or fifth, with a worried, or worse, a tearful, expression on their face. What would be the point? It is my job to support their process of developing their characters—in the parallel process of telling the story that the director wants.

Sometimes the result is a compromise between what the director asked for and what the actor imagined. But I always try to make sure that when the actor sees themselves in the mirror, they're smiling.

BEING NUMBER TWO

The design team on a Broadway show has an established hierarchy. This has developed historically over the last century, starting in the late nineteenth century. Originally the productions billed the designers—if they were indeed billed at all—as "production designed by" or "design by" or "settings by." The lighting was usually directed by the set designer; the costumes were supplied by various costume houses, and sound was rarely mentioned at all (before electricity through Ethel Merman, electronic sound design was not a possibility/necessity).

Therefore the marching order is now:

1. Sets
2. Costumes
3. Lighting
4. Sound

I explain it this way: the set designer creates the world; the costume designer peoples the world; the lighting designer tells you where to look, in addition to time and atmosphere; and the sound designer controls what your ears hear. In that order.

I do not mind being number two. The fact that I say it that way indicates a slight ruffling of feathers. But I respect the tradition; I respect the creation of the world as the first step.

I have an enormous respect for the set designer. As a student in stage design at the Yale School of Drama, I studied with the great designer Ming Cho Lee. If there is any man on earth who wears a halo, it is he.

He created an informal class in "collaboration studies." It was a special Saturday class in which directing students met to work on presentations with design students. It was not for credit, but anyone who was serious wanted to get involved. Of course this was not really a class about collaboration, but it was fostering a situation where a designer learned how to understand how to carry out a director's vision. The importance of this dialogue really hit home to me when I moved to New York and started trying to find work. Especially when I finally found work.

Ming also taught me always to think big. Thinking big works the same whether you are teaching a student or directing a creative team. If you want to ignite and encourage creative integrity, creative strength, creative knowhow, creative *anything*, you have to start with "the sky's the limit." You should not start a project being strictly pragmatic. You must encourage students to think. You have to expose them to the dream, to the poetry and to the art of the subject. You must start with "what if...?" If you don't teach at that level, your students (and future designers) will deliver designs consisting of unit flats lashed together.

Doorknobs and Pocketbooks

The set designers decide how much we are supposed to know about the world of the play, and what we're not supposed to know about it. And it goes far beyond whether we are inside or outside of four walls. The set designer decides the level of reality we are going to see on the stage. Will it be abstract or realistic?

For example: are there doorknobs? If there are doorknobs on the doors set within the walls of the stage design, that means that I have to give the ladies pocketbooks. One level of stage reality demands consistent stage reality in the costuming.

For example, in the 2003 revival of *Little Shop of Horrors*, there was a door that had to slam a lot, so it had to have a doorknob. That meant that Audrey had to have a pocketbook.

On the other hand, in *The Boy From Oz* and *Never Gonna Dance* (both from the 2003 season)—no doorknobs. Both of these two productions were impressionistic, so pocketbooks—and the detailed stage business surrounding that level of reality—were unnecessary. The singular exception was with the character of Liza Minnelli in *The Boy From Oz*. She made entrances and exits. The scarf, the stole, the pocketbook were necessary for the effect of those entrances and exits.

In 2004 I worked on a revival of the Ben Hecht/Charles MacArthur farce *Twentieth Century* for Broadway's Roundabout Theatre Company, directed by Walter Bobbie and starring Alec Baldwin and Anne Heche. The play takes place in the late 1920s in a luxury train. The setting was by John Lee Beatty, the master of the box set. He created luxury liner train compartments that had not only doorknobs, but locks on the doors as well. When I find myself in an environment that is fully and realistically conceived, I am totally at home—I relax, my shoulders drop about four inches. I know I better have, not only pocketbooks, but Kleenex and lipstick and compacts with mirrors in those pocketbooks for the ladies to take out. I knew exactly where I was. And so did the actor; and so did the audience.

And it doesn't stop there. We designers use the colors of the costumes to help tell the story. Lighting designers work hard to make sure everyone looks delicious in front of the set, so I need to make sure that, in addition to being real clothing, the clothes help certain people to "pop" when they are the focus of a scene. Colors need to be striking enough to pull the audience's attention to the most important character; but the color cannot be *too* striking. Bright colors have a duration quotient in your field of vision, or they might start burning your eyes out. Have you ever looked hard at a color and then turned away from that color and have seen its opposite color?

To avoid retina burn, you have to work with the lighting designer to help focus the audience in certain scenes containing bright costumes. It is choreography with color and intensity, choreography with clothing.

And usually it's pretty subtle. Sometimes I am free to mute and simplify the clothing of certain characters because I know they will be taken care of by the lighting designer, who will "discover" them. But sometimes I want to spice up a scene with color. It's like cooking. Here's some paprika! Whoosh! Here's some cayenne pepper! And I can bring a certain character across in a special way. But of course I don't do it arbitrarily. I think: How much is too much? How much is not enough?

MISSION IMPOSSIBLE

My most riveting and daunting assignment was the 1992 revival of *Guys and Dolls*, directed by Jerry Zaks, designed by Tony Walton, who created the most spectacular personal vision of Runyonland. Mr. Walton threw me a curve ball on that production: the color palette would be the A to Zed of Technicolor, with no single dominant color.

At first I was flummoxed and didn't know where to start. I began by placing strips of Pantone colored paper on top of an enlargement of Tony's sketch of the first scene. I then looked at the late work by Gauguin and found perfect complements to Tony's palette in the "Two Nudes on the Beach" and "In the Forest" by Gauguin. By staring carefully at the shadows in those paintings, I discovered in-between colors—browns and oranges and mauve—which would blend in and flesh out the range of dominant colors used by the painter. Walton and Gauguin—two artists besotted by vibrant color. But what to do next?

My biggest challenge then was how to let the audience find the leading man, Nathan Lane as Nathan Detroit, amid all the color madness. The answer was, of course, to put him—and only him—in black. And it worked. I did the opposite in the 2003 musical *Never Gonna Dance*, in which there was a number where everyone was in color. I put the leading lady all in white. Both times I had help from lighting designer Paul Gallo, who made it all pop.

Fifteen years later I'm still designing that *Guys and Dolls* in my mind, trying to find better ways to use all those colors to define characters.

FUNNY COSTUMES

Another lesson I learned on *Guys and Dolls* was from Jerry Zaks. He taught me how to work with characters. "Trust the material" is Jerry's mantra. Jerry also says, "Don't make funny costumes. Make real clothing, and the humor will come through with the material and the performance." So, ironically, while I am known for countless funny costumes, they were not meant to be funny costumes; they were meant to be clothing for that character to suit the time, the place and the story.

My work on *Guys and Dolls* was referred to as "cartoon," which cuts to the bone.

In defending my "no funny costumes" assignment, I want you to look at black and white production photographs from that show. By and large they look like a nearly proto-realist production. The silhouettes are absolutely spot-on for the period. Miss Adelaide is totally "late '48," as the lyric says. I was giving you the authentic clothing from the era, but I used Technicolor colors to give them a heightened reality to underscore Damon Runyon's and Frank Loesser's poetry. Perhaps that's what people interpreted as cartoon-like.

"Yes, Sir"

Sometimes your best designs are rejected by the director. Now, I could pull a hissy fit and say, "I'm the costume designer and I know what's right." Instead, the only word out of my mouth is "Yes," except when it is "Yes, sir" or "Yes, ma'am." The director wants to hear that one word only. And that's what they hear from me. You can't imagine how many confrontations this averts.

However, saying "Yes" doesn't solve the problem. Having said "Yes," I have to think, "What did I really mean?" "How am I going to do this 'Yes'?"

To solve this problem, I start by trying to get inside the director's head in order to understand what they really meant and to discover what kind of vision they are looking to fulfill.

This brings up another lesson from the production of *Twentieth Century*. I had to design a costume for the character of a young woman who is a Betty Grable-type floozy. It's what I call a classic "Red-Dress Character." But Walter didn't want her to be that and make a dumb-blonde misogynist sexist joke. We decided to try updating the sensibility a bit by making her quite professional and sophisticated—with no red dress. We tried that take for three and a half weeks in previews. However, we all soon saw that the script, even as reimagined and restyled by playwright Ken Ludwig, called for that image, and what we had done wasn't giving the needed spice to those quick farcical moments. We found we needed to add back a little bit of all those clichés. Walter finally said, "We were wrong. We really need to see the red dress." Unfortunately, by then I had rethought the palette and put Anne Heche in a red "Star" dress (actually, a dressing gown). So I had to think fast. I put the floozy character in a burgundy-brick-orangey-brown red dress. It still said, "I'm the Red-Dress character," and it enabled the actress to reach all the great farcical moments in the script, and it enabled Anne to keep the red Star Dress. Walter also waited until the Red Dress was ready to go on stage before he redirected the actress who was to wear it.

It was similar to the way we fleshed out the character of Ulla, the sexy receptionist in *The Producers*. Dumb-blonde jokes played straight just don't go over today. So Mel Brooks and Thomas Meehan built up all kinds of extra interest for Ulla in the script. She's still sexy, with a thick Swedish accent, but she's now also an aspiring actress who figures out Bialystock and Bloom's scheme, romances Bloom and marries the Producer.

Ordinarily you'd say she was the "Red Dress" character; and certainly that element remains in abundance. But, aha, I put her in a *white* dress. It automatically says, "There's more to me than you think."

All of this lighthearted talk of misogynist sexist jokes probably sounds politically incorrect—but you must keep it light. To this end, I keep an "order up" bell on each and every desk in my studio, and we ring it whenever someone says something politically incorrect. When we were working on *The Producers* and on *Hairspray*, we all became baby Mel Brookses and John Waterses—and the things were ringing all the time.

A side note: I've been privileged to design shows for the three great American satirical writers working in the theatre today: Mel Brooks, John Waters, and Paul Rudnick. And if you don't have a bell on your desk, you just can't work with them. Period.

STAIRWAY TO PARADISE

One of my biggest hits (and favorite shows) was the 1992 Tony-winning Best Musical *Crazy for You*, directed by Mike Ockrent, choreographed by Susan Stroman, book by Ken Ludwig, music by the Gershwins. I met Mike and Susan on the same fateful day in set designer Robin Wagner's studio.

One of the classic images of that show was to be a transition in which the chorus girls of the Zangler Follies make their entrance into the little desert town of Dead Rock, Nevada. The town is dusty and beige and grey; and these girls are gorgeous and full of line and color and, as they sashay downstage, the orchestra is playing "Stairway to Paradise" full out.

That image was the first piece of information about the show that Mike and Susan gave me that first day. Susan stood in front of me, locked arms with an imaginary girl on her right, and then with one on her left and said, "This is the most important moment in the show." The girls were going to be walking on a treadmill, and she wanted to see those fabulous feminine hips swaying as they walked. Mike said he wanted the audience to see them only in silhouette first, then, when the lights came up and they walked down stage, they had to look *spectacular*.

And that was fine by me. I'm a hip man, I love the shape. The straight-down reed-thin look just isn't interesting to me. Even a "va" isn't enough for me; I need the whole "va-va-va-voom."

I keep a photograph of that scene on the wall of my studio. When the girls were in silhouette, it looked like they were wearing authentic 1930s clothes. But when the lights came up, what did we see? Colors, Art Deco lines—all inspired by Art Deco jewelry, brooches, cigarette boxes, earrings, book bindings. And, mind you, all in fabrics that would allow them to dance, to kick up their legs to touch their noses. I was inspired by this assignment, and my costume shops were inspired. Those costumes were triumphs of construction, and all because Mike Ockrent and Susan Stroman had a very specific costume idea, and knew how to get their costume designer's blood racing.

WORKER BEES

In closing, let me say to any aspiring theatre artist: don't take yourself too seriously. Be extremely serious about your work; and take yourself seriously enough to wake up in the morning, put on your clothes, go to work and do your job to the best of your ability. If you can do each of those things slowly, carefully and effectively, then you can go out into the world and get started.

But don't get too full of yourself. Learn your craft and start practicing it. And, as you go through your day, look around, study what has been done in the past, see what is being done in the present and the dream, dream, dream what you want to deliver for the future.

And don't worry too much about being an artist. Rest assured, in a hundred years someone will decide, A, if they even remember you; and, B, if you were an artist. Right now, we're all just worker bees.

CHAPTER 21

JULES FISHER AND PEGGY EISENHAUER
LIGHTING DESIGNERS

The Tony-winning team of Jules Fisher and Peggy Eisenhauer began their collaboration in 1985 working together on Bob Fosse's *Big Deal*. Since then, they have created inventive designs for many Broadway productions, receiving Tony nominations for Best Lighting Design for *Jane Eyre*, *Marie Christine*, *The Wild Party*, *Ragtime*, and the hit revival of *Cabaret*. They received a 2004 Tony Award for the lighting design of *Assassins*, and the 1996 Tony and Drama Desk Awards for *Bring in 'Da Noise, Bring in 'Da Funk*. They have been honored with a combined twenty-seven Tony nominations, and designed the theatrical lighting sequences for the Oscar-winning film of *Chicago*. Having spent more than forty years in the business, Jules Fisher has designed lighting for more than one hundred and fifty Broadway productions, including landmark original productions *Hair*, *Jesus Christ Superstar*, *Pippin*,

Beatlemania, *La Cage aux Folles*, and *Chicago*. He earned additional Tony Awards for *Dancin'*, *Ulysses in Nighttown*, *Grand Hotel*, *The Will Rogers Follies*, and *Jelly's Last Jam*, the latter three in collaboration with Peggy Eisenhauer. Eisenhauer designed Betty Buckley's performance at Carnegie Hall and *Sweet Charity* at Avery Fisher Hall. In the music industry she has created concert production designs for Whitney Houston; Crosby, Stills, and Nash; Fishbone; Neil Young; and Tracy Chapman. Her designs have been seen internationally in twenty-six countries on six continents. Fisher and Eisenhauer formed their own company, Third Eye, in 1996. Other joint designs for Broadway include *Elaine Stritch: At Liberty*; *Chita Rivera: The Dancer's Life*; *Caroline, Or Change*; *Victor/Victoria*; and *A Christmas Carol* at Madison Square Garden.

Looking Out the Window

JULES FISHER: Designing Broadway shows is very difficult. There is tremendous pressure. It's not an easy life. It's not an easy career. It's something you're driven to do. There are a few things that make it easier, and one is your collaborations with fellow artists you admire. It's rare to have a partnership like mine with Peggy. I'm not advocating artistic partnerships in general, but this one works for me.

Peggy began as my assistant, which was very helpful, in that I had another person to do some of the chores. But I found that creatively it was also a gain. She understands musical timing, which is enormously useful because lighting is often very involved with music. It has the same rhythmic face, and it can have the same tonal effects. Peggy has a musical memory. She can hear a piece of music once and know it totally,

which is quite rare. She had a musical background and studied as a pianist. All of a sudden I saw that her influence on my work was better than the sum of the parts. Working together, we were able to come up with conceptual ideas and carry them out. We have continued to work in a manner that allows us to conceive of things together. We might go off separately and read the script but then come back together to create.

She'll say, "I think we'll do the play in red light." I might come back and say, "I thought all in blue," and then maybe together we figure out it should be magenta. We put the ideas together. I personally love our dialogues together. It makes the studio a lot less lonely when we are working. We have the same goals. By accident or by her innate view of lighting, we come up with similar concepts. That always impressed me. I can't quite figure it out, but we do it and we're happy.

PEGGY EISENHAUER: I grew up in the New York area and became enamored of theatre when I was child, thanks to the benefactors who took me to see Broadway plays and musicals. When I got a little older I simultaneously began helping out at my community theatre while, in New York, I was getting to see the lighting design work of some of the great talents of the time: Tharon Musser, Jennifer Tipton, Jean Rosenthal, Thomas R. Skelton, and, of course, Jules Fisher.

Jennifer Tipton is one of the pioneers of Broadway lighting design. She fought for recognition of our craft and I am the happy recipient of her pioneership, because things are certainly different now. We are brought on with the idea that we can really create a dynamic atmosphere rather than just to illuminate the faces on the stage. I tip my hat to her.

I decided early on that lighting was exciting. I admired Jules' work with Bob Fosse on Broadway and decided to pursue study at Carnegie Mellon University partly because that was where Jules had trained.

Jules, who was then a successful producer and master lighting designer, came back to the school in my sophomore year to give a series of talks, and I made a point of introducing myself. I think I was 18. Afterward I called my mother and howled into the phone that I had met Jules Fisher which I said was worth the whole price of tuition (which, by the way, was pretty expensive).

She then took it upon herself to write a little note, cold, to Jules at his New York office repeating what I said about it being worth the price of tuition and thanking him for being kind. He wrote back and offered to help me after graduation.

I cut my teeth on Broadway working with lighting designer Richard Nelson, and then Jules called. The first show we did together was Andrew Lloyd Webber's *Song and Dance* with Bernadette Peters, on which I was Jules' assistant. Immediately after that we worked on *Big Deal* with Bob Fosse. And at that point we decided it was working out well and I hung around—a long time.

In the early 1990s we finally got to a point where we decided we would become partners. Among our first shows were *A Christmas Carol* and *Victor/Victoria*.

FISHER: The first thing a lighting designer does, before we ever touch a spotlight, is to read the script—hopefully many times. To do our job we have to immerse ourselves in what the playwright is trying to say. What's the play about? What is he trying to communicate? What does he want you to feel when you leave the theatre? What should you get from the play?

Next, we meet with the director and find out his take on the play. How is he going to take what the playwright has done and interpret it? There are a hundred ways to do anything. There are a thousand ways to do *Hamlet*. Each director has his own take on it.

Once we know that, then we can start to ask ourselves, how will the light help tell that story? What is it that light itself can do to communicate all the things we've learned from the playwright and the director.

Lastly with our ideas in hand of how we are going to illuminate the story—no pun intended—we then meet with the other designers. From then on we work very closely with the people doing the sets, costumes and sound, because all our work needs to dovetail.

EISENHAUER: In the best creative collaborations the designers are all brought on at the same time, preferably early in the process. We want the time to learn and conceive, and we also want to start at the same time on the blank page with everybody else.

Even if our process times out differently than the scenic designer's, starting at the same time nourishes our end product because we've gone through all the steps with everybody, even though we won't be turning on a light on for maybe three months. Working with everybody on the same vision feeds towards the moment when we do turn that first light on.

Sometimes lighting designers are hired late in the process, which is an older tradition. It's really changed now and it's wonderful that we are part of the initial kernel of creation. It improves the final outcome tremendously.

Mechanics of Collaboration

FISHER: Here's a simple example of how we work. Take the vertical strip lights we used on the 2004 revival of *Assassins*. The show's concept is that it's set at an imaginary shooting gallery in a midway or carnival. Robert Brill's set was a wooden structure that looks like it might hold up a roller coaster from the old era of the Cyclone in Coney Island. It consisted of wooden structural beams painted white that faded into black at the bottom. It curved around the back of the stage and there was a big staircase.

I went off one weekend alone with the script—Peggy went away separately—and when we got together afterward I proposed that we light the whole structure, maybe forty feet high, with white light strips. A light strip is a long compartment shaped like rod with one light bulb after another in a straight line. It's one of the earliest devices used for the theatre in electric lighting. I proposed that we put these vertically outside the set to provide a huge area of light, but it wasn't a spotlight, which is the normal way you would do it. This would provide a wall of light and use an old-fashioned technology that would not look out of place at a carnival.

Peggy then took the idea and suggested that we break it up in color so the bottom is one color and it changes to another color by the time it gets to the top, to add both color and nuance. I never thought of that. Then she broke up the colors on the upstage and downstage beams as well. It added a whole new dimension.

EISENHAUER: An important dimension of partnership is that there is no pride of ownership. That is one of the cornerstones of the best collaborations. It's not your idea or my idea. It has to be *our* idea. When there's pride of ownership, it separates collaborators and there's a sort of psychic scorecard. In the best collaborations, when an idea is accepted by the group, it's accepted. It's no longer his or hers or mine. It's *our* idea.

On the other hand, if an idea is brought to the group that turns out to be no good, there's no shame and no fear of embarrassment. That's the mentality of a good collaboration. In our case, when we put an idea out there that gets accepted, it's immediately assimilated as both of ours. If Jules puts out this wonderful and simple idea of these flat planes of light, and I say, "Great idea," I can build on it without saying it wasn't really my idea but now I have to do something with it. It's instantly both of ours and that's transparent for us. That's the thing that generates a lot of design energy between us. An idea comes out and we can just build on it and we don't have to separate, idea for idea.

FISHER: We work out of a large office in the West 20s of Manhattan, but we do a lot of the actual creative work in a little twelve-by-twelve studio filled with a lot of lighting equipment. But ideas come in the most mundane of places: on the way to the restaurant or on the subway to the rehearsal. Sometimes it happens while we're talking on the phone. A lot of ideas also come to me in the middle of the night. I wake up and jot them down. I can't exactly say they come to me in my dreams, but something causes me to wake me up. I'm thinking about some area and

I can't go back to sleep until I resolve it in my brain. Once I've written it down, then I go back to sleep.

History

FISHER: Nowadays designers work together like a family—hopefully a nurturing family. In the ideal situation we like to think as one.

But there was a time when all these jobs were literally done by one person. A hundred years ago you didn't have separate lighting, costume, and scenery designers. One person did it all, and often it was the director, who also often served as playwright, manager, and sometimes also the star.

Individual designers began to appear just around the turn of the 20th century, when, often, great artists became involved. Diaghilev employed Léon Bakst as a scenic and costume designer for the Ballets Russes. But lighting was still thought of principally as illumination. In the 1910s, a couple of people, Adolphe Appia and Edward Gordon Craig, started to define the idea that light could have an equally important effect on the final picture on stage.

These developments were made possible by the advent of electric light. Before then they were just burning sticks of lime to make limelight or used candles and gaslight. The idea was just to get enough light so people could see what was happening on the stage.

At first even the electrical effects were very crude. But as electricity began to provide more sophisticated lighting control, many of the designers who were good at drawing pictures and designing scenery and costumes didn't grasp the technological issues and turned it over to other people. Lighting designers started out mainly being electricians and then evolved into artists who took the technology of electric light and used it as another way to tell the story.

A lot of lighting is carving away the darkness to put light somewhere because I want you to see one thing, and having no light somewhere else because I don't want you to see that. What you don't see can be as important to storytelling as what you do see.

In those early days, the production designer did it all. Jo Mielziner is one example. He was a scenic designer and also lit every show he ever did. He employed no separate lighting designer on his shows.

There are a lot of reasons why that changed. For one, scenery has gotten more complicated technically. Early scenery was painted flats or painted drops. The idea still hangs on that set designers are on a higher level, or that they dictate to the rest of the design team. But what's happening in recent years, directors are starting to realize that lighting could easily be the leading force in a production. You can do a production without any scenery but you can't do a production without light. And designers are taking more advantage of that.

Set designer Robin Wagner has been leading the way on that. He shows amazing restraint in not providing excessive scenery. He creates opportunities for light to set the scene as much as traditional scenery. He sees the whole picture, which enables him to serve the director very well. This is why Robin is a brilliant designer as well as a great collaborator.

EISENHAUER: Another good example of that would be Riccardo Hernandez's set for *Bring in 'Da Noise, Bring in 'Da Funk*, a non-conventional musical that George C. Wolfe developed with Savion Glover at the Public Theater, which is based on a very deep, very black box of a space. Single, carefully chosen fragmented pieces of real things were used to suggest time and place and period. The scene where the Chicago Defender letter is being read from a newspaper used just a single lightbulb, a suitcase on the floor, a hat rack and a chair. The playing space was carved with light from the deep black space around it.

That theme carried through the entire evening. The prime force of the show was the rhythm of tap dancing. So the lighting was presented rhythmically, as well: in flashes, in beats of light. We wanted the lighting to have an abstract, musical quality.

FISHER: Everyone knows what a drum is but no one thinks of light as being able to deliver the same kind of rhythmic pacing. We used light itself like a percussive instrument.

EISENHAUER: One of the great joys of a fully functioning collaboration with a director is that not everything has to be articulated. There is a flow of ideas that just happens by doing. We have that kind of collaboration with George C. Wolfe. *Noise/Funk* was one of our most memorable experiences with him. We decided to take a very modern, almost pop-world approach to the materials. We may have discussed that, or maybe we just innately felt it together. Working from a videotape of the rehearsals—a great luxury—we brought some lights down to the Public and started turning them on and off in rhythm, almost like musical instruments. He'd rehearse with the actors all day, then in the evening we would show him, without actors, light stabbing through the space. We simultaneously played the videotape and ran the lighting effects on the stage and hoped he could put it together in his mind. We didn't know what he was going to say the first time around. But we showed him maybe a minute and a half of the beginning of the opening number, and we saw him respond. He got excited and told us to just continue going down this path.

Once we started running it with the actors, George reshaped, reformed and modeled every bit of it. But the essence of it, the concept of it, remained. As an example, George would watch a segment, then tell us to go back and make one corner darker, and we'd adjust that.

FISHER: We'd mark out a rhythm of red light, blue light, red light, blue light, white light. George would say, "Instead of the white light, what if it was green?" And we'd change it.

We're always trying to get into the director's head, trying to understand what is it that the director is trying to communicate. It's not always easy for the director to say, particularly when it comes to light. It's always good to try what the director is saying, even if you don't initially agree, because it may show you something you never thought about. We might go back and say, "I don't think this really works." If he firmly feels one way, he'll tell us.

BOB FOSSE

FISHER: Bob Fosse very much appreciated what a lighting designer contributes. He knew that light could be used cinematically to focus on a single body or even a single gesture. He was so disciplined in his work that even when a dancer lifted a little finger, it meant something to him and he wanted to draw the audience's attention to it. His dancing was not large sweeping gestures. It was much more detailed and specific. It was about style, and he realized early in his career that lighting could help the audience understand that.

He was a tough taskmaster. He was demanding and sometimes impatient. He wanted results right away. He didn't like the idea that humans operated the lighting instruments and could make mistakes. In the period we worked with him he was doing more and more films. In the film medium he saw that he could have ultimate control. You could shoot it again and again until you got exactly what you wanted, and then it stayed that way forever.

In the theatre that doesn't exist. There are still humans doing it. There are musicians playing the music freshly every single night. So they hit the wrong note or they make the volume too loud or the electrician hits the lighting cue too early or a lightbulb burns out in the course of the play. Those things bothered him. He understood intellectually, but it still made him angry. He was difficult to deal with in that sense.

Everyone remembers his dance style, of course. But I believe he was a greater contributor as a director than as a choreographer. He had an unparalleled ability to tell a story dramatically and theatrically. Everything he did was theatrical.

EISENHAUER: It was almost as if he was trying to make the lighting design in the theatre provide as much control to the eye as the camera does. Jules worked with him a half dozen times, but I worked with him only once, on *Big Deal*, the last show he directed. He was trying to create close-ups in the theatre the way he could on film. Actually *Big Deal* was the first, or one of the first, times automated lighting was used on Broadway in that quantity. We were trying to step ahead with the idea of a beam of light that could move in a way that would make the audience feel that their perspective was moving.

FISHER: Fosse was taking the idea that he could move the camera around anything to force you look at something a certain way. He wanted to do that with light in the theatre. It was a challenge, but our collaboration with him was to go along with his experiments and see if we could introduce a new vocabulary of lighting.

EISENHAUER: We had much cruder means in 1986 than we do now, but we were still trying for the same idea of a moving panorama of some kind. Sometimes we did it with shadows. A dancer would move a short distance, but his shadow would travel a long distance based on a strategic angle. Sometimes we'd light something from behind so the audience would feel that they were looking at it from the back. Simple techniques were called into use for the strongest advantage.

FISHER: He would make requests that prior to that day we had never figured out how to solve. We would use present, available equipment or we would invent something. We are not scientists and we haven't studied engineering but we are both technologically versed and we both like to toy with lighting equipment.

In the opening scene of *Pippin*, Fosse wanted the white gloved hands to appear out of the darkness. The hands had to be clearly visible, but the bodies had to be invisible. I needed a beam that could be intensely bright, but tightly focused. I tried a number of things and finally discovered what I was looking for in an unlikely place: farm tractor headlamps. They were set in a narrow trough in the floor and they shot straight up so there was this permanent sheet of light. Think of the light coming out of a little crack in the floor going straight up but going no where else—not upstage or downstage. It was a curtain of light. All the actors did was put their hands in the light. The light didn't change. If they took their hands away, it went black.

You don't see light unless it hits something. Light itself is not visible. It has to either hit dust, dirt, atmosphere, smoke, raindrops, the human body or some other object. Otherwise light is invisible.

AUDIENCE

FISHER: The audience serves as our alter ego in a way. We represent the audience until they come into the theatre. When the audience does come in, particularly in the preview period, we see what they gasp at. If they gasp at one thing, maybe we will make it a little brighter. Or if they don't see it at all, maybe we *have* to make it brighter or something's wrong with our concept. They are very much essential to putting the play on. Previews allow us time to hone the light cues. Witnessing the audience reaction helps us finish the collaboration.

EISENHAUER: Being an artist is a way of life. It effects every waking moment. As visual artists we are alert visually to everything. It's a blessing to lead an artistic life, as hard as it may be, because it influences one's emotional view of everything.

FISHER: A friend of ours, Robert Rabinowitz, says that when an artist is looking out the window, he's working. That sums it up.

CHAPTER 22

TONY MEOLA
SOUND DESIGNER

Tony Meola's Broadway shows include *Wicked*; *Man of La Mancha*; *Sweet Smell of Success*; *The Wild Party*; *Copenhagen*; *Kiss Me, Kate*; *Footloose*; *High Society*; *The Lion King* (Drama Desk Award); *The Sound of Music*; *The Last Night of Ballyhoo*; *Juan Darien*; *A Christmas Carol* (Madison Square Garden); *Steel Pier*; *A Funny Thing Happened on the Way to the Forum*; *The King and I*; *Company*; *Chronicle of a Death Foretold*; *Moon Over Buffalo*; *Smokey Joe's Cafe*; *Face Value*; *Guys and Dolls*; *A Month in the Country*; *Picnic*; *Five Guys Named Moe*; *She Loves Me*; *The Best Little Whorehouse Goes Public*; *The Red Shoes*; *Anything Goes*; *A Grand Night for Singing*. London's West End: *Kiss Me, Kate*, *The Lion King*, *Smokey Joe's Café*, *Anything Goes*. International work includes *Driving Miss Daisy*, *Les Misérables*, *Mozart!*, Disney's *Hunchback of Notre Dame*. Off-Broadway includes *Love, Janis*; *A New Brain*; *Violet*; *Durang, Durang*; *One Man Band*. Meola is a graduate of Ithaca College's Department of Theatre Arts.

Finding Pianissimo

Most people are completely unaware of what a sound designer does, unless he does it wrong. Then, everybody knows. The music is tinny, the singing is flat, the orchestra is loud, and the audience can't hear the words. But if he does it right, you don't notice. It sounds great. It sounds *right*.

BECOMING A SOUND DESIGNER

When I was in high school in Middletown, New York, I played the clarinet and really wanted to do it professionally, despite my family's misgivings.

I was also into theatre. Thanks to my high school auditorium, which doubled as the local stop for bus-and-truck tours, I spent my teenage years working stage crew for tours of *Pippin*; *Godspell*; *Kiss Me, Kate*; *1776*; the Dance Theatre of Harlem; and other shows. My official title was stage manager, but I was most interested in lighting. When it came time to choose a college, my hours spent on my clarinet and in theatre—as opposed to the classroom—left me with limited choices, and I entered Orange County Community College in my hometown as a music major. My college grades were good enough for me to transfer to Ithaca College, again as a music major. But Ithaca College's prestigious theatre department was a major reason why I wanted to go there. In fact, I hadn't been there a week when I changed majors, eventually graduating with a degree in technical production in theatre, and an Associate Degree in Music.

Between my sophomore and junior years, I got a summer job as an electrician at the New York Shakespeare Festival in New York City. They were rehearsing a little show called *A Chorus Line*, and the production manager warned me that if *A Chorus Line* was not a hit, they might have to lay me off in August.

I didn't care. It was an exciting time to be down there, let me tell you. *A Chorus Line* completely changed my life. It told me, number one, that it was OK to work in theatre. And, number two, it was OK to be gay. That was a lot to learn the summer I turned 21.

In case you didn't hear, *A Chorus Line* was a huge hit, so I kept my job. And when the Shakespeare Festival needed someone to do sound on its mobile theatre, which used to take live theatre into all the poor communities of New York (sadly, it no longer exists), I was volunteered. That was my first time doing sound—and under the worst possible acoustical conditions—but it was a wonderful, wonderful thing. I liked it, and it stuck.

My first musical was a show called *On the Lock In*, a kind of *Chorus Line* show about prison inmates. The composer liked the fact that I had a musical background and could talk bars and tempos instead of just amplifiers and speakers. I started to get work.

Acoustics

In the traditional hierarchy of designers, sound designers were the most recently accepted into the business, and therefore the fourth in status after sets, costumes, and lighting. A lot of my work is a struggle to get the other collaborators to understand what I do and to make allowances for the equipment I need to do it.

A sound designer starts by speaking to the director and the rest of the creative team to find out what the show is about and what the concept of the sound might be. Will it be a natural sound? Will there be a lot of music? Will there be special sound effects?

The next job, however, is going into the theatre where the show will play. Every theatre has unique acoustics. Some are easier than others. Some have wonderful architectural detail that translates into wonderful aural detail like the New

Amsterdam, for instance—and, unlike the Gershwin. When you go into an older theatre and see all that ornate carving and relief on the walls and boxes, you may think they're just there for decoration. They're really there to spread high frequencies around so the sibilance of voices gets to every corner of the theatre, for clarity.

Once you know the strengths and weaknesses of the theatre, and you know the sound concept of the show you're working on, you can start to make equipment lists and you make drawings and you speak to the other designers and find what everybody's needs are.

In a typical show, *my* idea is to have the voices sound as natural as they can. But, honestly, audiences today don't really *know* or want to hear a truly natural sound. They're so used to hearing amplified sound, especially from popular music and movies, that they'd be very disappointed to hear what a pit orchestra sounds like completely unamplified. What they really want is something a little bit raised above what an original Rodgers and Hammerstein show would have been performed at—for a traditional musical, that is. Musicals with more contemporary music need to have a more contemporary sound, but not so loud that one notices the volume.

THE AUDIENCE IS NEVER AFRAID

The audience is always foremost in my planning. I spend technical rehearsals and previews sitting all around the theatre to make sure that I've covered it. The first place I go is the critics' seats and adjust the balance, if necessary. Then I move from corner to corner until I get the best balance of sound I can from every seat.

Contrary to what you probably think, the balcony is the easiest place to adjust the sound. The hardest places are the most expensive seats. They're right down front, and you can't put a speaker between the performer and the audience. I try to put speakers all around the proscenium and balance them so it sounds like its coming from the stage. But you get up the balcony and there's plenty of places to put them: on the ceiling, on the balcony rail, on the sides. It's much easier.

In many theatres the sound engineers are sitting at a big console in the back of the theatre. We are very visible. The audience is never afraid to tell us exactly what they think, especially if they can't hear the words. And I listen to them. Sometimes they think we control the lighting and say the lighting was great. Sometimes we smile and say thanks.

Microphones

Abe Jacobs and Otts Munderloh are two of the great pioneers of Broadway sound design. I learned most of what I know from Otts. I watched him for years to get actors to speak up and not rely so much on microphones.

Microphones can be wonderful things but they can also be horrible things. I abhor going to a Broadway show with an orchestra and hearing the downbeat come from the speaker on the proscenium. I work very hard not to do that because live theatre has to compete with movies and TV and even the Internet. The one thing we have over all those competing media is the fact that we're live. We have real people in the orchestra pit and we have real people on the stage. There is a visceral reaction to hearing a real voice and a real instrument. It goes to somewhere deep within us. And that's the only thing the theatre has left where no one can touch us.

Special effects have improved. There are great special effects in *Wicked*. But we still can't do what they can do in the movies. We can't sketch out on a computer a body double that falls into a burning pit, or show car crashes or all those fantastic things they can do on the screen. So we have to keep real in the theatre. The more stuff we put between an actor's voice and the audience's ear, the more we take away from the last thing we have going for us.

I love to find creative ways to hide microphones. I don't think the audience should see microphones unless they are part of the story, or the ambience of the show. They usually aren't.

There was one time I used visible mikes intentionally: *Smokey Joe's Café.* I put the cast in headset mikes because director Jerry Zaks wanted a close mike sound without their having to hold microphones.

I have a microphone that's so small that if you put it under a regular hairnet you can't see it under stage lighting. It's great. But on *Wicked*, costume designer Susan Hilferty wanted to use film-grade hairnets, which are much finer than theatrical-grade and you can see mikes underneath. That's one place where we collided a little bit. For people like Kristin Chenoweth you could see the microphone. Idina Menzel was a challenge because she has the pointed black witch hat.

But on *Kiss Me, Kate* we were able most of the time to hide microphones. The material is great—Cole Porter—so I wanted the audience to get every word. Luckily, I was part of a great team on that show, and we were at my favorite Broadway theatre, the Martin Beck, now the Al Hirschfeld. It's got the best orchestra pit I've ever used. The Don Sebesky orchestrations were marvelous, and he won a well-deserved Tony Award for them. The musical director was Paul Gemignani who understands better than anyone in the business the importance of pianissimo and fortissimo and the importance of hearing lyrics. He's brilliant, and a pleasure to work with because he understands the nuances of sound like few others.

PROJECTING

Sound design can help actors only to a degree. You have to have performers who face downstage and project. You have to have performers who haven't just danced for thirty-two bars and are out of breath. You have to have a musical director who is keeping the orchestra volume below a certain level so that you don't have to make the vocals so loud. You have to explain this to everyone to achieve a good sound balance and not everyone understands it.

Television actors often create the biggest problems. They're used to speaking into microphones and don't know how to project. I did a revival of *Picnic* in 1994 at the Roundabout Theatre Company. We had Debra Monk, Ann Pitoniak, and Larry Bryggman from the old school. You could hear those three in every corner of that 499-seat theatre. But then you had Ashley Judd and Tate Donovan and the other young people in the show who were not properly trained to speak on stage. Every time Scott Ellis, the director, would ask them to be louder, they'd say, "But I feel like I'm shouting!" They never learned the technique.

All the same, it's my job to help the audience hear all the actors. If you have one person on stage who's projecting and another person who's not projecting, the one not projecting will be louder in the speakers and therefore more disembodied. I depend on the trained actor for "source"—original sound—so you hear them first, and then you fill in the quieter parts with speakers. But you have to do it carefully, otherwise it sounds like some lines are coming from the actors and some lines are coming from the wall or wherever the speakers are. Part of the sound designer's collaboration is encouraging everyone on stage to speak up.

COMPRESSION

I try very hard not to use a process called compression. You might not recognize the term, but if you've listened to recorded rock music or popular music, you've heard it. Compression takes the highest of the highs and compresses them down so there's not much difference between the very quiet parts and the very loud parts. They do that so you hear everything all the time at a specific volume setting. If you are dancing you don't want to hear quiet stuff, you want to hear "boom, boom, boom" coming at you the same way all the time. Radio stations compress so you don't have to keep adjusting your volume. But that's not the way you were meant to hear sound. You're meant to hear loud sounds fortissimo and soft sounds pianissimo.

I am a classically trained musician. I love to go to the symphony. I am reminded what pianissimo is at the symphony. I almost never hear pianissimo in the theatre anymore. People complain that they can't hear. But they're hearing fine. What they're hearing is *quiet sounds*. On most modern musicals we never get below a mezzo forte. But when your quietest is a mezzo forte, fortissimo isn't loud enough and you get charged with making it louder to make it more exciting. If we could just get back to pianissimo then fortissimo would be loud enough.

On *Wicked* I was fortunate to have as collaborators composer Stephen Schwartz, director Joe Mantello, orchestrator William David Brohn, musical director Stephen Oremus, and others who understand and agree with all of that. So *Wicked* has pianissimos but they're getting rarer on Broadway. I know other shows where they just don't care about it. The director wants it to sound like a very loud, compressed CD, and that's just what they do.

Stereo

A scary thing I heard from one director a few years ago was, "I was sitting in the second row during rehearsal last night and I couldn't hear anything coming out of the loudspeaker."

I said, "Could you hear the actors?"

He said, "I could hear them fine, but nothing was coming out of the loudspeaker near me." That was a little frightening. In the live theatre speakers should be used to help boost sound where necessary, or to create a special effect, but they shouldn't be the source of all sound, like a stereo.

Musicians will sometimes ask me if I'm going to do the orchestra in stereo. People forget that stereo isn't something that we do in real life. Stereo is something that we do in our homes to try to *duplicate* real life. In the theatre, stereo works for about four seats in the dead center of the orchestra. For everybody else, they're going to hear just the instruments in the one speaker closest to them. It will actually sound unbalanced.

If I do stereo at all, it's to enhance reality. Because if most of the strings are on one side of the orchestra pit, people on that side would naturally hear the strings a little more anyway. That's real. I don't like it to be superfluous. I don't like it to be cool and fun and groovy—unless it has a purpose and helps, rather than distracts from, the story.

Among the greatest collaborators I've ever worked with are director Michael

Blakemore, whom I worked with on *Kiss Me, Kate*, and the lighting design team of Jules Fisher and Peggy Eisenhauer, with whom I collaborated on *Love, Janis*.

Everyone should learn from Blakemore how to get people to do what you want. He is brilliant at it and you don't ever feel that you are taken advantage of.

As for Peggy, she was the first one who taught me you can turn off the color scrollers on stage lights. They have to be on during technical rehearsals and, of course, when they are rolling. But they don't have to be on throughout every scene. We did *Love, Janis* in a tiny Off-Broadway space where I had to fight for real estate on the stage for loudspeakers amid the lighting instruments and scenery. By working together we were able to fit everything in and be quite successful, all things considered.

Wicked was in many ways an ideal situation. All members of the design team consulted one another and put together the show in a way that served everyone— which meant it served the audience. In addition to Ken Posner and Susan Hilferty, there was set designer Eugene Lee and his associate Eddie Pierce. If I told them I needed to put a speaker somewhere, they'd say, "I could cut a hole there and put something on it so you wouldn't see it." Or they'd say, "We actually wouldn't mind seeing a loudspeaker there because it fits in with the nature of the scene." The whole collaboration was like that. Most of the time the designer is asked last, but on *Wicked*, it was all part of the same job.

Joe Mantello was also instrumental in keeping the team together. Joe knows what he wants and expresses it. It isn't necessary (or helpful) at times for a director to know technically what I am doing. I can interpret the director's ideas and Joe's are very clear.

Noise and Light

Another great collaborative lighting designer is Ken Posner, with whom I did *Wicked*. There's a great example of a collaborator thinking outside his own particular area. Varilite, a company that makes lights with little motors so you can turn and point and pivot them remotely, came and demonstrated its latest model for Ken. At the end of their presentation he said, "This lamp does everything single thing I want it to do. Congratulations on your design. But I cannot use it for *Wicked*."

They were flabbergasted and asked why. He said because its cooling fan was too loud. This is something I've been fighting since moving lights moved into the theatre. People don't realize that theatres are generally quiet. Sometimes the ventilation systems are a little noisy. But when you put one hundred moving lights and color scrollers on nearly every other light in the theatre, it creates a significant amount of ambient noise. That's one of the reasons you can't get a pianissimo.

On the Patrick Stewart revival of *The Tempest* which debuted in Central Park and then moved to Broadway, Stewart walked on stage for the first technical rehearsal and said, "What's all that noise?" When they told him it was the lighting, he said, "I'll leave until you get rid of that noise." If it wasn't my show, I would be thrilled to hear an actor say that.

On *Wicked*, accoustician Sam Berkow took the cover off one of the Varilites, wrapped a scarf around it, put it back on, and that simple step reduced the noise coming out of that light by at least thirty percent. He also discovered that the fan was cooling the whole fixture when it only needed to cool the one part that got warm. It's a small thing, but anything we can do to decrease noise pollution inside theatres, I'm all for.

Piano in a Box

On the other hand, it's been my unfortunate experience to be part of collaborative teams that had no unified idea of what kind of sound they wanted for the show, and no idea of what sound design requires. This can create chaos.

For example, I was asked to do a show called *Here Lies Jenny: The Songs of Kurt Weill*, with Bebe Neuwirth. At the first meeting I was told that Bebe didn't want to be miked, and I was told by the musical director/pianist that she wanted a monitor of herself and Bebe. How can you give her a monitor if Bebe doesn't have a microphone? And shouldn't you involve the sound designer in the formulation of these decisions in the first place?

And then there was the piano itself. None of the old pianos that they tried sounded good, so they decided to get a piano they really liked and build a box around it to make it look like an old piano. I told them that a piano in a box *sounds* like a piano in a box and when you don't have a full orchestra, you just have the piano, it's not a good idea to have bad-sounding piano. You might as well use one of those old pianos because a good piano sitting in a box is not going to sound very good.

The problem initially was that decisions were made about the sound design before the sound designer was hired. Fortunately, we were able to communicate and collaborate and in the end, I am very proud of the sound design of *Here Lies Jenny* and the experience was wonderful.

I've had the great good fortune to work with wonderful directors who can sit at a table and talk out their issues rather than bark orders from above. I'm a good enough communicator that I can sit down with almost any director and resolve any differences that may arise.

I only once remember getting frustrated with a director's wishes. It was Stanley Donen on Jule Styne's last musical, *The Red Shoes*. Nearing opening night at a full dress rehearsal, he kept telling me to make it louder and louder. I tried to explain that the show had gotten too loud, to the point where people were starting to get concerned about their hearing. As soon as that happens you've stopped telling the story. The sound has gotten in the way of the story.

But he kept saying, "Make it louder!"

Finally I said, "Stanley I will make it louder, but I won't make it louder with my name on it!"

In any collaboration you sometimes have to do things you don't believe in. But only up to a point. Nevertheless, I later apologized and we came to agree on levels. Sometimes that's part of a collaboration, too.

ORCHESTRA PITS

The Hirschfeld Theatre's orchestra pit is great because it's all wood, shaped like a band shell, and has a beautiful wooden balustrade in front of it. The musicians love it, too, because there's plenty of room and it's open, not pushed under the stage like in most houses. During the run of the 2002 *Man of La Mancha* revival there I used to love and go sit in the pit and listen to how great the orchestra sounded there, especially under Bob Billig's musical direction.

Economics have pushed orchestra pits further and further under the stage. If you go to the opera house, you see a great big open pit. You can see all the musicians. On Broadway they want to sell as many top-price tickets as possible, so they cover over the front of the pit, and add rows AA and BB and such. The orchestra has no place to go but under the stage. In some theatres, there's barely enough room for the conductor squeeze between the front row and the stage. As soon as you move something under the stage, of course, you have to mike the orchestra *more*, which kills the natural sound. You are virtually putting it in another room. You no longer have the visceral sound you get from an open orchestra pit.

Sometimes it's a good thing to have a drummer underneath because that can be too loud. A good orchestrator can help by balancing the orchestra acoustically. For instance, on *Sweet Smell of Success*, which I did with Bill Brohn orchestrating, the orchestra was in balance in the rehearsal studio. Another recent show that I did had five percussionists and four string players. Guess who won that volume battle? To begin the process with an out of balance orchestra makes it very difficult to maintain a truly live sound. You must isolate too many instruments, creating a more electronic sound and this takes away from the visceral reaction that I wrote of earlier. The orchestra is not unlike the chorus. In a live situation: it is always better to have them in balance before you add microphones so that you are merely lifting the natural sound, not creating a sound like one does in a recording studio. A studio sound can be wonderful, but it's certainly not organic.

SPECIAL EFFECTS

There *are* a lot of cool things you can do with sound. I love sound effects and special effects. You can pitch somebody up or down a half step. You can put reverb on it, you can put echo on it, you can make it tinny, you can make it bassy, you can throw it around the room. You can do whatever you want with it. But doing it just because its cool isn't necessarily a reason to do it. Everything has to have reason, and has to enhance or forward the story.

I have a lot of special effects in *Wicked*. The Wizard in the play has his voice overamplified and dropped in pitch to make him sound scarier. There's a part where the Wicked Witch hears her sister's voice in the wind. It comes from the speakers in the rear of the house, so it sounds very distant.

There are atmospheric effects: rain and wind. I love wind. And there are birds. Birds usually tell you it's morning. A barking dog indicates night and loneliness. There's a lot of little things I can add to set the scene and help it along

I also like reverb. I used it on "He Lives in You" in *The Lion King* to create an ethereal sound. If you put reverb on someone's voice it's a way of telling the audience that the character is inside their own head. The character is thinking or resolving a conflict within themselves.

I did sound for *A Christmas Carol*, which ran at the Theatre at Madison Square Garden for ten holiday seasons. That was the hardest show I have ever done. The first year we had fifty-five microphones and we were putting sound out to more than six thousand seats spread very wide. The people on the left side wanted the sound to be coming from there, and the people on the right side wanted the sound to be coming from there.

Composer Alan Mencken, lyricist Lynn Ahrens, director Mike Ockrent, and choreographer Susan Stroman were very good collaborators on that production because they had a vision of the show and they knew what they wanted. When the creators are very clear about what they want, it makes all our jobs very easy.

ADVICE

When a young person tells me they want to be a sound designer, I tell them to study theatre, not only sound design. It's great to know a lot about the technology of sound. In pop music venues, the sound guy is the number one tech person. Everybody has to do things to your specs.

Unfortunately, it's the last thing in the theatre. A lot of people who come to work for me from the rock 'n' roll world have too much attitude. They don't understand why the set designer doesn't want a speaker there or the costume designer doesn't want a microphone in somebody's face. It's hard to cross over and accept that, in theatre, the storytelling comes first.

CHAPTER 23

William David Brohn

Orchestrator

Over a twenty-year career, William David Brohn has worked with major composers such as Boublil and Schönberg on *Miss Saigon*, Ahrens and Flaherty on *Ragtime* (Tony Award-Best Orchestrations), Stephen Schwartz on *Wicked*, and has given new life to works by George Gershwin (*Crazy for You*), Jerome Kern (*Show Boat*), Richard Rodgers (*Carousel*), The Sherman Brothers (*Mary Poppins*), and many more. Working with the composer to varying degrees, the orchestrator chooses which instruments will play which notes in the score, helping to illustrate the music. Many orchestrators do much more besides. Brohn has his own definition, which follows.

The Three Commandments

The first thing you have to understand: when the show isn't working they fire the orchestrator.

That somewhat flip remark is attributed to Hershy Kay, first known for his work with Leonard Bernstein and then for orchestrating an impressive boodle of Broadway musicals including *On the Town*, *A Chorus Line*, and *Evita*. Maybe it's an apocryphal attribution (although knowing and working briefly with Hershy, I can believe he said it...and more than once).

Such a remark highlights the reality that no one really understands how music achieves its magical effect, but everyone is an expert re: Music, that supreme mistress of all non-verbal communication in the arts. And frankly everyone has the right to feel a proprietary claim on something that indulges the brain in such powerful responses . . . its effect is at once personal and interpersonal.

So it's 9 a.m.; the creative team collaborating on a musical sits in a clutch of chairs destined to cradle the bums of a paying audience at 8 p.m. and tries to figure out what went so woefully wrong in last night's preview, and then nagged their fitful dreams until dawn. And, if the muses are rooting for them, this team may come up with some fixes that will go into rehearsal around noon when the cast is assembled, and into the show that night. Maybe the song will still embarrass the hell out of them, but something might just click and the road to salvation will beckon enticingly. Or amputation could be a pressing option. All of this actively concerns the orchestrator who awaits a collective decision from his colleagues as anxiously as the gaggle of scientists in 1942 watched Enrico Fermi with his slide-rule on the fateful night the first atomic reaction reached critical mass.

When I am lucky enough to be that orchestrator-arm of a cracking good team I haven't got a second to spare. My whole being is ready to jump and my writing arm quivers. It's after the show has opened for better or worse that I scratch my head asking, " How did I get into this intriguing firestorm?"

I am bound to report that the nascent orchestrator lingered longer *in utero* than an elephant. Maybe it was planted when, as a kid, I heard the overture to *South Pacific* on the original cast album. How that orchestra soared on the wings of orchestrator Robert Russell Bennett! Can I ever express the fulfillment that flooded my life when many years later I was privileged to work with him? But that's jumping the story because many years of music lessons, schools and conservatories lay ahead, and it was not until 1950-something that I got into the orchestra pit of a summer music theatre and the bolt to this amazing world slipped open.

In those days a summer music theatre was a seething cauldron of talent: people from all the crafts and flocks of actors including big stars all worked heatedly together to get one new show a week on the stage. There wasn't an instant to think about highfalutin concepts; just get that show on. Many years later I can see that this was collaboration at work of almost Biblical proportions. That nascent pen-pusher in me voluntarily took on the task of getting the existing orchestrations—which usually arrived in all their coffee-stained glory and replete with New York pit musicians' graffiti and often with many of the wrong notes intact—and quickly shrinking them to a one-size-fits-all reduction for our local barefoot Philharmonic (in which I played bass for all shows). I really played the role of arranger by default in reducing these sleek orchestrations. I would never

ever boast that they were any good, but I probably got some serious on-the-job training.

Funny how years later I am still perplexed at a definition of what an orchestrator does. Oh well, here goes another try: simply put (for once) the orchestrator is merely a facilitator; he's there to help the composer to say what he wants. That's not far removed from the role of a translator of languages. It's just converting the notes as given by the composer into a different medium (e.g., from piano into orchestra). Any new musical filament such as harmony or rhythm or counterpoint (independent ancillary lines that help glorify the Goddess Melody) are the work of an arranger. But I hasten to point out that most often the orchestrator wears the arranger-hat, and without any fanfare or discussion. It's just part of the job.

You begin to see that my concept of the smoothly functioning arranger/orchestrator (I will occasionally use the slash here) is of a craftsman who brings his whole kit with him and is ready to fit into the collaborative scheme in a trice. How that fit is achieved is part learned, part improvised, but fit he must or he may as well take a hike.

This may be a surge of rhetorical fancy, but I've imposed a first commandment on myself; it's not one handed down from some cloudy biblical mountain peak, but simply hewn by hard observation and abbreviated to summarize years of labor in the vineyards of the Musical Theatre:

I. Thou Shalt Not Try To Do The Other Guy's Job

It is fundamental that this commandment is the *ur*-consideration for me as orchestrator in the collaborative process with the composer. "How could the orchestrator possibly imagine he could do the composer's job?" you quickly interject. Easily. Exhibit A: all arrangers (this includes orchestrators, who are usually arrangers to boot) are closet composers. Their training and disposition makes them composers but the job they're trying to deliver must emphatically put them in that closet with the door firmly slammed shut. Exhibit B: I give you Old Man Ego. Everyone has it—without it there'd be no creative thought—the job is to subsume it to the collaborative process. So if I fancy myself a composer of musicals, I'd better get cracking and get my own show on somewhere else and see what it's like wearing those shoes. Not here—I am the composer's handmaiden; I put her work in orchestral garb and then step quietly away. Not that I exactly hate the odd rave or a proffered Tony Award.

This commandment is so basic that, for my part, I believe it can be applied to all phases of a getting a show on. Maybe we want to back up and consider that the first job in music theatre is to collaborate with the producer. He's probably the one who called you in the first place. I get shivers of happiness when the rest of the team seem to tacitly agree on observation of this commandment. They make life easier when the battle is joined.

Which leads us to another commandment, specifically wrought for me, the orchestrator:

II. THOU SHALT HONOR AND LOVE THY COMPOSER ABOVE ALL OTHERS

You'd think there's no need to go into the primacy of the composer. It's so basic that it is missed in a lot of the cases. This is the lady or gentleman who is the prime mover for you...they came up with the music, and no matter how they convey it to you (by writing out completely, banging out on a keyboard or humming) that music is the reason for your existence at this moment, and the central focus for you is to help the composer say what he wants to say. So we can dispense with all the gossip about who hums, who gives you a full-blown demo recording, or who writes out a completely harmonized short-score...there's no pecking order involved. This score, however conveyed to you, needs orchestrating, and how appropriately beautiful it sounds with an orchestra is the only paying part of your job. I can truly say that hearing the composer play and sing is the most thrilling moment for me, and perhaps the most telling. Lucy Simon hooked me on *Secret Garden* when she sat down at my piano and sang "How Can I Ever Tell You." I will always cherish that moment. There is chemistry that takes over at some moment in the collaboration. For Claude-Michel Schönberg and me it came in the first week of getting acquainted with his score for *Miss Saigon*. He was singing (in the original French) the exquisite wedding scene and playing it in his special way. Before long he could hardly sing, so overcome by the emotion of that moment, and he turned to me only to see that I was crying too. Talk about bonding.

So we see this special relationship and its need (my credo) for an unwritten oath of loyalty between composer and orchestrator. If there is even a scintilla of competition between these two parties, something in the collaboration will go sour. This neutral position takes restraint, humility, strength and dedication to one's own job. It is not taught; it has to be what's bred in the bones.

At the same time, that unique collaboration asks for openness from the composer, who having handed the job of orchestration over, wants to exploit whatever special creativity his orchestrator offers. A clever and wise writer of song will always know when to stroke and when to demand. It is one of the most intimate of relationships.

A third commandment might read:

III. Thou Shalt Trust Thy Colleague

Margo Fonteyn appeared as guest ballerina for American Ballet Theatre in the 1960s when I was a young associate conductor with them. I was assigned to conduct a set of variations from *The Nutcracker*, but had been unable to rehearse directly with her as she flew into New York only hours before the performance (which was across the river in New Jersey) and had gotten a briefing by the music director and ballet master as to tempi. Enter trembling stripling conductor backstage where that magnificent lady was having a go at the barre and rosin-box. "Miss Fonteyn, I am William Brohn and I am conducting the variations and would like to check the tempi with you. It starts *molto moderato* about beat beat beat dum-de-dum dum dum dum de-de-dum and then picks up ever so slightly at the middle part but not too much then drifts back to the opening tempo...." An elegant arm glides out and an ethereally beautiful hand rests on the liveried arm that was nervously ticking gestures accompanying the fear-struck voice that I didn't recognize as mine. "My darling," intones the voice at the end of that arm, "you shall simply make beautiful music...and I shall dance to it."

Trust me, trust yourself, and trust the music. That was the universe she flung open to me in a moment of such dazzling perception and summation that my eyes always tear up when remembering it.

Such is trust among colleagues. Collaborations in music theatre are lumpy by their very nature...a rather disparate group of volatile creative folk are foregathered to storm Troy. They drop all hopes of a normal life for the ensuing months and must indulge in a massive game of improvised give-and-take. Trust in each other is the marching order.

Marching to the same drumbeat of course. There has to be a simpatico with each other's sensibilities, and that always starts with respect for each other. And of course you've got to try to suss out what their expectations are of you.

Show me a team that harbors suspicion within and I'll show you a show that ain't gonna show. We've all had such episodes in our careers and they're best taken as life's lessons. No face would be redder than mine if I had to abide a recounting of some loser of a show that I was involved with. We are supposed to work as a team, and therefore it's the team that bears the responsibility as an entity.

If it's a team we are talking about, it's surely a group of specialists. But there is a first among equals in this team, and that is the director. (For the moment, we'll put aside that primal relationship of composer and orchestrator.) This person is captain of the ship, and believe me, it's good to see him on the bridge when that ship is plowing through heavy seas! The wise director probably knows a lot about all the things going on, but limits his words to the specialists on the team (Commandment I) and spends gobs of time with the actors. From my point of view it's best when he allows the music-director to do his job (Commandment III) and talks to his orchestrator only on well-chosen occasions. Trevor Nunn and Hal Prince are the two that know how and when to push my buttons. A word, an arm (there goes that arm again) placed on my shoulder, a look, an anecdote...all with that exquisite sense of the moment that defines the genius for knowing when to shoot the arrow that always makes its mark.

That aforementioned music director needs a word too. He, along with the rehearsal-pianist, has been at all the production meetings, backers' auditions, actors' auditions, and then the rehearsals. In short, he knows where all the bodies are buried. Paul Gemignani is the ace here. Nobody knows the musical-dramatic moment as instinctively as Paul, and no one has conveyed it to me with more dispatch, ease and understanding. It would have taken me six months (instead of six weeks) to finish the orchestrations to *Crazy For You* without Paul Gemignani as my extraordinary colleague. Also when I've done the orchestrations, nobody brings them to life like Paul. He can make an orchestra (and an audience) pay attention!

When there is a separate lyricist (as in most cases) I like to have a special moments with that person too. Lynn Ahrens has a way of sensing an orchestrator's needs. I will credit her among other things with getting me on the right track on the song "Back To Before" from *Ragtime*. (That is not taking anything away from the brilliance of Steve's composition... most hours were spent with him and, in fact, I believe the two write together more than separately.) But in this one instance she suggested to me in an orchestra-reading that I had not gotten the surge of the sea which is a metaphor (I believe) to the momentous surge of feeling and cardinal decision-making that the character Mother goes through and I went to my study with a clear brief to rewrite it (they say) successfully. When I reflect on composer/lyricist duos that I have known, Steve and Lynn are the clearest to me. They just have a way of saying the same thing, but each contributes an illuminating skein.

Bob and Chet (a.k.a. Wright and Forrest) had the same creative joined-at-the-hip gift and I was privileged to observe it when I orchestrated *Timbuktu* for them. My *Miss Saigon* and *Martin Guerre* experiences with the Boublil-Schonberg team were that Alain always met with me privately and made the very necessary eloquent intellectual connections in superb English that he knew my particular psyche needed. As I noted above, Claude-Michel always provided me with all the visceral nuance I ever wanted. I never knew such passion.

Passion is a key word here. It informs all of the process of collaborating, and such guidelines as I propose (keeping to your own job, honoring the composer, and trusting your colleagues) are only glow-in-the-dark markers, but this *passion* is the engine driving all of music theatre—behind the scenes, on the stage and in front of the stage. You of the audience are a major component of that alchemy.

And to those in that audience who are passionately intent on jumping the quantum leap—remember an atom's electrons do it constantly!—to the other side and join us who labor here, just a word. Keep your eye on the ball. Amid the alchemy going on right before our eyes, we on this side of the curtain often miss things going on that affect us profoundly. A good case for this statement is how we in the of music theatre have buried our heads in the sand when it comes to computer-based substitutes for acoustic instruments. Brought up as my generation was in the Romantic tradition of the Orchestra—yes, the theatre orchestra of Robert Russell Bennett is a direct descendant of Berlioz—we at first ignored electronics then hoped they'd go away. Well, they are here; the sea change they have wrought is upon us. I would be happy if the aspiring young orchestrator learned the tools of the trade as ever—from the many competent schools and teachers, studied scores of the masters (classic and theatre) and apprenticed as all musicians for centuries have done. I would be exultant if that young person faced the era of electronics head-on and became its master. If I'm around, I'll be in that same classroom.

CHAPTER 24

ANGELINA AVALLONE
MAKEUP DESIGNER

Angelina Avallone has designed makeup for many Broadway productions, including *The Color Purple*; *Chitty Chitty Bang Bang*; *A Touch of the Poet*; *Thoroughly Modern Millie*; *Wonderful Town*; *Sweeney Todd*; *Gypsy*; *Sweet Charity*; *All Shook Up*; *Lennon*; *Bombay Dreams*; *Dracula: The Musical*; *Little Shop of Horrors*; *The Caretaker*; *Enchanted April*; *Henry IV*; *The Boys From Syracuse*; *Kiss Me, Kate*; *A Thousand Clowns*; *Frozen*; *The Sound of Music*; *High Society*; *The Last Night of Bally-hoo*; *The Scarlet Pimpernel*; and *Once Upon a Mattress*. Regional: *Dracula* (La Jolla); *The Importance of Being Earnest*, *Hedda Gabler* (Long Wharf). Off-Broadway: *Quartet* (Brooklyn Academy of Music); *Blur*, *Captains Courageous* (Manhattan Theatre Club); *Troilus and Cressida* (Theatre for a New Audience); *Cellini* (Second Stage). Opera: *Marco Polo* (New York City Opera, Hong Kong Festival, Munich); Eos Orchestra.

I fell in love with the stage at an early age. I love everything about it. I love the performers and the fact that actors can become these amazing creatures who leap in the air. You walk into a theatre and for those two or three hours you are elsewhere. You are transported. Anything is possible. I think it's the magic that really captivated me.

I began my introduction to theatre at age 5. My mother loved the theatre and she used to read us plays, along with fairy tales. We had a lot of books. We had Greek mythology. We had the Indian epics, the *Mahabharata* and *Ramayana*. I remember one of my first theatrical experiments was putting on a show with my friends when I was about 7 or 8 years old. We needed costumes, so I decided to take down the curtains in the house and sewed them into costumes on my grandmother's sewing machine. We painted our faces with watercolors and we had become the characters of the story.

I loved to draw as a child. I went to art

school early on and we frequented the theatre and the opera. I remember, at age 6, falling asleep in the middle of *Aida* but then waking up in Act Three, which is full of magic. I didn't know if I was dreaming or if it was reality.

COLOR AND LIGHT

My journey to Broadway was very interesting. I started out as a painter. I went on to fashion school in Florence, Italy. I began working with photographers, and that's where I began to do makeup. I liked it. It was exciting. But I felt something was missing. I realized I was missing "story." I missed theatre. So I came back.

I was accepted at the Yale School of Drama and studied theatre and design. It was very inspiring. I studied with some wonderful teachers: Ming Cho Lee, Jane Greenwood and Jess Goldstein. After graduating I had the great opportunity to work with Jane Greenwood as her assistant costume designer on many productions on and Off-Broadway and around the U.S. It was an incredible education and experience. I was greatly inspired by her talent and her vision as a designer. We eventually did *Scarlet Pimpernel*, *Once Upon a Mattress*, shows at the Kennedy Center, even some opera productions. She's an amazing and inspiring person. She loves theatre, and loves what she does.

My first Broadway show as a makeup designer was with Jane. Jane asked me to design the make-up for several other productions as well. Soon afterwards I was requested to design makeup for other Broadway productions by other great costume designers such as Martin Pakledinaz, Catherine Zuber, William Ivey Long, Jess Goldstein, Ann Hould-Ward, Anthony Ward, and Mark Thompson. Designing makeup involves a close relationship and collaboration with the wig designer. I have been very fortunate to have worked on several Broadway productions with some very talented and creative wig designers such as Paul Huntley, David Brian Brown, and Tom Watson.

My art background helped me tremendously. Understanding color, understanding light, understanding what you can do with shadow and light. How you can pull out a feature or push back a feature, or make something vanish entirely. If I need to make a prosthetic, I can draw on my background in sculpture.

Makeup designers must design for a certain performing space. If the audience is forty feet away, the features appear in a certain way. If you're working at the Metropolitan Opera, it's a whole different story. It's fascinating how little you really are able to see and how big a certain feature has to become in order for somebody sitting in the orchestra of a Broadway theatre to see it. So you adjust and exaggerate the effect. Of course, in a very intimate space on the other hand, you must be extremely realistic.

I worked on a revival of *The Normal Heart* with Larry Kramer, which takes place in the early years of the AIDS epidemic, before any treatment was available. I had to create prosthetics for characters who had these really awful lesions that were one of the symptoms. Larry was very nervous about it because he said no production had ever been really successful at creating that without it looking like a painted spot.

That was a huge challenge. You are so close in the theatre sometimes. In *Normal Heart*, the actors were about two feet from the audience. How to do it in a small theatrical space so it would look realistic to an audience that may have seen such things it real life, so that it would convey the horror people were feeling at what was happening to them and their friends, and yet would not drive people out of the theatre?

I went back and I looked at all the research and looked at the way the lesions invaded the flesh. I decided not to just draw the lesions on, but to sculpt them and apply them on the actor. The first time we walked the actor to the stage under lights, Larry came down and he said, "Oh my God. This looks so real. You are going to make a lot of people cry. It's heartbreaking."

I thought, "OK, we've done our job. It's effective and it's subtle enough. It works. It's real." Those moments are so rewarding.

See Me in Light

In creating the makeup look for a character, the makeup designer works with the director, costume designer, wig designer, and the actor. The director has the overall vision of the production. The discussions between the director and makeup designer involve primarily the story and the specific characters and their needs for the production.

In a way, makeup is an extension of the costume, so you work very closely with the costume designer and the actor. The lighting designer's contribution is also very important once the actor is on stage. The lights can age an actor significantly or add a youthful glow to their skin. Once the actor is under lights on stage and is in full costume and wig, this is the time when the director has the chance to see the actor and give notes for changes. Sometimes you'll get just a few words: "It's too much" or "I love it, it's great."

Sometimes the director hates it, or it just doesn't work, and you have to do it all over again. That's just part of the process and you have to expect it. Sometimes whole numbers get cut out of the production, and they may contain your best work. You deal with it.

If something looks great in the dressing room, but doesn't work under lights, you need to figure out *why* it's not working. Maybe you've done too much, and need to pull back. Maybe you haven't done enough, so it needs to get bigger. Maybe it's a conversation you need to have with the lighting designer.

One big challenge I'm constantly dealing with is actors, especially younger actors, who are used to street makeup, or they've done film or television, where they use very natural makeup. They come to do stage work and suddenly they find the eyes are much bigger on stage, and we use brighter and bolder colors. What you see in the dressing room or from a camera about a foot away is not what you see from sixty feet away in a theatre under the stage lights. All of a sudden you are putting orange, coral, or shocking pink on them and they are terrified. You have to build the trust of the actor and the confidence of the actor sometimes to let you do your work.

Kiss Me, Kate was an interesting example. Marin Mazzie, who played Kate, ended up wearing this incredibly pink makeup in that show. The first time we did the makeup I did a very natural base but it didn't work under the stage lights. It did not look pretty. She looked washed out. I tried warmer colors, and they still didn't look right on stage. There was a lot of amber in the lighting, a lot of warm light.

So I had to find pigment and custom-mix it to come up with a formula that worked for her. I tried a very pink base with hot pink cheeks. The problem was, in the dressing room it looked big and bold and frightening. But when she put on the wig and stood under the stage lighting she looked absolutely glorious. Marin trusted me, and it paid off.

THE TRANSFORMATION

What I find fascinating is the transformation. My collaboration is to understand the character, and then use makeup or prosthetics to help the actor get into the character.

Actors sometimes must go on an incredible journey to become somebody else. Sometimes they have to age thirty years. It's not an easy thing. Makeup helps. You work with the actor. You start playing. You change his features. If the look is successful, you can see the character being born. You see the actor look at their new brows or see how their mouths can make new grimaces, and they suddenly discover a new face staring back at them that's the character. And they work to become that character.

When I worked with Kevin Kline on *Henry IV*, Kevin was playing portly, jolly Falstaff. Kevin is an amazing actor, and he loves makeup. He can spend hours working on detail. He said that helps him get into the character.

Kevin is not a heavy man. He is slender. You need a full, robust face for Falstaff.

Kevin was going to wear a fat suit, but what could we do with his slender face?

He said, "I think we can do it with makeup. It's important to me."

I said, "Let's try."

So we did. There were no prosthetics involved in Kevin's makeup. He grew his own beard. We created a very round shape and combed the beard out with a lot of product. He grew his own hair and took the color out. We used the tiniest of brushes to paint little veins and spots on his nose and cheeks. It was a two-hour makeup and he was willing to do it. And it was very effective.

In most theatres, once the show is established the actors take over doing the makeup for themselves. I was a little nervous creating all these complicated tiny little effects. But I said, no, he's great and he wants to do it. He is willing to spend the time. For me, that was another wonderful moment.

CREATING TRACKS

Makeup isn't just me or the makeup team. Makeup is a collaboration between yourself and the director, the designer, the actor, and the wig designer. Sometimes the director hires me, or an actor requests me. But usually it's the costume designer.

For example, Martin Pakledinaz hired me for *Thoroughly Modern Millie*. That show was set in the 1920s, one of the most fun periods for makeup. It was time of liberation for women after the Victorian Age, so the makeup was very colorful and dramatic. There was an explosion of experimentation in makeup for women. And it wound up being very bold because makeup was not very refined at that point. There were only so many shades of powder available. Makeup was over the top, clothes were over the top, and women, for the first time, were bobbing their hair. Women began to look like what we think of as modern.

During the design phase, you design the look of each character. For actors with multiple roles, you have to design a look for each costume change and you have to check to make sure it looks right under lights with each wig and costume. And, of course, the looks have to be approved by the director, and by the costume designer.

Millie is a girl who comes from Kansas City to New York to meet Mr. Right and experience big city life. She goes to Hotel Priscilla, which is a hotel for aspiring young actors, and meets all these different characters. We had an ensemble of great young actresses who played a variety of parts. When they were at the hotel, they were the Priscilla Girls. But when the scene shifted to a speakeasy, they became flappers. And when we visited Millie's office, they became the office workers. The scenes constantly shifted between a variety of places, so the girls constantly had to change their costumes—and makeup.

The challenge was making all these quick changes. First I had to work with the costume designer to find out what color palette he was working with. Then I had to work with the actors, to find out how much time they had from one scene to the next.

You create a "track" for their various looks throughout the show. You start by timing the changes. You work out a system of what goes on first, what comes off first. What can go on top of the makeup? Sometimes you layer the makeup one on top of the previous. Sometimes you take off makeup. You preset makeup baskets backstage so they can find the products quickly and easily. What's in the basket? How many products? What kind of brushes do you need? Who is changing where? If they start in the dressing rooms but they change their hair downstairs, where do you preset that basket? You have to figure out all the logistics of that.

MAKEUP AND CHARACTER

Makeup must be very specific, not only to the character, but to the actress playing the character. Even when I work with an ensemble, I always try to customize the makeup to each of the girls. To the audience, it may all read like a red mouth, it's actually a slightly different kind of red or the eye makeup is in the range of coral and pink perhaps. There is always some variation to suit the face or match the wig. When it comes to helping develop character with the actors, I am very willing to change the makeup and explore new alternatives.

Here's another example from *Millie*. Over the course of the run, several major actresses played the villain, Mrs. Meers. The character is a Caucasian former actress who is passing herself off as a Chinese manager of the Hotel Priscilla, while actually kidnapping the girls and selling them into white slavery.

The role was originated on Broadway by Harriet Harris, who went on to win the Tony Award for it. We looked at Marty Pakledinaz's designs and we talked to the director about what he wanted for Mrs. Meers. She's kind of a cartoon, but she needs to be believable. So I asked myself, what would Mrs. Meers do? How would *she* create her look? She had been an actress in the '20s. She knew stage makeup. She's resourceful. She's clever. She probably styled her own wig. I brought in some books on Peking Opera. Obviously it couldn't just be Peking Opera. It had to be Peking Opera from a '20s American point of view.

And she's vain. She wouldn't see herself playing a character part. She thinks she's playing a leading lady. So she'll perhaps give herself the mouth of the '20s, that leading lady mouth, plus a Chinese eyebrow and then some black eyeliner. It became this weird blend of real Peking Opera, '20s beauty makeup, and sort of her *idea* of Peking Opera.

Later in the run she was replaced by Dixie Carter and Delta Burke. I couldn't just put Harriet's makeup on them.

Delta is a beautiful woman who has always played these glamorous characters and has the "Delta Look." We created something that complemented her look, but was still Mrs. Meers. It took her a long time to learn how to do the elaborate makeup by herself, but she wound up doing a great job.

When Dixie took over she had her own ideas. She said, "Mrs. Meers is the villain and that's the way I'm going to play her." Her costume was slightly different than Delta's, and Dixie decided Mrs. Meers was going to move in a distinctly reptilian way.

I said, "Dixie, perhaps we should do something shiny."

We got waterproof, semi-permanent makeup, and put it on the palms of her hands. Her character did a lot of movements with her hands. The makeup caught the light and gave it an evil sort of sheen. Instead of hot pink, we went with emerald green and gold, and it worked.

Choreographing the Teeth

On *Millie*, like most shows, the actors had to put on their own makeup. It's rare on Broadway today to have a makeup crew on a big show, unless there are heavy prosthetics.

Dance of the Vampires, for instance, was a makeup artist's dream. I was asked to stay on with two assistants to help Michael Crawford and the ensemble get through the show every night. It's too bad that show had such a short run, because doing the makeup was a lot of fun.

We had many cast members with full body makeup and we were painting bodies throughout the performance every single day. We had to paint the entire ensemble, get the principals ready and then run the show.

It's amazing the choreography that took place backstage—just for the vampire teeth alone! It was putting ultraviolet glow on legs and arms and faces. It was making sure teeth that came off at stage right were ready to go back in at stage left.

There was one number where the vampires rose from their graves. Costumer Ann Hould-Ward and I decided we wanted them to look like really horrific cadavers. Her beautiful period costumes consisted of patchwork metallic silks, and I wanted the faces and the arms to be an extension of the costumes. The makeup consisted of layers of runny pewtery silver makeup on top of the already existing layers of makeup from previous scenes, which was right for the look of that particular moment. They did look pretty scary and amazing.

Leading lady Mandy Gonzalez had to look sweet and lovable for most of the show, then really terrifying at the end when she turns into a vampire. We put a piece of prosthetic in her wig. When she got bitten by Michael Crawford, the prosthetic piece activated and blood began flowing down from behind her ear and down her neck and onto her lovely costume.

That brings up another practicality issue. You need to be aware of your collaborators. Effects like that are great, but how do you preserve the costumes? It's not a film: you can't cut and stop and go and clean. You have costumes that may cost thousands and thousands of dollars.

In that case we were lucky because the dress was red. But we still had the issue of the flowing blood. It travels and you don't want it getting all over the place. I had to work some kind of magic to trap the blood.

In this case, Ann designed a corseted dress, the blood flowed down into the décolletage where I put a padded piece that absorbed the blood.

These types of situations make you very creative. You start thinking: OK, what do I do? Do I mix the blood to make it dry really fast? You actually time how long it takes for the blood to flow down, then you become a bit of a chemist. In our makeup room we had all kinds of pots and blenders. We were like mad scientists trying to figure things out.

You troubleshoot. You call other people. I worked extensively with Dana Nye of Ben Nye Makeup Company in California. His father, Ben Nye, worked in Hollywood in the '30s and the '40s. He is from a family of makeup artists. He has his own cosmetic line and also custom-makes makeup. He helped us custom-make our body makeup. It had to be the kind of makeup that didn't sweat off easily and didn't get all over the costumes. We had to find a sealer so the makeup could go on fast, dry fast, and didn't come off with sweat and hot lights. We also worked with MAC Cosmetics in creating the characters. MAC Cosmetics has also been a very generous sponsor of makeup products for several Broadway productions that I designed.

TWENTIETH CENTURY

When I worked on the Roundabout Theatre Company's 1994 revival of *Twentieth Century*, I found myself designing for two major movie stars, Alec Baldwin and Anne Heche. And it was a bit of a culture shock because film actors are used to a different kind of makeup.

Interestingly enough, Alec did not need much makeup at all. Anne had worked on film and television and she'd never done anything in this period, the 1930s.

She said, "I don't normally put my makeup on. I usually have somebody else do it."

I said, "Anne, we are going to have a big makeup session and I'll teach you."

She said, "That sounds exciting."

I said, "Let's go shopping!"

We ran around Barneys department story and tried all the different makeup lines. We picked out some colors and I bought some products from the MAC line.

We had had a meeting with the costume designer, William Ivey Long who had done a lot of research into movie stars of the period and what they wore and what were the trendy "looks" of the time. We looked at his costume designs, and he showed us color swatches. Wig designer Paul Huntley was there as well. He brought some hair colors and we looked at wigs.

Then I brought out the makeup kit and I picked colors and products that would go with what we'd just seen, and which were right for Anne's coloring. We sat down and began to play. I extended her brows, changed the lip shape, and gave her a very full foundation. I also changed the shape of her eyes. We created that smoky look—soft, a lot of highlight. Anne came with her hair curled. She mocked a hairstyle from the period by pinning it up.

Anne was amazing. She grabbed a mirror and started saying her lines into it, in a way that matched her look. And there, in front of my eyes, she became Lily Garland.

She said, "I love it!"

I said, "Now put lashes on."

She said, "I've never worn lashes."

"Put the lashes on!"

She did, and batted her eyes and found all kinds of movements and expressions and things you can do with your eyes when you have big lashes. She played at being Lily Garland in a great big mirror they have there.

She said, "This is great. I want to learn how to do this." And she learned how to do it, and she loved it.

Honesty

I think honesty is the best thing in any collaboration. Two key things to remember if you're an artist and want to survive in the theatre: don't take things so personally, and don't get too attached to any one idea.

Sometimes you do a great makeup and there are makeups you love, but maybe that particular makeup may get cut. Or it may be too much for the character. Or all of a sudden the character goes on stage and it's too perfect.

That's right: sometimes your best work maybe *too perfect* for that character because perhaps that character would not have done their makeup so well. Even though it is work well done, it's not right for the character. Then there's nothing for you to do but take it off and chalk it up to experience. Makeup is only right if it's right for the character as a whole, and for the play as a whole.

That doesn't mean you don't experiment. Playing it safe is perhaps the worst thing you can do. It's good to be pushed by your collaborators because experimental work is great. It may be scary and you may make mistakes. But you should be willing to go and try something different. If it turns out not to be right, have the confidence to try something else.

CHAPTER 25

NANCY COYNE

ADVERTISING

Nancy Coyne is a partner in Serino Coyne Inc., the largest full-service advertising and marketing agency in the live entertainment industry. In its nearly thirty years of existence, the company has counted among its clients original Broadway productions of *Cats*, *A Chorus Line*, *The Producers*, *Les Misérables*, *42nd Street*, *Movin' Out*, *Smokey Joe's Café*, *Wicked*, *The Lion King*, *Beauty and the Beast*, *The Phantom of the Opera*, *Miss Saigon*, *Mamma Mia!*, *Annie*, *Angels in America*, *Grease*, *Titanic*, *Urinetown*, *The Who's Tommy*, *Dreamgirls*, *The Radio City Music Hall Christmas Spectacular*, and dozens more.

At the end of the remarkable one-woman show that Jane Wagner wrote for Lily Tomlin, *The Search for Signs of Intelligent Life in the Universe*, Lily is playing Trudy, the bag lady, who is being visited by aliens. Trying to explain to them the difference between a can of Campbell's soup and Andy Warhol's painting of a can of Campbell's soup, Trudy points to each: "Soup... Art... Soup... Art...." Later, she takes her space chums to see a Broadway show. At the end of the show, she asks them what they thought of what they had seen on the stage. The aliens reply that they weren't watching the stage. They were watching the entranced audience. "The play is Soup," they tell Trudy. "The *audience* is Art!"

As a creator of theatrical advertising, I concern myself

with the audience; my job is to get them to the theatre. The show's job is to engage them to the extent that the next day, they will talk about the experience and excite others. Even though the advertising budgets for shows are a fraction of those for products costing infinitely less than a Broadway ticket (colas, fast food, cosmetics, etc.), we are able to sell a good show quite effectively as long as we can create ambassadors of good will. You don't talk about the pizza you had for dinner at the water cooler the next day. But you do talk about the show you and your boyfriend saw. And if you took your kids to Broadway you will be especially vocal. Parents are proud of themselves for making *The Lion King* or *Wicked* or *Hairspray* a family experience. They know instinctively that it is quality time away from the computer or videogame screen, removed from the TV and unplugged from the iPod. It is shared time. It is Art!

I fell in love with the theatre on my first trip to Broadway. Watching Ethel Merman as Mama Rose in *Gypsy*, I related to my own stage mother and, like Baby June, I yearned to give all my toe shoes to someone. When intermission came, I counted the seconds until Act II began. So, when in my early twenties I was offered a job writing advertising copy for TV and radio spots for every show on the Great White Way, I couldn't believe my good fortune. Like most "theatre people" I had ambitions to be on the stage. But just recently, at the Disney offices, I ran into a young girl who was changing into a dress to audition for a role in a Disney touring production. She asked if I was there to audition too, and I said no, that I did the advertising for the Disney shows. "Oh wow, you're so lucky," she said, so genuinely that I knew she wasn't kidding.

And while the pressure is always on us to come up with a campaign that will put a line at the box office, I realize how nice it is to make my living off a skill that improves with age and experience. We bring people to the theatre as surely as the name above the title, but with none of the attendant problems of being an actor. Our accountability is tangible: we take an ad, we count the tickets it sells. We measure our every effort against the box office numbers. The weekly grosses and daily wraps are our report card, and the immediate nature of the business means that we feel like we're in the cast, constantly peeking out at the audience from behind the curtain...counting the house.

My job, and the job of the hundred-person advertising agency I started with my partner, Matthew Serino, is to take a script and—in collaboration with the client, the producer of the upcoming show—create a strategy for attracting the greatest initial audience at the most efficient cost. Every show is different; every show must be treated as a unique entity. Ascertaining a show's greatest strengths is crucial at this stage in deciding to whom to appeal and how. If the music is compelling, radio can be more efficient than TV. If the visuals are astonishing, it might well require TV to tell the story. If a star is present, one good photo can be worth much more than a thousand words.

Once a strategy, budget, and timeline are in place, the ad agency creates the sales materials: the logo, title treatment, artwork, print ad adaptations, outdoor billboards, and transit ads—bus sides, taxi tops, phone kiosks, and posters at train stations and on subway platforms. We then create the front-of-the-theatre displays, the CD packaging, the tourist and group-sales brochures, the merchandising designs, the radio spots, television spots, and the direct mail campaigns. Frequently, at this stage of development, focus group research is done to determine the public's perceptions before the show opens, and how advertising materials might help shape them. Then, in collaboration with the producers, the general manager (who is charged with keeping the budget under control) and the press agent (whose strategy for dealing with the media is frequently a correlative of the ad agency's strategy for the public), the campaign rolls out and a new product—a Broadway show—is introduced.

It sounds relatively business-like, but every decision is fraught with personalities. Directors, writers, set designers, stars, and their wives all weigh in with the producers, whether asked or not. After all, everyone has an opinion about advertising, and sometimes it's difficult to understand that all opinions are not created equal. Just as everyone on a show brings a unique skill to the production, my skill—my agency's strength—is that through twenty-five years of trial and error, we have developed unparalleled instincts for serving our constituency: our audience. And we never forget that although we're paid by the producer, we're speaking to the public.

The agency itself looks like a cross section of a theatre audience: lots of women, gay men, and other intelligent people, all with a keen appreciation of the arts, and many with their own kids whom they wish to introduce to the joy of live entertainment. Each of us is committed to the premise that encouraging a customer to spend up to one hundred and ten hard-earned dollars on a theatre ticket is an honorable endeavor and the aforementioned customer would surely thank us if he knew how to find us. Our product doesn't cause cancer, make you fat, make you drunk, or suggest that all you are good for is doing the laundry and getting stains out of the carpet. The product that we sell can make children more inventive, adults more thoughtful, boyfriends more romantic, girlfriends more appreciative, and makes everyone realize the power of a collective audience all imagining the same thing at the same time. Our product cannot be rewound or replayed and is not easily available anytime or anywhere. Only about one thousand people at 8 p.m. on 45th Street between Broadway and Eighth Avenue can have the exact experience of watching a show in the Schoenfeld Theatre tonight, an experience audiences call "priceless."

The planning that takes place for a show is usually divided into stages: first, pre-opening, in which we appeal to those early hard-core "see-everything" buyers, patrons who like to be the first in the know. These are invariably people who want the best seats and buy early to get them. Then, opening-night has a strategy unto itself, with the exploitation of the best reviews, and an extra effort to remind people who don't read reviews (or who will read only one) that many reputable sources had favorable things to say about the show. And third, there is the strategy for the first year of the run with the original cast. Much of the impression the world will get of this show is dependent on the success of this first crucial year. Ancillary campaigns are devised to appeal to tourists or specialized smaller audiences and to help secure awards. But an important measure of a Broadway show is its longevity. While we are proud that twenty-one of the past twenty-five Tony award Best Musical winners have been our clients, we are prouder that only eight shows have played over three-thousand performances in the last three decades—and Serino Coyne has handled all eight.

Perhaps the greatest collaboration that we, as an advertising agency, participate in is our internal strategy sessions wherein the account supervisor, charged with adhering to the budget and expressing the producer's point of view (and the director's and writer's and star's, if the producer has given them any say in the ad campaign) meets with the agency's creative director, art director, media director and marketing director to craft our approach to the public. We identify each person for whom we are creating a campaign: for instance, with *Wicked* we felt we had remarkable tween appeal (young girls aged 8 to 16).

We invented one target and named her "Katie," sent her to Greenwich Academy from her home nearby where she lives with her mother, an interior designer, and her father, a broker. We gave her a younger brother, a dog, and an extensive wardrobe. We let her watch TV and spend hours on the Internet and telephone, all simultaneously every day. We knew her friends were her number-one priority and that she was taken to school in an SUV, and played soccer after school. We explored her favorite websites, magazines, television shows, and radio stations, because we knew Katie had the power to *sell* to thirty other consumers exactly like herself. She is more social than perhaps any other demographic in the country. So we designed with her in mind, wrote for her, and bought air time and space for her—and, when we got her, we got her mother, too. And because *Wicked* is also male-friendly, we also got her father.

This is not to say that a Broadway poster should look like a page out of Seventeen Magazine—after all, her parents are buying the ticket. It should look like a Broadway show. But one that is accessible and appealing to Katie. One that Katie will want the poster for...and the baseball cap, the tee shirt, and the CD. And here's the best part: one that Katie will want to go back to with a few friends on her birthday.

The best collaborations between producer and agency are the ones in which the producers have agreed among themselves on a single point of view. To pick a direction and then to *stay with it* is the first great marketing decision a producer can make. One truth remains constant, no matter how much the industry has changed over the years: the advertising for a show is exactly as good as the client who picked it. Because, while the client isn't always right, the client is always the client. You can suggest that perhaps he would look better in the single-breasted jacket, but when he demands the double-breasted one, you'd have to be a pretty bad businessperson to refuse. Of course, we have come to blows with producers over the years; no more than three or four times, when, wishing to communicate how deeply we felt a certain campaign was in the show's best interest, we did not acquiesce to the client's suggestions. But those instances were rare and many years ago, and usually the result of clients not understanding that to target an audience was not to exclude all other audiences, but rather to position the show rightly for the audience most inclined to love and *talk about* the show.

Word of mouth is the ultimate sales tool, and cultivating it is our specialty. It is very much a matter of managing expectation. The advertising must promise an experience well worth the price of a ticket; in other words, we must promise value. But we must also position the show accurately. One Off-Broadway play that we did not handle was *Jeffrey*. Our concept, the statue of David in a chastity belt with the copy line, "Abstinence makes the heart grow fonder," was deemed too explicit. They wanted something more "Neil Simon." Our feeling was that if the wrong people wandered into *Jeffrey* expecting a family comedy, they would be shocked by the adult nature of the material and not speak highly of this very funny show. But people knowing what to expect would love it, talk it up, and send more people like themselves to see it.

Similarly, while the darkest of plays sometimes has very funny moments, to sell such a show on the surface accessibility of its laughs is to do the show an enormous disservice. If we deliver more than an audience expects, word of mouth is good. Less, and word of mouth closes the show. There have been occasions where an appealing ad campaign caused a lot of people to rush to a show, only to rush out and tell their friends, "Don't go." These shows closed faster than if they'd never advertised at all.

Bad collaborations are usually a result of a lack of trust or an insecurity that cannot be overcome. In a difficult agency-producer collaboration, you hear things like, "My doorman said he doesn't get it," or, "My babysitter said it reminded her of that movie she hated." Bad collaborations are also the result of frustrations with the show itself. Sometimes it seems easier to fix the poster than the second act. Even though the poster isn't broken.

Theatrical advertising and marketing have many challenges. Your product can close on Saturday night. And there's no shelf life to a theatre ticket. If you don't sell B101 tonight, you can't sell it tomorrow; it won't wait for you to have a better idea. But there's nothing else in the world that I would sell. Because in this technologically advanced day and age, being part of something that is hand-crafted, multigenerational, personal and, in so many ways, exactly the same as it was in the days of Aristophanes and Euripides is enormously satisfying. And despite the *New York Times*' never-ending predictions that Broadway is dying, the numbers have never been better and the art form never healthier.

After all, theatre exists whenever anyone telling a story pretends for a moment that he *is* the wolf. The moment a line of "dialogue" is acted and not merely described is the moment an invitation is extended to abandon reality and participate in collective imagining. It is my great pleasure to extol the virtues of sitting out there in the dark with hundreds of others, traveling to wherever the people on stage choose to take us.

CHAPTER 26

ADRIAN BRYAN-BROWN
PUBLIC RELATIONS

Boneau/Bryan-Brown, Inc., was formed in 1991 by Chris Boneau and Adrian Bryan-Brown, who jointly bring more than forty years experience serving as press representatives on more than two hundred productions on and Off-Broadway, on national tour, and in Europe. A representative collection of Boneau/Bryan-Brown's current, recent and upcoming clients include *The Boy From Oz* starring Hugh Jackman; *Brooklyn*; *Caroline, Or Change*; *Cabaret* at Studio 54; *A Day in the Death of Joe Egg* starring Eddie Izzard; *Debbie Does Dallas*; Disney's *Aida, Beauty and the Beast, Tarzan, Mary Poppins, The Little Mermaid* and *The Lion King*; the Pulitzer Prize-winning *Doubt*; *The Drowsy Chaperone*; *Drumstruck*; *Flower Drum Song* starring Lea Salonga; *42nd Street*; Terrence McNally's *Frankie and Johnny in the Clair de Lune*; *Gypsy* starring Bernadette Peters and directed by Sam Mendes; *Hedda Gabler* starring Kate Burton; the National Theatre's *The History Boys*; *Into the Woods* starring Vanessa Williams; *Jersey Boys*; *Jumpers* by Tom Stoppard; *La Bohème* directed by Baz Luhrmann; *Lennon*; Yasmina Reza's *Life x 3*; *The Look of Love* directed by Scott Ellis; *The Lord of the Rings* (Toronto World Premiere); *Mamma Mia!* (11 productions worldwide); *Match*; *The Music Man* directed by Susan Stroman; *Nine* starring Antonio Banderas; *Never Gonna Dance* directed by Michael Greif; Boublil and Schonberg's *The Pirate Queen*; *The Play What I Wrote*; the Pulitzer Prize-winning *Proof*; *Puppetry of the Penis*; *The Real Thing* directed by David Leveaux; *Red Light Winter*; *Ring of Fire*; *The Smell of the Kill* directed by Mark Brokaw; *Monty Python's Spamalot* directed by Mike Nichols; *Steel Magnolias*; *Stomp*; Richard Greenberg's *Take Me Out*; *The Tale of the Allergist's Wife*; Pulitzer Prize-winner *Top Dog/Underdog*; *A Touch of the Poet* starring Gabriel Byrne; *True West* directed by Matthew Warchus; *Twentieth Century* starring Alec Baldwin and Anne Heche; and *Well*. Institutions Boneau/Bryan-Brown represents include Atlantic Theater Company, Broadway Cares/Equity Fights AIDS, Dodger Theatricals, LAByrinth Theater Company, Littlestar Services, Manhattan Theatre Club, the Roundabout Theatre Company, and Walt Disney Theatrical Productions. From 1991 to 2005 Boneau/Bryan-Brown's Broadway and Off-Broadway productions have won 98 Tony Awards, 5 Pulitzer Prizes, 75 Drama Desk Awards, and 52 Outer Critics Circle Awards.

A press agent's responsibility is to assemble information about a production, put it in a form that makes it clear and concise, and distribute it to as many people as possible at the appropriate time. This is much easier said than done.

Press agents don't just deal with the press. Yes, we speak to members of the press and give out press tickets, of course. But we're responsible for collecting all kinds of information, like biographies and background about the production, for dissemination quite often to the members of the company as well as to the press and he public. We are also responsible for keeping our producers informed about what is being said and written about their show and the environment around it.

We act as a clearinghouse—as a broker, if you like—of information about the show. A press agent is probably the one element of a production that has to be involved in

almost every aspect of the show, creative, business, and marketing. To do our job, we have to collaborate, in our own way, with everyone inside and outside the production.

LOOKING FOR SOMETHING NEW

I started out not realizing I wanted to be a press agent at all. I wanted to make movies. I had a degree in biology and I went to UCLA. Believe it or not, I often relate it to what I do today. Biology is the most artistic of the sciences: 1) It's the most exploratory. 2) It's so open to interpretation. 3) It's the least scientific of the sciences. Which I think is a great application for marketing and press because you're always looking for different things, looking for something new, looking a point of interest.

I was very lucky, as a kid, to go to school in England and live in New York. I went to a lot of theatre. I saw all the greats in the 1970s in the West End: Olivier, Richardson, Gielgud, all those big-name knights. At the same time I was very lucky to see *A Chorus Line* the week it opened in New York. I had a very schizophrenic—but lucky—background in commercial theatre that was also combined with a huge love of movies. My ideal day was to do a couple of movies in the afternoon and then see a stage show in the evening, and I was lucky enough to be able to do that.

At no point did I think of working in theatre. I fell into it. After a summer in Los Angeles I returned home to New York and somebody said to me, "Susan Bloch's office is looking for help. It's a press office." I didn't even know what that was, but I immediately found it a congenial place to work. I liked the communications, the minutiae in looking for a clipping, making the connection between putting out a press release and then seeing the result in print. The requirements of the job complemented all my skills and interests. I caught on very quickly.

Growing up I always kept newspaper and magazine clippings. If there was an article that interested me, about a movie or something I liked, I'd save it. I had an innate interest in the sort of things that are important for a press agent.

Susan Bloch had been the press agent for producer Jules Irving, who was producer of the Repertory Theatre of Lincoln Center, the first legitimate theatre company there. They had a pretty disastrous three or four-year run. The company had extraordinary people like Blythe Danner, Philip Bosco and such—all doing these amazing productions. But it never quite clicked. I joined her after that, when she was representing the Chelsea Theater Company and the Phoenix Theater Company, which are no longer with us, and, ironically, Roundabout Theatre Company, which has since moved to Broadway and is now a client of mine again. We did a lot of dance companies, too. I was suddenly immersed in Off-Broadway and dance, and I quickly learned the responsibilities of a press agent.

My job usually begins with a call from a producer. They'll generally call a press agent they've worked with before, or perhaps they'll call a number of press agents and talk to them about a project. Sometimes we'll hear buzz from London about a show, and we'll be very eager to do it. So we often initiate a call ourselves about an exciting production happening out of town.

Ideally this happens several years out, but quite often happens at the last minute. The producer will want to know if a press agent has a feel for the project, and if the press agent has a plan to describe their project to the world.

If you're meeting cold for the first time, even if you've gotten to read the script ahead of time, you're winging it, because you really don't know what the producer thinks about that show, except that it's their baby. It's very hard to read a new script and know exactly how to market the show, because if the producer brings along a genius director, or brings along an extraordinary designer or if the casting is phenomenal, a script that might not read so well can become amazing theatre.

At this very early stage, when all you have to go on is the script, all a press agent can do is inform the producer about what I call the "environment" for a project. That means, what people are likely to be thinking about when it opens, what other similar projects like this are happening, what elements make it sellable or interesting. We have to show them how, in that environment, our publicity campaign could work.

Every show opens in a unique media environment, and it can have a big impact on how a show is perceived. You have to be aware of what's going to be happening in movies around the time of the opening, what new TV series people will be watching, what's likely to be happening in publishing, what other stage shows will be around at that time.

You take this information into your "audition" with the producers. Sometimes you also meet with the creative team if it's particularly high-powered. If the director is very involved in the producing side, you'll meet with them too. Sometimes if it's a star-driven vehicle you'll meet with the star. Hopefully you know a year or so out that everyone is committed and you can start on the project.

Most celebrities and stars have personal press agents, which is very shrewd of them. When stars come to do Broadway they want to do it partly because they want to do theatre, but often also as a "positioning" step for them. There is a prestige to doing theatre, and they want it to be seen as doing it because they love the live experience—but they also want to get it done so they can get back into that $20 million movie salary. On the whole, I find that most personal press agents get it. They understand that this is a commitment to what is actually a very small community that generates a lot of media attention. If they are going to do it they need to really understand that. They need to know that there is an obligation to make sure their client goes out their and represents the show in the press.

Over the last twenty years the press has become a lot more aggressive in their interaction with celebrities, so it's a delicate game. The reason why a lot of celebrities don't talk to the press is because they feel they are fodder. And so the personal press agents have become very sensitive to that. We are playing a very defensive game, which can be misinterpreted as actually keeping information away. In fact it is protecting someone who is feeling vulnerable.

STARTING THE CAMPAIGN

There are two layers of education to a publicity campaign: educating the media, and educating the ticket buyer. They are different campaigns. You want the public to talk and buy tickets. You want the press to talk.

After hiring a press agent, the producer's next step is to choose an advertising agency. The ad agency buys ad space, often in newspapers, magazines, billboards, train stations, TV, radio, etc., to get the message out directly to the public. The press agent's job is to work with reporters and editors in the media to present Broadway shows as news, and to get coverage. We also deal with critics, but that comes later.

The campaign begins when producers decide they want to let the world know they are doing their production. We will put out a press release or call a key columnist or media outlet to outline the main points of the new show: its cast (if any at this point), its creators, and its subject matter.

Sometimes it's not just to create buzz, but to attract other investors in order to get the money to put a show on its feet. A producer may say "I want this announced but we don't have an opening date set, we don't have a venue (a theatre) booked, we just need to get the word out there."

It used to be that the priority was making sure you got some kind of a break in the *New York Times*' Friday theatre column. The industry people who mattered saw that as the "trade" column. If a producer announced there, you knew that every potential investor would see that. In recent years this has changed, and not just because the *Times* cancelled the Friday column. The trade angle has changed a lot. The prominence of Variety and the online news websites is now considerable. The reach of a story on the Associated Press is remarkable—literally hundreds of websites and small (and large) papers around the world. People interested in theatre today monitor sites like Playbill.com all the time.

Journalists used to be more dependent on the information we sent. If they wanted more information on a show, they'd have to trek to a library or make twenty phone calls. But now, a couple of clicks of the mouse and you can pull up all kinds of background on a show or a star or a writer. This can create problems, especially if the background material contains errors. An error in a previous report gets repeated and compounded. We spend a lot of our time now making sure that people not only have information but the correct information.

Another change is the luxury that a producer used to have in deciding when they were going to announce something. That has disappeared. The rumbling in chat rooms has the power to make something "real." Someone hears a rumor and posts it on the web. Next, a call will come into my office to ask, "Is this happening?" Our "no comment" or even denial will still register as a possibility. There's a lot more speculative reporting today. I'm fine about that, I suppose. But it certainly makes it a different game for a press agent and a producer. You have to adopt a different strategy. The problem we now have is trying to have fresh information to present all the time. If information is published too early, it's kind of played out. It's no longer news. Our job is to constantly suggest fresh news angles to keep the buzz going. I call it "liquid news," and we constantly have to stay on top of it.

There is a positive side, too. Broadway can be a very formal and stodgy industry. This constant focus and constant change has helped loosen things up incredibly. "Trade" news—news for people in the industry—used to be separate from consumer news. Now, the separation between the two is disappearing. The consumer is now plugged in, which is fantastic, really, because it conveys an excitement about what's happening on Broadway. But it's changed what we as press agents have to do.

RIPPLES

Once the word gets out, the ripples begin to spread.

A "look" for the show's image—the posters, the print ads, the commercials—is developed by the ad agency, with our input. When casting begins, we may be asked by the casting agency and by the producers for our opinion on certain actors—but only to the extent of what kind of a Q-rating (popular recognition) someone has. Will they be bookable on Regis? Will they be bookable on Letterman? What value, from a press point of view, do they have? Our advice helps set an expectation level for what kind of press kick they can expect from a casting choice. It goes into the mix. If someone is well-known enough to be "announceable" we will put out another press release saying so and so is joining the company.

If a casting announcement goes into one of the trade papers like Back Stage or Variety, immediately other journalists will call up and say, "We hear you are opening a new show. Is this true? What are the details? What exclusive angle can I write about?"

Now the "press" part of our "press agent" title really begins to kick in. If there are still important questions about the show, you start to get a lot of speculation in the press—which may not be something the producer wants. They may not want it known that they haven't fully cast the show. They may still be talking to some stars and don't want that confusion.

Sometimes a star's own agent will call up a columnist and try to build the impression that they are already cast. It's a pressure tactic. Sometimes they just want to get attention for their client, which is their job.

And we like to make announcements widely when we can, rather than in just one outlet.

MEDIA TRAINING

We have to be very reactive to inevitable changes in the environment around a show. We have to be ready if a cast member drops out, or a choreographer is fired. How you handle each of these situations and whom you tell is something you learn with experience.

Normally a show will rehearse in New York. Sometimes we'll invite the press in to see a bit of the rehearsal, get some interesting footage that we hope they'll use, and meet and interview some of the people doing the show. Pressure only increases in the coming weeks, so this may be the last time the cast and creative team can really focus on helping us do press.

The rehearsal event creates an awareness about the production in the press. It gives us a chance to help shape an image. We can say, "This is going to be a fun musical that will remind people of the great days of Broadway and will appeal to audiences from 8 to 88."

Our job becomes working with the creative team on shaping specific information about the production. And we are under a microscope from our clients. We hear immediately any time anything appears in the press about their show. Part of my job is explaining to the producer and management that we read everything, good and bad, but the consumers out there get only traces, if anything. That's why it's important to keep everyone "on message" about the show. Everything we put out there should have an educational goal.

When you send an actor into an interview, it's important that they know about who is interviewing them, and that they understand what they are supposed to be talking about. I don't mean that in a patronizing way. But if they are doing something controversial, they don't necessarily have to jump right into that. You give them talking points. I think of it as "Media training." It's not censoring. It's teaching them to think clearly and not get flustered by tough or manipulative questions. You go over what is interesting about the show and emphasize those points. Actors appreciate getting a little bit of a script. That's how they work. After that, it's like they're improvising, but on a theme.

Next, your show either goes right into previews, or heads for an out-of-town tryout. The challenge now becomes to convince the press that this show is *in development* and not fully formed yet. Without apologizing for your show, you try to promote an understanding that these are artists in the process of creating something. Our focus is to make sure that the show is judged for its merits rather than what's around it.

This is also the point where the stress level really begins to rise, rewrites are happening every day, personality conflicts emerge, we're pushing them to do interviews when they've been rehearsing a hundred and thirty-two hours a day, the producers run low on money and people get cranky. That's when everyone starts reading tea leaves. The slightest blip or negative comment in a column sends them haywire. It's our job to do some hand-holding at this point.

Back in New York, you get to the gypsy run-through, the final dress rehearsal and the first preview. These tend to be ecstatic. It's all friends and adrenaline, and everyone says, "We're OK!" This is dangerous, too, because the *second* preview lacks that adrenaline buzz and it lands on the counter like a dead fish. And suddenly, we're in panic time. "What happened!? Should we delay the opening?" Again, we do hand-holding.

A new element has been added in the last ten years. With the rise of the Internet, people start posting critical commentary from the very first preview. It means there is no room, from your first preview, for any kind of freedom to experiment. Once upon a time the previews were time to tweak a show and get it right. Now your show is judged from the first preview. It's a challenge for us in many ways, not the least of which is convincing the producers and the company that once you're up, that's it, the gloves are off.

THE LAST WEEKS

During the last weeks before opening night, it's our job to bring in a camera crew to shoot B-roll—video clips of a limited union-defined length—which are used for the TV news and other marketing purposes, like online clips on entertainment websites. We've also had photographers come, hopefully to a final dress rehearsal, to get production shots that show the actors in their costumes and on the set.

As the opening approaches, we start to field all kinds of questions from the press—sometimes nasty questions if there are rumors that the show is in trouble in some way. It's our job to put the best possible face on whatever situation may come up. While it's not true that all publicity is good publicity, the public *can* hear about all sorts of backstage misbehavior and it won't affect ticket sales a bit. It sometimes even helps. What you don't want to see in print is that the show is boring or that people will not, in some way, get their money's worth. That's death. So, as long as you answer questions in a way that shows how interesting the show is, you are doing your job.

On the last week before opening, the critics begin coming. The general public still has the image that critics go on opening night, then rush up the aisle to meet the deadline for the next day's paper. That scenario has been pretty much extinct for more than a decade. Late in his career, former *New York Times* critic Walter Kerr asked for more time to write a review, and he was allowed to come to one of the final previews. Since then, there's been an etiquette that people who review for overnight papers and overnight broadcast outlets are invited to come before the actual opening. So we now issue press tickets for the three or four performances before opening, in consultation with the director and the producers. Reviews must still be held until after the official opening night—a practice called an embargo. But even that courtesy is beginning to crack.

You lose something and gain something by spreading out the critics' performances. Once upon a time there was the adrenaline rush of having the critics mixed with producers' families and their friends coming on opening night. Now, you've got three or four performances that spread out the stress of having the adjudicators in. As a result, opening night is actually much more fun. It's a party, because everyone in the room is wishing you well—with sincerity! You still have the nerves of opening night because you're going to have to pick up the papers later that evening. Still, it's much more fun because there isn't that tension of feeling that half the room is out to "get ya'."

Thursday night is the best night to open because the review appears in the Friday papers, which generally allot more room for entertainment coverage. So the feeling is, you get bigger play in the Friday papers if you schedule your opening for a Thursday night. Of course, that's a double-edged sword. If you have a hit, everybody in the world sees the rave review. But if you have a flop, well, everybody sees that, too.

CROSS YOUR FINGERS

And so, at last, we get to opening night.

Quite often we know the tenor of most of the reviews. We don't know precisely, but we generally have a pretty good feeling about how it's going to go. We let our producers know, if they want us to. We don't let anyone else know. We feel everyone should be allowed to just enjoy that Broadway opening night moment.

That evening, while the show is up, we normally go back to the office and begin sifting through the early wire reviews to see what's there. We make sure the ad agency has copies because normally they're doing some kind of radio flight immediately. Even as early as midnight they'll have live copy going out to radio people in the tri-state area.

Around ten o'clock we will receive the *Times* review on our Blackberrys or on our email. Normally we will sequester with the producers and have a little discussion on how it went and maybe tell the director.

Back at the party, some of our people are still coordinating photographers and guests, and doing some press in the way of interviews and so forth.

But then nothing happens until the next morning when we, along with the ad agency, are responsible for collecting as many reviews as we can so the producers can put together some kind of quote ad. Normally this takes the form of a full-page (or larger) ad in the *New York Times*, but it can also be an email blast of some kind of ticket offer with quotes from the overnight reviews.

We also see that the front of the theatre gets decorated with some of those quotes. It's very expensive making those front-of-house pieces, putting quotes in the display cases in front of the house, and hanging the underslings, which are banners that hang down from the marquee. But it creates an atmosphere of excitement and is a permanent (for the run of the show) billboard.

Along with the ad agency we'll advise as to what is effective for how to play quotes from the reviews. It's easy, of course, when they're all good. But you can build a marketing campaign even if they're not unanimously great. Normally the producers have very strong opinions about that. The reviews appear on only one day, and are read mostly by people who are interested enough to look for that review. On the other hand, the producer can get his own message out every day in advertising. So it becomes my job and that of the advertising company and the producers to pick what's most appealing about a show, and get it out there to the public. The book or script may have been panned, but the lead actor may have gotten raves. So you get that actor's face in the ads and on the talk shows. Great special effects? Make sure they are front and center!!

KEEPING THE BALL ROLLING

If the press agent has done the job right, the noise of the opening will seem like part of an ongoing celebration of the show, not just one night. From the earlier feature articles through the reviews and then the follow-up articles, it should all just feel like one curve of news and information about a worthwhile cultural event—one that you've got to get tickets to.

If you have very bad reviews you have to be even more ingenious, more aggressive in finding particular angles. Not that you do any less when you get good reviews—it's just that people are less inclined to help you.

Whether the reviews are good or bad, the opening night is a trigger for many potential ticket buyers. Opening night stories accelerate word-of-mouth. So you need to try to keep the editorial flowing if you can.

Here's how we collaborate with ticket buyers. I believe potential ticket buyers have a kind of list in their heads—not only for theatre, but all forms of entertainment—even if they're not aware of it. They know that if they go to see a Broadway show, there's one they want to see. If a friend tells them a show is great, it moves higher on that unconscious list. If they see an excerpt they like on *The Today Show*, and it looks like people are clapping and having a good time, it can't help but move higher on that list. After the opening, my job becomes how to get my client higher on that list. Quite often we find ourselves saying, "OK, I can't get my client to that number one *Lion King* or *Spamalot* or *Mamma Mia!* slot. But those shows may be sold out. How can I get my client into that number two slot?

The awards season, culminating in the Tony Awards, gives us some great attention after opening night. But that's only one part of the year. We keep thinking: What can I do to make my show distinct from the competition? Is there a story on the director who has three other exciting projects coming up? Does the star have a pet charity? Should we create a great flyer to hand out on the TKTS line? Should we invite a columnist to have a part in the show? Later in the run you're faced with the task of making an older show still seem exciting. Is the third anniversary a sign the show is getting old—or that it's becoming a classic? You've got to constantly find new angles, create new buzz, and keep the ball rolling.

What gives me a real charge, as a press agent? When you book your actors on a talk show and the next day there's a big bump at the box office, you really feel you've had an effect. Two days later you still feel a sense of pride.

THE CHALLENGE

We have reached a very challenging period for the commercial theatre. We have created an environment where tickets can be bought at great discount, at the same time offering premium seating for hundreds of dollars. We are in danger of cheapening the product, especially for the avid theatregoer who we repeatedly offer the cheapest tickets to by e-mail and direct mail in an attempt to build an early audience. Out of financial necessity we've created a scenario where the perception for many (including the press) is that tickets for Broadway cost more than a hundred bucks, yet in reality many people don't pay that much.

We have a value perception problem. Industry-wide we are trying to address this. There are so many barriers beyond cost that have to be overcome. Many of these are way more perceived than real: that buying a ticket at the box office is an intimidating experience, which is why the majority of sales will soon be online; that getting to the theatre in Times Square is mentally traumatic for many people; knowing the dress etiquette in the theatre; being punctual; the time commitment made to see a two-act musical; uncomfortable seating; too few lavatories; etc.

My focus has to be on the particular production I am working on. To fill seats we will often make discount offers. We will do things to promote one show that are not beneficial for the industry as a whole.

Entertainment options today are extraordinary—interactive and participatory in a way that wasn't even dreamed of a decade ago. We have to reinforce the live communal experience that you can only find in a theatre. Theatre is truly live. Theatre is good medicine. Theatre is inspirational and cathartic. It's also really fun. This is not something you can convey in a TV commercial or a print ad—those are valuable reminders and signs to let you know what's out there and where it's playing. I do believe that passionate writing and intriguing broadcast stories can do more than that. Smart editorial accelerates word of mouth. Reviews, both good and bad, stimulate debate. Mostly the press can take away any stigma of Broadway being stuffy, old-fashioned and for the privileged, and remind us all that the theatre is a vital and relevant cornerstone of our culture.

INDEX

South Essex College
Further & Higher Education, Southend Campus
Luker Road Southend-on-Sea Essex SS1 1ND
Tel: 01702 220400 Fax: 01702 432320
Minicom 01702 220642

Practical Photography

Practical Photography

How to get the best picture every time

JOHN FREEMAN

ACROPOLIS BOOKS

DEDICATION
FOR MY MOTHER
AND IN MEMORY
OF MY FATHER

THANKS TO
LEEDS PHOTOVISUAL LIMITED
NIKON UK LIMITED
PUSH ONE LIMITED
THE STUDIO WORKSHOP LIMITED
TAPESTRY LIMITED
MORTIMER AND RHONA AT MANIQUE MODELS
MEL FOR HER MAKE-UP SKILLS

ACKNOWLEDGEMENTS

This book would not have been possible without the help and support of numerous friends, colleagues and organizations. In particular I would like to thank Joanna Lorenz, who saw it as a good idea, and Penelope Cream, my editor, who made it all happen, sometimes in circumstances when it appeared it might not! Also, Mike Morey for his design skills, my assistants Alex Freeman, Octavia Hedley-Dent, Kate Freeman, Luke Freeman, Sue Sharpe and a special thank you to Vanessa Ephson for being there.

Many thanks also to Isabelle Blondiau, Paul Cochrane, Stuart Davies, Jack Dooley, Melanie Ephson, Teresa Freeman, Roe Freeman, Frome Photo Centre, Samuel Greenhill, Sandra Hadfield, Lisa Haleran, Ami Hanson, George Heap, Dom Linell, John Mair, Yvonne and Luz Mosquera, Lorenzo Nardo, Theresa Neenan, Tarjit, Gurmeet and Jaspreet Parmar, Megan and Briony Plant, Denise and Lizzie Reynolds, Rikki Sarah, Meg, Jessica and Emma Simmonds, Jen Sherrin, Laila Walker, the Wapping Playgroup, Charlie Whiteside, Patrick and Rainbow Wiseman, David White and Carol Yun.

All photographs by John Freeman.

The photograph of the Palace of Holyroodhouse is reproduced by gracious permission of Her Majesty Queen Elizabeth II.

The illustrations for the video still camera and photocopying sections by Al Morrison.

This edition first published by Acropolis Books
Desford Road, Enderby,
Leicestershire LE9 5AD
United Kingdom

This edition exclusively
distributed in Canada by
Book Express, an imprint of
Raincoast Books Distribution Limited
112 East 3rd Avenue, Vancouver
British Columbia, V5T 1C8

Distributed in Australia by Treasure Press

Typeset by MC Typeset Limited
Printed and bound in Hong Kong

Photographs © John Freeman
© Anness Publishing Limited 1993
Boundary Row Studios
1 Boundary Row
London SE1 8HP
Reprinted in 1994

ISBN 1 873762 90 9

Editorial Director Joanna Lorenz
Project Editor Penelope Cream
Designer Michael Morey
Illustrator John Hutchinson

770 FRE

16955

CONTENTS

Getting Started

INTRODUCTION

Photography is probably the world's greatest hobby. It is difficult to imagine a family where at least one member of the family does not own a camera or has not appeared in a photograph. Even with the popularity of the video camera, nothing can compare to looking at a photograph which has captured for ever a moment in time. It was George Eastman, the founder of Kodak, who first made cameras at a price that increasing numbers of people could afford. The transition in terms of technology from those simple box Brownies to today's sophisticated 35 mm single lens reflex cameras is phenomenal. Yet even with these advances, the single most important factor behind a great picture is the photographer. With a basic knowledge of the principles of camera technology everyone can take full advantage of all that the art of photography can offer.

The question that professional photographers are probably asked most frequently is, 'What is the best camera I can buy?' Unfortunately there is no simple answer. Even though many people consider the Rolls-Royce to be the best motor car in the world, it is not suited to all uses: it would be at a distinct disadvantage in a Formula One race. In the same way, there are some cameras that some photographers consider the 'Rolls-Royce' of their kind yet it does not always follow that these are the best choice for all shooting situations. Undoubtedly the camera that has proved most popular is the 35 mm SLR.

The important aspects to consider when choosing a camera are application, variety of accessories and cost. The range of cameras available is wide, yet each type is very distinct in

its uses. Photographers should examine the different models and decide which might be the most suitable for their requirements. Ultimately, however, whichever camera is used, the elements that go to make up the final image will be those that the photographer brings to the camera, rather than the number of dials or knobs it has. Even a disposable camera can produce a good picture in the hands of an attentive and enthusiastic photographer who takes care with composition, gives thought to foreground and background, and notes the prevailing lighting conditions. Great shots can be achieved with even the most modest budget and a little technical knowledge.

The more money the photographer is prepared to spend, the more sophisticated the camera can be; usually

the different models will include autoexposure and built-in flash (although this may not always be very powerful), motor drive, zoom lens, autofocus, and automatic rewinding of the film back into the cassette when the reel is complete. Models at the cheaper end of the range have a fixed lens and focus limit so that bright daylight conditions are required. The more expensive models obviously expand the creative possibilities of the 35 mm camera, although even the basic models are reliable and will produce effective shots.

THE 35 MM CAMERA

The compact 35 mm camera (so-called because it uses 35 mm film) is an ideal

● The range of 35 mm cameras is enormous, from a disposable model, BOTTOM LEFT, through to the most sophisticated autometering and autofocusing types, FAR RIGHT.

model for those beginning photography or those who want a simple all-in-one with the minimum of accessories and adjustments. There is a vast range of different models within the 35 mm category. The simplest, and cheapest, will be a 'point-and-shoot' version without a built-in exposure meter or flash where the film is loaded and advanced manually.

THE SINGLE REFLEX (SLR) CAMERA

This camera is portable and extremely adaptable. Since its introduction approximately 50 years ago, the SLR (single lens reflex) has proved to be one of the most popular cameras available. The original design has now evolved into a multiplicity of models, the majority of which have a formidable array of lenses and accessories.

When you look through the viewfinder of an SLR camera what you see is what the lens 'sees'. This is because there is a mirror behind the lens that reflects the image up to a device called a pentaprism. This turns the image the right way up and the correct way round, and is situated on the top of the camera in front of the viewfinder. In normal conditions, when the shutter release button is pressed several functions operate in a fraction of a second. First the mirror flips up 45 degrees so that light can pass through the lens onto the film. The aperture you have chosen stops down. The focal plane shutter opens for the amount of time you have chosen on the shutter speed dial and then closes, then the aperture opens up to its full extent and the mirror comes back down so that you can view the scene again.

Using readily available 35 mm film, the basic SLR model can be adapted by the addition of all sorts of equipment, including telephoto or zoom lenses, motor drive and flash units. This means that it is the ideal 'system' camera; it can be adapted as quickly or as slowly as budget allows. An extra advantage to

the SLR is that the top-of-the-range models and accessories popular with professional photographers can be hired at specialist camera shops. In this way, a vast amount of equipment is available for minimum financial outlay.

THE RANGEFINDER CAMERA

This is another model of camera which has proved very popular with professional photographers. The most famous brand of rangefinder is the Leica; the French photojournalist Henri Cartier-Bresson shot nearly all his most memorable pictures using one.

In contrast to the SLR camera, the rangefinder allows the subject to be seen through a separate viewfinder rather than through the lens. In the centre of the viewfinder are two images. When the lens is focused on the subject these two images become aligned with one another and the picture will then be sharp. This method of working is preferred by some photographers who find that the camera is quieter to operate and is less prone to being affected by vibration as there is no mirror to flip up. Although the rangefinder does not have quite as wide

a range of accessories as the SLR, it is a sturdy and reliable camera with extremely high-quality lenses. The rangefinder is available in 35 mm or medium format models.

THE SLR MEDIUM FORMAT CAMERA

These cameras come between the 35 mm and the large format cameras in size and application. They take pictures in a variety of formats including 6 × 4.5 cm, 6 × 6 cm and 6 × 7 cm. These cameras have extensive ranges of lenses and accessories and are much favoured by professional photographers. They are much bulkier than 35 mm cameras and are usually used on a tripod, although they can be hand-held. They are the only cameras that use 120 or 220 ISO film, available in roll or cassette form.

THE 5 × 4 CAMERA

This is a large format, tripod-mounted camera which takes photographs where the transparencies or negatives are 5 × 4 in (12.5 × 10 cm). The film is loaded into dark slides, each one holding just two sheets. There is no viewfinder in the conventional sense: the image is seen upside-down and back-to-front on a ground glass screen. In order to see the image and keep out any stray light the photographer covers the camera and his head with a dark cloth. Despite the rather old-fashioned appearance of the camera, many models are in fact brand-new, extremely sophisticated and can be very expensive.

The range of applications of the 5 × 4 camera is very varied both in the studio and on location. It produces pictures with excellent clarity and sharpness of detail. However, it would

● Medium format and large format cameras, such as the 5 × 4 in, FAR RIGHT, are generally favoured by professionals.

not be the best choice for spontaneous or action shots where a more portable camera with speedy shooting capability might be more suitable.

THE INSTANT AND POLAROID CAMERA

Instant picture cameras such as the Polaroid offer another dimension to picture-taking. After the picture is taken, the film is impregnated with the chemicals required for processing the image and the picture begins to appear only seconds after the shutter is pressed; development is complete within minutes. As well as providing an immediate image of the subject, these cameras also offer as many possibilities for creative photography as their conventional counterparts. Many professional photographers attach special Polaroid backs to their standard cameras; once they have composed the image and calculated the exposure they will take a Polaroid picture to ensure everything is perfect before shooting on conventional film. Polaroid backs are available for all cameras from 35 mm size to 10 × 8 models.

THE VIDEO STILL CAMERA

The video still camera is a relatively new type of camera; it uses a computer disk instead of conventional film and the pictures can be viewed on a television screen or video monitor, or sent away to be made into prints. Although still in its early stages, this form of photography could change the nature of picture-taking in the future.

Just as there is no one camera that is ideal for every shooting situation, the same is true of lenses. Some lenses in certain situations have distinct advantages over others. An extra element of challenge can be added to photography by experimentation with different lenses, perhaps applying a particular lens to a situation in which it is not normally used.

LENSES FOR 35 MM SLR CAMERAS

Most 35 mm SLR cameras are purchased with what is known as a 'standard' lens. This has a focal length of about 50 mm and will give an angle of view roughly equivalent to what we see with our own eyes. Its maximum aperture in the region of f1.8, but faster lenses such as f1.4 and f1.2 are

available. At a later date one of these faster lenses could prove useful.

LENS MOUNTS

All SLR cameras have interchangeable lenses, attached to the camera by means of a mount. There are several different sorts of mount, the most popular being the bayonet mount. This is operated by depressing or sliding a small button positioned on the camera body near the

lens. The lens can then be turned 45 degrees in a clockwise direction and pulled gently forward from the camera body, and another lens inserted using the reverse procedure.

CHOICE OF LENSES

Interchangeability of lenses opens up a

● A selection of zoom and telephoto lenses.

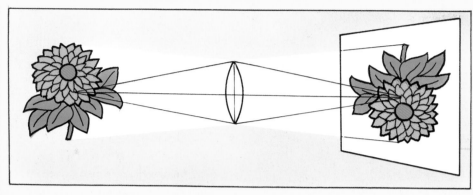

• ABOVE The subject is reproduced through a lens upside-down on the film.

vast array of options and is probably the biggest single factor in improving photographic creativity. Having chosen a camera and standard lens, it is advisable to consider purchasing two other lenses at the same time or very shortly after. These would probably be a wide angle lens in the focal range of 28–35 mm, and a telephoto lens in the 85–135 mm range.

WIDE ANGLE LENSES

A wide angle lens gives a wider angle of view, so more of the area in front of the camera will appear in the shot. Like any piece of equipment there are disadvantages as well as benefits; the

• Wide angle and medium telephoto lenses.

most common in the case of the wide angle lens occurs in landscape photography where the foreground may lack interest so the eye is not naturally led to the central point of the picture.

On the other hand, a wide angle lens allows subjects to be photographed much closer to the lens than usual, while at the same time keeping the background in focus. In some cases this effect can greatly enhance a composition.

TELEPHOTO LENSES
A medium telephoto lens has many advantages. As well as bringing distant objects closer, it is a superb lens for portraits. It has definite advantages over a wide angle lens in this situation as, when used straight onto someone's face, a wide angle lens will add an unflattering, albeit at times amusing, bulbous quality. A telephoto lens in the region of 100 mm enables the photographer to stand some distance away, making the subject more relaxed and allowing an unblocked light source. The lens will very slightly compress the image, making for a far more pleasing portrait. The depth of field will be less, so the background can be put out of focus and a part of the subject's face, such as the eyes, can be highlighted.

ZOOM LENSES
Many photographers find these lenses very convenient; they give the benefit of being adjustable to an infinite variety of focal lengths which can make composition of pictures much easier. Although in a technical sense a zoom lens will not produce the same quality as a prime lens of a given focal length, under most conditions the difference will be apparent only to an eagle eye.

Depending on the type of photography that is of interest, wide angle and telephoto lenses that are of a very extreme range have limited applications and can easily be under-used; their purchase should therefore be considered very seriously.

FISHEYE LENSES
A fisheye lens can be used to dramatic effect, but as an everyday piece of equipment it has limited applications and its novelty value can quickly wear off.

● Ultra-telephoto lenses.

A MACRO LENS

The macro lens allows the photographer to get very close to the subject without the need for special close-up attachments. Depending on the lens used, small objects can be magnified to produce a final print which shows them life-size. Many of the lenses mentioned here in the 28–300 mm range have this facility built in and it is often worth considering paying a bit extra at the outset if this is of interest.

SHIFT OR PERSPECTIVE CONTROL LENS

The shift or perspective control lens allows photography of a subject that is very tall, without the problem of converging verticals; this occurs when the sides of the subject taper toward the top of the picture. The conventional rule for preventing this from happening is to ensure that the film plane is parallel to the vertical plane of the subject and then all vertical lines will remain straight in the final shot. However, with a fixed lens the top of a very tall subject is usually cut off, but with a shift lens the axis can be altered, allowing the camera to remain straight while the lens is moved upwards: the top of the building will then come into view.

● Fisheye, ultra-wide angle and macro lenses.

● BELOW By using a shift, or perspective control, lens, as opposed to moving the camera, subjects such as tall buildings can be perfectly framed.

◉ ACCESSORIES

There are many accessories that can be added to a basic camera unit when building up a comprehensive 'system'. It is important to bear in mind that no accessory on its own is going to provide a magic formula for improving photographic skills. Accessories lend technical help, yet it is the photographer's eye for seeing a good picture that is the essence of photography.

A UV FILTER

Having decided on and purchased the camera, the next thing to buy is an UV filter. This can be kept on the lens at all times, whether you are using colour or black and white film. As well as reducing the amount of ultraviolet light passing through the lens (cutting down haze and minimizing the risk of a blue cast appearing on the film), it will also protect the lens itself. It is much cheaper to replace even a good quality glass filter if it gets scratched than a scratched lens. Consider buying a UV filter for each lens.

As well as the UV filter, there is a whole selection of special filters and holders available. These range from colour correction and colour-balancing filters to special effect filters and masks.

THE LENS HOOD

This should be bought at the same time as the camera. Look at any picture of professional photographers at work and they will all be using lens hoods. The hood prevents most stray light from entering the lens. Stray light causes flare and can ruin the picture. It may be caused by sunlight falling directly into the lens or being reflected off a building or shiny surface. If you are in any doubt as to the necessity of a lens hood, next time you are walking or driving into the sun, notice how you need to shield your eyes from the light with a hand or

the sun visor in the car. A lens hood works in exactly the same way for the camera lens.

A TRIPOD

A tripod keeps the camera steady during shooting at long exposures. To be effective the tripod must be rigid. Some tripods are very flimsy when fully extended so it is often well worth paying a little extra money for a truly sturdy model. Tripods are

available in many sizes from the smallest, which are about 15 cm (6 in) high, to much larger, heavy-duty models which can extend to well over 3 m (10 ft).

Some tripods come complete with all attachments; others need a head, the part that fixes the camera to the tripod. Heads can vary and it is important to look at several before making a final choice. The most common type is the 'pan and tilt' head which allows the

● A combination of accessories aids the able photographer to enhance shots, and to be more versatile in a variety of situations.

adjusted to different heights. Obviously, a monopod will not stand unaided but it can be used to help brace the camera. Professional photographers at a football match, for example, nearly always use a monopod.

A Cable Release

A cable release can be attached to any camera which allows it to be screwed into the shutter release button; when the plunger on the end of the cable is depressed it fires the shutter without the need for any direct manual contact. It is often used in conjunction with a tripod when shooting at slow speeds to reduce the vibration that often occurs when the shutter is released manually.

Some cable releases are now available for SLR cameras. When the cable is depressed half-way the mirror-up mechanism is activated. Any vibration that occurs when the mirror goes up is then eliminated by this intermediate stage in the shutter release process. When the cable plunger is depressed fully the shutter is fired and the camera remains steady.

A Carrying Case

A case to carry all the accessories is convenient and also provides protection for equipment. The most effective cases have hard outer shells, and compartments moulded from foam rubber to hold the individual accessories. Soft cases are also available but these may not be suitable for very delicate items. Many cases are obviously meant for carrying cameras; this attracts thieves, so do lock them out of sight if left in a car. Insuring expensive photographic equipment is becoming increasingly costly; if you think that you may have to leave equipment in a locked vehicle, make sure that the insurance policy covers theft from cars.

camera to be moved smoothly through 360 degrees – the 'pan' movement. At the same time it can be adjusted vertically; this is usually in the range of 90 degrees forwards and 45 degrees backwards – this is the 'tilt' movement. (If an angle of 45 degrees is not sufficient, turn the camera round and use the head back-to-front.)

Another useful head is the 'ball and socket' version. Normally this has two knobs that allow the camera to be

moved when fixed to the tripod in much the same direction as the pan and tilt head, yet is far less cumbersome.

A Monopod

Since many tripods are often bulky, some places such as churches, buildings of historical interest and museums do not allow their use without a permit. One solution to this may be to use a monopod. As its name suggests, it consists of a single leg which can be

Flash guns

Ring flash

*F*LASH *A*TTACHMENTS

Most SLR cameras do not have built-in flash so it is certainly worth purchasing a flash unit to attach to the 'hot shoe' or accessory shoe on the camera. Some are quite compact but are nevertheless sophisticated and powerful.

The more powerful flash units are mounted on a bracket that is screwed into the base plate of the camera, and linked to the flash synchronization socket on the camera by means of a cable. When the shutter is activated a signal is sent to fire the flash.

*E*XPOSURE *M*ETERS

Although most cameras now have some sort of built-in mechanism for evaluating exposure, a separate hand-held exposure meter is very useful. Basic photoelectric meters need no batteries and register the amount of light available. Although reliable, they are not as powerful nor as sensitive as the battery-powered meters; many of these can be used as flash meters as well as for reading ambient light.

Bellows

Flash and ambient
light meter

Set of extension rings

Battery-powered
exposure meter

Photoelectric meter

In ambient light mode, they can be used to take incident light readings as well as reflected light readings. An incident light reading is taken when the meter is placed on or near the subject and pointed towards the light source to take a reading. A reflected light reading is taken when the meter is directed at the subject from the camera position.

It will take a little practice to be able to evaluate the various benefits of the different types of reading.

EXTENSION RINGS OR BELLOWS

These are used in conjunction with SLR cameras and allow close-up photography of detail in stunning clarity. Close-up lenses can be used for the same purpose but extension rings give a far better result.

The rings or bellows are attached to the body of the camera on the lens mounting; the lens is then attached to the front of these. The rings offer a single magnification whereas with the bellows the magnification is variable.

CARE OF EQUIPMENT

Cameras and lenses are delicate and expensive instruments that need to be treated with care. Water, dust, dirt and grit are the worst enemies, although leaving a camera in bright sunlight or in the glove compartment of a car will not do it any good either, and so any strong heat should be avoided. If the camera is taken to a sandy beach, keep it wrapped in a plastic bag when not in use. Even on the calmest days sand seems to get into every crack; extra care needs to be taken as sand can easily ruin expensive equipment.

When a camera is not in use it should be kept in its case or together with the other pieces of equipment in a proper camera case. If it is not going to be used for some time the batteries should be removed; if left in the camera they may corrode the contacts and cause irreparable damage.

LENSES AND FILTERS

Always keep a skylight UV filter on the lenses. This will keep out UV light and will help protect the lenses themselves. This filter can be kept on the lenses permanently, with either colour or black and white film. A scratched filter is cheaper to replace than a damaged lens. If the filter or lens becomes dirty first blow away the dust and any other particles of dirt. The most efficient way of doing this is to use a pressurized can of air. Many of these products are ozone-friendly and do not contain CFC propellants. Alternatively, use a soft brush with a blower attached to it. If neither of these pieces of equipment is available, simply blow gently onto the surface. The next stage is to remove any grease by gently wiping the lens or filter with a soft lens tissue or lens cloth.

If something jams in or on the camera and the fault is not apparent never force the piece, as more serious damage could be caused. If the lens or camera develops a serious fault send it

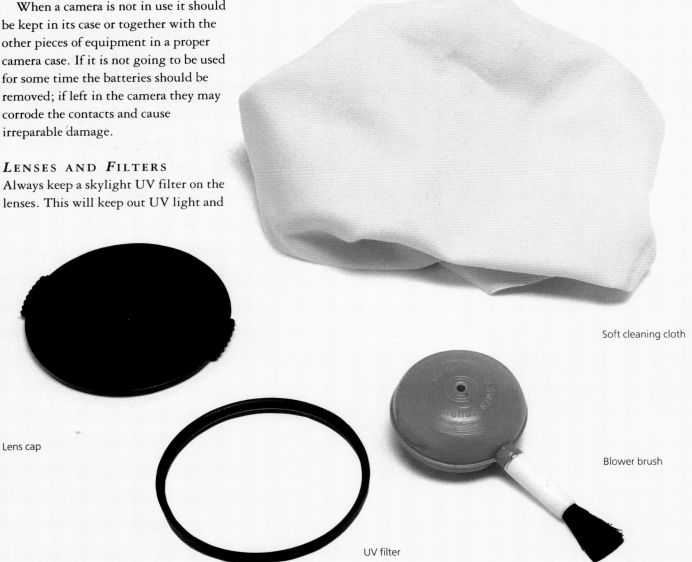

Soft cleaning cloth

Lens cap

UV filter

Blower brush

to a reputable camera repair shop. If it is still under guarantee, return it to the dealer or direct to the manufacturer.

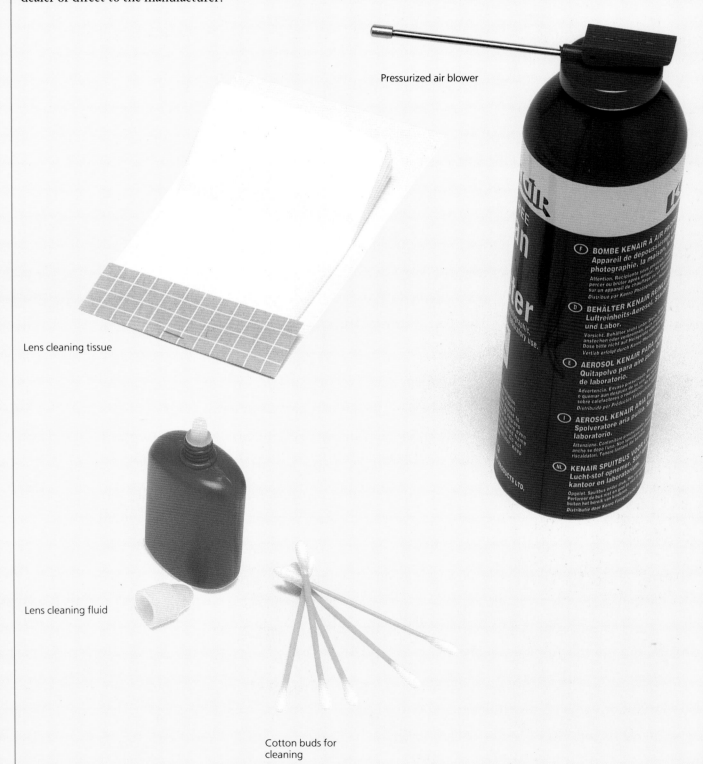

Pressurized air blower

Lens cleaning tissue

Lens cleaning fluid

Cotton buds for cleaning

Negatives and transparencies form an archive of images, preserving memories and moments forever. A visual diary of children can be built up from birth. These children may well have children of their own, and even grandchildren. What better way of seeing a family's development, a history of its background, even the country it has come from, than in a series of photographs? If all the negatives have been kept in good condition, then future generations can assemble a fascinating visual family tree.

It is only too easy to mislay colour negatives and transparencies. This can be a great pity; if prints are destroyed, or friends or relatives would like copies of pictures, others can always be produced from the negatives. While it is possible to reproduce an image from an existing print the quality will not be as good.

STORAGE OF NEGATIVES

Negatives are returned with prints in a wallet. If they are dated and catalogued properly these provide a perfectly adequate storage system. The wallets can be filed in a drawer with a simple log of what they are. Alternatively, special negative storage filing systems are available; these consist of double-thickness plastic or paper sheets with pockets or channels for holding the transparencies. The sheets are then stored in binders or hung from metal rods in filing cabinet drawers.

STORAGE OF TRANSPARENCIES

If they are mounted as slides, transparencies can be stored in slide boxes, grooved to take a mounted slide, with an index for cataloguing the pictures. If the slides are for projection, they can be kept in a slide projector magazine or tray. These have dust covers and can be indexed as before.

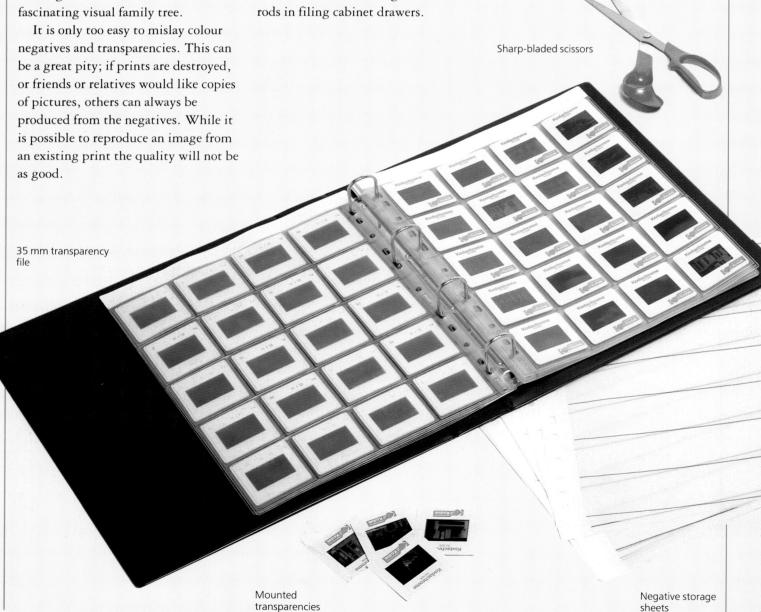

Sharp-bladed scissors

35 mm transparency file

Mounted transparencies

Negative storage sheets

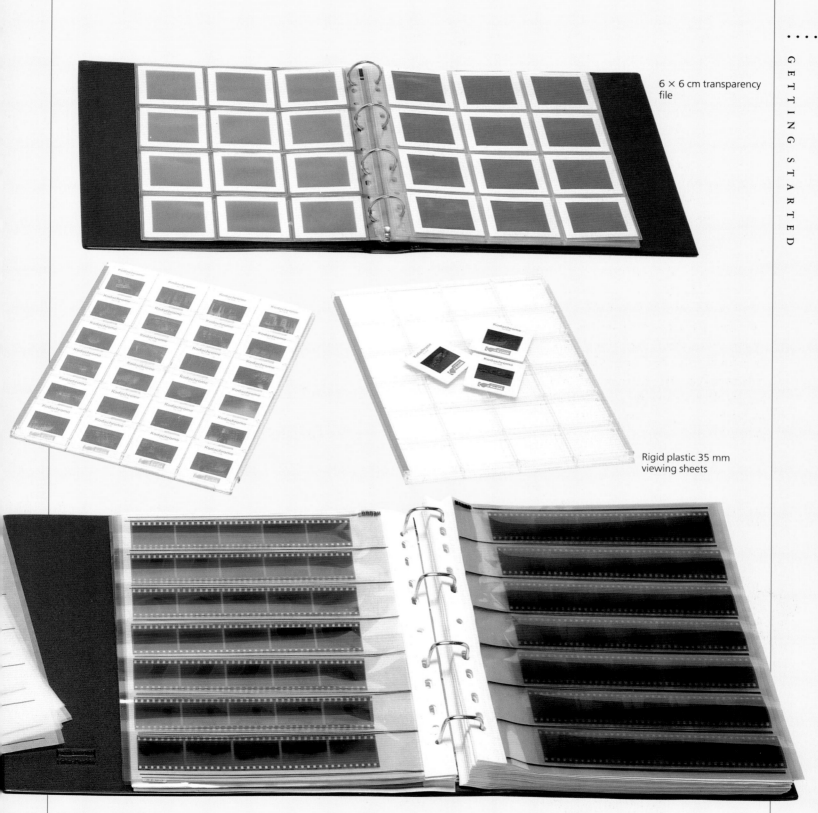

6 × 6 cm transparency file

Rigid plastic 35 mm viewing sheets

Negative storage file

There are two main types of colour film used.

● Colour reversal film produces transparencies that can be mounted as slides and projected or viewed with a slide viewer or on a light box. Transparencies can also be made into prints, either directly, or from what is called an internegative, which involves photographing the transparency onto the other kind of film, colour negative film.

● Colour negative film is the type used to make prints.

Most professional photographers use colour reversal film, whereas most amateurs prefer colour negative.

Both types of film come in a full range of sizes, from the small 110 up through 35 mm to 10 × 8 in (30 × 20 cm) sheet film. They also come in various speeds. These are given as an ISO (International Standards Organization) number from about 25 for the slowest up to 1600 and beyond for the fastest. The slower the film, the finer the grain and sharpness, and the greater the colour saturation and contrast. 1600 ISO film can be uprated to 3200 ISO and more for work in low light but the result will be very grainy – an effect which may be sought deliberately.

UPRATING FILM AND DX CODING

Uprating, also called speed readjustment, means using film as if it had a higher ISO rating than it actually does, and so shortening exposure time. Uprated film needs a longer development time, and if you uprate any film you must let the laboratory know that you have done this so that they can 'push', or extend, development. Some laboratories charge extra for handling uprated film. Generally only colour reversal film is uprated since the processing for all colour negative films is the same. However, a few colour negative films are now made in such a way that they can be uprated.

35 mm film is now DX coded: this means that the film cassette has a bar code on it. Nearly all new cameras have tiny sensors that read the code and automatically change the camera's ISO setting to the appropriate speed. If you

want to uprate the film you should buy bar code override stickers to put on the cassette. Alternatively, if your camera has an exposure compensating dial, you can adjust this to uprate the film. In either case you must inform the laboratory of what you have done.

LIGHTING

There are two types of colour reversal film: one for daylight and electronic flash, the other for tungsten light (ordinary lamps). If daylight film is used in tungsten light the shots will come out very warm, with an orange and red glow to them. If tungsten-balanced film is used in daylight the pictures will have a blue cast. Although both these films are made for the specified lighting

conditions there is no reason why they should not be used in different lighting to create a special effect. Either of them can also be used with a light-balancing filter. Using an 85B filter, which looks orange, on a camera allows tungsten film to be used in daylight or with electronic flash to get a normal colour balance. An 80B filter, which is bluish, allows daylight film to be used in tungsten film with normal results.

Until recently there was only one kind of colour negative film which was used in both daylight and tungsten light. Any colour cast was corrected at the printing stage. However, there are now several colour negative films available that are made specifically for use in tungsten light.

ACCURATE EXPOSURE

Exposure needs to be far more accurate for colour reversal film than for colour negative because the transparency is the final result. With colour negative film any inaccuracies in the negative can be corrected at the print stage. Where accuracy is required it is a great help to make a test with an instant film such as Polaroid so that any adjustments can be made on the spot.

INFRARED FILM

You might also like to experiment with infrared film. This gives unusual though unpredictable results, quite different from the colours we normally see. For example, foliage becomes magenta and pale skin tones green.

Over the last two decades shooting in colour has become the norm in photography, and amateurs have almost abandoned black and white. This is a great pity, for many colour photographs would look better in monochrome. Some of today's best known photographers, such as Steven Miesels, Herb Ritts and the late Robert Mapplethorpe, are famous for their work in black and white, and exhibitions and books of their work consist almost entirely of black and white prints.

Undoubtedly most people relate immediately to a colour photograph, which is hardly surprising as we see the world in colour. Therefore any colour image is relatively acceptable, while an image in black and white has to be spot on for it to get the attention it deserves. Another reason for the neglect of black and white is that the film is now almost as expensive to buy and more expensive to process than colour. It also takes longer to process: you cannot get your prints back in an hour!

Unlike colour film, which has negative and reversal types, black and white film is almost always negative. There is no need to worry about colour balance, as black and white film can be used under any lighting conditions. It comes in speeds from very slow, such as 25 ISO, to ultra-fast at 3200 ISO – and even this can be 'push processed' to increase the speed still further. Slow film gives very fine grain and good shadow detail, and pictures can be enlarged with little loss of quality. In contrast the faster films are generally very grainy and the shadow detail inferior.

BLACK AND WHITE FILM

When black and white film is processed it is usual to make a contact sheet. This means that, for instance, a 36 exposure roll of film is cut into six strips of six negatives. These are placed on a 10 × 8 in (30 × 20 cm) sheet of printing paper to make a positive print. On this contact sheet you select and mark the negatives you want to have made into enlarged prints. In making this selection you can ask for unwanted parts

of the negative to be cropped out — draw the area you want on the contact sheet as a guide. You can also ask the printer to angle the masking frame, which holds the printing paper in place on the enlarger, to tilt the picture. This can often improve the overall composition. Some laboratories can produce enlarged 'contacts' which give a better idea of how enlargements will look. The whole film is printed on a 16 × 12 in (40 × 30 cm), 20 × 16 in (50 × 30 cm) or 24 × 20 in (60 × 50 cm) sheet.

Prints can be ordered in different finishes, from matt to glossy. Paper types include resin-coated, which has a plastic surface that gives faster development, needs less washing and

dries faster than the traditional type. The older fibre-based paper, which gives a more subtle effect, is favoured by photographers for exhibitions and portfolios. On both these papers you can have toned prints. Sepia is the best known tone, but there are others. Some are more suitable for fibre-based paper, others for resin-coated. You can also hand colour your prints. This old technique is now enjoying a revival. It calls for special colouring media.

SPECIAL BLACK AND WHITE FILM

Black and white slides for projection are made on special 'positive' black and white film. There is also black and

white instant film, made by Polaroid. Infrared black and white film gives unusual results: pictures taken in daylight look like night scenes. This film should be tested before you use it in earnest, to avoid unexpected results.

FILTERS FOR BLACK AND WHITE

Although you do not need to use light balancing filters for black and white film, some coloured filters can add interest to your images. For example, a yellow filter will darken a blue sky and make the clouds stand out sharply. A red filter will exaggerate the effect: even a blue sky with white clouds will look positively stormy.

THE HUMAN EYE AND THE CAMERA

We see the world in colour, so it is hardly surprising that most people tend to load their cameras with colour film. Even before the invention of colour film black and white prints were toned or sometimes hand coloured to add realism.

Technical improvements in colour film have made it possible for everyone to get a reasonably exposed photograph. But exposure is not the only element of a successful colour image. In the same way as a painter controls the colours on his palette, the way we combine colours in photographs, and juxtapose different and complementary hues, plays a vital role in achieving a successful image.

THE HUMAN EYE AND FILM

The colours we see are reflected off the objects we look at. The light that falls on these objects constantly changes, and with it their colours. Daylight is warmer – that is, redder – at the beginning and end of the day than at midday. Weather also changes the quality of daylight. On an overcast day we see colour as cooler – bluer – than in bright sunshine. Hazy sunlight gives muted colours. However, the most important element in colour vision is not the eye but the brain. If we know that a jacket is a particular shade of red we will see that shade of red at any time of day, in any weather, and even indoors under artificial light – ordinary tungsten bulbs throw out a light strongly biased towards the orange and red end of the spectrum, and give colours markedly different from those produced by sunlight.

Film reacts differently. When we move indoors from daylight our vision adjusts to the change in light quality. But if we load a camera with a film made for use in daylight, and use it to photograph the red jacket first out of doors then indoors under tungsten light, the first shot will look about right but the second shot will have a strong orange cast to it. If we use film balanced for tungsten light, the indoor shot will look fine but the outdoor one will be skewed towards the other end of the spectrum, with a blue-violet cast.

It is important to understand how our eyes record colour, and how colour film does it, and to experiment with these effects, in order to create successful colour photographs.

● The juxtaposition of varied coloured images produces a startlingly vibrant collage of contrasting and complementary shades and tones.

SEEING IN BLACK AND WHITE

Taking photographs in black and white is a most rewarding exercise. It is sad that most people today would not dream of putting anything other than colour film in their cameras. Undoubtedly this is because they want their photographs to record the way they remember a particular scene. Yet the absence of colour in a black and white photograph can make a far more striking interpretation of that scene. And since black and white imagery is an interpretation rather than a mere record, the onus is on the photographer to create a picture through the use of texture and tone; these are important considerations in colour photography, but in black and white they are paramount.

If you have two cameras, try loading one with black and white and the other with colour. When you compare your prints you might be surprised at the power of the black and white images.

TONAL RANGE

The tonal range from black through various shades of grey to white is known as the grey scale. Professional photographic stores sell charts of these scales called step wedges, which can be used to analyse a photograph. A black and white print where most of the tones are from the extremes of the scale —without any mid-tones — is referred to as a high-contrast print. If these tones are mostly towards the white end it is called a high-key picture. A picture where most of the tones are near the black end is a low-key print. One that uses the full range of tones is called a full-tone print.

One of the great exponents of black and white photography was the American Ansel Adams. His landscapes combine stunning composition with a powerful grasp of tonal range. They are worth studying.

● ABOVE This picture emphasizes the soft, velvety appearance of the girl's skin. She is lit using a single studio flash unit fitted with a large diffuser or soft box. As its name suggests, this gives a very soft and even light. The picture was shot on the same film, 100 ISO, as was used for the image of the older man.

● LEFT By shooting this ship-building dock threatened with closure in black and white, the mood is emphasized much more than it would be in colour. The print was deliberately made darker to reinforce this image of despair.

● LEFT This studio picture shows a good tonal range. The black at the extreme end of the scale is rich and even, and the mid-tones show a well-defined gradation. The lines and wrinkles of the man's skin are enhanced by the use of black and white. One main light was used to the right with a fill-in light on the other side. A light above the head was used to illuminate the hair. The shot was taken on 100 ISO film.

● BELOW If you are in doubt as to whether a shot should be in colour or black and white and you have two cameras, shoot both as here. The black and white print was deliberately printed on a hard paper to bring out the contrast in the grass. Both shots were taken with the same wide angle lens within minutes of each other.

PROCESSING YOUR FILM

Once you have taken your photographs you will want to see the results as soon as possible. Many places now offer film processing and claim that they give a unique and professional service; but in fact often the film is collected and sent to a central processing laboratory. Here each film is given a computer identification code and they are all joined together in one huge reel like a movie film. The films are processed and printed in rapid succession, the prints cut up and put in wallets, and back everything goes to the shop where you handed in the film.

This sort of processing does not produce results of very good quality, nor is it consistent. If you send the same negative to be printed at the same laboratory several times, the chances are that each time it will come back with a different colour cast. In order to obtain the best results with expensive equipment, or when you have taken the greatest care in composing and exposing your pictures make sure the processing laboratory is a good one.

THE PROFESSIONAL WAY

A professional photographer, especially one who uses colour reversal film, has a close relationship with the technicians at his laboratory. The laboratory will maintain the highest standards, simply because if it does not, photographers will not use it any more.

A professional laboratory can clip test film: before the technicians process the whole film they will cut off the first few frames and process them. You can then check these and ask for adjustments to the rest of the batch. They can adjust the processing in increments of as little as $\frac{1}{8}$ of a stop (one stop is equivalent to the difference between f8 and f11, or between exposure times of $\frac{1}{60}$ and $\frac{1}{125}$ second).

Of course, for this to be worthwhile the film must be consistently exposed, and where the film is cut one or two frames will be lost. There is also a small extra charge for the clip test on top of the cost of processing the rest of the film. Kodachrome Professional film is bought with the processing paid for, but even this can now be clip tested and settings adjusted as necessary.

HOME PROCESSING

The more adventurous can buy home processing kits for both colour negative and colour reversal film, and also for black and white. You do not need to have a fully equipped darkroom to process film. Apart from the equipment in the kit all you need is a processing tank – these come in various sizes, depending on how many films you want to process at once – and a light-tight room or cupboard where you can load the film into the tank. Once this is done, the rest of the process is carried out in normal light, though of course you have to go back into the dark to make prints.

PUSHING AND PULLING

If a film is underexposed, for instance if it is uprated, it needs to be given a longer than normal development time. This is called 'pushing'. Overexposed film is 'pulled' by being developed for a shorter time than normal. These techniques are common, but they should not be used where they can be avoided because both of them cause a certain loss of picture quality: the harder a film has been pushed or pulled, the greater the loss. There is no substitute for getting your exposures spot on.

ENLARGED PRINTS

Again, a professional laboratory will give you substantially better enlarged prints. You will be able to discuss how you want your picture cropped and positioned on the masking frame of the enlarger. If a transparency that is to be printed has a colour cast you can ask for this to be corrected. You can even have particular areas of a negative or transparency shaded or printed up to darken or brighten them. This can be important if there is a large discrepancy between the tones in highlighted areas and shadows.

● Colour or black and white, transparency or negative – after you have taken your shots, good processing is essential.

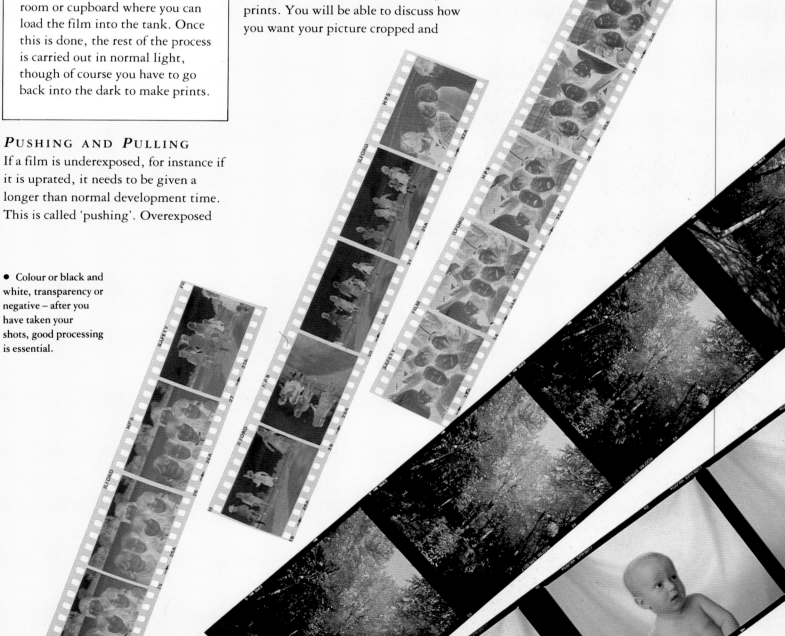

WHAT THE APERTURE DOES

There are different sized apertures on a camera to allow different amounts of light to pass through onto the film. When the shutter is released it allows light to pass through the aperture. It is necessary to have a shutter as well as an aperture because the aperture controls depth of field as well as contributing to the exposure of a film.

The correlation between shutter speed and aperture size is a direct one; the immediate situation or the effect required dictates the necessary combination of shutter speed and size of aperture. If, for instance, an exposure of $\frac{1}{15}$ second and an aperture of f22 are needed, the aperture would get wider as the shutter speed increases

e.g. $\frac{1}{30}$ second   f16
        $\frac{1}{60}$ second   f11
        $\frac{1}{125}$ second   f8

DEPTH OF FIELD

The depth of field is the distance in front of and beyond the sharply focused subject of the picture. With a standard lens set on its widest aperture of f1.8, for example, and a subject 2 yards (1.8 m) from the camera, very little of the background and even less of the foreground would be in focus. However, if the lens is stopped down and the aperture is set to f16 or f22 much more of the background and foreground will be sharp.

With a wide angle lens depth of field will be greater even at wider apertures than it would be with a telephoto lens.

Depth of field plays an important part of the creation of a finished photograph. If, for example, the subject of the picture is a head and shoulders portrait of a person, yet with a distracting or unattractive background, it can be the depth of field that can be altered to put the background out of focus so that the person is the only clear part of the shot. If, on the other hand, the background is important or the subject is a group of people or objects at different distances from the camera where each one must appear sharp, a small aperture is needed. A small aperture would bring more of the picture into sharp focus.

AUTOMATIC CAMERAS

Some automatic cameras have a system called aperture priority. When the aperture is set the camera automatically adjusts the shutter speed. Care must be taken in cases where the chosen aperture is quite small, e.g. f11 or f16, as the shutter speed selected may be too slow to take an accurate shot without the steadying aid of a tripod or other support.

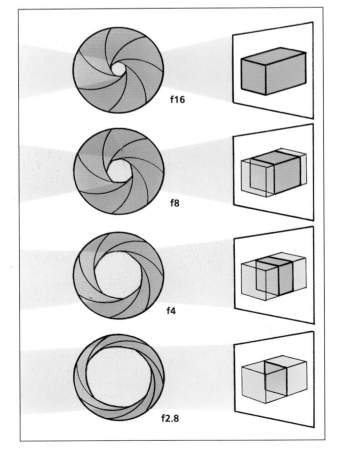

● LEFT There is a direct correlation between aperture size and depth of field. As the aperture decreases, more of the subject is in focus.

- This picture was taken using a standard lens at an aperture of f2.8. The girl is in focus and so is the front arm of the seat but everything else is out of focus.

- In this picture a medium telephoto lens was used and focused on the girl. Depth of field is minimal at an aperture of f4.5.

- In this picture an aperture of f8 was used. More of the seat and background are sharper but the distance is still unclear.

- Using the same telephoto lens an aperture of f11 has been used but the background still remains very soft.

- Here the lens was stopped down to f22 and all the seat is sharp and the far distance is only slightly soft. By reducing the size of the aperture more of the picture is brought into focus i.e. the depth of field increases.

- With the lens stopped right down to f32 much more of the picture is in focus, yet it is not as sharp as in the first picture. Depth of field is greater with wide angle lenses than it is with telephoto lenses.

WHAT THE SHUTTER SPEED DOES

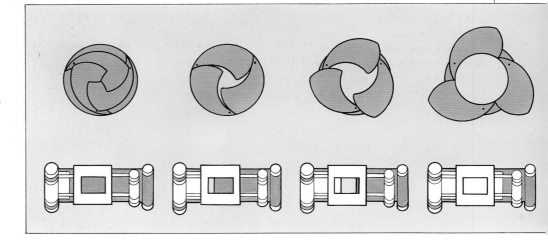

● BELOW A leaf shutter (top) and a focal plane shutter (below) in the process of opening.

The opening of the shutter of a camera determines the amount of time light is allowed to pass through the lens onto the film. As well as affecting exposure, the shutter speed can also freeze a moving object as a sharp image on film and reduce camera shake.

PORTRAYING FAST-MOVING OBJECTS

For hand-held shots it is virtually impossible to hold the camera completely steady at shutter speeds of ⅟₃₀ second or less without mounting the camera on a tripod or bracing it against a solid support, such as a wall.

Imagine a car or a person passing quickly across a chosen viewpoint. If the shutter speed is set at ⅟₆₀ second or less the moving object would appear blurred on the photograph. However, if the shutter speed were ⅟₂₅₀ second or more the moving object would be clear, 'frozen' in action. In the case of the car, it can be difficult to tell whether it is moving or stationary; this may result in a dull picture. A better way to illustrate action is to use a slower shutter speed and 'pan' the camera, following the moving object and taking the picture when it is directly in front. This type of photography may take a little practice to perfect but it produces striking images where the background is blurred and the moving object sharp, illustrating very effectively the speed at which it was travelling.

USING FLASH WITH SLR CAMERAS

With SLR cameras the shutter speed should be set to the manufacturers' recommended setting when using flash. This is usually ⅟₆₀ or ⅟₁₂₅ second. If a faster speed is used, only part of the film will be exposed as the flash will fire before the blinds of the shutter have

● LEFT Shutters at various stages of opening. TOP A leaf shutter. BOTTOM A focal plane shutter.

● BELOW When using flash with a camera that has a focal plane shutter it is important to set the camera at the manufacturer's designated speed. This might be ¹/₁₂₅ second, for instance, or there might be a flash symbol on the shutter speed dial for this. If the speed used is in excess of this setting, only part of the frame will be exposed.

● BELOW LEFT In this picture the camera was mounted on a tripod and a slow shutter speed, ¼ second, was used.

● RIGHT When a long exposure is required, in this case 20 seconds, the shutter was set to the T setting. This meant that when the shutter was fired it remained open until it was depressed again. If the camera only has a setting on the shutter speed dial marked B, the shutter release has to remain depressed.

fully opened. With cameras that have a leaf shutter or a shutter between the lens the flash can be synchronized to any speed. This is a great advantage in situations where flash has to be balanced with daylight.

B AND *T* SETTINGS

On some shutter speed dials there are two settings marked B and T. When the shutter ring is set to B the shutter will remain open for as long as the shutter release button is depressed. If it is set to T, the shutter will remain open even when the shutter release button is released, closing when the button is depressed again. Both these settings are for use with pictures that require a long exposure.

*A*UTOMATIC *S*HUTTER *S*PEED *S*ELECTION

Some automatic cameras have metering modes called shutter priority. This means that when the shutter speed is adjusted manually the camera selects the aperture automatically.

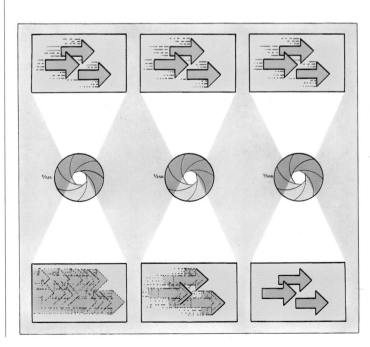

● LEFT If the camera is moved in line with a moving object and a shutter speed of ¹/₆₀ second is used, the object will remain sharp but the background will be blurred. This technique is called panning.

● LEFT By contrast, a shutter speed of ¹/₂₅₀ second was used to photograph this bird in flight, and it has 'frozen' virtually all movement.

Most cameras today have built-in exposure metering systems. These should enable the photographer to get the correct exposure every time. However, in many situations the metering system is led astray by the general level of light, so that the subject of the photograph is over- or underexposed. This is because many systems take an average reading of the illumination over the whole frame. If you are photographing a person against a white wall, or if there is a lot of sky in the frame, these big light areas will have the greatest influence on the meter. Unless you compensate for this the person will come out underexposed, in extreme cases reduced to a silhouette. Conversely, if you place a person against a dark background the metering system will read mainly for this area, and if you do not make an adjustment the person will come out overexposed.

THE AUTOMATIC EXPOSURE LOCK

This problem can be resolved by using the camera's automatic exposure lock. This sets itself when the shutter release is lightly pressed. It holds the current exposure setting until the release is pressed to fire the shutter, or until the button is released altogether. So you can go up close to your subject, take an accurate reading from their flesh tones, hold down the shutter release and go back to your chosen viewpoint for the

● ABOVE Bracketing exposures lets you make slight variations in exposure that may make all the difference to the final picture. In this case the difference was ⅓ of a stop between each one. Here, TOP, the meter gave a reading that has slightly underexposed the girl, making her eyes look heavy and dark.

With the aperture increased slightly, MIDDLE, the skin tones are more natural and the shadowiness of the eyes has been eliminated.

A further increase in the exposure has made the facial features begin to burn out. So the picture on the BOTTOM would be chosen for the final print.

composition. If you want to take several shots you will have to follow the same procedure for each one.

SPOT METERING

If your camera has a variable metering system, you can use spot metering in such cases. This restricts the meter to measuring the light falling on a small spot in the centre of the viewfinder.

USING A HAND-HELD METER

There are two main ways of taking a reading with a hand-held meter:

● For a reflected light reading, point the meter at the subject and take a reading of the light reflected from it.

● For an incident light reading, place a small white disc, or invercone, over the meter cell. Some meters have a white blind which can be slid over the cell. Hold the meter against the subject and point it back towards the camera. This gives a more accurate reading of the light falling on the subject.

BRACKETING

Another way of getting the correct exposure is to bracket. For example, imagine that the metering system is giving a reading of ¹⁄₁₂₅ at f8. If you take one shot at this setting, one slightly over it and one slightly under, when the film is processed you can judge which exposure has worked best and make a print from that negative.

● ABOVE The camera meter took an average reading. As there was so much sky, which even on a dull day is bright in comparison to other areas of the picture, the girl has come out underexposed. ABOVE RIGHT Going in close and using the camera's exposure lock has given a truer reading of the flesh tones and a far more flattering exposure.

● RIGHT Spot metering has given an accurate exposure of the girl. If your camera does not have this feature you will have to use the exposure lock or a hand-held meter.

GENERAL COMPOSITION

Cameras are becoming increasingly sophisticated with their built-in exposure metering systems, and it would seem to follow that the photographer has more time to concentrate on areas such as composition. However, this is often not the case. Unwanted intrusions confuse and distract the eye; backgrounds that are irrelevant or dominating overpower the foreground, and foregrounds that should lead the eye into the picture either occupy too great an area or appear merely because of incorrect framing. All these faults can be corrected with very little effort and only minimal preparation.

● ABOVE Even when a photographic opportunity occurs by chance, it pays to take time to consider the general composition. Here the chess board fills the centre of the foreground and the two subjects are positioned on either side, creating a perfect balance. The scene captures a particular image of society, especially with the inclusion of the third man in the background; although not deliberately arranged, the three people and the juxtaposed chess board have become key elements in the final photograph.

● ABOVE This nutseller is the centre of interest and as such occupies the middle position in the shot. Do not be afraid of placing the subject in a prominent position within the frame of the picture. Here the subject sits among a display of his wares; this helps draw the eye towards him yet also around him as more and more items become apparent. Always retain an even balance between the subject and his surroundings.

● ABOVE This very simple shot has all the ingredients of a good composition. The foreground is uncluttered, and the pathway leads from the foreground directly to the centre of interest, the house. The house is set against a backdrop of small hills, which do not overpower the house but provide a contrast and add interest by breaking up the uniform stretch of blue sky.

THREE KEY AREAS TO BE CONSIDERED IN COMPOSITION:

1 The centre of interest – having decided what the central subject of the photograph is to be, ascertain where the photograph is to be shot from to achieve the most effective background.

2 Possible distractions or intrusions – examine carefully the subject, background and foreground to ensure the picture will not be spoilt by an unwanted object. It is only too easy to mar a beautiful building with a traffic sign in the foreground, or to produce a portrait of some friends complete with a telegraph pole emerging from the top of one of their heads. Usually an intruding object can be removed from the composition simply by moving slightly to one side. It is worth waiting for any moving vehicles to pass by.

3 Enhancing the foreground – it is important to decide if there is anything that might add to the foreground without detracting from or obscuring the centre of interest.

USING FOREGROUND

Foregrounds can play an important part in the general composition of photographs. A point of interest in the foreground close to the camera can be used either as a framing device or as a tool to lead the eye into the picture. This type of added interest can make all the difference between the exciting and the mediocre.

USING FOREGROUND AS A DISGUISE

Foregrounds can also be used to hide untidy objects or unwanted intrusions in the middle or background of the picture. However, it is important to make sure that the foreground does not dominate the picture as then it will detract from the main subject of the photograph, becoming as much of an intrusion as the detail it is attempting to disguise.

OBJECTS IN THE FOREGROUND

Although objects in the foreground of a picture can add interest, it is all too easy to let them appear with monotonous regularity. This is a danger with a series of pictures taken from similar viewpoints, yet can be easily avoided with a little thought. Take time to evaluate what is in front of the camera; use all the components to their best advantage in the final shot.

When objects are included in the foreground care must be taken with the exposure. Check to see if the objects are in shadow compared to the central portion of the shot and background as this may produce an ugly dark shape with no detail visible. If the shadow is unavoidable try correcting it using a reflector or fill-in flash.

Also check to see if the camera needs to be higher than the object in the foreground. If not, make sure the object is not filling too much of the frame.

● LEFT This picture of a formal garden has been enhanced by the use of the foliage of the outer trees as a framing device. The gates at the bottom of the frame complete the foreground interest. The result gives the impression of peering into a 'secret' garden. If the camera had been positioned further forward and the foreground lost, the picture would have looked entirely different.

USE OF PERSPECTIVE TO CREATE FOREGROUND INTEREST

Additional foreground interest can be created by the use of perspective, for example the furrows in a ploughed field stretching out into the distance. In this case, a low viewpoint might be best. When taking a landscape shot the sky can often be a dominating factor so that the landscape scene itself is overpowered. If this happens, perhaps the addition of a tree with overhanging branches within the shot could frame the top of the picture and diminish the impact of the sky.

• ABOVE Foreground objects do not always need to be placed dead centre. Here the boat is in the bottom right-hand corner of the frame and creates an added degree of foreground interest. The colour of the boat complements the colour of the lush green grass without providing too harsh a contrast. If a picture of this sort is to be part of a series, try to vary the position of the object in the foreground so that it does not become a dull motif, detracting from the shots themselves.

• ABOVE The strong lines of the strata shoot out from the foreground and pierce the sea, leading the eye straight into the picture and creating a powerful composition. If the photograph had been taken from a position at the end of the rocks, the foreground would have been merely a dull stretch of sea with no added interest.

• ABOVE Not all historical buildings are always at their best – as here in Reims, France, where the cathedral was covered in scaffolding. Added to this the early-morning sun rose behind the cathedral and since there was no time to wait for the sun's position to alter a viewpoint was found some distance from the front of the building. A telephoto lens, 200 mm, was used and by having as a framing device the trees in the foreground the untidy scaffolding was concealed and the direct sunlight was blocked.

USING BACKGROUND

The background of a picture can enhance the overall composition of an image in ways similar to the effects of the foreground. As a general rule, backgrounds should not dominate the photograph, obscuring the main subject. This jars the eye and gives an overall impression of a cluttered photograph. Similarly, a flat, dull background can influence the whole picture so that all interest is lost. A telephoto lens can produce a compressed image, bringing the background forward and reducing the depth between the middle- and foreground.

The weather can create dramatic effects; if dark clouds are hanging in the sky watch out for isolated bursts of sunlight which can spotlight areas of the foreground, underexposing and making the dark areas even darker.

When taking a shot of an apparently tranquil landscape, check to see if there are any roads or tracks running through. If there are, wait until traffic has dispersed as an unsightly track can ruin an otherwise beautiful scene.

G E T T I N G   S T A R T E D

• ABOVE LEFT The cows form an almost monochromatic background to this picture. The track that comes down to the gate balances the picture and enhances the general composition, yet nothing detracts from the young girl. Her bright raincoat and hat are set off by the black and white cows, and the juxtaposition of her diminutive size alongside the cows adds a subtle touch of humour to the shot.

• ABOVE RIGHT The ever-burning flame of this oil refinery on the banks of the Mississippi at New Orleans relieves an otherwise dull background. It also provides a powerful contrast with the more traditional technology of the old paddle steamer in the foreground. It always pays to be alert to pictures where the back- and foregrounds provide not only a visual contrast but can also make a wider abstract statement in visual terms.

• RIGHT This picture was taken using only the available light coming in through a small window and with an exposure of ⅛ second, bracing the camera against the bar. It is a clear example of how the background can provide information about the subject while at the same time adding extra interest and detail.

• LEFT This salmon fisherman is holding a putcher, a funnel-shaped basket used to catch salmon as they swim out to sea. The stakes stretching out behind echo the mood of the putcher, and convey a greater sense of the man and his work.

KEY POINTS TO NOTE ABOUT BACKGROUNDS:

1 Is the background overpowering? Will it overshadow the subject of the picture? On the other hand, does it have enough interest to prevent it from being dull?

2 Does the background behind a human subject represent anything about the person's work or environment?

3 Are the background colours harmonious or unusual in some way? A telephoto lens can push the background out of focus, throwing up some interesting shapes and muted colours.

4 Does the sky appear in the background? If there are any clouds, try to retain their clarity and detail, perhaps by using a graduated neutral density filter or polarizing filter, or a yellow filter with black and white film.

CHOOSING A VIEWPOINT

There are many situations when taking a photograph where a simple alteration of viewpoint can make all the difference. Viewpoint can be defined as the position from which a photograph is taken, and takes into account the background and foreground, and any interesting angles that will lead the eye naturally towards the emphasis of the image. By using different viewpoints the photographer can dramatically alter the impact of a picture.

Often people will say to a professional photographer something along the lines of, 'But you've got all the equipment!' In fact, all that it takes to achieve a better view is a little thought of where one should stand and how the foreground can be utilized to the greatest effect. On many occasions it may be possible to utilize detail in the foreground by either tilting the camera downward or by moving slightly to one side. These small shifts of position or angle, that may seem insignificant at the time, can produce the difference between the dramatic and the dull.

● BELOW The choice of lens is important for the composition of a picture.

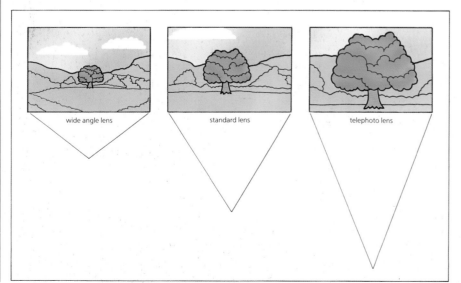

wide angle lens   standard lens   telephoto lens

● ABOVE AND INSET Viewed individually there may seem little to choose between these two pictures of Brooklyn Bridge. The shots were taken within 46 m (150 ft) of one another and within a short space of time. The upper picture was taken from further away than the lower one; much of its impact is lost by the inclusion of too much sky at the top of the frame, and the cloud is an added distraction.

The lower picture was taken from much nearer to the bridge using a slightly lower viewpoint. This means that the verticals have converged to a greater degree than they would have done had the shot been taken from a higher position, and the tension cables fill the frame, fanning out in all directions to draw the eye into the shot. The cloud has been cropped out which extends the symmetry of the shot; with fewer distractions the graphic qualities of the composition are enhanced.

EASY ESTIMATING

To help judge your choice of viewpoint, simply form a rectangle between the thumbs and forefingers of both hands, and look through to judge your chosen image.

To tighten the 'frame', slide the right hand closer to the left, keeping the rectangle steady. In order to create a 'zoom' effect, extend your arms so that the background is removed and the

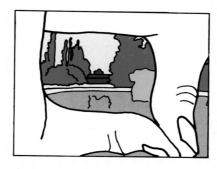

subject of the picture appears larger in relation to the rectangle.

● ABOVE Standing close to one element of a photograph can add extra emphasis. The viewpoint for this picture was created by standing close to the canyon wall that appears on the left. The dramatic sweep of the wall and its horizontal strata lead the eye straight into the picture. If taken from a different position or angle the effect would have been weaker.

● RIGHT By tilting the camera downward the lilies on the water are brought into the picture. This provides extra interest in the foreground without detracting from the mountains and sky beyond. If the camera had been horizontal or tilted upward slightly, without including the lilies, the result would have been a rather dull stretch of water and reflected cloud in the foreground.

Daylight colour film, as its name suggests, is for use with daylight-lit subjects or with electronic flash. If daylight film is used indoors where the main source of illumination is provided by domestic light bulbs, the resulting pictures will have a predominantly orange cast to them. This is because what is known as the 'colour temperature' of the light source would be at variance with the colour balance of the film.

COLOUR TEMPERATURE

Colour temperature is usually measured in values of kelvin. To achieve the correct balance when using daylight film in artificial light of 3200 kelvin requires the use of an 80A filter. This is a blue-coloured filter which corrects the orange cast that is otherwise created. However, the blue-coloured filter is quite a dense filter and will cut down the amount of light passing through the lens onto the film; to compensate for this, 64 ISO film must be rated at 16 ISO. Care must be taken when adjusting for these factors as a long exposure is needed – yet most daylight-balanced colour film suffers from reciprocity failure at exposures of 1 second or longer.

When you expose daylight-balanced colour film for exposures of longer than approximately 1 second, the film will suffer from reciprocity failure i.e. where the stated ISO rating no longer applies. An example of this is where a 100 ISO film may only be 25 ISO at an exposure of 10 seconds. Owing to the unpredictable nature of the film in these circumstances, the only sure way of getting the right exposure is to test the film in the prevailing light conditions to see what ISO it should be rated at.

When using tungsten-balanced colour reversal films and the few tungsten-balanced colour negative films available these problems are solved. There is no need to add a filter to the camera when shooting in situations where the colour temperature is 3200 kelvin, and tungsten-balanced film can be used at far longer exposures than daylight film without suffering from reciprocity failure.

If daylight-balanced colour negative film is used in tungsten light it can always be corrected at printing stage. If daylight-balanced colour reversal film is used in tungsten light without an 80A filter the resulting transparencies would have to be duplicated and corrected at the printing stage. This is expensive, and, however good the duplicates are, some of the quality will inevitably be lost.

● TOP LEFT If daylight-balanced colour film is used in artificial light the results will have an orange cast. To correct this imbalance an 80A filter needs to be used, TOP RIGHT. Alternatively, tungsten-balanced film used in artificial light does not require a colour-balanced filter.

● BOTTOM LEFT Using tungsten film in daylight or with electronic flash will result in pictures with a blue cast. To correct this, use an 85B filter, BOTTOM RIGHT. As an alternative, use daylight-balanced film in daylight or with electronic flash as this does not need a colour-balanced filter.

● ABOVE When shooting in artificial light it is often necessary to use long exposures. This picture required the shutter to be open for 30 seconds. Since the lighting was tungsten, tungsten-balanced colour film was used. Apart from the fact that it rendered the colour correctly, tungsten film suffers far less from reciprocity failure than daylight-balanced film.

average tungsten light   average daylight

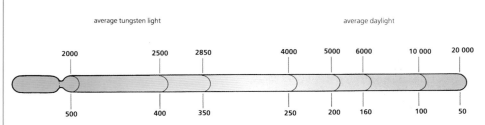

2000	2500	2850	4000	5000	6000	10 000	20 000

| 500 | 400 | 350 | 250 | 200 | 160 | 100 | 50 |

● LEFT Light is measured in values of kelvin. The measurements change according to the type of light, from warm to cool.

51

SHOOTING IN MIXED LIGHT

Occasionally there are situations, especially indoors, when the light comes from many different light sources. These light sources may all have different colour temperatures, so using just tungsten-balanced film or filtering daylight-balanced film to 3200 kelvin may not be adequate.

FLUORESCENT LIGHT

One of the most difficult lights to balance is fluorescent light. This is because there are many different types of fluorescent light tubes ranging from cool to warm white. When a tube wears out it might be replaced with a tube of a different colour temperature. To the naked eye, all the tubes may look the same yet they are in fact giving off different temperatures of colour which makes choosing the correct filter very difficult.

DAYLIGHT MIXED WITH ARTIFICIAL LIGHT

Sometimes with two different light sources, such as tungsten light and daylight or fluorescent light and daylight, the only practical solution may be to expose for the greater light source. A more elaborate method – when shooting in a room lit by tungsten light with windows that let in daylight – is to place light-balancing material over the windows to convert the daylight to the same balance as the tungsten light.

In mixed light situations that combine daylight with tungsten, the warmth of the tungsten light can add a mellow tone. If the situation is one which combines daylight, tungsten and flash, the trick is to make all of these elements balance. The best method to achieve this is to work out the exposure for the daylight coming in through the windows. For example, it may be 1 second at f16. If so, adjust the power of the flash to give an exposure of f16. (Shooting at speeds slower than the flash setting on the camera will not alter the flash exposure; this will only happen if a faster speed is used than is recommended for the camera.) Set the shutter speed to 1 second and take the shot. At this exposure tungsten light (coming, for example, from a table lamp) will be recorded without causing an unnatural colour cast.

● ABOVE In the TOP shot daylight predominates and the picture comes out well on the daylight film in the camera. BOTTOM, using the same film and pointing the camera down to a small area of the building lit by tungsten light without the use of an 80A filter has created a definite orange cast.

● LEFT This picture, taken outdoors at dusk, shows several different light sources but because of the expanse of the picture and its varied elements it appears correctly exposed even though the lights have differing colour balances.

● ABOVE This picture of the famous food halls of Harrods in London is a good example of a mixed light situation: the ceramic well set into the ceiling is lit by fluorescent lighting yet the rest of the store is lit by tungsten. In the time available it was impossible to put colour correction gels over all the fluorescent tubes so a compromise had to be reached. Since the fluorescent light was illuminating an isolated area, the whole shot was exposed for tungsten.

● FAR LEFT This museum room has fluorescent light as the dominant source which has given the shot a green cast. LEFT An FLD (fluorescent daylight) filter removes this and adds a natural tone.

USING FLASH

Flash has become as commonplace as the cameras that use it. It provides a convenient, renewable, instant and often adjustable extra light source. Some cameras have built-in flash while other models take flash unit attachments. Professional photographers use large free-standing flash units for studio work yet excellent results can be obtained with less expensive equipment.

BUILT-IN FLASH

Built-in flash is very convenient, yet like any piece of equipment it has its drawbacks. The flash tends to be rather weak and any subject beyond approximately 10 ft (3 m) will be underexposed. The output of the flash may be constant and no adjustment available; the disadvantage of this is that anything very close to the flash will be burnt out. The most common problem is that of 'red eye'. 'Red eye' occurs when the flash is fired near the axis of the lens. If a shot is taken of a person looking at the camera, the flash will bounce off the retina of the eye and produce a red spot in the final picture. The remedy is to move the flash away from the axis of the lens. This cannot be done with built-in flash. If the flash is of the type that flashes several times in quick succession when the shutter release button is depressed, finally firing at full strength, the pupil of the eye contracts so that there is less of the retina from which the flash can be reflected and it does not appear red.

SEPARATE FLASH UNITS

Separate flash units may be more powerful than built-in flash. They are attached to the camera hot shoe or to a special bracket and sync lead. Many units have heads that can be angled upwards to varying degrees so that the light can be bounced off a ceiling or

● TOP LEFT Using a flash gun attached to the side of the camera creates a harsh light with a shadow to one side.

● BOTTOM LEFT Placing a diffuser over the flash softens the shadow but it is still quite obvious.

● TOP RIGHT By moving the flash even further to one side the shadow is accentuated.

● BOTTOM RIGHT By bouncing the light off the ceiling the shadow on the wall has been eliminated, but at the expense of a shadow under the chin.

other pale material. If this type of angled flash is used for a portrait the light will be softer but might result in dark shadows under the eyes, nose and chin. These can be avoided by using fill-in flash.

FILL-IN FLASH

A built-in fill-in flash unit is positioned under the main flash attachment. When the flash is fired on 'bounce mode' with the fill-in flash, 80 per cent of the power passes through the main flash while the remaining 20 per cent goes through the fill-in unit. This removes most of the shadows from under the eyes, nose and chin. Another method of softening flash light is to diffuse it. This can be done very simply by placing a small cloth such as a handkerchief over the flash, or even by holding a piece of tracing paper just in front of the flash itself.

● TOP LEFT Sometimes daylight is not enough even though a built-in meter may advise you to the contrary.

● BOTTOM LEFT Fill-in balanced flash helps eliminate the problem by bringing the exposure required for the person to the same level as that required for the background.

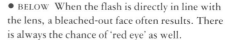

● BELOW When the flash is directly in line with the lens, a bleached-out face often results. There is always the chance of 'red eye' as well.

● LEFT By bouncing the flash in this picture and using a fill-in flash as well a more acceptable picture is achieved.

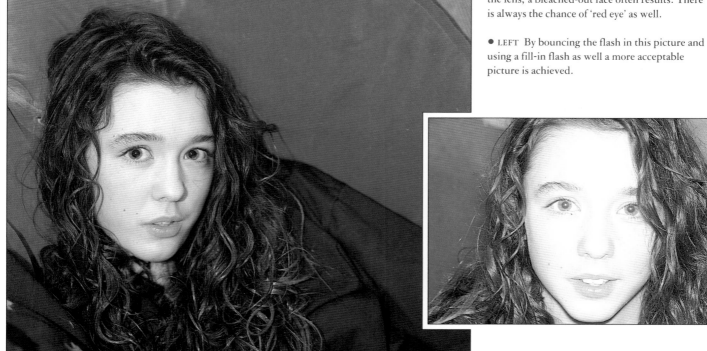

USING WIDE ANGLE LENSES

Additional lenses are the accessories that will probably do the most to improve your photography. A wide angle lens offers you a completely different perspective on a traditional view. Not only will its wider angle of view get more into the picture, but it also has a greater depth of field than a normal or telephoto lens, so that more of the shot will be sharp.

You can have an object relatively close to the lens and still keep the background in focus. If the object is close enough it will look much larger in proportion to the rest of the picture than it really is. With extreme wide angle lenses, distortion can be a problem and you should not photograph people from too close in, to avoid unflattering results. For instance, a 21 mm lens pointed directly at someone's face will make the nose look enormous, the cheeks puffed out, and the ears as if they have moved round towards the back of their head. This might be fun at first, but the novelty will soon wear off and it will be time to turn to more serious applications.

● ABOVE The impact of this shot relies on the feeling of the 'big' landscape. The wide field of view gives a feeling of overwhelming space and loneliness. The lines marked on the road exaggerate the already strong perspective and give the impression that the road goes on endlessly.

● RIGHT Using a low viewpoint with a wide angle lens makes it look as if the windmill sails are soaring into the sky. The great depth of field offered by the lens makes the whole picture sharp even though the bottom of the sail is quite close to the lens. It is very important to choose the correct viewpoint when using a lens of this kind.

● LEFT A drought has dried up this lake, exposing an old tree stump. Again, the wide angle lens keeps the whole picture sharp. Placing the stump at one side of the frame gives it an almost living quality, as if it is walking towards what remains of the lake.

● RIGHT When photographing people, take great care to avoid unflattering distortion. In this picture, although the hands and arms are distorted this is within tolerable limits and does not unbalance the composition as the viewpoint and angle of the shot have been carefully chosen. Although the arms look long and the hands, which are closest to the lens, enormous, the imbalance is acceptable because the strong hands represent the nature of the fisherman's work. His arms lead the eye straight to his face, which is framed in turn by a backdrop of his working environment. The busy background keeps the eye from dwelling too long on his hands so that, large as they are, they simply appear to be part of the composition.

USING TELEPHOTO LENSES

Telephoto lenses do much more than just bring distant objects closer. They can greatly enhance general composition. Their shallow depth of field can blur the background in a portrait to isolate and emphasize the subject. In contrast to wide angle lenses, going in close to people has a positively flattering effect. This is because a telephoto lens slightly compresses the picture so that prominent features such as the nose and ears stay in proportion. Careful use of a telephoto lens can also help to cut out unwanted foreground clutter, allowing you to get to the heart of the picture.

EXPOSURE AND APERTURE SETTINGS

Some compensation has to be made in settings when using a telephoto lens, especially a long one. This is because the magnifying effect of the lens spreads the available light out more thinly, and the longer the lens the greater the effect. With cameras that have TTL metering this is no problem, but a manual camera will have to be adjusted.

Telephoto lenses also tend to have smaller apertures than normal or wide angle lenses, so that exposure must be longer. There are exceptions: some of the latest telephoto lenses have apertures as big as f2.8, but these lenses are very expensive, and few amateur photographers will consider that their usefulness justifies the price. If you need a fast long lens for a particular shot it would be more sensible to hire one.

USING A TRIPOD

The image made by a telephoto lens shifts very rapidly when the camera is moved. This fact together with the long exposure time may call for the use of a tripod or monopod. With a lens over 300 mm this will be essential: it is almost impossible to hold the camera still enough to avoid shake and a blurred image.

CONVERTERS

You would need to use a very long lens such as a 500 mm very often to justify its high price. If not, you might consider using a converter. This fits between the camera body and an existing lens. A 2 x converter will increase the focal length of a 250 mm lens to 500 mm. The price is reasonable and the image almost as sharp as that of a long lens. Most camera manufacturers make converters.

● This was shot with a 28 mm wide angle lens. It has stretched the telephone boxes apart and given a very elongated effect.

● Here a 135 mm telephoto lens has been used. It has compressed the boxes so that they look closer together. The composition is far tighter and cuts out much unwanted detail from the frame.

● RIGHT The use of a 200 mm telephoto lens has cropped a lot of clutter out of the picture. The lens has compressed the picture, reducing the apparent space between buildings. Such a composition emphasizes the contrasts between the various architectural styles, from the Victorian classical façade to the modern skyscrapers in the background.

● BELOW A 100 mm telephoto lens is ideal for portraiture. Its short depth of field, especially at wide apertures, can put the background out of focus and thus allow the viewer to concentrate on the main subject. In such shots it is best to focus on the eyes and expose for the skin tones.

INSTANT OR POLAROID CAMERAS

Polaroid cameras are unique among cameras as they provide an instant print within a few minutes. The prints can be either colour or black and white and begin to develop as soon as the film sheet appears from the camera; the sheets are impregnated with developing chemicals activated by pressure. Reprints can be made from the originals if they are sent away and copied. These, like the film itself, can be expensive.

The variety of Polaroids available range from the inexpensive 'point-and-shoot' models to those that have interchangeable lenses, built-in metering and flash. In the mid-price range is the image system; this has autoexposure, autofocusing and built-in flash, together with a range of accessories including a close-up lens. The film used in the image system model is supplied with a built-in battery that powers the camera: every time the film is replaced the battery is also renewed.

POLAROID BACKS

As well as the conventional camera unit, Polaroid backs which fit onto a range of more traditional cameras from 35 mm SLRs to large format 5 × 4s are also available. These backs allow the photographer to view the composition and make adjustments before taking the final shot on conventional film. The lighting can be checked and corrected if necessary and the exposure assessed. Prints can be collected and displayed in an album as a visual and technical record of how a shot was taken; this is especially useful as a reference when a similar composition is needed again.

Some of the film used in Polaroid backs produces a negative as well as a print. This means that it is not necessary to obtain copies from prints, where quality may be lost.

October - Lucy's birthday party

The Gang

The prizewinning entry!

The leaves beginning to turn

Signor Serafino at the restaurant

Surprise, Surprise!

Almost perfect symmetry!

Mr Jackson and chemistry class

Tiger looking fierce

Tom and Jim in the park

Waiting for the furniture — to arrive

A balcony shot of Sarah's party

Dinah posing for her portrait

The happy couple

A lucky snap - the portico background matches the sky

Many compact cameras now have an autofocus facility built in; this allows for even more spontaneity in instant shots. The autofocus camera emits an invisible infrared beam which bounces back off the subject to the camera in much the same way that radar works. The camera analyses this information and sets the focus to the correct distance by means of a small electric motor.

It sounds simple and it is, but there are a few points to remember before shooting the picture. On the most simple autofocus cameras the area analysed by the autofocus mechanism will be in the centre of the frame; it will be this part that the camera focuses on even if the main subject is to one side and therefore out of the autofocus range. It is very simple to learn how to alter the focus by manually overriding this mechanism.

Some of the more sophisticated cameras have a larger area of focus than that of the central spot found in the more simple models. These more sophisticated cameras send out three separate beams and make a 'judgement', either from one of these or from a combination. Many of the single lens reflex cameras that take interchangeable lenses are now of the autofocusing type. Most of these have a manual override for focusing but when in the autofocus mode the same alterations may be required.

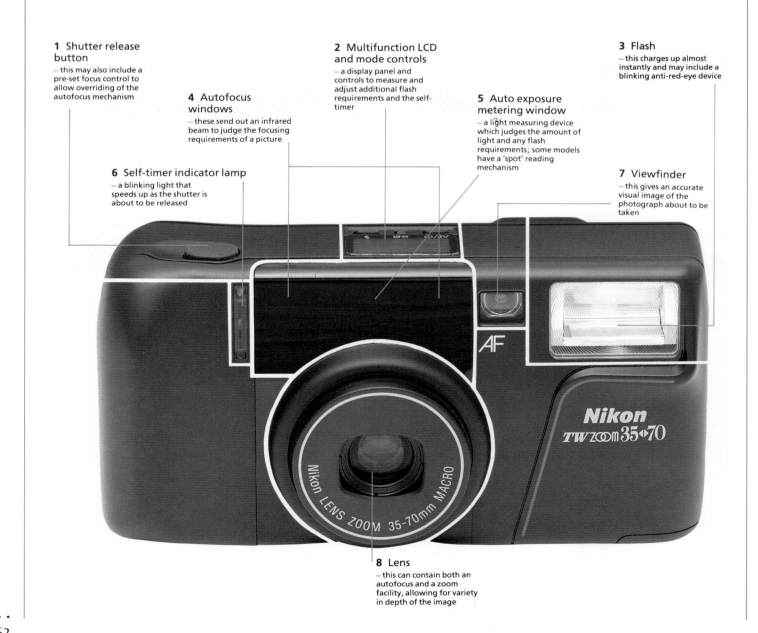

1 Shutter release button
– this may also include a pre-set focus control to allow overriding of the autofocus mechanism

2 Multifunction LCD and mode controls
– a display panel and controls to measure and adjust additional flash requirements and the self-timer

3 Flash
– this charges up almost instantly and may include a blinking anti-red-eye device

4 Autofocus windows
– these send out an infrared beam to judge the focusing requirements of a picture

5 Auto exposure metering window
– a light measuring device which judges the amount of light and any flash requirements; some models have a 'spot' reading mechanism

6 Self-timer indicator lamp
– a blinking light that speeds up as the shutter is about to be released

7 Viewfinder
– this gives an accurate visual image of the photograph about to be taken

8 Lens
– this can contain both an autofocus and a zoom facility, allowing for variety in depth of the image

• In this shot the person is in the centre of the frame and is perfectly sharp. The background is out of focus as the automatic focusing mechanism has 'fixed' onto the subject in the foreground. Perhaps the subject needs to be moved to one side in order to reveal or conceal part of the background.

• By repositioning the camera so that the person is at one side of the picture the background comes into sharp focus but the girl is now blurred.

• To eliminate the problem is quite simple. First point the camera at the person and gently depress the shutter release button to a half-way position. This will fix the autofocus mechanism on the subject in the foreground. Keeping the shutter release button depressed, move the camera to the desired position so that the picture is composed satisfactorily. Now depress the shutter release button fully. The picture has now been taken and the person is in focus.

• BELOW Autofocus is excellent for capturing instant and spontaneous shots that retain the essence of a particular moment.

ADVANTAGES OF AUTOMATIC CAMERAS

• Automatic focusing allows spontaneous pictures to be captured instantly without time-consuming dial adjustments.

• The built-in flash provides quick, on-the-spot lighting for every occasion.

• Light exposure is metered automatically, saving on adjustment and measuring time.

• 'Hands-free' pictures can be taken using the self-timer; even the photographer can appear in the shot.

• The small, compact shape makes the camera easily portable in all situations.

WHEN THINGS GO WRONG

Even when you think you have taken every possible care with your photography, things can still go disappointingly wrong. Often these errors are caused by a momentary lapse of concentration, but in extreme cases the fault can be traced to a malfunction in the camera or other equipment.

Do not be discouraged by faults in your photography; problems are nearly always easy to rectify. Look at the examples shown here and compare your own pictures to diagnose and correct the fault.

Probably the most common fault is fogging of the film. This occurs when the camera back is opened before the film has been fully rewound into the cassette, or because light is leaking into the camera. If light is leaking in, take the camera to a reputable repairer.

If the film is blank when it comes back from the processors, the most likely fault is that the film has not been advancing. When you load the camera, always check to make sure the rewind crank turns when you advance the film; if it does not turn, the film will stay in the cassette.

Consistent overexposure of film may be caused by a defective meter. However, it may also occur if the wrong speed is set or the metering system is set to the wrong ISO speed. Alternatively, this may take place if the aperture on the lens is not stopping down when the shot is taken; this means that the lens needs repairing.

Blurred shots are usually caused by camera shake. This will occur if you are using a slow shutter speed without securing the camera to a tripod. If the camera has aperture priority mode and you are shooting in dull light, the camera will select a slow shutter speed if you choose a small aperture.

● Flash overexposure. Cause: the sensor that determines the power of the flash was covered by part of a hand. To correct: always leave the sensor clear.

● Flare and marks on the film. Cause: after loading, the film has not been wound on two or three frames before shooting begins. The laboratory's processing marks and number are visible over the image. To correct: always be sure to wind on the film for at least a couple of frames before beginning photography.

● Incorrect framing. Cause: parallax error. When shooting with a compact camera the viewfinder does not see exactly what the lens sees. To correct: refer to the manufacturer's parallax adjustment guide.

● Out of focus. Cause: going too close or incorrect use of an autofocus mechanism so that the middle distance is measured, in this case the plants behind the subject. To correct: semi-depress the shutter on the main foreground subject before framing the shot.

● ABOVE Under-exposure. Cause: the auto-exposure meter has read the reading from the sky rather than from the person. To correct: be sure to take a reading from the main subject.

● ABOVE Marks on prints. Cause: the camera back was opened before the film was wound back into the cassette. To correct: ensure the cassette is fully rewound before opening the camera back.

● ABOVE 'Red eye'. Cause: the flash is too close to the lens. To correct: move the flash to one side if possible, or activate the anti-red-eye flash mechanism if one is fitted.

● ABOVE Over-exposed background. Cause: the auto-exposure meter in the camera has taken a reading for the trees in the foreground and over-exposed for the background. To correct: ensure the readings are taken from the main area of interest.

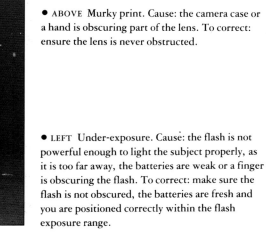

● ABOVE Murky print. Cause: the camera case or a hand is obscuring part of the lens. To correct: ensure the lens is never obstructed.

● LEFT Under-exposure. Cause: the flash is not powerful enough to light the subject properly, as it is too far away, the batteries are weak or a finger is obscuring the flash. To correct: make sure the flash is not obscured, the batteries are fresh and you are positioned correctly within the flash exposure range.

Travel
Photography

INTRODUCTION

Going on holiday, especially abroad, provides the photographer with many different sights and renewed creative energy. Not only are there new geographical vistas to be shot but also local people and colourful environments. Unusual architecture and local or national parades and carnivals also provide a wealth of possibilities. Although it is true that travel to foreign and faraway places can prove to be inspirational there are many exciting photographic opportunities nearer to home as well. A few simple basics and a good eye are all that is needed to get the best out of photography – whether it is around the corner or half-way around the world.

TRAVEL PREPARED

Before travelling away from home, especially for a holiday, collect together all the photographic equipment needed to record the journey. Do not try to take every piece of equipment and all additional lenses, lighting and accessories: just take enough to cover most situations.

HOLIDAY CHECKLIST

● How long have the batteries been in the camera? Do they need replacing? Make sure spares are packed; it is still difficult to find certain types of battery in some countries. If the camera uses rechargeable batteries, be sure to pack the charger, together with an international plug converter.

● Take one or two zoom lenses; these will cover most of the focal lengths required and will save on the weight and space that a number of prime lenses would take up.

● Two camera bodies will mean faster work as the time taken to change lenses will be reduced; one camera could be fitted with a 28–80 mm lens and the other with a 100–300 mm lens.

● Consider having black and white film in one camera and colour in the other; alternatively try loading one body with fast film and the other with slow.

● Try to purchase all film likely to be needed from a reputable supplier before leaving. The film will be fresh and probably cheaper. In some countries it is difficult to obtain very fresh film, and in hot climates it may have been on a shelf in bright sunshine. If you are concerned about it passing through the X-ray security machine at an airport there are protective bags available from specialist shops.

● Think about taking one or two filters; an 81A will help add a little warmth to the pictures, while a polarizing filter will enhance the quality of the sky and sea while also cutting down on or eliminating unwanted reflections. A graduated neutral density filter will help balance the areas of the picture that require different exposures, for instance a bright sky above a dark landscape. A yellow filter when used with black and white film will help retain the clarity of clouds.

● A flash gun is useful in cases where the light is low as well as in bright sun as a fill-in light. As with the camera, make sure the batteries are fresh and that a spare supply is packed.

● A small portable reflector is an asset, especially for portraits.

● It is worth taking a tripod, together with a cable release. If the tripod is too

● Take everything you are likely to need for a trip. This camera case contains the essential items for travel photography: a compact but sturdy tripod, a variety of film for colour as well as black and white shots, a camera body and lenses, and filters and flash equipment. Always check everything thoroughly before setting off on your travels, and remember to pack spare batteries!

bulky, consider a monopod instead.
● Lens cleaning tissue and a blower brush are essential, especially in sandy or dusty locations. Wrap the camera in a plastic bag to protect it from dust or sand particles, and as a general measure against the effects of the environment

and extreme weather conditions.
● A camera case to hold all this equipment is extremely useful; when travelling by air and not keeping the case as hand luggage, it is best to have a hard aluminium case for maximum protection.

WHEN THE LIGHT IS LOW

Low light, whether due to the time of day or prevailing weather conditions, does not mean that good photographs cannot be taken. It is sometimes even possible to obtain more dramatic shots in low light than in brilliant sunshine. If the weather is misty or foggy, moody pictures can be taken. If the sun is low, at the beginning or end of the day, for instance, the colour of the light will be much warmer, and can be used to dramatic advantage, emphasizing the sky and clouds. Even indoors, light filtering through a window is often perfectly adequate to light a subject without using flash.

A tripod is an asset in many low light conditions where slow shutter speeds are necessary. An alternative is to use a fast film, although the results will be grainier. Graininess can be used to creative effect but often it will detract from the final image if not used carefully. Instead of using fast film, ordinary film can be uprated. If the film in the camera is 100 ISO, for instance, the speed dial on the camera can be altered to 200 or 400 ISO. Remember, though, to tell the laboratory this when the film is sent in for processing so that it can be developed accordingly. The disadvantage of this method is that the whole film has to be rated at the same ISO and any increase in development will result in loss of shadow detail, increase in contrast and a grainier texture.

● BELOW The late evening light bathes this building in a wonderful reddish glow. The anonymous figure at the window lends an air of mystery to the overall composition. Always be on the look-out for the unexpected, especially when the light is low and hopes of a good shot are fading.

● ABOVE This shot was taken using only available light coming in from a window. The shutter speed required was ¹⁄₁₅ second; this was too slow to allow the camera to be held by hand so a column in the restaurant was used as a support. It is virtually impossible to hold a camera steady at ¹⁄₃₀ second or less without suffering camera shake; with a little ingenuity it is usually possible to find something to support the camera.

● RIGHT Here the setting sun has painted the sky completely red and the clouds lend it extra depth. No tripod was available here so the camera was braced on the defensive wall of the river.

● LEFT Even adverse weather conditions can be used to the photographer's advantage. This picture of Bodiam Castle in Great Britain was taken early on a misty morning. The mist rose and fell, sometimes completely obscuring the castle. By waiting for the right moment it was possible to take a shot in which the light had an ethereal quality. The mirror image reflected in the still waters of the moat adds to the general composition.

Any accessory used while taking a photograph can enhance the final image; however, care must always be taken to ensure the images produced are effective. One of the least expensive and yet most important of accessories is a filter. Certain filters improve the colour saturation of the film or enhance the sky or quality of water. Before deciding on any filter, indeed any accessory, test it in similar situations before using it for a specific shot.

COLOUR CORRECTION FILTERS

Some manufacturers' film may have a natural bias towards results that are too blue or green, giving an unwanted coldness to the photographs. On the other hand, the film may be too warm and the results will then tend towards red or yellow. To correct these tendencies there is a huge range of CC (colour correction) filters; for most photographers one or two colour balancing filters will prove more than adequate.

POLARIZING FILTERS

A polarizing filter is a useful accessory; not only will it enhance the quality of the blueness of a sky, making any clouds stand out with greater clarity, it can also be used to cut out unwanted reflections, such as those in shop windows or on shiny tabletops.

EXPOSURE COMPENSATION

Since many filters cut down the amount of light passing through the lens, compensation in exposure must be made. With cameras that have TTL meters this will be done automatically, but for manually operated cameras this must be taken into account before the final exposure is made. This is quite easy as each filter comes with a number known as a filter factor which indicates the amount of compensation required for each exposure. For instance a filter factor of 1 requires one stop increase in exposure.

● TOP RIGHT In this picture no filter was used. Although the image is correctly exposed it has a slightly blue cast which makes it look rather cold. The sky lacks definition and appears flat.

● TOP, FAR RIGHT By adding an 81A filter the blue cast has been reduced, the picture appears warmer and the contrast between the different tones is increased.

● BOTTOM RIGHT In this picture an 81EF filter was used to eradicate the blueness of the overall picture. The grass and tree are well defined and the clouds and sky have body.

● BOTTOM, FAR RIGHT As well as using an 81EF filter, a neutral density graduated filter has been added. This filter allows two differing areas of brightness to be brought into line with one another. In this case the hill and background required an exposure of 1/125 second at f8, but the sky only needed an exposure of 1/125 at f11. The graduated filter brings both areas into line so that the sky is well defined yet the land area is not underexposed.

● RIGHT Here a polarizing filter has been used. This has made the blue sky darker and the wispy white clouds stand out with great clarity. If this filter is used with an SLR camera the effect can be seen in the viewfinder as the filter is rotated.

LANDSCAPES: GENERAL COMPOSITION

The main subject matter of photographs taken while travelling will probably be landscapes. In landscape photography it is very important to take care with composition to avoid producing dull shots, for example of a lot of sky with only a thin strip of land. A commonplace image can be transformed very simply by paying attention to shadow, colour and detail, all of which are paramount in producing good landscape shots.

● LEFT This grouping of trees is common around the River Po in northern Italy. The planting arrangement is exaggerated by going in close using a wide angle lens so that the long lines between the rows form a focal point for the composition. The evening light helps to create a pleasant atmosphere.

● ABOVE Give some thought to which lens to use when composing a landscape shot: it is one of the most important factors in a successful composition. By using a 200 mm telephoto lens this picture has been framed without any sky. The eye is drawn to the slightly pink terrain of the foreground while the grey rock of the canyon forms the background. The long lens has compressed the shot, further emphasizing the foreground. The trees in the foreground look like tiny bushes and this gives an indication of the scale of the canyon.

● LEFT AND BELOW Although these two shots were taken very close to each other, one is a far better composition than the other. In the upright picture the road and tree balance one another, drawing the eye to the centre. The tree is a bold dominant feature; the way the narrow road converges adds a sense of curiosity – what lies beyond? In the horizontal picture the tree appears to lose its dominance and the expanse of fields on either side diminishes the power of the converging sides of the road. It is clear that the smallest adjustment can make a considerable difference to the overall composition.

VARYING A LANDSCAPE SHOT

- Rotate the camera slightly to one side; this may cut out unwanted scenery or bring in an added point of interest.

- Move the camera from a horizontal to a vertical position; sometimes the smallest of movements which does not even involve moving your feet can have a dramatic effect.

- Try isolating a portion of the landscape against a backdrop from a different part of the image; this can emphasize scale or make a coloured field, for example, stand out from surrounding pastures.

- Notice the position of any trees; a single isolated tree or a group of trees apart from a wood or forest can be used as a device for leading the eye into the scene. Tractor furrows or a meandering stream or river have a similar effect.

- An object in one corner of the picture adds to the composition; be careful that there is enough variety in a sequence of shots – do not always place an object in the same corner or the series begins to look dull.

Often the view that looks most spectacular to your eyes does not come out nearly so well on film. This is not necessarily because of any technical fault: it may be just that the wrong viewpoint was chosen when pressing the shutter. All the time you look at anything, your eyes are editing the scene and suppressing uninteresting details. In contrast, the camera records just what is in front of it, and unless you have taken care to exclude things you do not want, they will appear on the print.

In many cases the picture could be improved beyond recognition by moving a short distance. The basic viewpoint may be fine, but perhaps a higher or lower viewpoint is needed; try standing on a step, or crouching down. It is worth taking time to explore a variety of viewpoints. Even when you have taken your shot and are walking away you may suddenly see a better shot. If you do, take it. After all, film is the least expensive component in photography. You may never return to that place, or the light may never be the same again – so do not worry about using up another couple of frames.

PARALLAX ERROR

One common reason for not getting the picture wanted is parallax error. A camera with a separate viewfinder for the lens – that is, most cameras except single lens reflex cameras – gives a slight difference in framing between what you see and the picture you take. This makes no noticeable difference when photographing a distant object or a landscape, but the closer you go in, the greater the error. If the landscape shot has a foreground you will certainly have to allow for parallax. If you do not, a detail you expect to be in your photograph may simply not appear, and vice versa.

● BELOW, LEFT AND RIGHT From looking at the background of the buildings and cliffs it is clear that both these pictures were taken from almost the same place. But the foregrounds are quite different. This shows the effect that altering the viewpoint slightly can have on the finished picture. Although both compositions work well, the one on the LEFT is taken from a better viewpoint in relation to the sun.

● RIGHT A central viewpoint from a bridge over both the railway track and the canal has created an interesting composition. A fairly slow shutter speed of ⅟₆₀ of a second was used. This has made the express train slightly blurred. But instead of being a fault, it adds an air of movement and speed. In contrast the canal looks calm and tranquil, a bygone and slower mode of transport. The viewpoint contributes greatly to the juxtaposition.

● BELOW Taking this shot from a viewpoint some way up the bank of the lake has brought the pavilion on the far side into clear view. A view from near the water's edge would have made the bridge in the middle distance cut into the pavilion, spoiling the composition.

LANDSCAPES: THE WEATHER

There is no such thing as perfect weather for photography. Of course, photographing people on a beach holiday in the pouring rain may present a few difficulties, but many inclement weather situations are in fact the basis for original and dramatic photographs. Overcast skies can be used to advantage and reveal more about the immediate environment than if the sun were shining on a clear day. Rain can be evocative, portraying isolation and stormy conditions. Wintry, and especially snow-covered views provide good, clear images; these are best shot in sunshine to obtain the best view of the shadows cast on crisp snow — an effect which is lost if the sky is heavy.

Predicting where light will fall is important; try to look at a map to gauge where the sun will shine strongly, and rise and set. Make sure the camera is in position at the right time to get the full effect of the quality of light required, particularly if unusual weather conditions produce dramatic cloud formations.

CAMERA CARE IN EXTREME CONDITIONS

If the weather is very cold the shutter on the camera may freeze and valuable picture opportunities may be lost. Extreme heat can ruin film so keep it wrapped in aluminium foil as this will keep it a little cooler. As big a lens hood as possible may help to shield the lens from the rain; beware of cutting off the corners, or 'vignetting' the picture. Do not let weather conditions prevent photography — be prepared to have a go: the results could be surprising!

● ABOVE AND RIGHT Snow creates wonderful picture possibilities. Take care not to underexpose: there is so much reflected light that exposure meters may read the conditions as being much brighter than they are. Try waiting for different light on snowscenes. Here the picture with the sun shining brightly, RIGHT, certainly enhances the overall effect.

● ABOVE Even in the rain dramatic pictures can be taken. This storm over the Atlantic illustrates the qualities of cold and isolation. A slow shutter speed can help to emphasize the driving rain.

● LEFT Prior calculation of where the sun is going to set means that full advantage can be taken of warm evening light, as here where the sun falls on the shapes of the clouds. The same shot taken earlier in the day would have lacked such intensity, warmth and atmosphere.

● LEFT Mist and fog should not be a deterrent to photographers. This almost monochromatic picture has a strange eerie quality to it. Is the boat perhaps drifting and abandoned? Hazy air can add an enigmatic quality to shots.

● LEFT The heavy rain cloud hanging over the limestone pavement illustrates perfectly the visual effect overcast weather can produce. Here it is particularly apt as the cloud hangs over rock which has been eroded by rainfall over the centuries, so the image has a double purpose, it is visually pleasing as well as instructive.

LANDSCAPES: TIME OF DAY

Throughout the day the sun constantly changes position. In photographic terms this movement is more than one from east to west: any change in the sun will produce a different effect on any landscape. In the early morning and evening the sun will be quite low; the shadows it casts will be long and dramatic. In winter the sun will be lower still and these shadows will be even more exaggerated. At midday the sun will be high and the shadows cast will be shorter. In some cases this can lead to flat and featureless shots, so care must be taken at this time of day.

The other factor to consider is that the light cast by the sun in the early morning and late afternoon will have a warmer tone than that of midday light, so pictures taken at these times will appear redder or more orange than those taken in the middle of the day. It is well worth making the effort to get up early, before the sun rises, to be in position to capture the quality of light as dawn breaks. A little research beforehand will show where the sun will be and what it will fall on, depending on the time of year. Early and late rays of sunlight can illuminate an isolated area of a landscape in much the same way as a giant spotlight trained on the scene.

● ABOVE LEFT This shot was taken at mid-morning, yet there is enough of an angle in the light from the sun to create shadow detail. The well-defined clouds have broken up what could have been a bland sky so that the general result has equal focus and visual impact in all areas.

● ABOVE RIGHT The early evening sun was very low on the horizon when this picture was taken. It has just started to tinge the clouds with red and darken the golden sand. By using a wide aperture, a fast enough shutter speed could be used to capture the gently breaking waves.

● RIGHT AND BELOW RIGHT These two pictures were taken from the same viewpoint, the one BELOW after the sun had set. The sky is bathed in a dramatic red-orange light. In contrast the shot taken in the morning, on the RIGHT, had the sun behind the camera and the quality of light is much cooler. A polarizing filter was used to enhance the colour of the sea.

● LEFT This picture was taken just after the sun has risen and the quality of light is very warm, casting a golden reflection on the River Thames. The early morning mist has diffused the sun and gently bathed the scene with a sense of calm. A little prior research meant that the picture was taken at exactly the time the sun appeared between the dome of St Paul's Cathedral and the National Westminster Bank Tower. If the shot had been taken two months earlier, the sun would have appeared to the right of the tower; four months later it would have been to the left of the cathedral dome.

PEOPLE IN LANDSCAPES

Landscape photography is often enhanced by the inclusion of a human figure. This technique of combining people with landscapes can be used to illustrate a particular activity in a certain area, or to show the type of landscape a person may work or live in. Human figures add scale to a particular feature of a landscape, such as a large rock or the height of a tree. Showing a person isolated within a landscape is an effective way of showing the desolate or lonely aspect of a region. On overcast days a person can help to enliven an otherwise dull situation. If the person is working try to let them continue with the task already started. Reassure the subject that he or she is a welcome part of the shot – many people assume that they are in the way and try to move out of the picture.

On a walking holiday, for instance, it might be better if your companions were seen coming through a gate or along a path while the camera is positioned on higher ground than the people to be included; but also remember not to let your shadow creep into the picture. In the early morning or late afternoon shadows will be well defined and long. If people are to feature in the foreground of a picture make sure that they do not block out an important point of interest in the middle or background. On the other hand, if there is something unsightly in the background the inclusion of a person can help conceal the object.

● RIGHT The shepherd in the foreground helps to create a sense of space between himself and his village. He also diverts the eye away from the overcast weather. Local people are often very pleased to be in photographs; do not be afraid to ask them to pose.

● ABOVE The man has been included in this picture to give a sense of scale; without him it would be almost impossible to tell accurately how high the waterfall is. Consider the picture without the man: as well as losing the sense of scale, the composition would be entirely different without the added point of interest which makes an intriguing juxtaposition to the waterfall.

● LEFT This shot was taken in the early morning light. The warm tones of the sun highlight every feature of the man's face while the cliffs behind provide both an interesting backdrop and a sense of location. This type of light would be too harsh for some people, and it may be better to wait for the position of the sun to move or to move the person into a shaded area.

● BELOW This shot was taken in winter; the people standing by the seashore add a clear sense of the desolation of the beach at this time of year, yet in contrast the setting sun bathes the sky and surrounding landscape with a warm glow.

BLACK AND WHITE LANDSCAPES

Often a black and white photograph of a landscape or seascape can be far more evocative and dramatic than one taken in colour.

One important thing to remember is that some detail, for instance in a cloudy sky, can become flat and grey if a filter is not used. To make white puffy clouds stand out against the sky use a yellow filter. For even greater drama use a red one, which will turn the sky very dark.

Provided there is detail on the negative, the sky can be 'burnt in' at printing stage. This means giving certain areas of a print more exposure ('printing them up') or less exposure ('holding them back') than the rest of the picture by partly masking the print under the darkroom enlarger.

Another advantage of black and white for print making is that there is a variety of paper grades to choose from. A print made on grade 1 paper will be soft, and one made on grade 3 much harder. The whole feel of a picture can be altered by choice of paper alone.

In colour photography there is contrast between different colours as well as different tones. The essence of a good black and white picture is its tonal range. This does not mean that there have to be extremes of white at one end and black at the other. That would be a high contrast print, and it might be interesting; but it is the subtlety of gradations of tone that make a rich print. Fine-grained film, 100 ISO or less, will give better shadow detail than faster film, and will allow far bigger enlargements to be made.

To see how good a black and white landscape can be, study the work of the late American photographer Ansel Adams whose studies are epitomized by their starkly contrasting tones.

● ABOVE Keeping the rooftops in the foreground has increased the feeling of depth in this picture. A medium telephoto lens, 150 mm, was used and this has very slightly compressed the picture, bringing the town on the other side of the river closer in.

● TOP LEFT This picture shows a good tonal range. The camera was fitted with a wide angle lens and pointed downward to emphasize the texture of the rock in the foreground. A neutral density graduated filter was used to retain detail in the sky, and this was further emphasized when the print was made.

● BOTTOM LEFT This high-key picture of sand dunes has an almost tactile quality. Keeping the tones to the lighter end of the range has enhanced the softness of the windswept sand and given the picture a feeling of peace. When working in conditions like these be careful that sand does not get into equipment.

● LEFT Filters can make a dramatic difference to black and white photographs, as this shot shows. A red filter has turned the sky very dark. For a less extreme effect, a yellow filter will help to retain detail of white clouds.

SEASCAPES

Special care must be taken when photographing seascapes as misleading exposure meter readings can occur. In an environment with so many reflective surfaces the meter can be fooled into measuring the scene as brighter than it is. This can lead to underexposure and disappointing results. To overcome this problem take a meter reading close up of some mid-tone detail.

If the camera is one with built-in autoexposure but no manual override, first decide on the composition. Then point the camera to an area of mid-tone detail such as grey rock. Depress the shutter release button half-way; this will activate the meter and the camera will record the reading. Keeping the shutter depressed in this position, move the camera back to the scene of the original composition. Now gently depress the shutter release button fully and take the picture. To take a similar picture from a slightly different viewpoint, you will have to repeat the process for each shot.

Some cameras with a built-in autoexposure meter have a special mark on the shutter ring labelled AEL, or autoexposure lock, for taking readings like this. Its action is similar to semi-depressing the shutter release button.

● LEFT Movement in the sea at the Giants' Causeway in Northern Ireland is captured and emphasized by a slow shutter speed, to make it look as if the sea is really pounding at the unusual hexagonal rocks that are a famous landmark in this area. The rocks are lit by warm light as sunset approaches, and the strong shadows bring out these strange forms.

● BELOW This picture was taken as a hurricane approached; in high winds it is important to hold the camera steady, perhaps bracing it on a firm surface such as a rock or low wall if you do not have a tripod. Even at relatively fast shutter speeds, such as $^1/_{125}$ second, camera shake will lead to blurred pictures.

● ABOVE Always look for points of interest when shooting a seascape. This unusual high tide marker creates a focal point in the foreground while the bright colours of the windsurfer's sail help to create a balance in the overall composition without dominating the scene. Try to imagine the same picture without these two elements. Would it have been as interesting?

● BELOW The addition of a polarizing filter for this shot gives the sea a translucent quality. In order to check the effect of a polarizing filter when using an SLR camera, rotate the filter while looking through the viewfinder, until the desired effect has been achieved.

SPECIAL EQUIPMENT FOR SEASCAPE SHOTS

1 A lens hood – this should be fitted at all times, whether or not beside the sea, but is particularly important in cutting down any unwanted reflections which may flare on the lens.

2 A polarizing filter – this makes the blue colours of the sky much richer and enhances the clarity of any small white clouds. The filter will also change the reflective nature of the surface of the sea.

WATERWAYS

Lakes, rivers, streams or canals offer an entirely different variety of photographic opportunities from those found by the sea and in coastal regions. The surrounding areas are often reflected in the surface of the water, adding an extra dimension to the shot and reproducing what is often the most spectacular scenery twice over.

The same problems of measuring exposure encountered when taking seascapes also apply to pictures of large stretches of fresh or inland water; the exposure metering system may judge light as being brighter than it is because of the light coming from the expanse of reflective water. As with sea shots, compensation must be made for this in order to avoid underexposure and ruined pictures.

Take care when choosing a viewpoint for water photography. Make sure the surface, especially of rivers or canals, is free of factory effluent, waste products and debris, unless this is the detail to be highlighted.

● LEFT If a shot is taken very early in the morning the water surface is often quite still. This creates a perfect mirroring medium. The inclusion of the single cloud adds depth to the image as well as providing an extra point of interest, drawing the eye upwards as well as to the reflection in the water.

● RIGHT Colour and detail are not always easy to find in the composition of a water shot. Here the canal boats add bright spots of colour in what would otherwise be a rather dull stretch of water. The trees help block out unwanted buildings and provide a neat frame for the picture.

● LEFT This shot was taken from a rock set slightly out from the bank. The exposure used here was calculated to give maximum depth of field and the slowest possible shutter speed. This means that the rock in the foreground is very sharp while the water is blurred, emphasizing the speed at which the river is flowing.

● BELOW Choice of viewpoint is always of paramount importance when photographing water, especially where reflection is included. Here the dramatic picture of the reflected snow-capped mountain is altered by the plants growing beneath the water. Make sure there are no unwanted intrusions in the final shot.

SHOOTING STILL WATER

Water is usually at its stillest very early in the morning before the wind, if there is any, has begun to blow. If the surface of the water is completely still, the surrounding scenery reflected in it can produce a striking mirror image. Try mounting the final prints vertically instead of in the conventional horizontal fashion. At first glance the picture will be a striking abstract image and many unusual and often amusing effects can be produced by a little experimentation with presentation angles.

According to the time of year, the ever-changing light, weather conditions, cloud formations and seasonal changes provide an endless range of photographic opportunities when taking pictures of the sky. Although sunsets are a favourite subject for many photographers, not all sky shots need be taken at dusk, and in fact many of the most effective shots are captured at different times of the day.

The essential point to remember when photographing skies is to judge the exposure so that the important details, such as clouds, are recorded. A polarizing filter will help to darken the sky while retaining the detail if the shot is of a blue sky with puffy white clouds. A neutral density graduated filter could be used to similar effect or, for real drama, combined with the polarizing filter. As well as the neutral density graduated filter, a graduated colour filter such as a tobacco graduated filter can be added. This will turn the sky a sepia colour while retaining the natural colour of the land.

When photographing an area you know well, try to be in position early to take advantage of the changing light patterns and the different effects this has on the sky.

When shooting at sunset be prepared to work rapidly as the sun sets very quickly. Also be on the lookout for the changing colour of the sky. Once the sun has set the sky can deepen in colour considerably. At sunset watch for light playing on clouds; an aura of light from these will look far more dramatic than a clear sky. As exposures will be quite long at this time of day a tripod is essential, and a cable release preferable.

● BELOW Here there is an almost perfect mirror image of the sky captured in the surface of the sea. It is best to take this kind of picture when the water is very calm. Watch out for unsightly objects or rubbish floating in the foreground.

● ABOVE This picture was taken just before the sun sank beneath the horizon and its light bathes the few clouds that remain in a golden aura. At this time of day a tripod is essential as the exposure required will be quite long.

REFLECTED SKIES

Skies that reflect into water, for example, make very good subjects. Either try to photograph the water when the air is completely still so that a perfect mirror image is achieved, or isolate a small area of water such as a puddle or pond to create foreground interest.

● LEFT By using a medium neutral density graduated filter all the detail of the clouds has been retained. A wide angle lens combined with a low viewpoint has emphasized the sky and it dominates the picture.

● RIGHT This shot was taken just before sunset. By using the small amount of water in the foreground interest is focused on the sky and the composition greatly enhanced. The backlighting on the ripples of the wet sand has added texture. In a situation like this carefully consider the reflective surface from various positions to obtain the best viewpoint.

REFLECTIONS

Reflected images, whether in buildings, water or glass, can make intriguing pictures. The majority of these can be made to look very abstract and as such can be very rewarding photographs. Shop windows, car body work, modern buildings: a close look at any of these will yield a surprising number of opportunities. Examine the materials buildings are constructed from; different types of glass will reflect in a variety of ways, for example. The many panes in an older window, for instance, will provide a multiple-image reflection. The many angles of a modern glass building mean that the image can be photographed reflected into itself. As well as creating fascinating shots of modern architecture the eye is led into a visual conundrum. Try having several prints made of such images and have half of them reversed. When they are mounted together the effect can be quite startling and a whole new range of creative possibilities opens up. This effect works equally well in black and white as well as colour.

Rain, or rather the puddles it creates, also offers many opportunities for interesting reflections. A wet road, too, can provide a strong reflective surface, but beware of flare.

● RIGHT Well-known landmarks can look refreshingly different when photographed reflected in another surface. Always be on the look-out for modern buildings with mirror glass which, depending on the angles, will reflect itself or typical aspects of a city in a new way. Here the familiar London bus is blurred but quite recognizable although it has taken on an abstract quality.

● ABOVE A multiplicity of reflections and neon light make this picture into a strong graphic image. This shot was taken at dusk; the same scene in daylight lacked impact. Always think about the surrounding lighting: the bright colours of neon lights, especially those in signs which are constantly changing, can give extraordinary results reflected in wet surfaces.

● TOP RIGHT This picture of the Rio Grande illustrates just how perfect some mirror images can be. If viewed on its side it takes on a completely different dimension. Many images lend themselves to this treatment and it is worth experimenting with aspects of presentation for a varied effect.

● BOTTOM RIGHT This shot was taken into a shop window in Chinatown, Los Angeles. At first the images are confusing as it is not immediately obvious what is reflected in which surface. The green flag with the strong Chinese lettering is the backdrop to the shop window, and the street scene is reflected into the window. Optical illusions of this type arouse curiosity as well as providing unique photographic images.

● ABOVE This shot is a combination of reflected neon light, glass and steel which has several visual layers to it. By choosing the viewpoint with care, a strong geometrical composition is created.

Each season has its unique characteristics but autumn provides the photographer with a range of colours that lend themselves immediately to composition. Of all the seasons it is the one that lasts the shortest. Just when a tree is at its peak a strong gust of wind can blow off most of its leaves leaving it stark and bare. Even without wind a tree will take a little over two weeks to shed its leaves so it is important to seize the opportunity quickly for photographing these tremendous colours. As well as photographing large swathes of broad-leafed trees try to look for spots of isolated colour to provide contrast. These might be provided by a lone tree set in a landscape or a single leaf blown onto the ground.

Experiment by being aware of situations from different angles. Looking up towards a blue sky can make a wonderful backdrop to golden leaves, while the use of a wide angle lens in a forest can, from a low viewpoint, make trees appear to soar skyward.

● LEFT It is not only trees and leaves that present an image of autumn: these windfall apples show what can be found by the alert photographer. Always be on the lookout for the unexpected.

● BELOW A low viewpoint is used to its full advantage here. The slender tree trunks soar skyward and their golden leaves form a colourful canopy. There is just enough light filtering through onto the foliage below to form some interesting patterns and keep the exposure even.

PHOTOGRAPHING AUTUMN LEAVES

● Try to place leaves together and examine the contrasts in their colours, shapes and sizes.

● Consider what the leaves might look like backlit.

● When photographing leaves in close-up so that the detail of the veins as well as the colour becomes a vital part of the image, extension rings or bellows will probably be necessary.

● When backlighting leaves or photographing from very close up, the leaf must be kept still. Some sort of windbreak may be needed; alternatively a modest lighting set-up can be erected indoors and the leaves arranged there. Whichever method is used, always watch out for large uninteresting shadows; these may not be very noticeable at first, but once photographed in close-up a small area may look ugly if one leaf casts a long shadow onto another.

● FAR LEFT Autumn is a rapidly changing season and the photographer needs to be aware of this to take full advantage of the range of shots available. A few days before this shot was taken these ferns were green. Now, the early morning light has intensified their deep rust colour. The tree in the foreground leads the eye into the picture and helps break up an almost entirely blue sky.

● ABOVE Autumn leaves provide very good detail for close-up shots. These were photographed against the sky. If a slow shutter speed is used wind may be a problem unless the subject is shielded.

If you study travel photographs you will be surprised at how often you can recognize the country, even a particular city, by looking at the people in the shots. This may be something as obvious as a shot of a guard outside Buckingham Palace or a portrait of someone in front of the Eiffel Tower. But other, more ordinary forms of dress can also convey location – especially when combined with architecture.

Thanks not only to our own travels but also to television, newspapers and magazines, many parts of the world are now more familiar. Photographs which in the past would have been fascinating glimpses of exotic places are in danger

of becoming mere clichés, but adding people to these views can lift them out of the ordinary.

Most local people do not mind having their photographs taken and some, such as uniformed guards, positively expect it. In all these pictures the people were unknown to the photographer, but in three of them it is clear that they were well aware of being the main focus of interest.

Always look out for the unexpected detail that gives the key to the location. It could be a sign on a door or a detail of a building, even something as mundane as an advertising hoarding. Clothing, as well as the overall lighting of the

picture, gives a good idea of the climate of a place.

Think about viewpoint when taking pictures like these. It may be worthwhile to crouch down and take the shot from below. It will make people look more dominant than if you are looking down on them. Consider also whether it is best to have them in the centre of the frame or to one side. In the latter case, if you are using autofocus and your camera has an autoexposure lock, first point the camera at the people, semi-depress the shutter release and hold it down to lock the setting, then move the camera to the desired position and take your shot.

● ABOVE By restricting the depth of field, the buildings in the background have been put out of focus very slightly. This has helped emphasize the guard's vivid red uniform and the fine detail on his helmet so that he becomes the focal point.

● ABOVE The girl is small, but a low viewpoint has made her the centre of interest. Always think carefully about the angle from which you take your portraits. The slightest change can alter the emphasis.

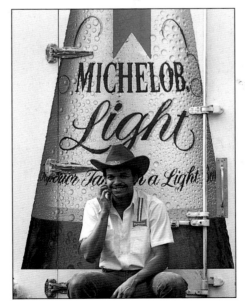

● LEFT These people in Orvieto in Italy made a diverse group. Shots like this one can be used in a series of pictures of an area to lend it human interest.

South Essex College
Further & Higher Education, Southend Campus
Luker Road Southend-on-Sea Essex SS1 1ND
Tel: 01702 220400 Fax: 01702 432320
Minicom: 01702 220642

● LEFT The beer truck made an interesting background. Always be aware of unusual possibilities. The man was a complete stranger, but he was perfectly happy to be photographed. His clothing and the background positively shout 'America!'

PEOPLE AT WORK

When travelling, good shots of people in their working environment can complement scenic pictures and add an extra dimension to a record of a journey. These pictures will often provide a more intimate insight into places visited and show what is special about a particular area. They can be displayed in an album beside pictures of landscapes, buildings and family. Shots of factories or farms which offer tours,

waiters serving in a favourite restaurant, or a craft centre with unusual items – these may all capture the essence of the holiday or trip and serve as a useful reference later on.

If the work that people are engaged in is very detailed, try to get in close so you can see what they are doing. Remember not to get in their way and so become a nuisance or they may refuse to allow the picture to be taken.

If you are indoors and the light is low flash may be needed. Try to bounce it off the ceiling or diffuse it. Nothing is worse than a harsh blast of strong flashlight that burns out the foreground but leaves the background dark and murky. Pay attention to the background, too; does it add something to the shot? Does it provide any information about the work being done, or is it a useful plain backdrop?

● RIGHT The waiters and waitresses in this café in New Orleans are relaxing while off duty. This type of shot shows not only people in their work environment but also helps to build up an overall picture of life in a particular town or city. Try to think ahead and decide which aspects of a trip will be the most memorable and descriptive.

● BELOW These men work in the malting room of a whisky distillery on the Orkney Islands of Scotland. By including their work implements in the picture a clear image of their job is captured as well as adding an air of spontaneous activity. The same implements also served as convenient resting posts while the men steadied themselves during the long exposure.

● BELOW Always look around to examine what props are available; these are usually part of the person's work and add extra visual interest to the picture as well as providing information about the job itself. If the people to be featured in the shot seem shy, start by taking pictures of the surroundings so that they become used to a photographer's presence. Talk to them about their work. If they sense genuine interest they will soon gain confidence and appear naturally relaxed in the picture.

● LEFT This man is one of the few professional lute makers in existence. The work is very delicate and slow; one slip of a chisel and the whole instrument could be ruined. This shot was taken by a window using the available daylight that is filtering through. The intensity of the work is reflected in his expression. A 100 mm lens was used to afford a clear view of what he was doing while still keeping some distance from him.

LOCAL PEOPLE

People will add colour to travel pictures, especially when featured in shots presented alongside others concentrating on landscape, architecture or the sea. A series of pictures of the people of a locality can form a portrait of life in that region. To catch the spirit of local activities, go in close so that people are related to their work or environment.

When photographing strangers politeness is the key. If people are approached in a friendly and reassuring way only the most recalcitrant will object to being photographed. Remember, though, that in some parts of the world it is inadvisable to photograph people – or even to make drawings of them. In some cultures there is a belief that if people are photographed their soul is removed. However strange such an opinion may seem it is important to respect it. Remonstrating with people will only make matters worse. It would be far more productive to find someone in authority and use your best diplomatic skills to get them to reassure and persuade your subjects to give their assent. In most cases such an approach, aided perhaps by a small gift, will win the day. A very effective method is to offer them a Polaroid portrait.

● BELOW Being quick to spot a good shot and seize the moment is the essence of a good travel shot. This grape grower was seen driving his tractor laden with grapes down a country lane. He agreed to be photographed, and a series of portraits was taken in the late afternoon sun.

● RIGHT Using a wide angle lens together with a small aperture has given good depth of field. This means that the spices are in focus as well as the two stall holders. The vivid colours of the spices create strong foreground interest and lead the eye into the picture.

● RIGHT Careful selection of colour will say much about the climate of a locality. It does not always have to be vivid; here the colours are muted but give a feeling of warmth. This shepherd was spotted by chance on a drive through a remote part of Sicily. Although his sheep were giving him and his dog problems he readily agreed to be photographed. His clothes convey the feeling of someone who works out of doors, and his hat indicates that the climate is hot, protecting him from the strong sunlight. Such ingredients in photographs put across a sense of place.

● LEFT Close cropping of these soldiers emphasizes their rich uniforms, and the gold of the gates behind them forms an effective backdrop. As events like this happen on a daily basis in most capital cities, you will have many opportunities to shoot local ceremonies.

Buildings present the photographer with an inexhaustible supply of imagery. The most important part of photographing any building is the general composition. The weather can be perfect, the exposure correct and the time of day just right, but a badly-framed picture will ruin everything. Here, equipment can be a great help:

● a telephoto lens will not only bring closer a distant building but also, depending on the power of the lens, compress the overall view and so reduce the illusion of space between the main building in the shot and those that may be behind or in front of it.

● a wide angle lens allows a close-up shot with an exaggerated perspective. A tall building such as a skyscraper can appear even taller if the camera is pointed upwards because the verticals will converge.

● a shift lens allows the photographer to avoid converging verticals in situations where these are not wanted as part of the shot. A shift lens alters the axis of view without the need to move the camera, yet allows movement of the lens in relationship to the film plane.

Choosing the correct viewpoint is a vital ingredient for general composition. Position the camera so that there are no unwanted objects within the frame. This may mean simply moving a short distance or using a different lens. If the camera is fitted with a zoom lens all that may be needed is a small adjustment in its focal length.

● ABOVE A telephoto lens was used for this shot of an isolated Scottish house; the top of the mountains that form the backdrop was deliberately cropped out. By composing a picture in this way the isolation of the subject is emphasized and becomes a particular point of focal interest.

● LEFT A small telephoto lens of 100 mm was used for this shot. This slightly compresses the buildings making the composition very tight. Ensure that any vehicles or other unwanted intrusions have been moved before taking the shot, or try to stand in a position where they would be cropped out of the frame.

● ABOVE The railings around the church form a frame for this picture and produce a pleasing composition. Although a wide angle lens was used the viewpoint was close enough to prevent the church receding too far into the distance. The puffy white clouds help to break up the blue sky and enhance the composition, adding another visual element.

● ABOVE By waiting until dusk a certain quality of light is captured; here the tower is bathed in a warm glow. The reflection of the building in the water helps to give a greater illusion of height. The use of a shift lens means that there are no converging verticals, yet the whole building still fits the frame. Remember to ensure that when photographing modern buildings light is not reflected off their exterior surfaces and into the camera lens.

BUILDINGS: EXTERIORS

Sometimes it seems enough to simply stand in front of a great building, point the camera and press the shutter, especially if the building is so famous that there does not seem to be anything to add. In many cases this may be true, but if everyone followed this path the results would be repetitive and tedious. There are always new ways of representing a familiar object: unusual angles, different lighting conditions, a section of an exterior. All these elements can enhance any photograph of a building.

ATMOSPHERIC DETAILS

- Time of day is an important consideration when photographing buildings. If, from a chosen viewpoint, the sun rises behind the building, this could result in a hazy image making the building look rather flat. If there is time, wait until the sun moves round, perhaps bathing the building in a warm afternoon light and creating strong shadow detail.

- Clouds can provide an added dimension. Sometimes even a radiantly blue sky will benefit from a few puffy white clouds above a building. Also, billowing storm clouds will add drama and perhaps a somewhat theatrical appearance to the shot.

● LEFT The New University in Moscow was photographed when the sun was at its highest and therefore illuminating the exterior evenly. A shift lens was used so that the full height of the tower could be included in the shot without needing to tilt the camera upwards. This would have caused converging verticals.

● LEFT Isolated in a mountain range, this white church stands out in a shaft of sunlight. This shot was taken after waiting for half an hour while a cloud obscured the sun; without the sunlight the scene was flat and uninteresting. It is always worth waiting for changes in the light to obtain a better photograph.

● BELOW By standing to one side of this street a rather ugly wall was cropped out. A medium telephoto lens, 135 mm, was used and has slightly compressed the buildings and brought closer the fields in the background. This has produced a tight composition with the emphasis on the row of housing without any unsightly distractions.

● ABOVE This shot was taken using a medium telephoto lens. The buildings in the foreground have been retained in the frame to enhance the cathedral of Siena as it stands majestically over them, dominating the skyline. The whole city is bathed in late afternoon light which adds warmth and enhances the predominantly terracotta hues of the buildings.

● ABOVE The white puffy clouds, enhanced by a polarizing filter, hang gently over these adobe buildings at Taos, New Mexico, and help to provide extra detail. They also break up the otherwise somewhat monochromatic shot.

SHOOTING VERTICALS

Different lenses can completely alter the perspective of a building. Pointing the camera upwards, at a skyscraper for instance, will make the verticals converge. This can add greatly to the dynamic qualities of the image.

On the other hand, another building could be shown with converging verticals and might look distorted, seeming to be in danger of toppling over. Every building composition should be assessed individually.

A telephoto lens can be used to photograph a building from a distance. The building can be brought closer and the foreground compressed. This will give the impression of increased grandeur to the main building in the shot.

For more specialist photography of very tall buildings a shift lens can be used. This allows a building to be photographed so that its vertical lines remain upright without needing to tilt the camera upwards. This would create converging verticals.

● ABOVE This picture of a skyscraper shows the extreme effect of converging verticals. By pointing the camera upwards the height of the building has been exaggerated and its sides appear to meet at a point in the sky. A wide angle lens has helped to emphasize this effect.

BUILDINGS: INTERIORS

One of the main points to consider before photographing the interior of a building is the amount of light available. In the majority of cases this is very little compared to that available outdoors. Our eyes are adept at adjusting to different light conditions, so adept that we soon cease to notice that certain conditions are in fact rather dull. With film, however, even relatively fast film, there is no such natural adjustment. The only way to record a usable image is to increase the exposure or to light the interior artificially by using flash.

Many cameras have built-in flash or a flash attachment connected to the hot shoe of the camera or to a bracket on one side of the camera body. However, even with the most powerful of these flash units there still may not be enough light to illuminate the interiors of very large and grand buildings. Even where a fast film is used with available light the result is very grainy and much of the shadow detail will be lost. A far better solution is to mount the camera on a tripod and use a long exposure. Of the pictures shown on this page none was shot on film faster than 64 ISO, and in only one picture was flash used as well.

Inside great monuments crowded with visitors some extra thought should be given to viewpoint so that the shot will not include other people. In some monuments tripods are not permitted; in this case use a monopod or find a suitable surface, such as a pew, floor, table or window sill, on which to rest the camera.

• ABOVE This interior was shot entirely in natural light. The blinds were angled to let in as much sun as possible while at the same time using them as a creative tool to cast interesting shadows. The result is a thoroughly modern interior bathed in bright sunlight.

• LEFT In this shot the window is illuminated by the daylight outside. This was not powerful enough to illuminate the walls inside without burning out the detail of the stained glass. By balancing the exposure of the flash on the walls with the light coming in through the window an even exposure was achieved.

● RIGHT By using a fisheye lens, an unusual angle of the ceiling of Westminster Abbey has been achieved. Even though the Abbey was opened to the public, tilting the camera upwards means that people have been cropped out. The day was overcast so there are no strong shadows on the sides of the buildings. This made the exposure relatively even, although long, and no other lighting was required.

● RIGHT Flash is forbidden in the Long Room in the Old Library of Trinity College, Dublin, so available light was used. The shot was taken from the balcony to add a feeling of greater depth. If the shot had been taken from ground level the camera would have to have been tilted upwards and this would have led to converging verticals, giving the impression that the room was leaning inwards.

Buildings provide many opportunities for the photographer to create exciting and, in many ways, unusual images of scenes that are always present but which the majority of people pass by without noticing. Sometimes it is not always possible or indeed beneficial to include a building in its entirety in a single photograph. In some cases the building may be quite dull and it is only by isolating a small section of carving or ceramics, for instance, that a strong shot will be obtained.

The time of day can play an important part in photographing details. When the sun is low or at an acute angle to the subject strong shadows will be created. This can enhance the graphic qualities and result in unusual, if not abstract, images.

It will be rare that an interesting angle cannot be found for even the most mundane building, and in the majority of cases what makes a photograph 'good' is the amount of time the photographer has spent looking for an unusual angle, going in close on detail and framing the picture to hide or crop unwanted intrusions. In certain cases close up shots of architectural detail may, over a period of time, provide a series of pictures that could be used together or to form a collection of individual themes or styles. With interior details precise framing can be important and it would be beneficial to use a tripod. This is not just in instances where there will probably be less light and so longer exposures will be necessary, but also in situations where symmetry is a key element, for example with a ceiling. Nothing is worse than seeing a final image where care has been taken with exposure and general composition but where one of four pillars, for example, is not quite square. With a tripod this 'squaring up' can be achieved with a greater degree of precision than can be expected with a hand-held camera.

● ABOVE It was impossible to fit the whole of Florence cathedral into a single shot. Also there were all the unsightly aspects of mass tourism that seemed at odds with this majestic building. By concentrating on one section and pointing the camera up above ground level the shot shows the uninterrupted beauty of the stone work.

● LEFT The hallway of the old *Daily Express* newspaper building in London's Fleet Street is one of the capital's greatest Art Deco interiors. Although the hallway is still intact many such interiors have been lost forever and photographs remain the only historical document of their existence. Needless to say these photographs could be very valuable in the years to come. To show the detail of this metallic mural it was lit from one side. If the light had been directly in front the picture would have looked flat and 'hot spots' would inevitably have appeared.

● ABOVE By going in close on these New York fire escapes and taking advantage of the low afternoon winter sun, a strong graphic image has been created. If the lower part of the building had been included the result would have been less abstract and therefore less dramatic.

● ABOVE The ground floor of this building had been converted into the most mundane offices with uninspiring furniture. The ceiling, in contrast, had been preserved and by choosing the viewpoint with precision and mounting the camera on a tripod a perfectly symmetrical image was achieved.

● RIGHT Churches in particular provide many photographic opportunities. Details of figures, columns, masks and stone work could over a period of time form the basis of a historical collection.

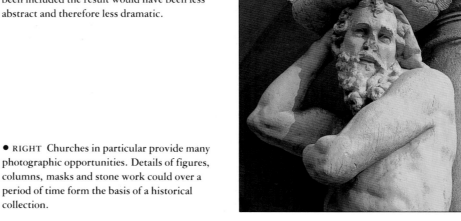

BUILDINGS AT NIGHT

Buildings seen at night can often be far more evocative of a cityscape than they appear to be in daylight hours. Some cities, such as New York, literally throb at night and are lit for the great part by garish neon light which looks strangely fitting.

The best time to take modern cityscape shots is about half an hour after sunset when the sky takes on a deep blue hue, which is far more attractive as a backdrop than a completely black sky. This quality of light lasts for a very short time, usually only 10–15 minutes. If you are prepared, such a length of time will be adequate, except of course that it will only provide perhaps one or two shots an evening. Because the light is low, exposures will be long and a tripod will be essential in most cases.

MAKING USE OF ADDITIONAL LIGHTS

- If the composition of the building includes a street the head- and tail-lights of passing cars can be an added ingredient. By using a slow shutter speed the lights will appear as trails of light snaking through the man-made canyons of the city.

- Be careful to avoid flare from external lighting such as street lamps. Sometimes a standard lens hood will be inadequate and a shield may need to be improvised from a piece of card, a book or a map, for instance; alternatively, shift position to stand between the camera and the light.

● ABOVE This shot was taken at the premium twilight hour. The camera viewpoint looks upwards. This has caused the two skyscrapers to converge but this has the effect of exaggerating their height and adding an impression of enclosure within the city.

The bus fills the bottom of the frame horizontally and reinforces the sense of movement. The thin side windows of the bus, turned green as they are lit by the fluorescent tubes, add to the theme of nightime and its artificial lighting in the city.

● BELOW This picture was taken when the sky was quite dark. As the building is well illuminated on the outside and fills most of the frame, the blackness of the sky forms a contrasting backdrop without being overpowering or dull.

● BELOW The main shot of the Coliseum in Rome strikes a perfect balance between the illumination of the stone of the building and the colour of the twilight sky. The trails of the head- and tail-lights of the traffic help to fill the void created by the road. The other shot, INSET, taken from the same viewpoint, shows the effect of inadequate lens shading as the flare from a street light has flawed the picture.

FLORA

● BELOW By using extension rings it was possible to get very close to this marigold. Depth of field was very limited and a long exposure was needed. This meant that the camera had to be mounted on a tripod and a shield used to protect the plant from wind, so that it did not move and blur the picture.

Plants provide good material for the photographer. It is worth considering not only exotic plants but also more commonplace varieties. Apart from colour, texture plays an important part in a striking image. All plants look their best at a certain time of year. If any plant is of particular interest, check when it is in season, especially if you have to travel any distance to photograph it.

Original effects can be created by isolating one plant in a mass of others, perhaps using the shallow depth of field afforded by a telephoto lens. There are other opportunities for unusual viewpoints; for instance a plant or group of flowers, or even trees in the foreground of a scene adds interest in its own right and can also mask an unwanted object that would otherwise spoil the picture.

CLOSE-UPS

- If you are taking close-ups of flowers, depth of field will be very small, especially if you are using extension rings or bellows. You will therefore need to stop down as much as possible, and to use a long exposure. If there is even the slightest breeze the plant will have to be sheltered from it, or it will sway and blur the picture.

- Lighting can also be a problem when working so close. If you are using available daylight you must take care not to cast a shadow from yourself or your equipment. A ring flash could be a useful accessory. This gives powerful but almost shadowless illumination. The flash tube forms a complete ring around the lens. Units for 35 mm cameras are quite compact and do not weigh very much.

- A tripod is essential because of the length of exposures.

- Details of trees and other plants are also excellent subjects for close-up shots. The texture of bark can be fascinating, and different shots can be mounted together to make a striking collage.

● ABOVE RIGHT Look for the unusual. There will always be something of interest on a country walk. This whitebell was growing alone in a sea of ordinary bluebells. Careful use of depth of field has put the background out of focus, making the flower even more prominent in the picture.

● RIGHT The texture of tree bark can be very satisfying, especially when several varieties are mounted together. A whole series of pictures can be built up over the years. This applies equally to many other natural forms.

● LEFT These cacti in the foreground frame the view. Not only do plants in the foreground add to the general composition, they can also be used to hide unsightly objects such as telegraph poles.

F A U N A

● BELOW Safari parks provide ample opportunity for photographing wildlife. A telephoto lens is essential as animals like this lion can only be photographed from a safe distance. Sometimes autofocus lenses do not work effectively when photographing through glass objects like car windows. Manual focusing can overcome this problem.

One of the most demanding areas of photography is that of wild or semi-wild animals. Patience is required, and a certain amount of forward planning is useful if not essential. Despite the arduous nature of this area, the rewards can certainly make it worthwhile. While most people do not have the opportunity to travel to the regions best suited to photography of big game or endangered species, many may live within reach of a farm or a safari or wildlife park. Safari parks have many exotic animals and with some peaceful species such as the zebra or giraffe it is sometimes possible to leave the vehicle and stand in the same area to take the shot with a medium telephoto lens of 100–200 mm.

● ABOVE If taking a photograph in a safari or wildlife park or zoo, a natural image is perfectly possible as long as the background includes relevant vegetation rather than an unsightly man-made intrusion. A close-up shot can be obtained without frightening the animal by using a 100 mm lens.

● ABOVE Small details are always most effective, especially when photographing fauna. These flamingoes look as if they are asleep yet a careful look at the far bird shows that its eye is open. This shot was taken with a 250 mm lens since if the camera had been positioned any closer the birds would have moved away.

PHOTOGRAPHING WILD ANIMALS

● Spend some time observing the behaviour of the animal; watch to see whether it is easily startled, or whether it appears to move in a constant direction.

● Try to select a viewpoint with an interesting background without unsightly fences or buildings.

● Be patient. Calling or gesturing to an animal will probably cause it to run in the opposite direction. Upsetting wild animals can also be dangerous: however docile they may seem it is important to remember that they are wild. It is best to avoid annoying both the animal and the farmer or ranger.

● BELOW Always be on the look out for spontaneous pictures. A quick check for any unsightly intrusions is usually all that is needed towards the composition of such shots.

● ABOVE This shot of cattle was taken in close from a higher viewpoint. All detail has been cropped out leaving only the black and white hides visible. This technique produces some effective graphic images that usually need a second look before the viewer realizes what the apparently abstract image is.

● RIGHT This shot was taken from a low viewpoint with a wide angle lens. This produces a dramatic image of the sky. By getting into position and being patient it is relatively easy to obtain effective and at times amusing shots of certain animals, whose natural curiosity means that they eventually come close to the camera for a better look. In this shot, the shutter was fired when the cow was about 3 ft (1 m) from the camera.

STILL LIFE

● BELOW By cropping the picture tightly – a medium telephoto lens was used – any extraneous details can be excluded. The texture of the wall provides a perfect canvas for setting off the doorway, the shrub and the traffic sign.

Travel often has the effect of making us more visually alert. Many things in our day-to-day lives may pass us by without us giving them a second glance. However, a new environment provides visual stimuli; to the photographer these stimuli provide a new awareness of photographic possibilities. Many items around us may not be very interesting in themselves, but gathered together in a collection, perhaps as a grouping of souvenirs from a particular place and photographed in an attractive way, a still life picture is created.

Still life arrangements have inspired painters throughout time and the same inspiration provides photographers with numerous creative opportunities. It is a useful discipline to look closely at, and arrange and light a group of inanimate objects. Sometimes these arrangements already exist and all that is required is to see the potential for an attractive shot.

● LEFT This is a good example of a ready-made still life. All the objects were fixed to the side of a barn on a ranch in Arizona. This shot frames them to their best advantage; no other preparation was needed. To the ranch owners this was just an assortment of objects rather than a creative arrangement. It is often worth looking around at familiar objects to view them with a fresh eye.

● RIGHT Some still life arrangements present themselves; this collection of African craft objects and furniture was lying in the corner of a room, lit by weak sunlight coming through an open window. A white reflector to the right helped throw back just enough light to illuminate the shadow areas.

● BELOW RIGHT A large aperture was used to emphasize the colour of these flowers by minimizing depth of field and throwing the background out of focus. The lines of the steps beyond are still just discernible and lift the background so that it remains a composite part of the picture without being too bland.

CHECKLIST FOR STILL LIFE SHOTS

- Should the arrangement be lit with flash or is there enough available light?

- Examine the available light for any creative elements: does a shaft of light fall at just the right angle?

- Which angle would look best for the shot? Imagine the arrangement in the centre of a circle. Stand a certain distance from the objects and walk around them slowly, stopping at regular intervals. Every pause provides a new visual angle and a different shot.

- Which viewpoint? Consider the arrangement from eye level, as well as from above and from below.

- Every visual angle provides a different background: which one is most suitable and complements the objects most effectively?

- Consider the depth of field: should the background be sharp or blurred?

PATTERNS

The refreshingly new viewpoints that travel often provides may reveal scenes or details that appear isolated from their immediate surroundings. This might be due to the way the light falls or may be because of an object's texture, or a combination of both these elements. Such images need not be confined to a documentary record of a place but can be used to startling creative effect. Examine the patterns created by an object or group of objects; often when such objects or scenes are carefully framed they form an interesting composition. Sometimes the pictures have a very abstract appearance or they may need careful viewing to see exactly what they are.

It is important to examine all the possibilities of a scene before taking the shot:

- Would it look best if framed symmetrically?

- Do the lines of perspective increase or decrease with the chosen viewpoint? If so, which is best?

- Is texture an important part of the picture? If so, does the light need to come from the back or the side to emphasize the texture?

- Would going in close help to achieve the effect better than being positioned further back?

- Would using a wide angle or a fisheye lens create a more interesting or subtle effect? This can be especially striking when looking up at the ceiling of a building, for instance, particularly if all the horizontal and vertical lines have been carefully aligned.

- Consider using prints or transparencies in a collage of different patterns. Try reversing one of the pictures and butting it up to one that is the correct way round.

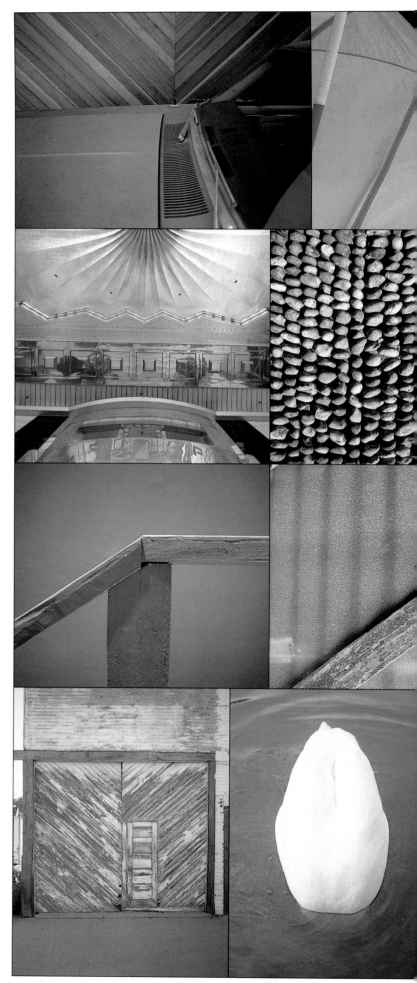

120

EVENTS

All over the world events take place which are worth a special journey. One such is London's Notting Hill Carnival, the largest street festival in Europe. People flock from far afield to see the parade, dance and share the street parties. Some come for that reason alone, others as part of a wider tour of the city or the country.

GETTING IT RIGHT

If you decide to make an event the high point of your trip, a little planning will avoid disappointment. Make sure you arrive at the right time: this may sound obvious, but events do not always happen on the same date each year, especially if they are associated with a movable festival such as Easter (which also happens on a later date for the Orthodox Church).

Take plenty of film. This will help to keep your pictures consistent, as they will all be from the same emulsion batch. With film bought locally you can never be sure how long it has been lying around in the shop, perhaps exposed to damaging heat. You often see film being hawked around tourist sites unshielded from the blazing sun.

Professionals keep their film refrigerated. You cannot take a refrigerator with you, but at least you can keep your film as cool as possible.

CHOOSING A THEME

At huge and varied events it is difficult to get just one picture that says everything. That is not to say that you should not look out for such a shot. A better approach might be to shoot as much as you possibly can, and to assemble these pictures as a montage on a particular theme, or a diary of events. Themes could be faces, floats, costumes, food, or the onlookers themselves. Many events last for several days, so you will have plenty of time to get all your shots.

SECURITY

Events such as the Carnival are also a magnet for pickpockets. If you are carrying a case for accessories keep it properly secured at all times. Be alert for children who beg you to take their picture. It sometimes happens that, while you are concentrating on the shot, one of their colleagues is lifting your valuables.

● A collection of images placed together effectively captures the atmosphere of London's Notting Hill Carnival. Small details can be placed next to wider shots of dancers and street scenes to convey the sense of colour and exuberance.

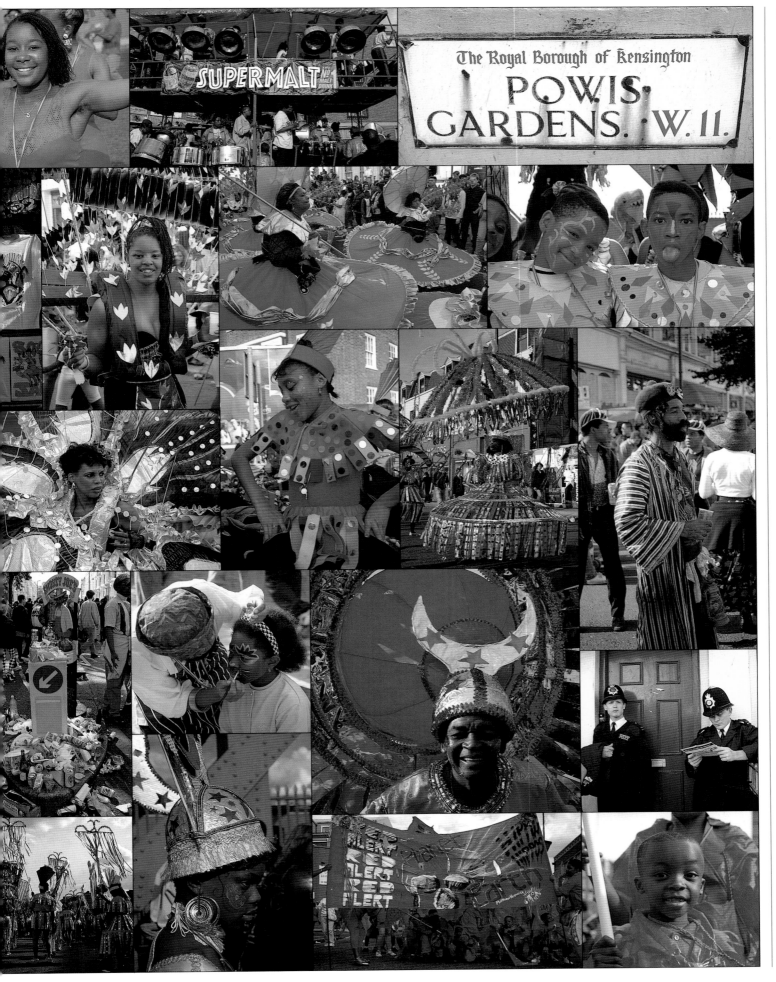

MAKING A PICTURE SERIES

When you are photographing an event you need to consider how many different things are happening. Sometimes there is so much diversity that you are spoilt for choice. In other instances the focus of interest may be narrow, and you will need to shoot from as many viewpoints as possible to give an informative account of the occasion.

PLANNING IN ADVANCE

It is always helpful to try to reconnoitre the place beforehand. Once the event begins you may not be able to move about easily, especially if you are burdened with a camera case and a tripod. In such a situation, try to pick a spot that will give you a good view of the main action. Also find out when the event is to begin, so that you can be there

● ABOVE As well as taking a formal picture of the troops standing to attention, for instance, try to move in close so that either the detail of the uniforms is visible or so that the impression of them marching close together is conveyed.

● ABOVE A crowd scene completes the picture. However, instead of merely photographing a mass of people, try to find a point of focus such as the young girl on her father's shoulders.

● LEFT At an event such as London's the Trooping the Colour, try to look for an unobtrusive background so that a group, such as these soldiers, stand out clearly. Sometimes extra height is needed for a particular shot: here the photographer stood on a strong camera case to gain an uninterrupted view over the heads of the people in front.

in plenty of time to get a good position at the front of the crowd. It is surprising how early people start to congregate for spectacles such as London's Trooping the Colour shown here.

If you cannot get a commanding view, try to take a small, lightweight set of steps. Not only will you be able to see over people's heads, you may also get an unusual angle on the proceedings.

Also try to work out beforehand which will be the key shots that you simply must have. You could make a list just in case, in the heat of the moment, you forget what you meant to do. This may seem obsessive, but hardly anyone makes a movie without a script. For example, at the Trooping the Colour you might plan to capture:

● the main participant – the Queen;
● a range of shots of the soldiers – individual guardsmen, and rows marching and standing to attention;
● the crowd itself.

This does not sound like a lot, but it is amazing how quickly an event can pass by and suddenly be over; it can seem like seconds if you have stood waiting for it for hours.

EQUIPMENT

Have a range of lenses, or if possible two camera bodies with zoom lenses – one could be 28–80 mm, the other 100–300 mm. In this way you will be able to work quickly with the minimum of weight. A monopod will help you to brace the camera. This is especially important if the weather is dull so that a long exposure is needed.

● LEFT An essential shot at an event like this is the main participant – in this case, the Queen. Try to plan ahead and think where the person will be: here she is taking the salute before retiring to Buckingham Palace.

● BELOW By using a more powerful telephoto lens it is possible to photograph the other participants, such as the members of the Royal Family.

Photographing People

INTRODUCTION

Probably more pictures are taken of people than of any other subject. Nowadays it is possible to record a person's life on film from the moment of birth, providing a visual diary for the future. There are so many different areas to explore through photographs: babies, children and older people, in groups, as individuals, in the studio or outdoors. With even the most basic equipment good portraits are within everyone's grasp.

PORTRAITS: BACKGROUNDS

A key element in shooting a portrait is the care given to the background. Yet so often it is given very little thought and the finished photograph is spoilt by unwanted distractions. In some situations, such as in a studio, the background can be altered at will and could range from a simple plain white or black backdrop to a more elaborate purpose-built set, or even a back screen projection.

When photographing people in their homes, at the workplace or outdoors, it is important to use the existing environment to the best advantage. This may mean including the work the person does – or even a relevant hobby or collection – without letting the subject become a secondary element within the picture. Positioning plays a key role in creating a background: thought should be given to where the subject of the portrait is to sit or stand, as well as the distance and angle of the camera in relation to both the person and the background. Choice of aperture is another consideration to be taken into account; a small aperture will produce a greater depth of field than a large one, and so more of the background will be in focus which may well prove distracting.

● ABOVE Here the glass panels of the door make an interesting background without becoming an intrusion. They are slightly out of focus but they are still identifiable. This makes the child's face appear to spring out from the doorway as if one has captured her in a game of hide and seek.

● ABOVE The Russian poet Yevgeny
Yevtushenko in his Moscow apartment. Although
the background is very busy his collection of
paintings is highlighted as well as him. By placing
the poet in the centre of the frame with the
relative neutrality of his dining table directly
behind, he stands out and the eye is immediately
drawn to him.

● RIGHT This picture of a model was achieved by
placing her on a background of shiny plastic. The
lighter blue stripes were placed diagonally on the
darker stripes and the colours were chosen to
complement her make up. This hardly elaborate
but highly effective background shows what can
be done to obtain an eyecatching shot without
spending a great deal of money.

● LEFT This shot of a woman on a fairground stall
in Tenerife illustrates an instance where the
exception proves the rule. The background
dominates the picture and the stallholder looks
completely lost. However, because of the
garishness of the display and its overwhelming
dimensions the woman appears about to be buried
in an avalanche of her own wares – adding a touch
of humour to an otherwise rather mundane
fairground scene.

PORTRAITS: PROPS

Props are items introduced into photographs that can either add something to the composition or tell us more about the person featured, perhaps providing information about a job or a hobby. Used successfully, props should enhance the picture without overpowering the person. In their simplest form props might be an addition to the clothes someone is wearing – a hat or a flower for instance. Sometimes a bunch of flowers placed in a vase near the subject will give a certain 'lift' to the shot. It could be that by placing people against a backdrop of their work the item they produce or create becomes a prop in itself.

In a working environment there are endless possibilities for adding available props to a shot. These may take the form of a background or may completely surround the subject. If the people featured are in an active position, do not pull back so far that they become insignificant. In situations like this it is possible that the prop can subtly convey the atmosphere rather than becoming a visually dominating part of the picture.

For instance, if a man is involved in working with molten metal, heated in a furnace, it would be the sensation of the intense heat rather than a prominent shot of the furnace that would say far more about the atmosphere. Going in close to the man and showing the heat reflected on his brow while keeping the furnace in the background, you could create an evocative composition.

As a photographer, always look for props in the immediate situation and employ them in the same way as an imported accessory.

● LEFT This shot was taken in a 'smoker', the room in which kippers are cured. The room had jet black walls and was quite small. By placing the owner in front of several rows of newly-smoked kippers the fish themselves provided the props to illustrate his work.

● LEFT Upon entering this tobacconist's shop it seemed that the entire place was full of props. Positioning the owner, lighting his pipe, among his wares added an extra visual dimension to the shot as well as conveying his character.

● ABOVE Costume can provide effective props in portraits; here the simple inclusion of an unusual hat changes the character of the shot and its subject.

● ABOVE This woman lived in a small apartment. She made exotic and expensive clothes and the purpose of the shot is to show her and her work together. Since her work is so colourful, it was decided to use it to fill the room and to cover the kitchen worktop in the foreground. The room takes on a swirl of colour but the woman remains a prominent part of the shot.

PORTRAITS: SELECTING A VIEWPOINT

Taking good shots of people depends on many factors. One of the most important is where you take the picture from. It is difficult to set down hard and fast rules about this, and obviously it depends on the situation. But one or two general points are always worth bearing in mind.

If you choose a high viewpoint to photograph a person full length this will have the effect of shortening them. But if you kneel down you will exaggerate their height. A quick look in any fashion magazine shows many examples of this stance, with models who appear to have legs that go on and on. With young children and babies it may be necessary to get down on the ground and choose an extremely low viewpoint for an effective shot.

When photographing groups or crowds of people it is generally best if you can remove yourself from the throng and view them from a distance, or perhaps from above.

At a special event you may be able to emphasize the detail of a uniform or costume to make an individual or small group stand out from the rest.

When you go in close the viewpoint you take can emphasize or exaggerate a person's expression. But remember that if you go too close with a wide angle lens it is very easy to get distortion, which may not look too flattering.

Your next consideration is exposure. If people are moving about rapidly TTL metering may be an asset, but when taking shots by this method beware: the meter is reading for the general scene and not for a predominantly dark or light area which may be the centre of interest of the picture. You may need to compensate for this to get a correct exposure.

● ABOVE At formal events like the Trooping the Colour in London it sometimes pays to look for a different angle as well as the more obvious shots. A viewpoint behind this guardsman emphasizes the colour and detail of his uniform. The line of soldiers can be seen out of focus in the background, which helps to concentrate attention on him.

● LEFT Going low and looking up at this man's face has helped to highlight his features and expression. He is playing chess and I wanted to capture his concentration. If people are wearing hats be careful that the brim does not cast an unwanted shadow across their face.

● LEFT This shot was taken from ground level, lying in a similar position to that of the boy. The emphasis is on his face and this has been exaggerated by going in close. Using an 85 mm lens at this distance has helped to reduce distortion and has put the background slightly out of focus so that nothing distracts us from his gaze.

● BELOW It is very difficult to get a general shot of people from ground level in a crowded place, such as a bustling market scene. This shot shows as many people as possible, with the stalls and some of the goods they sold and was taken from a communal balcony. From here a downwards viewpoint was obtained of the shoppers milling back and forth. The angle the shot was taken from makes a strong diagonal of the crowd that enhances the overall composition.

MAKE-UP

Taking spontaneous pictures of friends and relatives produces natural and pleasing results. The appeal may come from seeing them in an unexpected situation, pulling a face, or seeing something that makes their hair stand on end. But often when taking a special portrait a little extra is required. A girlfriend, wife or daughter may be seen as an attractive person, but will the camera see her in the same way?

Often what is needed is suitable make-up. The subject may already wear make-up, but often this is inappropriate for photographic purposes. Professional photographers taking fashion and beauty pictures work with make-up artists and hair stylists. These highly trained people have spent years perfecting their craft and they can literally transform a model to give any required look.

Obviously this is the top end of the market, and no amateur would be expected to know or hire such experts. But it is worthwhile studying fashion magazines to get an idea of current looks, so that these can be discussed with the subject so that there is a good chance of getting the required effect.

Pay attention to detail. Even with the simplest make-up the shot can be ruined by a stray hair or crooked parting. Also make-up can be too reflective and cause unattractive highlights.

Men also need to take care with grooming. Messy hair and grubby fingernails are hardly the way to enhance a portrait, especially when going in close.

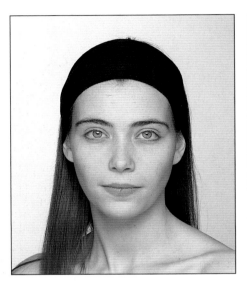

● At this stage the model is not wearing any make-up. She has used a cleanser to clean her face thoroughly, and is now ready to be made up.

● A little foundation has been applied. This gives the skin an all-over even tone. Translucent foundation cream has been used, matching the model's own natural skin colouring. Skin concealer cream can be used to cover any blemishes or shadows under the eyes. Powder is then applied to seal the foundation and to give the face a matt finish.

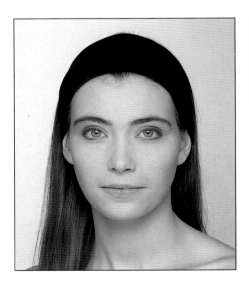

● The next stage is eye make-up. Here a little eye shadow and mascara have been used. Depending on the look required, false eyelashes could be added.

● Here the eyes have been finished with more mascara, and blusher has been applied. The lips have been outlined and covered in a pale base.

● The lips have been finished with lipstick. The model's hair has been brushed and she is now ready to be photographed.

Many people are daunted by the idea of taking photographs in the studio. But generally speaking, the majority find that handling studio lights is an easy skill to pick up.

Look through various magazines which feature pictures taken in a studio. The lighting techniques are as varied as the subjects they light. In some only one light is used, in others five or more.

The least expensive light available is a photoflood with a reflector and stand. But many people find the glare and heat from such lights uncomfortable. An alternative is studio flash. The units work from the mains and are much more powerful than a camera's built-in flash unit or one that fits onto a camera hot shoe. Each unit has its own power supply; some of the most powerful have attachments for additional flash heads.

As well as the standard reflector there is a whole variety of different attachments that can alter the character of the light. These include large umbrella-type reflectors in white, silver or gold, which bounce diffused light onto the subject, giving a softer light than a standard reflector.

An even softer light can be obtained by using a 'softbox'. These come in various sizes, but all work on the same principle. The box fits over the flash head. It has a highly reflective silver lining, and a diffusing material stretched over the front. Other diffusers can be stretched over the first one to diffuse the light even further.

Another lighting attachment is called a 'snoot'. This directs a thin beam of light onto the subject. It is not the same as a conventional spotlight, which has a broader beam which can be focused. Spotlights can also have inserts placed between the lamp and the lens, which throw patterns onto the lit area.

As with all accessories, special lights have to be used carefully and creatively. Used by themselves they will not produce miracles.

● LEFT Here only the background is lit, to make it white and silhouette the subject. This technique has to be used with care, because an overlit background can cause flare. When framing the subject take care that the light sources themselves do not creep into the picture.

● RIGHT Using just one light has lit one side of the model's face. This has left the other side of her face with dark, unattractive shadows, especially by the nose and eyes.

● LEFT A 'fill-in' light has been introduced on the left side. This is less powerful than the main light. It has softened the shadows without making the face look flat. A reflector would have a similar effect.

● RIGHT Another light has been used over the model's head to give more body to the hair. It was attached to a stand with a boom, an arm extending sideways. A boom allows a light to be brought close to a model without the stand appearing in the picture.

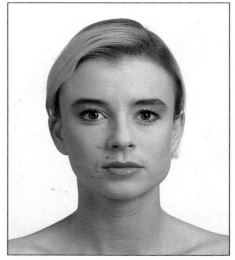

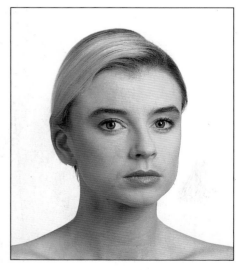

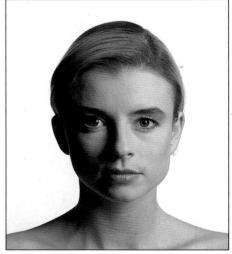

● The final picture has the addition of a white reflector placed under the model's face. This slightly softens the shadow under her chin, and to a lesser extent under her eyes.

PORTRAITS IN THE STUDIO

There are many advantages to taking portraits in a studio. For a start, the photographer has total control of the lighting, and the choice of backgrounds and props. Also, depending on the type of photograph, make-up and dress can be specified or chosen and altered.

Some photographers, and even more so their models, can feel inhibited by the studio environment, however. A bare room with only a few lights and rolls of background paper can seem an impossible setting for the creation of an interesting picture. But it only takes a little know-how and a measure of confidence to achieve a whole new dimension in photography.

Studios do not have to be elaborate, lofty or spacious. In fact, a reasonable-sized room in an ordinary house can work just as well as a studio, as the shot of the girl against a white background demonstrates.

To improvise a studio at home, hire lights from a professional photographic dealer, or perhaps buy one or two modest units as a start. However, good flash equipment would be a better investment than floodlights. It is generally more powerful, which allows shorter exposures than are possible with photofloods. It is also more comfortable to work with. Photofloods get very hot, and after a while this can make conditions uncomfortable. People also find the constant glare irritating.

An alternative is to hire a purpose-built studio. There are quite a number of these and they are advertised in photographic magazines. It is often a good idea to join a local photographic society, which can probably provide access to such facilities as well as equipment, assistance and even models.

● BELOW One of the advantages of taking pictures in a studio is that seamless backgrounds can be made with long rolls of paper. These can be hung from the wall or ceiling, and extended along the ground to conceal visible corners. A hired studio should normally provide such backgrounds, though all the paper that is used has to be paid for.

● LEFT This man's face is lit with a very low-key light. This has heightened his features and given him an enigmatic expression. Working in a studio gives total control of light, and allows the mood of a picture to be altered. Another light with a snoot (this gives a directional beam) was projected onto the background to give a graduated appearance.

● BELOW This picture shows what can be done in the home. A length of white cotton material was pinned to the wall and draped over a sofa. One flash was used, fitted with a large diffuser called a softbox. This was powerful enough to illuminate both the girl and the background. Some people – both photographers and models – find it less intimidating to work in an ordinary home than in a proper photographic studio. But as confidence and adventurousness increase, an improvised home studio can become a restriction, unless of course the room is very large.

FORMAL PORTRAITS

Formal portraits do not mean that subjects have to sit or stand to attention so that they look stiff and uncomfortable. In the early days of photography when exposure times were measured in minutes people did have to sit very still to avoid blurring the picture. Photographers even used special clamps at the back of their sitter's neck and waist to brace them in position. Fortunately these days are long past.

The most important thing in any portrait, formal or otherwise, is to capture the expression that best illustrates a person's character or status, or both. However formal the portrait might be, try to enter into a dialogue with the sitter. Discover a common interest, and the conversation will become easy and relaxed.

Even if the sitter is a complete stranger, try to plan the general nature of the shot in advance. It makes a bad impression if the first thing the photographer does after meeting the sitter is to stare hard at him, as if undecided what to do. But it is also important to plan wisely; it produces an even worse impression if, after a few shots, it becomes clear that the setting does not work, so that all the equipment has to be altered.

Often, time is of the essence. Some people, such as businessmen and public figures, are very busy, and they may be under the impression that photographs can be taken as quickly as if they had walked into an automatic photo booth. Knowing what is wanted, and directing sitters with flair and firmness, can yield strong portraits in a relatively short time. The results will please them and enhance the photographer's reputation and they are more likely to return.

● ABOVE Although this portrait of a young girl was taken in a studio, it is full of flair and vitality. An immediate rapport was struck up with her so that she felt confident and relaxed. Atmosphere is very important in any situation where there is close communication between photographer and model. It would be disastrous to start a session in an atmosphere of tension; this is as true in the studio as it is on location.

● LEFT This room looks grand and formal, yet the woman's expression gives the portrait warmth and there is the impression that it was a relaxed photographic session. Both the room and the hallway which is visible through the far doorway had to be lit. If the door had been shut the atmosphere might have seemed a little claustrophobic. Being able to see beyond the room adds space and light. Although the picture takes a wide view, there is no doubt that the woman is the centre of attention.

● RIGHT Formality need not mean rigidity. In this portrait of the photographer Terence Donovan the composition's formality and symmetry give him an enigmatic quality. For those who do not know his reputation as a photographer there are a few props to give a clue to his profession. Terence Donovan also runs a very successful film production company, and there is just a hint of the entrepreneur here.

● RIGHT The portrait of the former Speaker of the House of Commons in London had to be taken in a 10-minute session. His gown and wig might have made him look intimidating and rigid; instead they signify the status of his position and are in keeping with a portrait that is both formal and interesting. Although the Speaker appears small this is in effective contrast to the grandeur of the room.

INFORMAL PORTRAITS

Many portraits work because they have an informal look that most people would call 'natural'. But even pictures like these need thought to make them successful. For instance, it is pointless to take lots of pictures in a casual manner if the exposure or focus are incorrect or the shot is badly composed. With a little forethought all these problems can be avoided, but at the same time there is no need to be so preoccupied with the mechanics of photography that it causes inhibition and the pictures become rigid and unspontaneous.

As with all aspects of photography, the most important thing is being so familiar with the equipment that all the controls become second nature. Once these are mastered it is possible to concentrate on technique and become more adventurous.

This might mean experimenting with a different type of film. Try a high-speed one such as 1600 ISO. This will give very grainy results, but that is by no means an unattractive effect, as one of the pictures here shows. Also, using such a fast film allows pictures to be taken in almost any conditions. The film can even be uprated to 3200 ISO. (Remember that if this is done the whole film has to be shot at this rating, and when giving the film to the processing laboratory the technicians must be told that it has been uprated so that they can increase development time.)

A zoom lens, especially when combined with an autofocus mechanism, makes for faster work since focal length can be changed without the need to swap lenses.

Ultimately, of course, it is the photographer's eye that seizes upon that good shot, however much advanced equipment may be available!

● ABOVE This picture radiates spontaneity, warmth and humour. It is a good example of capturing the moment, which swiftly passes when dealing with animals. Going in close helps the general composition and focuses attention on the woman and the chicken.

● BELOW Pictures like these come readily to the alert photographer. Always have the camera loaded with film to avoid wasting time. The person might move away – or in this case merely put on his socks and shoes.

● ABOVE An ultra-fast film, 1600 ISO, has perfectly caught this young boy's cheeky expression. The grainy quality of the film, far from being a drawback, adds to the picture. The day was dull and the area surrounded by trees, so it is unlikely that a slow film would have given an adequate picture. Especially with informal portraits, be ready to try something different and do not be afraid to push film to its limits.

● RIGHT This couple was photographed informally at a barbecue. Using a 100 mm lens makes them fill the frame without the need to go so close as to make them feel uncomfortable. Her vivacious smile contrasts attractively with his rather whimsical expression. The result is a natural look that is relaxed and charming.

● BELOW Even when going in close, it is still possible to achieve a relaxed portrait. The old man's weathered face is set against a plain background which isolates and emphasizes his face. The ladder acts as a prop and introduces an informal element into the composition. The man's open-necked shirt adds a carefree element without looking untidy.

FULL-LENGTH PORTRAITS

Not all portraits of people need to be head and shoulders or full face. Sometimes the only way of achieving a good portrait is to photograph a person full length, and to include some of their environment.

When choosing a viewpoint for full-length portraits it is important to remember that photographing a standing person from low down will accentuate their height and make their legs look longer. Conversely, photographing the same person from a high viewpoint, looking down on them, will foreshorten them and make their legs look shorter.

When using a wide angle lens, care must be taken if the person is placed at the side of the frame. Some wide angle lenses, especially very wide angle ones, distort the extreme edges so that, for instance, a face will look 'stretched'.

When photographing a group of people full length, make sure that all

● LEFT This spontaneous full-length portrait was taken on a drive through Greece. The low viewpoint makes the bale of hay look even larger. The vibrant colour of the hay also makes an interesting background for the boy.

● BELOW In bright sunlight, be careful that ugly shadows do not fall across the faces of the subjects. In this picture the man was positioned in the doorway to keep the light evenly spread. Just moving someone back or forward could make all the difference. Do not be afraid to take control of the shot and direct people to the position where they will be seen to the best advantage.

● LEFT This picture of distillery workers was lit by flash. The warehouse was large, so they were grouped tightly in a confined space to give more or less even lighting. Also, they are placed quite close to the background so that the light does not fall off sharply behind them. In such situations, look carefully and try to get the best out of the environment.

● BELOW This full-length portrait was taken from a high viewpoint. By sitting the woman in a chair the problem of foreshortening has been avoided. The camera was on a tripod in a fixed position, so that items could be moved around the room till they looked right in the viewfinder. Even the dog let itself be placed so that it looks as if it was posing for the camera.

their faces can be seen. This is not just a case of careful positioning, but also of making sure that the shadow cast by one person does not fall across the face of another.

If the portrait is lit by flash make sure that this is spread evenly. Many built-in flash systems do not produce a very powerful light. A person standing in a large room may be well lit but the background will be dark and murky, because the flash was not powerful enough to light the whole room.

When photographing people full length outdoors in bright sunshine, be careful if anyone is wearing a hat. The brim can cast a dark shadow on the face. If necessary use fill-in flash to soften this shadow and eliminate the possibility of obscuring the facial expression.

PEOPLE IN THE HOME

● BELOW Children like helping around the house and such occasions can provide good opportunities for pictures, especially if there is a camera loaded and ready. Even better, this should be a simple model that anyone can use. If it is loaded with medium to fast film such as 200 ISO, it should cope with most situations without flash being necessary.

Many people do not take pictures at home except on special occasions such as a birthday or Christmas. But there are many other times when opportunities for photographs present themselves, and often these can lead to excellent portraits. One advantage of taking pictures at home is that people feel relaxed because they are in their normal environment. Another is that they are surrounded by objects that reflect their personality, which can be brought into pictures as props or backgrounds; these will reveal the varied aspects of their way of life, and their interests.

There is plenty of opportunity for spontaneous pictures in the home, especially of children. They may be doing the most ordinary, everyday things but even these, when viewed through the camera, can be seen in a new light, and spontaneous actions captured. This is one reason why it is so important to be ready with your camera. If it seems laborious to get out all your equipment, one solution is to buy an inexpensive compact camera for use around the house. This can always be kept loaded and ready to hand. It should have a built-in flash for quick shots in all conditions. In this way there will never be a reason to miss a picture — and many pictures will be well worth the effort.

● BELOW This informal picture of a young girl at the piano needed flash. The piano keys make an interesting background. The high viewpoint adds to the picture's informality.

● BELOW LEFT This couple photographed in their conservatory is a good example of balancing flash with daylight. The picture looks as if everything is lit by daylight, but in fact if flash had not been added the foreground and the couple's faces would have been in deep shadow. It was a day of patchy cloud with the sun going in and out, so it needed patience to wait for the sun to shine – but the result was worth it.

● BELOW Although this portrait is posed it has a relaxed feel to it. The musical scores in the foreground hint that the subject is a composer, or at least that music is important to him. Two flash units were used. One was directed at the man and the foreground, the other to light the area behind. These were balanced so that the scene outside the window was correctly exposed as well.

● BELOW Even on a dull overcast day good pictures can be taken. Photographing this person out walking her dog against a wooded background has cut out the dull sky. A 250 mm lens has reduced the depth of field, so that the focus is firmly on the subject.

Bright, sunny days offer good opportunities for taking portraits outdoors. But they can cause problems too. Bright sunlight can create harsh shadows. It can also make people screw up their eyes and squint, which looks most unattractive. To get round this problem, try to move the person being photographed into an area of shade. Alternatively, turn them away from direct sunlight and use a reflector to throw light back into their face. If the person is wearing a hat and the brim is casting a shadow across their face, use fill-in flash to soften the shadow.

Another problem with portraits outdoors is that the wind blows people's hair about and leaves it looking messy. If possible, look for an area sheltered from the wind.

Be on the look-out for appealing backgrounds. This could be something with an interesting texture, such as a stone wall, or it might be a view into a landscape. If the background is not photogenic, consider ways of cutting it out. This can be done by going in close and framing the picture tightly, or by using a large aperture to throw the background out of focus.

When photographing groups of people make sure that one does not cast an ugly shadow on another.

Bright but hazy days give an even, shadowless light, but in certain conditions and with some colour films the results may be a little cool. To alleviate this problem try using an 81A filter. This will slightly warm up the tones.

● RIGHT These young girls form a well-proportioned group. They were photographed with the sun to one side and slightly behind them. This has avoided ugly shadows under their eyes, and stopped any one of them from shading another. The background is dominated by the pool; the wall is unobtrusive and does not spoil the composition.

● LEFT Focusing directly on this man's eyes shows the full character of his face. Every detail of his beard is sharp. He was photographed under a white blind that acted as a diffuser so that the light, although bright, does not cast any shadows on his face.

● ABOVE In this picture of an elderly woman, a 100 mm medium telephoto lens combined with a wide aperture has put the background out of focus. It has made the splash of green behind the subject unobtrusive, but the colour complements that of her headscarf. She is in a relatively shaded area, so that her face glows with an even, natural light.

● RIGHT A low viewpoint and going in quite close lets this boy dominate the picture. The surrounding landscape gives a feeling of spring, and the boy's expression is one of playfulness. When taking portraits out of doors experiment with different viewpoints. Otherwise pictures will have an air of sameness.

PEOPLE IN THEIR ENVIRONMENT

PHOTOGRAPHING PEOPLE

Photographing people in their own environment can be very rewarding, especially when you are on holiday. Generally strangers are only too willing to be in your shots – particularly if they are in an area where tourists are commonplace. However, if you want to photograph someone close in you should always ask their permission first. There are several reasons for this:

● It is polite. If your manner is friendly they will not feel threatened.

● Once they know they are the centre of interest in your photograph, they are much more likely to do what you ask of them. This is important because, although they may be attractive and their environment interesting, they may be standing in a less than ideal place and would be much better framed if you asked them to move slightly to one side, or perhaps onto a step. You might be able to get a better background by moving yourself, but if you creep about in a furtive manner you are likely to upset them and make them uncooperative if you do finally decide to ask them to move. In this case you will have lost the chance of a good photograph.

● Once you have gained their confidence, they may show you another area or aspect of their lives which you would otherwise overlook. This may well prove more interesting than the original scene.

● Having gained their cooperation and moved them into the position you want, look carefully at the light falling on their faces. Are they in bright sun which creates ugly shadows under their eyes and noses? Or is the sun behind them and shining into the lens? In either case do not be afraid to move them again. You may never get another chance.

● BELOW This woman was cracking almonds outside her house. Her position was fine, but she was in strong shadow. By placing a small portable reflector to the right of the camera, just enough light was bounced back onto her. This is an example of a situation where a very bright background can give a misleading exposure reading.

● BELOW This shot is a good example of the advantages of taking people into your confidence. This shop was a good photographic setting but inside, where this couple was, it was too dark. The couple agreed to move into the doorway where the light was better than within the shop, but the shot still needed something more, so they also agreed to hang sausages around the doorway. As a final touch, they are holding one of their whole hams. A bit of friendly discussion produced a shot which would not have existed otherwise.

● ABOVE Markets, like this souk in Agadir, Morocco, provide a wealth of opportunities for the alert photographer. This young boy was leading his camel through the throng of people gathered around the vendors. He is dwarfed by his camel, which has a typically arrogant expression. In situations like this feel free to move around the person until he is in the best position with the light. The other people in the souk fill the background, but are out of focus so they do not intrude.

● LEFT Although the picture was taken from some distance, these security guards at the Museum of Art in Washington DC were well aware that they were being photographed, and they played to the camera. Their presence emphasized the monumentality of the bronze sculpture that serves as a backdrop. Always be on the look-out for such a juxtaposition.

Poor weather does not have to deter you from photographing people. Sometimes it can actually add to and animate a photograph. But before taking your camera out in pouring rain, remember that cameras should not get wet. A camera that gets thoroughly soaked – or worse still, dropped in the sea – will probably be irreparably damaged.

If the skies are full of fast-moving clouds with quick bursts of intermittent sunshine, extra care will have to be taken with exposure. If the sun is out when you take your reading but behind cloud when you take your shot, the photograph will be underexposed. The reverse will be true if the sun is obscured when you take your reading but then comes out before you take your shot.

Look out for something unusual that will lift your shots in poor weather, and give them a point of interest. An isolated colour, or a solitary figure in a landscape, will dispel the grey look. Whatever happens, do not be deterred by poor weather conditions.

● LEFT Here is a good example of making the best of a picture in poor weather, as people cross Dublin's Halfpenny Bridge in the pouring rain, their umbrellas jostling for space. The two large coloured umbrellas stand out in an otherwise monochromatic scene. The picture was taken inside a doorway which helped protect the camera from the rain.

● ABOVE As you go for a walk on a dull, overcast day, you are all the more likely to notice a splash of colour that can make all the difference to a photograph. The flag on the beach marked the area of safe bathing. It was pure coincidence that the red and yellow of the flag matched the colours of the children's oilskins. Even something as simple as a patch of colour can enliven the dullest of scenes. Be prepared at all times for the chance of a spontaneous shot.

● BELOW Although slightly posed, this picture of a young girl at a swimming pool is an attractive holiday portrait. The line of the white wall adds to the composition and makes an effective contrast with the blue of the pool. Shots like this can be fun, but it is important to work quickly so that being photographed does not become a chore for the child – boredom cannot be disguised.

● BELOW In the holiday season most countries provide good set-piece events. Events can happen spontaneously, so be prepared. It is important to get the best viewpoint for a shot, as far as this can be done without being rude or pushy. Failing this, hold the camera above the heads of the crowd and point it at the action – it may be an outside chance, but it could work!

● ABOVE This picture taken from a high viewpoint shows what can be achieved by looking for a new and striking angle. Seen from above, the water is translucent. The dinghy adds a splash of colour. The two boys did not know they were being photographed, and the spontaneity of this simple shot adds to its effect.

● RIGHT This couple fits in well with most people's idea of the British on holiday. The photographer did not know the people, but they happily agreed to be photographed. The picture is full of good-natured humour. Only a camera ready for instant use will capture the mood in this way.

When photographing children it is often a good idea to include their mother. She is usually the closest person to the child and the best suited to allay its fears and put it at ease, and help it to adopt the best position.

Use a photographer's eye to look for the best viewpoint and lighting to show the natural bond between mother and child. As in any situation when photographing more than one person, be careful that the mother's head does not cast a shadow on the child's face.

If working indoors try to use available light. This will be less distracting to the child, which may be alarmed if flash is used. If flash is necessary, soften the light as much as possible. This can be done by bouncing the light off a suitable surface such as a white ceiling or board. Alternatively

put a diffuser over the light. This can be tracing paper or even a handkerchief. Take care here not to underexpose the photograph. The best way to avoid this is to use a flash meter, which shows exactly how much light is falling on the subject. If the mother and child are sitting by a window, a reflector can be used to throw some natural light back on them.

When working out of doors make sure that neither the mother or child gets cold. Not only is it uncomfortable for them, but they might be shown with red hands and dripping noses.

Above all, be aware that most children can only concentrate for a short time. This may mean working quickly. Conversely, a good deal of patience may be required to catch the child at the best moment.

● ABOVE This was taken in a studio. Care was needed to keep the light from casting the mother's shadow onto the child. Placing the child behind the mother has created an informal mood and it looks as if a game is in progress. Try to make pictures look fun, especially in the artificial conditions of the studio.

● LEFT This picture was taken against the light and a reflector was used to bounce light back onto the mother and child. This has given a soft halo effect to their hair and made the picture look warm and summery. Asking them to lie down on the grass has further increased the air of a natural bond between mother and child. The low viewpoint makes the viewer feel part of the picture.

● RIGHT Draping a white sheet over the window has created a very soft background. The mother and child were lit by flash softened by a diffuser. This has softened the overall effect even more, perfectly fitting the mood. In this case the baby was fascinated by the flash light, and it proved a useful diversion for him. Using a 100 mm lens allowed a comfortable distance between the camera and the subject.

● LEFT Going in very close has achieved an intimate picture of a mother and her son. It was taken on a chilly autumn day, and they are huddled together to give a snug effect. In such situations take care that the child does not get too cold and become distressed.

BABIES AND YOUNG CHILDREN

Photographs of young children can bring pleasure to many people, not only their parents and close relatives.

The important thing to remember is that young children tire easily. Patience will be needed to get the best out of what might be a very brief photographic session. If the child seems to be becoming unhappy it is best to take a break and restart at a later time. Try to avoid dressing young children up in strange costumes, as these can humiliate them. The child should be having fun, and not be made fun of.

Natural light is probably the best, as it will not distract or distress the child. Very young babies are often upset by flashlight.

Try to think ahead about backgrounds. An ugly intrusion can ruin what would otherwise be a great shot, and there may not be a chance to move the subject. As well as more formal portraits, try to photograph the young child engaged in some activity — playing, or perhaps at bathtime.

When photographing small children in a studio or away from home, have a few toys around for them to play with. They may well not be able to understand a request to go to a particular place or do something specific. Often the only way of getting the right expression from a child is to play the fool.

With children who are two years old or more, Polaroid pictures can be a great help at the photography session. They will be fascinated by seeing the results instantly, and the pictures are also useful for checking exposure, lighting and general composition.

● BELOW Bathing can be fun for young children and provide plenty of opportunity for natural-looking pictures. This one was taken by standing directly over the bath and using the light coming in through a window. A standard focal length lens was used. By working quickly several good shots were taken with the minimum of fuss.

● ABOVE This child acted spontaneously for the camera in a studio which other children would have found daunting. Several shots were taken, each one with a different expression. They were lit by a flash unit which had a fast recycling time so that shots could be taken in close succession. Editing the pictures was difficult as each one had its own character, but this one was finally declared the winner.

● RIGHT Going in close on this baby's face has given full emphasis to his expression. Soft lighting has given a feeling of gentleness. A good deal of gesticulation, face pulling and cooing by the photographer and the child's parents were needed to maintain his interest. Never prolong a session with a young child to the point where it becomes upset. At the first sign of unhappiness, it is best to stop and try again later.

● LEFT The blanket makes an unusual and interesting background. Always look out for something new, so that shots taken over a period have variety. This picture was taken by natural light coming through a large window, with a reflector used to throw light back and give a fairly even level of illumination.

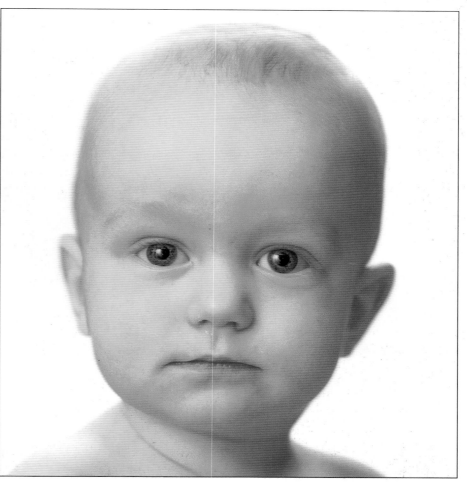

CHILDREN

Children are ideal subjects for photographs, for many reasons. First, such pictures tell the story of their lives. From the moment they are born there is a visual record of their development which will not only be a pleasure to their parents and grandparents but will also be fun for them to look back on, and to show their own children in years to come. Even with the arrival of home video cameras, it is hard to beat a still picture that captures a fleeting moment in a child's life. And last but not least, an unlimited number of copies can easily be made and sent to friends or relatives anywhere in the world.

There is no need to photograph every breath children take, but at least try to make a record of important events such as birthday parties. These in themselves will make a fascinating series of pictures that show the child growing and changing. It will also provide the children with pictures of their friends.

Often the best way to photograph children is to take a candid approach, especially when they are absorbed in some activity. A medium telephoto or zoom lens – 80 to 200 mm – will be useful in such cases, making it possible to keep at a certain distance but still fill the frame. A film with a speed of about 200 ISO should allow work in moderate lighting conditions without a tripod or flash, either of which could distract the child and destroy the spontaneity.

● RIGHT Special occasions such as birthday parties provide excellent opportunities for the photographer. This picture was lit entirely by the candles on the birthday cake. A 400 ISO film allowed an exposure just short enough for the camera to be hand-held. If flash had been used the atmosphere would have been killed, and the candles would have faded into insignificance. The picture also captures the birthday cake, over which a good deal of trouble has been taken.

● BELOW This portrait of a small girl captures a spontaneous expression that is at once both intimate and charming. The warm light and her yellow jumper make a pleasing contrast with her dark colouring. Always be on the look-out for quick shots like this.

● ABOVE Children's hobbies and pastimes provide many opportunities for pictures. Although this picture was taken in close the girl was not inhibited as she was happy to be photographed with her pony.

● RIGHT Children can become totally absorbed in what they are doing, shown in this picture of a young girl feeding pigeons. Standing back so as not to inhibit the subject usually makes for a better picture. A telephoto lens is useful in such situations, as it allows a frame-filling shot, perhaps without the child even being aware of the photographer. Patience is also needed, and can be richly rewarded.

CHILDREN AT PLAY

Children play naturally, so play gives good opportunities for natural pictures. Even in a favourite game children may lose interest in a few minutes, so quick work is needed to capture a good expression or gesture.

When working indoors, in the interests of speed it is probably best to use flash. This may upset a few children, but if they are busy they will probably take it in their stride. They may even be fascinated by it.

An alternative is to use a fast film and available light. If this is from an ordinary tungsten light bulb it will be necessary to balance daylight film with an 80A filter; otherwise the photograph will come out with an excessively warm, orange cast. There are now a few fast tungsten-balanced colour negative films, and a better selection of colour reversal ones. However, with these, if any other shots on the film are taken out of doors it will be necessary to use an 85B colour balancing filter to avoid a blue cast.

Try to think of different angles when photographing children at play. Consider a high viewpoint, looking down on them. This will make them look diminutive, but that may be an attractive effect. If the background is unsuitable, go in close to eliminate it, or use a large aperture so that it is out of focus. If the child is absorbed in painting or reading, try to get a shot that shows that concentration.

If the child gets bored, give up at once. Persistence will only produce tears of frustration and may put the child off further photographic sessions. A few Polaroid pictures taken to begin with will usually interest children and make them more patient when shots are taken with normal film.

● RIGHT, CENTRE AND BOTTOM LEFT These pictures were taken in a nursery school. The children liked being photographed; it was a new experience for them. However, young subjects can easily become bored and lose interest. Patience on the photographer's part is paramount in such situations.

● BELOW Although the ball is slightly blurred, this adds to the feeling of movement. The shot was taken at $1/125$ second. A faster speed might have frozen the ball and the feeling of action would have been lost.

● BELOW Sometimes the simplest shots are the most effective. This one of a young girl sitting on her bed surrounded by soft toys was taken using natural light streaming in from a window, diffused by a net curtain.

● RIGHT Colour plays an important part in giving a feeling of fun. The primary colours here convey excitement, aided by the boy's red sweater.

● ABOVE Look for different angles when photographing children. Looking down on this small girl has increased the sense of her diminutive size. The picture was lit with a flash attachment on the camera's hot shoe.

● LEFT When photographing children (or anyone) out of doors in bright sunlight look out for harsh shadows. Make sure the background does not dominate the picture, and is not ugly or uninteresting.

OLDER CHILDREN

Younger children can soon get bored and restless when being photographed, but older children can be awkward in front of the camera from the start — especially when in their early teens. It is often better to photograph older children in a group rather than singly. Having a friend along to support them will give them confidence.

If a teenage girl is being photographed she will probably have quite definite views on how she wants to look. Discuss what she wants to wear and the sort of make-up she wants, if any.

When shooting indoors, decide on the background. Will it be in the subject's room with a background of posters, or is it possible to rig up a small home studio?

When shooting out of doors in bright sun, watch for shadows on the face and use fill-in flash where necessary. Backlighting can be used to create a more romantic feel. Try using a reflector to throw light back onto the face.

When older boys are being photographed, they may feel more comfortable if they are pursuing one of their hobbies. You could take pictures of them making a model or working on a bike. If they play a musical instrument, this might be included as a useful prop.

With boys and girls alike, take care not to talk down to them or patronize them. This will create a bad atmosphere from the start. Ask what their interests are and talk to them on equal terms.

With groups of older children it is often difficult to get them all to do the right thing at once. Try to position them to ensure that no one obscures anyone else.

Experiment with different angles and lenses, and do not be afraid to bend a few rules. The result can certainly repay the trouble.

● ABOVE These children were on holiday. The older ones kept teasing one another, but eventually they got themselves together and formed this group. Care was taken to make sure that no one covered anyone else.

● RIGHT This picture of a teenage girl was taken using available light coming through her bedroom window. Photographing her in familiar surroundings made her feel relaxed and at ease from the start. The posters on the wall behind her were put out of focus so as not to distract from her, and the camera was focused on her eyes.

● LEFT The picture was taken in the two girls' room. It is one of a series of shots that were taken of them dressing up. This gave them something to do between shots, and allowed them to contribute their own ideas about how they wanted to be photographed. It is important to deal with older children on equal terms.

GROUPS

Very often when photographing groups of people there is always someone looking the wrong way, keeping their eyes shut or making a silly gesture or face. As a photographer it will take all your expertise as a director to get everyone to do what you want them to do when you want them to do it. The knack is to strike a happy medium between a jovial atmosphere and firmness. Of course not all groups of people that you photograph are going to be under your control. If this is the case it is then up to you to find the right angle and be ready for the right moment. You will need to get yourself into a position where the light is at its best.

It might be advantageous in certain circumstances to photograph people

● LEFT By including the overhanging foliage from the tree in the foreground a natural frame to the picture has been achieved. The people listening to the band have also added foreground interest. These details help to draw the eye to the main centre of interest, the group of bandsmen playing under the canopy of the bandstand.

● LEFT This shot was taken in a steam bath in Moscow. The attendants were only too willing to pose for the photograph and directing them to the required positions was quite easy. The lighting was a combination of flash and available light. The camera was mounted on a tripod and the shutter fired with a cable release. This meant that it was easier to keep an eye on the attendants' gestures and expressions and to direct them to adopt the pose required. Because of the style of the building – it looks more like a gothic church than a steam bath – a certain incongruity has been achieved.

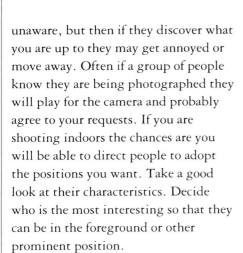

unaware, but then if they discover what you are up to they may get annoyed or move away. Often if a group of people know they are being photographed they will play for the camera and probably agree to your requests. If you are shooting indoors the chances are you will be able to direct people to adopt the positions you want. Take a good look at their characteristics. Decide who is the most interesting so that they can be in the foreground or other prominent position.

If there are many people to fit into the group, position them or take a viewpoint so that no one is obscured by anyone else. Consider whether some would be better sitting while others stand. It would be an advantage to work with the camera on a tripod and use a cable release. In this case you can position everyone to your liking. Also, when it comes to taking the actual shot, you can keep an eye on the group better from the camera viewpoint than looking through the viewfinder all the time. If you do use this method and your camera is set to auto exposure you will have to cover the viewfinder. On nearly all cameras there is a small button that brings a shield over the viewfinder. This cuts out light entering the eyepiece which would affect the camera metering mechanism and result in underexposure.

● RIGHT These men were playing cards on a terrace that was overlooked by a car park. It was a matter of chance that they were seen from this angle but full advantage has been taken of the viewpoint. Although the players became aware that they were being photographed they were too absorbed in their game to care. With a large group like this invariably someone will be looking the wrong way or making an unwanted gesture. Since it was not possible to direct them, several shots were taken so that a selection could be made.

● LEFT These five men were photographed at a barbecue being held at a ranch in Arizona. Either because of what they were drinking or because they were naturally confident, they had no inhibitions when it came to having their picture taken. Always be on the look-out for spontaneous situations but take care that unwanted details are cropped out of your shots.

Taking pictures of older people can be very rewarding for the creative photographer. Often they will have aged in a way which reflects their working life. For instance, a person with an outdoor occupation is likely to have a tanned, lined face – unlike an office worker. It is these physical characteristics that make such photographs so interesting.

At the same time, the photographer should show some sensitivity toward someone who is no longer young, not just in the way they are portrayed but also in the effect that a long photographic session, or even the use of flash, might have on them. If someone is a real character but frail, try several short sessions, and if possible use available light.

Older people are not only interesting in their own right but may well be surrounded by items collected over a lifetime, or they may be dressed in a way that reflects their life, as in the case of the Chelsea Pensioner shown here.

A serious approach may be required to illustrate inadequate living conditions or illness. But if it is not, look for humour in pictures. This is not the same as being humiliating or patronizing. An easy way to photograph an older person might be to strike up a conversation with them. If so, be patient and do not give the impression that they are repetitive or long winded.

Look for different viewpoints, or go in close and concentrate on a particular area such as hands. Black and white photography may be better than colour, since it allows greater expression and more evocative images.

● ABOVE These two men were photographed outside a café in Italy. They had no inhibitions about having their pictures taken, so that several angles could be explored. They were delighted with an instant Polaroid picture, which made them more receptive to being photographed. A medium telephoto lens, 100 mm, put the background slightly out of focus, drawing attention to their faces.

● LEFT The picture was taken from a high viewpoint, as the room was rather small and as much of it as possible was required for the photograph. The woman is Frances Partridge, the oldest surviving member of the Bloomsbury Group. She is surrounded by reminders of the group, including a portrait of Lytton Strachey.

● ABOVE Many older people wear clothes that symbolize their way of life, such as this Chelsea Pensioner. His hat and red coat add picturesque colour. His face is full of character and is lit by hazy sunlight. If the subject of the shot wears glasses, care should be taken with reflections, especially when using flash.

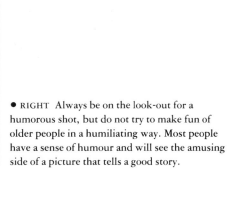

● RIGHT Always be on the look-out for a humorous shot, but do not try to make fun of older people in a humiliating way. Most people have a sense of humour and will see the amusing side of a picture that tells a good story.

CANDID SHOTS

● BELOW This is an example of being prepared for a spontaneous shot. The woman bending over the child makes the obvious comment on 'little and large'. However, the picture is taken in such a way that the woman's face is hidden, so she remains anonymous and not humiliated. The shot was taken using a 300 mm lens that kept a good distance between the woman and the camera.

Candid photography is when people are photographed in a natural or unposed way and may be unaware of the camera. Being prepared is essential – carry a camera at all times and have it ready for use. Since the opportunity for shots may occur when the light is low and there is no time for flash, or when flash might be intrusive, try a medium-fast film such as 200 or 400 ISO.

If you do take a photograph quickly and the subject is still in position, see if you can shoot from a different viewpoint that may be better. Even if the person moves away altogether you will still have that important first shot, but chances for improvement are usually available. Perhaps the best lens to use would be a 80–300 mm zoom lens. This means that the picture can be framed in such a way as to crop out any unwanted detail. It also means that you can get in close to the subject from some distance away without having to change lenses. In this way you can work unnoticed without inhibiting the person or people and ruining the spontaneity of the situation. In candid photography it is often the look, gesture or position of a person that makes the shot.

It is an advantage to have TTL metering, preferably with spot metering facilities. This means a reading can be taken from the subject's face and you can expose for the skin tone. If the person is against a white wall or bright reflective background then there is the risk of underexposure if the meter takes an average reading; this is because the background would be giving off the most light.

● LEFT This elderly man was quietly reading his book. After the initial photograph was taken another viewpoint was found. This made a better composition with the row of flower pots and added interest to his surroundings. Never think you have captured the perfect shot until you have exhausted all the possibilities.

● LEFT At first glance this picture looks like a man reading a newspaper but it is in fact a dummy. This plays a trick on the viewer and creates another dimension to candid photography.

● ABOVE Is it the unexpectedness of seeing a priest gambling that makes this candid picture a success? He was absorbed in selecting the winner in the next race and was oblivious to having his picture taken even though he was quite close to the camera.

● ABOVE Having had just a little too much to drink, this man fell asleep on the bonnet of his car. Shots like this abound for the alert photographer.

● RIGHT Even when people appear to be unaware of having their photograph taken, a second glance may contradict this. This boy in a Tunisian market appears to be asleep but a careful look shows that he is in fact watching from the corner of half-closed eyes.

GOING IN CLOSE

Pictures of people do not all have to be head and shoulders or full length. There are many other areas of the body that lend themselves to being photographed. Some of these pictures can be evocative and sensual. Others can be character studies, such as shots of gnarled hands and wrinkled skin.

Most standard lenses will not focus close enough, and a close-up attachment of some kind will be needed: extension rings, bellows or a macro lens. Close-up lenses that fit onto the front of an existing lens like a filter are available, but the quality of the image is not very good. Some telephoto lenses can also be focused to quite short distances and will give excellent close-up shots. With all these devices depth of field is very limited.

For close-up work the camera has to be kept perfectly still and it is advisable to use a tripod. In particular, extension tubes and bellows reduce the amount of light passing through the lens, so that exposures have to be long. They are made even longer by the need to use a small aperture to make the most of the available depth of field. When using available light, and with the lens stopped down to f22 or even f32, an exposure of 1 second or more may be needed. The subject also has to be kept still, which can be difficult.

If lighting a close-up picture with flash, be careful of shadows. What looks acceptable from a distance may be harsh and ugly in close-up and dominate the picture. As the camera will be only a short way from the subject, it is vital to ensure that it does not cast its own shadow onto the area.

Once the photographs have been developed, consider making enlarged prints. These could become many times larger than life size, with a strikingly abstract, sculptural quality.

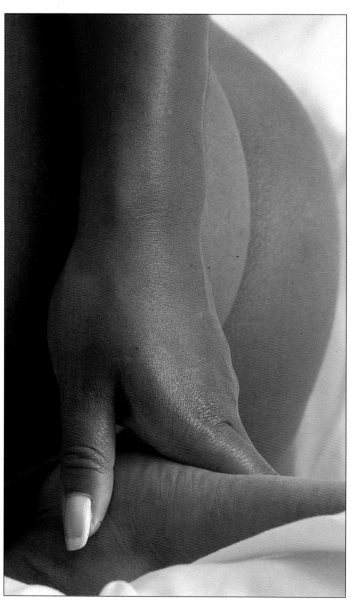

● RIGHT This picture was taken with a macro lens. The subject's feet were surrounded with a white sheet so that they became isolated and dominated the picture. They were lit with flash, using a 'softbox' to diffuse the light. The angle of view gives a sculptural effect.

● LEFT Going in close on this girl's hand, with her own body as the background, has created a sensual picture. A 100 mm lens focused at its nearest distance was used – this shows that close-ups are possible without special lenses or accessories.

● LEFT This picture was taken using a combination of extension rings and macro lens. The girl's eye was approximately 5 cm (2 in) from the front of the lens. It was essential to mount the lens on a tripod and to have a support for the girl's head. The picture was lit by flash and the depth of field, even at f22, was virtually non-existent.

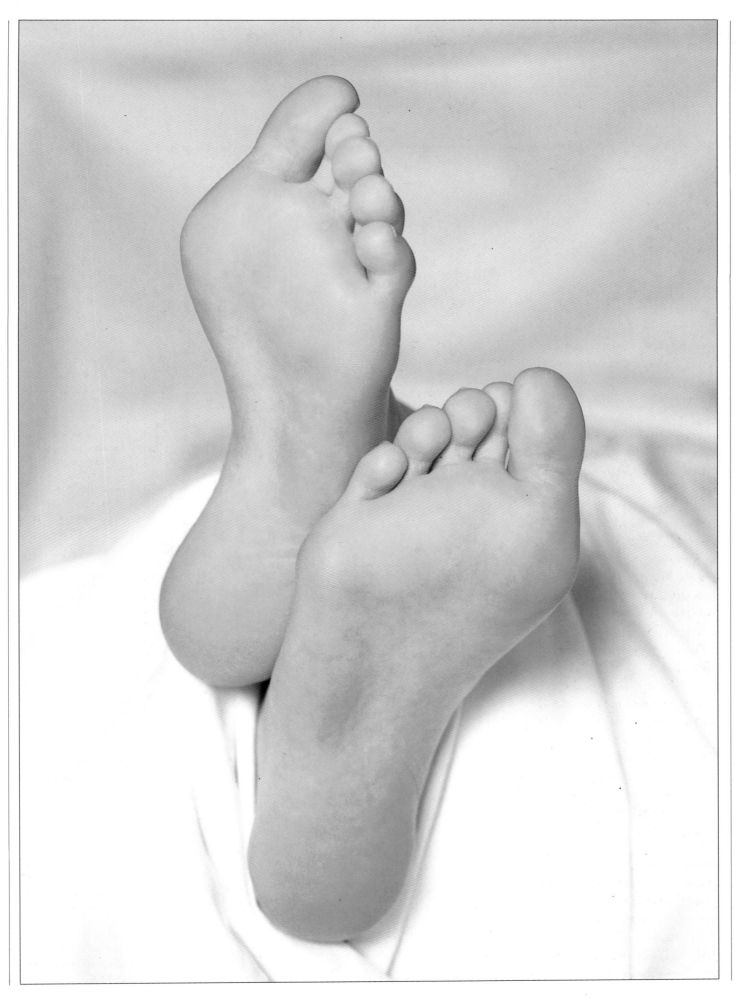

HIGH-KEY AND LOW-KEY PORTRAITS

High-key pictures are those where the tonal range is predominantly light. These are not to be confused with high-contrast pictures, which are images that have extremes of tone with few if any mid-tones. In contrast, low-key pictures have a tonal range mainly from the dark end of the scale. Again,

these are not the same as low-contrast pictures, which are images which have a narrow range of tone – this is probably due to underexposure, and the prints will have a muddy look.

When a full tonal range is easy to achieve, why, then, take high- or low-key pictures?

High-key pictures can look very romantic, and sometimes achieve an ethereal quality. If the background to a picture is uninteresting or intrusive it may be possible to fade it out by overexposing it. This may cause flare around the subject but, handled carefully, even this can be used to

● LEFT This low-key picture was taken in a studio, using just one light. This was placed to the side of, and slightly behind, the model. A reflector to the left and just in front of him bounced back just enough light to give detail in his face. The smoke from the cigarette shows up because it is backlit. If the light had been at the front the smoke would not have been visible.

● LEFT This is a high-key picture. The model is bathed in soft, diffused light and placed against a white background. A soft focus filter has been placed over the lens, further enhancing the romantic look.

creative advantage. High-key pictures can also portray freshness, a virginal quality, or the innocence of the newborn.

Conversely, low-key pictures can convey isolation or loneliness. They can be very atmospheric.

The easiest way to create low-key effects in the studio is with what is known as a 'rim light'. The light is positioned slightly behind the subject. This creates a slight halo effect on the side the light is coming from. Using a reflector or a fill-in light can give the shaded side of the face just enough tone. The result is an image with dark tones, but one in which the subject is easily discernible.

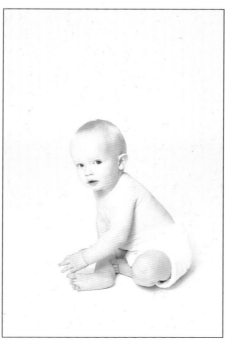

● ABOVE Although this young girl is wearing a medium coloured top the majority of the tones are from the lighter end of the scale. Her hair, backlit by the sun, adds to the high-key nature of the picture. A reflector was used to throw light back onto her face.

● LEFT This baby was photographed on a continuous roll of white background paper so that there is no line at the junction of the floor and wall. A large 'softbox' light was used, and this has created a very high-key picture.

BLACK AND WHITE PORTRAITS ON LOCATION

Photographing people out of doors or in their homes in black and white can give strong and incisive images. Unlike photographing in a studio, however, there is not full control of lighting.

When using available light, some thought is needed to make the lighting work. When a flashgun or a portable flash unit is used, the light can be put where it is needed. If bright sunlight is causing shadows on the person's face, there are several choices. One is to move the person to an area of shadow where the light is more even. Another is to use fill-in flash to soften the shadows.

If shooting against the light, a reflector can be used to bounce light back onto the subject's face. If, on the other hand, it seems that a silhouette

would make an evocative image, take the exposure reading from the light behind the subject.

When working out of doors, even if the light is bright, it can be interesting to use a film faster than would normally be chosen. This will give increased contrast and grain, even a 'gritty' look, as the picture of the youths shows.

Always look for a new angle, especially when photographing groups of people. There is nothing duller than a straight line of people rigidly sitting or standing. Keep watch for an unexpected chance, and always have the camera loaded and ready.

Remember that, unlike colour film, black and white is not affected by differences in light sources. Whether shooting in tungsten or fluorescent light or daylight, only the intensity of the light need be considered.

● LEFT When out and about, always be on the look-out for an unusual or spontaneous portrait, such as this one of a boy hiding behind his balloon. A camera loaded and at the ready allows the alert photographer to seize such moments.

● TOP LEFT Taking portraits in the studio allows complete control over lighting and composition. The possibilities are endless, as these three pictures show. Here the group is arranged to give prominence to the leader. The main light is coming from the right, but a weaker fill-in light has been put at the left. This arrangement shows some modelling in their faces. If the two lights had been of the same strength, ugly cross shadows would have occurred and their features would have looked flat.

● CENTRE LEFT Placing the main light directly in front of and below the group, shining upwards, gives an eerie effect. When positioning lights in a studio always return to the camera viewpoint to check the result.

● BOTTOM LEFT Standing on some steps and looking down on the group gives another angle. Whether photographing groups or individuals, always look for new viewpoints and lighting effects. The possibilities are limitless.

LEARNING TO USE LIGHTS

Explore the effect that one light can have on someone's face. If it is placed at an angle of 45 degrees to their face, set medium-high so that the shadow falls between the nose and half-way down the upper lip: the effect will be reasonably natural. If the light is straight in front and higher, there will be heavy shadows under the eyes, nose and chin. A light set below the face pointing upward will give a ghostly look. Practice, and a keen eye for where shadows fall, will soon make it easy to achieve a desired style. Once the basics have been mastered, all that is needed is a little imagination.

POLAROID MONTAGE

Polaroid film gives good instant portraits, but it is worth trying something different, such as making a montage portrait of several Polaroid prints stuck together. This technique was made famous by the artist David Hockney, who has exhibited works in this medium in major art galleries worldwide.

Making Polaroid montages is more than just a way of constructing an interesting image. It is a good exercise in looking and seeing. Consider having a conversation with someone. During this time one is aware that every part of the person is there, but at any one moment the eye is focused on only a single part. Moving one's gaze from the face to the feet gives a completely differently framed picture. You remain aware that the head is still there, but it is out of focus, as if it formed part of the background, and is not being concentrated on. Now compare a full-length portrait of that person. Every part is there and in focus, but it is not what the eye saw during the conversation. Even if it is a fine photograph it lacks something vital.

However, by building up a picture of that person from a series of quick Polaroid snaps, an image can be made that is like a series of glances. There is no attempt to make a smoothly connected picture where every part fits perfectly together. The assembled picture shows that there are ways of seeing that are more truthful to actual experience than a normal portrait. It reflects the way people actually see.

● ABOVE Not all the small pictures in this portrait align perfectly, but this makes the viewer look all the more closely at the girl's features. When the portrait is viewed as a whole, certain pictures in it may seem to jar and upset the conventional form of a close-up portrait. But think of talking to someone, perhaps across a dinner table. Visual emphasis changes throughout the conversation: one moment one is looking at their eyes, the next their mouth, or at a mole not previously noticed. The world is viewed not as a whole, but as a series of bits of information.

● LEFT At first glance this might look like a standard picture of someone sitting on a sofa, cut up and stuck together in a grid of rectangles. But a closer look reveals that each picture in the grid is taken from a slightly different viewpoint. For instance, the carpet and the things on it are seen from above. Ordinarily, a viewer standing in front of the sofa would be aware of the floor while looking at the person, or at the picture above her. But to see the floor clearly it would be necessary to look downward and look at it from a different viewpoint, which is the one shown here.

EDITING YOUR PICTURES

Once you have got your pictures back from the processing laboratory the next step is to edit them. How often you must have visited friends and been subjected to all their holiday snaps, with comments like, 'You can just see part of that church we told you about in the background,' or, 'This is a bit blurred but you can recognize John.' Not all their pictures may be like that, but they have not given enough thought to weeding out the unsuccessful or uninteresting ones. Even good pictures will make little impact if they are submerged in a flood of bad shots.

Look at any magazine and consider the pictures that have been used. In a

photo spread the few pictures that have been printed will have been chosen from several rolls of film. In a newspaper or news magazine, pictures of an event may have been chosen not just from many rolls but from the work of several photographers.

When looking through your pictures, discard those that are badly exposed. Next, look at subjects of which you have taken more than one shot. Select one or two that give a good overall view. If there are others where you have gone in close, choose the ones that give the most interesting details. After this initial editing, decide whether any pictures would be

improved by being cropped or differently framed when reprinted.

It is quite easy to select the best of a series of holiday pictures, but greater care is needed for a series of portraits or other studio pictures. These will have been taken in controlled conditions and will probably all be technically sound. Here you must look for the frames that show the model in the most flattering or arresting way.

It may seem wasteful to discard so many pictures, but the results will be that people actually look forward to seeing your pictures, and people you have photographed will be pleased with being seen at their best.

● ABOVE This frame has been printed virtually full frame. It was chosen in the initial selection to show an enlargement from a high viewpoint.

● RIGHT The printer was asked to angle the masking on the enlarger baseboard so that the model appears at a very slight angle.

● ABOVE RIGHT For this picture the printer was asked to crop in tight on the model. When having prints made at a professional laboratory it is a good idea to see if you can discuss your requirements with the printer beforehand.

Improving Your Technique

INTRODUCTION

Once the photographer gains confidence, the opportunities for improvement and experimentation are numerous. The methods of enhancing images are immensely varied and exciting: they range from the simple addition of a special effect filter or a specialized lens, or the more complicated manipulation of films and prints. The photographic techniques used to achieve original and extraordinary effects are available to everyone; do not be afraid of experimentation — it can produce some stunning shots.

PRESENTATION

When your pictures are processed and you have edited them you will want to decide how best to present them.

PRINTS

If the shots were made on negative film you will have prints. Many types of album are available: traditional ones where the prints are fixed to the leaves with corner mounts, and more modern kinds where the pictures are held in individual sheaths which are flipped over to view them.

For special photographs that you have cropped and had enlarged, and perhaps toned, there are folio books. These are spiral bound and come in various sizes. The prints are mounted on card and slid into transparent sleeves. When the book is opened the prints lie flat. This makes a very professional presentation. An alternative to this is to have your prints laminated. They are encapsulated between two layers of plastic – clear on the image side and black on the back – which are heat sealed. The prints can then be put individually into a folio case. The virtue of this method is that it can accommodate prints of different sizes.

TRANSPARENCIES

These can be made into prints, but there are other ways of presenting them. There are black masks that hold a single transparency, and which are slid into a clear plastic sleeve which protects them. These mounts are made for transparency sizes from 35 mm to 10 × 8 in. Mounts for pictures from 35 mm to 6 × 7 in can have the same overall size, and can be filed in a custom-made drawer for the best protection and access.

As well as individual mounts there are types that hold transparencies in groups. Typical mounts of this kind would hold 35 mm in groups of 24, or 5 × 4 in

transparencies in groups of 4. In all these cases the mounted transparencies have to be viewed on a light box.

Transparencies can also be made into slides, mounted in stiff holders, for projection. For the more advanced projectors the slides are put into magazines, which protect them and can be used as permanent boxes. Magazines may be straight or circular. The projector has a mechanism for picking out one slide at a time and projecting it; some machines have a remote control. For a really professional presentation two or more projectors can be synchronized and combined with a soundtrack or commentary or music, or both. Some shows use as many as 60 projectors, programmed with a soundtrack by means of a computer. These displays, which are known under

the general heading of AV (audio-visual), can be quite stunning.

A new way of viewing your photographs is to have them transferred to CD-ROM. They are recorded onto what looks like a CD, though it needs a special player which is connected to your television in the same way as a video recorder. At present each disc holds about 100 images. They can be viewed in any sequence, and a soundtrack is included on the disc. You can zoom into an interesting part of the image, pan from side to side and move up and down. A suitably equipped photographic dealer can make prints of any pictures on the disc. The scope for this system is enormous. You can have

Folio case for prints

images transferred from several existing discs to a single new one to make a record, say, of your children growing up. This may seem a startling advance, but when you recall that twenty years ago most people had not even heard of video you will appreciate how quickly new technology becomes the norm.

Projector

35 mm slide tray

Plastic 35 mm transparency mounts

Light box

Card transparency mounting masks

SPECIAL FILM TECHNIQUES

Special films can be used not only for their normal purpose, but also to enlarge a photographer's creative scope.

For example, tungsten-balanced film used in daylight gives pictures a predominantly blue cast. In some cases this can give a nightime look to a picture, or, if the film is slightly overexposed, a hard, slightly bleached look – this is often seen in fashion photography. Using daylight-balanced colour film in tungsten light gives results with a predominantly orange cast. This too can be exploited creatively, especially when the film is slightly overexposed. In either case, be imaginative and prepared to experiment with new effects.

Infrared film gives strangely coloured pictures. Black and white infrared film gives a night effect even on pictures taken in daylight. The results can be unpredictable, and some trial and error is needed to get good results – though there is always the possibility of getting a striking effect by accident. Processing infrared film can be a problem, since the chemical process required is the type known as E4. All ordinary laboratories now use a process called E6. It can be difficult to track down a laboratory with facilities for the older process. One of the main uses of infrared film is in medical photography, and the photographic laboratory of a large hospital may be able to advise you.

Very fast film can also be used to give special effects. It gives very grainy, high-contrast pictures, and if it is uprated the effect is exaggerated. 1600 ISO black and white film can be uprated to 3400 or even higher.

● LEFT Here 64 ISO daylight-balanced film was used. A meter reading was obtained, and the aperture was deliberately closed three stops from that setting. This has made the surroundings look as if it was nightime, though in fact the picture was taken at noon in full daylight. The girl dressed for Hallowe'en was then lit with flash, so that she alone is correctly exposed.

● RIGHT The same idea is carried a stage further. This picture was also taken in full daylight; 50 ISO tungsten-balanced film was used, under-exposed by two stops, which has made the sky deep blue. To both expose and light the girl correctly, a flash unit was used with an 85B filter placed over it instead of over the lens.

● LEFT Infrared film can produce un-expected results, and a certain amount of experimentation is required. The leaves of the trees and the grass appear magenta. At a different time of day or with a different light source the results would have been quite different.

● BELOW Using 1600 film rated at 3400 ISO has produced a very grainy but effective portrait. This shot was taken with available light from a window. Of course, if a film is uprated it is necessary to tell the processing laboratory that this has been done and what the increase is, so that the lab can adjust the processing time accordingly.

SHIFT LENSES

A shift lens, also called a perspective control (PC) lens, is a great addition to the photographer's equipment, and especially useful for architectural photography. With a 5 × 4 camera it is possible to move the front panel, on which the lens is mounted, up and down and from side to side, or to swing it vertically or tilt it horizontally. For 35 mm SLR and some medium format cameras there are lenses that can be moved up and down or across, and some lenses have a tilt facility as well. In the 35 mm range these lenses usually have a focal length of 28 or 35 mm.

When using one of these lenses to photograph a tall building, instead of tilting the camera up to fit in the whole building, the camera can be kept pointing straight ahead and the axis of the lens is shifted relative to the film plane – that is, the lens is moved upward but kept parallel to the film. This movement is known as a shift. The whole building now appears in the picture, but with a difference. With a normal lens and the camera angled up, the vertical lines of the building will converge towards the top of the frame. With a shift lens, as long as the camera is kept horizontal, all verticals in the picture will appear vertical and there will be no convergence, even when the lens is shifted as far as it can go.

Even when photographing things that are less strongly vertical, distortion can still be caused by angling the camera to cut out unwanted features such as an untidy foreground. Here, keeping the camera level and using a shift lens can eliminate unwanted areas at the bottom, top, left or right of the frame without causing distortion.

Before deciding to buy a shift lens, it is a good idea to hire one from a professional photography store and try out its effects.

● ABOVE To keep all the columns vertical in this shot of the Banqueting House in London, the camera had to be kept level. With a normal lens this would have cut out the wonderful ceiling painted by Rubens, and would have included a lot of the comparatively dull floor. Using the shift lens to its maximum has cut out much of the floor and brought in the ceiling.

● RIGHT A problem with photographing objects with shiny reflective surfaces, such as cars, is that the camera and photographer can appear in them. The effect can be corrected by standing to one side of the car, but by using the horizontal shift movement of the lens the car can be brought into the centre of the frame without the photographer or the camera appearing as a reflection.

• Using a conventional lens, the camera had to be tilted upward to fit the whole building into the frame. The vertical lines converge so that the building seems to be leaning.

• To keep the verticals straight the plane of the film must be parallel to the plane of the front of the building, which means that the camera body must be absolutely level. But here this results in the top of the tallest building being cut off.

• Here the camera is still level, but the shift lens has been moved upward. The whole building is now in view, but its sides are completely vertical. Also, a lot of uninteresting foreground detail has been cropped out of the picture.

FISHEYE LENSES

Among all the lenses that are available the fisheye lens is low on most people's list of priorities. The uses of this lens are limited and it is rather expensive. Nevertheless, it can be highly effective in the right situation.

It is sensible to hire a fisheye lens from a professional photographic dealer and try it out before deciding to buy one. If there seem to be many genuinely worthwhile uses for it, then and only then consider a purchase.

Most people looking through an SLR camera with a fisheye lens for the first time find it highly amusing to see the world through a 180-degree angle of vision. Objects appear severely distorted, and it is easy to get carried away by gimmicky shots of people's faces close to the lens, but used thoughtfully, a fisheye lens can produce uniquely striking images. The art of exploiting the lens is to make the photograph look as if a fisheye lens has not been used at all. Great care is needed in choosing a viewpoint and in framing the subject to obtain the best effect.

Because of their extremely wide angle of view, fisheye lenses cannot be used with lens hoods. Filters can be fitted, but these are special ones that are screwed in at the back of the lens. Graduated filters cannot be used.

There is a difficulty when using flash. Even when a flash gun is fitted with a wide angle attachment, the area that it illuminates is no wider than the field of view of a 28 mm lens. This falls far short of what is needed for a fisheye. If flash has to be used, at least two, even three or four flash heads are needed.

● ABOVE This hallway ceiling needed to be lit with flash, and four flash heads were necessary to give the required coverage. The symmetry of the design has created an interesting architectural conundrum.

● BELOW Like the domed British Museum Reading Room, the Olympic cycle track in Moscow lends itself well to being photographed with a fisheye lens. The banked curves at both ends look much as might be expected, and not unduly distorted. The ceiling panels add to a strong feeling of perspective.

● ABOVE A good example of how to use a fisheye lens without the result looking gimmicky. The Reading Room of the British Museum has a domed ceiling and the reading desks radiate out from the centre of the floor. Keeping the camera level allows the beautiful dome to be seen in its entirety, as well as including the floor in the shot. The curved lines of the room harmonize with the distortion caused by the lens, so that the shot looks as if it had been taken with a normal wide angle lens.

● LEFT Taken from the dome of the cathedral in Florence, Italy, this fisheye shot gives a striking panoramic view. The inclusion of the dome itself in the foreground leads the eye into the maze of streets below, and out into the Tuscan countryside beyond.

ZOOM LENSES

Zoom lenses allow the use of a continuous range of focal lengths without having to change lenses. If two zoom lenses are used, it is possible with only one change to go from 28 mm wide angle to 300 mm telephoto. The image quality is not quite as good as that of a prime lens, but the slight difference will be apparent only to the most critical viewer.

Many zoom lenses can now be used with autofocus systems, but some of these cannot take certain filter holders. It is as well to make sure what will fit before a problem arises.

As well as taking conventional pictures at any chosen focal length, a zoom lens can also be 'zoomed' during the exposure to create an interesting effect. This should be done during a moderately long exposure, say ⅛ second, to make the movement apparent. There will be a pattern of streaks radiating from the centre of the frame. Zooming from wide angle to telephoto will create a different effect from going the other way. The most effective shots with this technique are those which have strong highlights or colours which will make a noticeable pattern. This gives a feeling of movement, as if the objects are flying straight out of the frame. The slow shutter speed will require the camera to be mounted on a tripod. It may take a little practice to perfect the technique, but passable results should be achieved quite quickly. Like all special effects, this should not be over-used.

● ABOVE Here is a conventional view of a boy standing astride his bike. He is deliberately placed in front of a strongly coloured backdrop.

● ABOVE Here, he is in the same position, but this time a shutter speed of ⅛ second was chosen, and during the exposure the lens was zoomed half-way through its range of focal length. This created strong radiating lines of colour and gives a sense of speed.

● RIGHT The boy is still in the same position, but the lens has been moved from 80 mm to 300 mm. It looks as if he is going round a corner at speed.

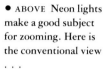

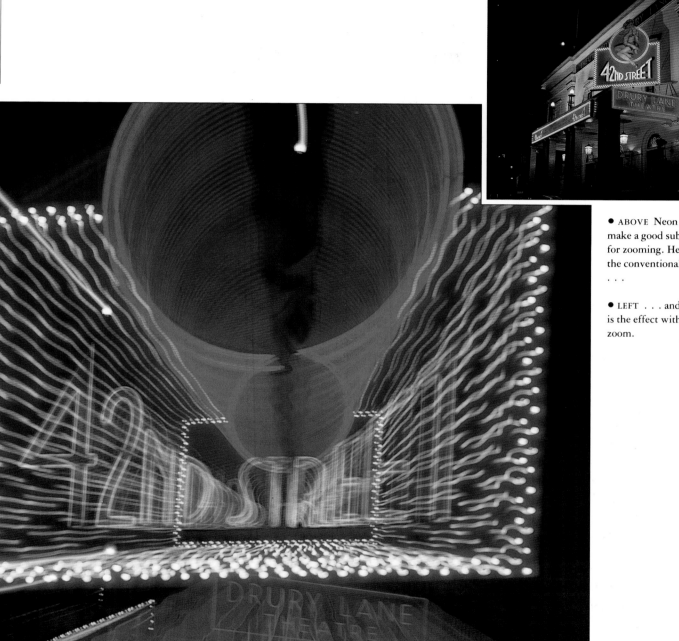

● ABOVE Neon lights make a good subject for zooming. Here is the conventional view . . .

● LEFT . . . and here is the effect with the zoom.

USING A MACRO LENS

Additional equipment may not be absolutely necessary, but it can offer new photographic possibilities. One of the most useful accessories is some means of taking close-up shots. There are several ways of doing this.

The cheapest is a close-up lens which is fitted over the normal camera lens. This does not, however, give a very high-quality image. When using such a lens on an SLR camera, focusing and framing are relatively easy, but when it is fitted to a camera with a viewfinder the distance to the subject must be measured. The lens will come with instructions about the correction to

make to the focus setting. Because the viewfinder is offset, an educated guess will have to be made about how to point the camera.

For some SLR cameras it is possible to buy a reversing ring. This allows the lens to be mounted back to front, which makes it possible to focus on closer objects. The lens is not designed to be used backwards, so the image will not be of the best quality.

The only really satisfactory methods are to use extension rings or bellows, or to buy a separate macro lens. The rings or bellows are fixed to the camera as a lens would be, and the lens is attached

to the front. Extension rings usually come in sets of three, and can be used singly or together. When using them with certain lenses 1:1 magnification can be obtained, which means that the image is the same size as the object. Bellows work in the same way, but can be moved smoothly in and out so that any degree of magnification within their range can be obtained.

A macro lens allows close-up work without having to fuss with these awkward devices. However, some macro lenses can be used with rings or bellows to give even greater magnification.

● ABOVE The two small leaves were photographed with a macro lens and extension rings. The magnification on the original film was 1:1, life-size. A soft focus filter was used on the lens and the leaves were lit by electronic flash with a very soft diffuser. When working at such high magnifications exposure time has to be increased considerably.

● LEFT This picture was taken with a macro lens at almost full magnification. A problem with any close-up work is depth of field, which at very high magnification is almost non-existent, as the picture shows. The nails are 6 cm (2½ in) long and quite thin, but when they are perfectly in focus the background, a mere 3 mm (⅛ in) away, is blurred.

● BELOW The section of lemon was photographed on a blue plate. The glaze is out of focus even though a tiny aperture of f45 was used, because the depth of field is so shallow. The high magnification and small aperture called for a very long exposure. The camera will always need to be mounted on a tripod, and it is advisable to use a cable release. If the camera has a mirror-up facility, operate this before firing the shutter, since even the slightest vibration caused by the mirror may blur the picture. It is also vital to make sure that the subject stays still.

SPECIAL FILTERS

Of all the accessories that are available, filters are the cheapest. Yet these simple attachments to the front of the lens – or sometimes to the rear – can radically alter the effect of a picture. There is a myriad of types to choose from. As with any camera accessory, you must pay attention to a few points in order to get a satisfying result.

Some filters cut down the amount of light entering the lens to such an extent that a longer exposure is needed. If your camera has TTL metering this will not be a problem, but with other cameras you will have to adjust exposure manually. Manufacturers of filters generally state the necessary amount of exposure adjustment: this is called the filter factor.

With a wide angle lens, vignetting may occur when a filter is put in front of the lens. This means that the corners of the frame are cut off, because the angle of view of the lens is so great that it takes in the filter holder ring. This usually happens only with lenses of 21 mm or wider.

It is possible to use more than one filter at a time, but do this only if it will enhance the image.

Some special effect filters, such as multiple image types, are fun but their use is strictly limited. Imagine looking at your holiday photographs and seeing them all as if through a kaleidoscope. You would quickly get bored. Even a graduated tobacco filter, which can help to lift a dull sky, would be tedious if all your pictures had this coloured sky.

● ABOVE A multiple image filter makes several tiger's heads appear. These filters come in different types, such as 2, 4 or 6 images. They can be used creatively but not too often.

● BELOW LEFT No filter has been used. BELOW RIGHT A soft focus filter has been added to diffuse the image.

● LEFT When this shot of Venice was taken the sky was rather grey and flat. A graduated tobacco filter has changed the colour of the sky, but the rest of the picture is unaffected. This is an effective filter but use it sparingly, or all your shots will look too alike.

● ABOVE An alternative to the tobacco filter is this pink graduated filter. Although this shot was taken at midday the filter, carefully used, makes it look like dawn.

● RIGHT A graduated neutral density filter will darken a sky without changing the colour. In this shot of Loch Torridon it has turned an already moody sky to a virtually night-time hue.

IMPROVING YOUR TECHNIQUE

Often a photograph can be greatly enhanced by the use of a reflector or what is called fill-in flash. To many people it seems odd that you would use flash in bright sunlight but it helps by reducing unattractive shadows. Suppose it is a bright day and the sun is quite high. Imagine that the people you are going to photograph are facing the sun. This will cause them to have dark shadows under their eyes and nose. Even if they turn to one side the shadows might still remain, or if they move to a different location they may be in total shadow while the background beyond is bathed in sunshine. In either case the use of fill-in flash will eliminate the shadows or balance the foreground with the background, creating a better shot.

To do this take an exposure meter reading of the highlight area of the picture. Let us imagine it is $\frac{1}{125}$ second at f11. Set the camera to this exposure. If you are using an automatic flash gun set the aperture dial on it to f 5.6, in other words two stops less than the highlight exposure. If you are using a manual flash gun you will have to work out a combination of aperture and speed from the guide numbers of your flash gun to give you the appropriate exposure. The guide number tells you how strong a flash gun's power is and will alter depending on the speed of the film you are using. For example a film rated at 200 ISO will give a higher guide number than a film rated at 64 ISO.

From the flash gun manufacturer's instructions you can work out the correct aperture to use. Roughly speaking, this is calculated by dividing the guide number by the flash-to-subject distance. Having done this you are now ready to take your shot. The important point to remember is always to underexpose the flash. If you do not do this then the light from the flash will look too harsh and burn out all the shadow detail. Many photographers are nervous of using fill-in flash because they cannot see the effect it is having until the film is processed, unless of course they have the benefit of Polaroid.

With a reflector, on the other hand, you can see the effect immediately. You can buy custom-made reflectors in a variety of sizes and effects. These range from white and silver through to bronze and gold. Of course you might find yourself in a situation where you do not have a reflector and therefore will have to improvise. A piece of white card, a white sheet or a piece of aluminium foil will do. Let us imagine that the sun is behind your subject. If you hold the reflector so that the sun shines directly onto it you can bounce this light back

● FAR LEFT This picture was taken without the addition of flash.

● LEFT Here the aperture setting on the automatic flash gun was deliberately set at a wider opening than what was required for the available light. This resulted in a weak burst of flash that was just enough to eliminate the shadows under this young woman's eyes. If the same power had been used as for the available light then her face would have been burnt out and the final picture would have looked most unflattering.

to your subject. By changing your position and the angle of the reflector you can redirect the light to exactly where you need it. A silver reflector will give a harsher light than a white one, and a gold one will give a very warm effect. Many photographers prefer using a reflector to fill-in flash as they feel it gives a more natural light.

The use of a reflector or fill-in flash is not just restricted to photographing people. Perhaps you are going to photograph a table outdoors laid for lunch. The table is in the shade but, if you expose for it, then the house in the background, for example, will be overexposed. By using the flash to illuminate the table the two different exposures can be bought into line with one another. Whichever method you decide to use it is of course best to practise before you take some important photographs.

● LEFT These pictures illustrate the difference a reflector makes. In the top picture a white reflector has been used. Although this has bounced the required amount of light back into the subjects' faces it is rather cool. In the second picture a gold reflector makes the quality of the light warmer, giving a more pleasing effect.

● BELOW LEFT In this picture it was important to retain the detail of the house in the background. The exposure for this has meant that some of the items on the table and the owner of the vineyard are in shadow. By using fill-in flash, BELOW RIGHT, these shadows have been softened while still retaining detail. The result is a more pleasing balance between foreground and background.

SLOW SYNC FLASH

Flash used normally will freeze a moving object, and, if the exposure is correct, will evenly illuminate everything within its range. But, as in every aspect of photography, creative rule-breaking can produce stunning results; and this is particularly true of the unorthodox technique of slow sync flash.

Most 35 mm SLR cameras have a mark on the shutter speed dial that synchronizes the flash when the picture is taken. Usually this speed is $\frac{1}{60}$ or $\frac{1}{125}$ second. If a shutter speed faster than this is used the blinds of the focal plane shutter will not have time to open fully, so that part of the picture comes out unexposed. However, it is possible to use a lower speed such as $\frac{1}{15}$ or $\frac{1}{18}$ second and still synchronize the flash. The flash will not last any longer than usual, which means that it will be illuminating the scene for only part of the time the shutter is open.

If a slow shutter speed is used with flash to photograph a moving object when there is a reasonable amount of ambient light, the subject will be marked by a faint trail looking like 'speed lines' in cartoons. This can look very effective in an action shot such as the picture of a roller skater here.

The important thing is to use a shutter speed compatible with both the ambient light and the desired flash effect. For example, the film is 100 ISO; a meter reading of the ambient light says $\frac{1}{125}$ at f5.6. To get the slow sync effect a shutter speed of $\frac{1}{15}$ second is needed. To compensate for the difference the aperture should be reduced to f16. Set the dial on the flashgun to f16 or, if it is a manually controlled one, work out the flash-to-subject distance that normally requires an aperture of f16. The result should be worth the effort.

● ABOVE The young boy is almost frozen in mid-flight, even though the shutter speed used was only $\frac{1}{15}$ second. This is because he was lit mostly by the flash, not by ambient light. However, the daylight has had a curious effect on his outline so that it looks as if the sky were directly behind him. The ambient light needed a full stop more, but it was decided to underexpose for this to give the shot more impact. The boy's friends in the background complete the composition perfectly.

● RIGHT A similar technique was used indoors to photograph the baby. Here a shutter speed of $\frac{1}{8}$ second was used. The baby turned his head as the shot was taken and the flash fired. There was enough ambient light to let this movement show up. It has created an attractive background which increases the effectiveness of the portrait.

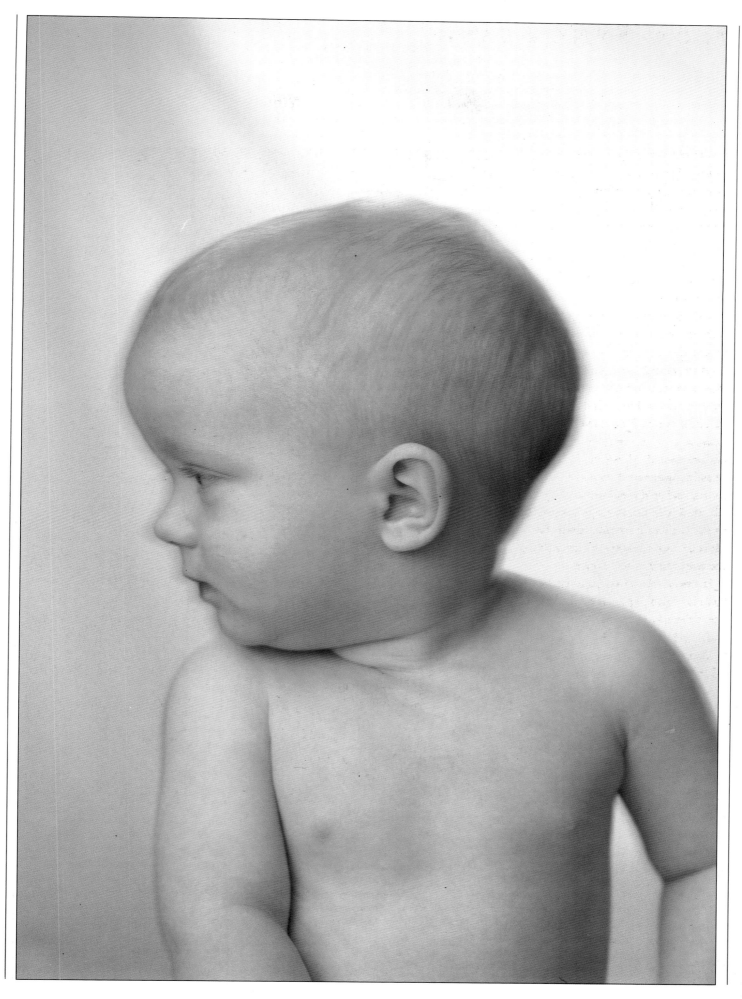

IMPROVING YOUR TECHNIQUE

Instant photographs from Polaroid cameras have the obvious advantage over traditional media that the picture can be seen within seconds. But Polaroid film also lends itself to a wide variety of manipulations. Many of these need no more than the camera, the film, and a blunt-ended instrument such as a pen.

With Polaroid image film, for instance, as soon the picture is ejected from the camera the dyes inside the picture 'sandwich' can be squeezed around before they set. This will create bizarre patterns which can, with practice, be controlled quite precisely. When the picture appears fully the results are amazing.

A Polaroid back fitted to a conventional camera offers another technique, which is known as image transfer. Once the film has been exposed, it is pulled through a pair of rollers built into the back. These squeeze and spread the chemicals that develop the film. Development of a conventional print usually takes 90 seconds. But as soon as the film emerges it can be peeled off its backing sheet and this sheet pressed face downward onto a piece of paper throughly dampened with water, and left for the remainder of the development time. This transfers the image to the paper, after which the original material is discarded. The result has none of the smoothness of a conventional Polaroid print. The effect is raw and blurred, but often stunning.

Apart from Polaroid cameras and backs there is also the Polaroid transparency printer, which makes instant prints from conventional slides. These can be manipulated in the same way as those from a Polaroid back.

These are only some of the techniques. There are many others, including immersing the film in boiling water and scratching the emulsion.

● ABOVE This Polaroid camera picture was allowed to develop in the conventional way. The image is attractive but the background is rather boring.

● ABOVE Careful manipulation with a blunt pen of the dyes around the girl while the print was developing has created a much more interesting, almost abstract background.

● LEFT A variation of the same technique: here only the faces of the three girls have been allowed to develop normally.

● ABOVE A conventional print from a Polaroid camera back.

● RIGHT Before the print could develop, the backing sheet was separated and laid on wet paper. It was pressed into the paper with a rubber roller and left to develop. Peeling away the backing left this striking image.

● BELOW This still life was created in the same way, but a different textured paper was used.

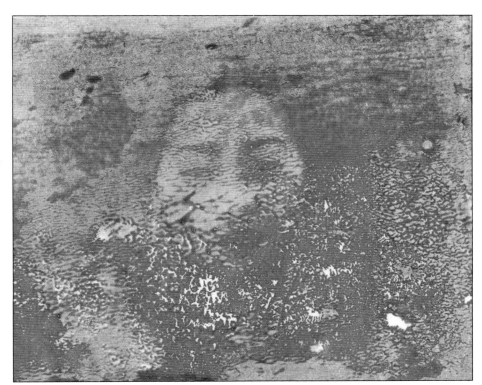

PERSPECTIVE

In photography, perspective means creating a feeling of depth. There are several ways to get this effect and all of them are quite simple. It is strange, then, that so many photographs lack this element which can make all the difference to a shot.

In landscape photography the easiest way of gaining a sense of perspective is to use a foreground. Often you can add a tree at one side of the frame, or with its foliage filling the top of the picture.

This simple addition creates an illusion, the impression that there is space between the viewpoint, the foreground and the background. Compare this to a picture with no foreground features – it will look flat and dull.

Strong, naturally-formed lines can create a powerful sense of 'linear' perspective. Try standing at the end of a recently ploughed field. Look at the lines of the furrows running away from you. They will converge towards a

central point in the distance – what in the formal study of perspective is called a vanishing point. Taken from a low viewpoint these lines will create a strong feeling of depth.

When photographing buildings it is not difficult to exaggerate perspective. A shot of the front of a building taken straight on may lack impact whereas a more dramatic effect may be achieved by moving in close and looking up so the verticals converge.

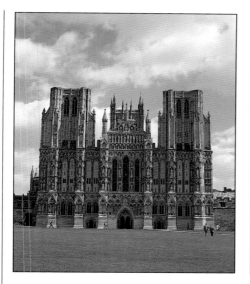

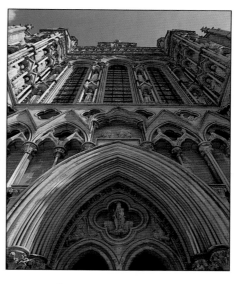

● ABOVE In this picture of Wells Cathedral the viewpoint was directly to the front. Although it shows all the façade it lacks depth. There is no sense of perspective at all.

● ABOVE Here the viewpoint is much closer. The camera is tilted upwards and the two towers converge towards the top centre of the frame. This creates a much more powerful image.

● ABOVE The viewpoint is nearer still and the verticals converge even more sharply. This slight change of viewpoint and camera angle greatly increases the perspective effect.

● ABOVE Another example of linear perspective: the bicycles create a seemingly endless line converging at an infinite distance. Lines of objects of any kind are one of the most effective ways of conveying perspective.

● RIGHT These red buses snaking down London's Oxford Street give a good sense of linear perspective. The uniformity of their colour adds to the feeling of depth.

● LEFT Placing this bale in the foreground and going quite close to it with a 21 mm wide angle lens creates a feeling of separation between it and the other bales, and the farm buildings beyond. This is a simple technique for adding perspective to your photographs.

MULTIPLE EXPOSURES

A camera with a facility for multiple exposures – that is, taking more than one picture on the same piece of film – allows unusual images and in the right hands can give stunning effects.

When planning a multiple image shot it is important to remember that light subjects will show up on dark areas. Try to frame the subjects so that a dark area is placed where a subsequent image will have a light subject, or vice versa. Images with large amounts of light areas are not suitable for multiple exposures. For instance, a great area of sky in one image will more or less obliterate anything else that appears in that part of the picture. As with any new technique, practice is necessary.

HOW TO USE VIEWFINDER SCREENS

A range of screens is available for many SLR cameras. A grid screen is best for multiple image shots. It is marked with a grid of vertical and horizontal lines which allows exact positioning of each image. The screen fits under the pentaprism on top of the camera. Release this, take out the existing screen, drop in the new one and put back the prism.

● BELOW At first glance this picture of the Palace of Holyroodhouse in Scotland may not look like a multiple image. But look at the sky. It is in fact a sequence of ten separate exposures taken at 30 second intervals. Each time the clouds were in a different position. By the final exposure they had moved a considerable way, giving the effect of a celestial explosion.

MULTIPLE EXPOSURES WITHOUT SPECIAL FACILITIES

This can be done on many ordinary SLR cameras. It needs some practice to get it right. To take three pictures on one frame, take the first picture in the normal way. Turn the film rewind crank as though rewinding the film back into the cassette, but *do not* press the rewind button. When the slack in the film has been taken up, then press the rewind button. Turn the rewind crank 1½ turns and release the rewind button. Take the next picture and repeat the process. Next take the third picture and then advance the film in the normal way.

● RIGHT This multiple exposure shot was taken indoors against a black background and lit by flash. First, the model was positioned at the left side of the frame, looking to the right. Then he was positioned looking the other way, and the camera was moved so that he was at the right of the frame. The result is a striking shot of both sides of his face in a single image.

● RIGHT The same technique was used in this picture, except that the first image was taken much closer in than the next two. This has made the central image much more dominant than the others. With such a technique care must be taken that the close-up image does not come out distorted.

● LEFT In this sequence of four exposures the camera was moved slightly sideways after each exposure. It is important to avoid making multiple exposure shots simply confusing.

SHOOTING AGAINST THE LIGHT

Many people think that you can only take good photographs if the sun is directly behind or to one side of the camera. Admittedly, by taking shots straight into the sun, flare and incorrect exposure may result, but if handled carefully these can be avoided or used to dramatic effect. To eliminate flare, a good lens hood should suffice. In fact you should always have a lens hood attached to your camera whichever way you are shooting. Flare can result from light indirectly reflecting off a shiny surface such as a car or window as well as directly from the sun.

Calculating exposure needs careful consideration as, if your subject is strongly backlit, it could appear as a silhouette. Although this may be the effect you are after, an adjustment to exposure will be necessary if you want your subject to be visible. If you are using a camera with built-in metering that has a choice of exposure modes such as average, centre-weighted or spot metering, then the spot metering mode will give a more accurate reading. If your camera only has metering in the average exposure mode, the chances are that it will underexpose your subject.

It is possible to overcome this if you can move in close so that the viewfinder is covering only the subject and take your meter reading at this distance. This means depressing the shutter release button about half-way. If your camera has an autoexposure lock you now keep the shutter release button

● BELOW In this picture the sun is at about 45 degrees behind the young girl. A reflector was used to bounce back a small amount of light into her face. Without this she would have been almost silhouetted against the background. Although a lens hood was used, flare can still be seen in the top left-hand corner of the picture.

● ABOVE By exposing for the light reflecting off the water behind this boy fishing, he is shown almost in silhouette. In this case it works well because it is still obvious what activity he is involved in and the quality of the sparkling light bouncing off the water adds a romantic feel.

● LEFT A combination of a long lens and small aperture have resulted in isolating this plant from its surroundings. The back light has helped to emphasize this effect and the eye is drawn immediately to its delicate blooms.

● LEFT Often there is no time to use fill-in flash or a reflector to throw light back onto a subject, and this is often the case with animals. By exposing for the shadows enough detail has been retained to record this cat's peaceful posture in the shade.

slightly depressed and return to your original viewpoint. Without taking your finger off the button take your shot. Your subject will now be correctly exposed although the background will be overexposed. If you are taking more than one shot from this viewpoint you will have to repeat the procedure with each shot.

Another way round this problem is to use the exposure compensation dial – if applicable – on your camera. Set the dial to give two stops more exposure than the reading on the camera meter. If you can operate your camera manually and you have a separate exposure meter then, as above, you could move in close to your subject to take a reading.

If you do use this method with your camera or a hand-held meter, care must be taken not to cast a shadow on your subject, otherwise an incorrect reading will be obtained and overexposure will result. The preferred method of taking a reading with a hand-held meter is to use the incident light method. This means attaching an invercone – a white disc – to the exposure meter sensor. The meter is then pointed to the camera and a reading taken. This method records the amount of light falling on your subject as opposed to reflecting from it.

One word of warning when taking photographs into the light: the sun is very powerful and can be greatly magnified by camera lenses, so if these are pointed to the sun damage to your eyes could result – be careful!

● BELOW By shooting straight into the sun a very dramatic backlit picture has been obtained. A lens hood is essential in a case like this to eliminate flare. Be careful when shooting into the sun that you do not point the camera directly towards it, to avoid damage to your eye.

THROUGH GLASS

There are many ways of changing the appearance of a subject. One of the easiest is to photograph through glass. This can create a whole range of fascinating images with a minimum of equipment. The technique can also be used to change the appearance of photographs taken previously, by copying them through glass.

Both plain and patterned glass can be used. Many patterns are on sale, and some of them produce interesting distortions or multiple images. Colour can be introduced by adding a 'gel' – a sheet of coloured acetate.

There are several techniques for photographing an object through glass. The object may be placed on the glass and backlit, perhaps with a gel under the glass. The object may be put under the glass; a sheet of plain glass can be

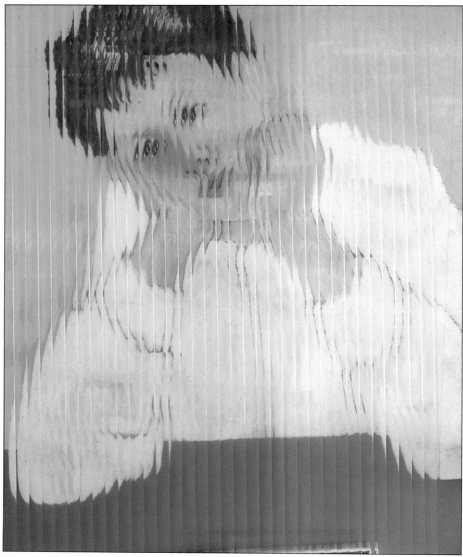

spattered with water to give the effect of looking through a window on a rainy day. An autofocus camera may not be able to decide whether to focus on the object or the glass. If the camera has a focus lock, mount it on a tripod, remove the sheet of glass, lock the focus on the object and replace the glass.

Such photographs are often taken from quite close in. A macro lens or extension rings or bellows will allow really close shots which can often give new effects.

When backlighting a subject, make sure that the front lighting is weaker, otherwise the backlight may not show up sufficiently.

As with any special technique, there is no limit to the effects that may be obtained by exercising a little imagination and being prepared to experiment.

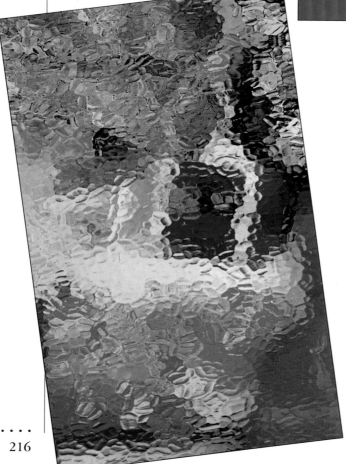

● ABOVE This painting was photographed through glass and was lit by available light. The distance of the glass from the subject alters the final effect. The nearer the glass, the more defined the subject; the further away it is, the more obscure the image will seem.

● FAR LEFT This abstract image resembles a painter's palette and was created by placing brightly coloured objects under a sheet of glass.

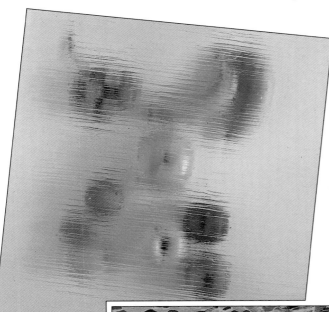

● LEFT Attractive still life images can be produced through glass. Here fruit is lit by available light using a reflector. Many different objects lend themselves to this concept; the effects can be seen immediately and can be altered as required.

● RIGHT By using a different pattern of glass over a painting another effect is achieved. Here the glass is placed further from the subject and the degree of obfuscation is increased.

ABSTRACT VIEWS

There are many ways of photographing everyday objects to give them a completely new and unfamiliar look. Sometimes the images may be so transformed that the picture becomes abstract or surreal. To achieve such an effect calls for an eye for composition and an understanding of how the image will appear on film, rather than how it looks to the eye.

One example is a moving object such as a flag fluttering in the breeze. To the eye it simply looks like a moving flag. It is not blurred, nor is it frozen into a particular momentary shape; however, if it is photographed it will appear in one of these ways. If a fairly slow shutter speed is used, and the moment is well judged so that the flag falls subtly into the frame, a strikingly dynamic image will result. A fast shutter speed could freeze the flag into a sharp image, but in comparison this will look stiff and lifeless.

This is only one example of seeing in an abstract way. Other images can be created by selecting part of an object, for example a building, which in isolation forms an abstract shape. Often the most ordinary objects or views can take on an abstract quality when viewed from a new angle.

There are no hard and fast rules as to what makes a good abstract picture. An acute eye will see the photographic potential in any scene.

● LEFT Taken at dusk from a low viewpoint, the white gate stands out from its darker surroundings. The angle exaggerates the perspective and gives a strong lead into the picture. The slow shutter speed has allowed the tail-light of a passing car to leave a red streak. This dash of vivid colour adds a curious, almost surreal feel to the picture.

● BELOW LEFT The American flag was flying near the Washington Monument. The camera was angled upward so that part of the monument could be seen, forming a background and giving the one hard edge in the picture. The flag was moving gently in the wind. A series of pictures was taken at a shutter speed of ⅛ second. This created a swirling blur in the picture. Although it is abstract it expresses the movement of the flag in a way which a frozen image taken with a faster shutter speed could never have achieved.

● BELOW AND BOTTOM Both these pictures are sections of a building taken at slightly different angles and at different times of day. Both form abstract images, but the quality of light in each one has produced quite different results. There is an endless variety of ways of seeing an object. Re-examine familiar sights – there will always be a fresh way of looking at them.

Look at a magazine feature on travel at home or abroad. What strikes you about the photographs? More often than not, as well as the large scenic shots of landscapes and buildings there will be many smaller photographs. These may be used individually over several pages, or in a block on one page or double-page spread. Individually, any one of these little pictures may not make a great impression, but in their context all these small pictures unite to bring the photo documentary to life. They not only complement the big set pieces, they become important to the narrative as a whole.

The lesson to be learnt here is that wherever you are, you should be alert to the chance of getting these small but vital shots. Think of how they might fit into an album of your travels. You could even mount them as a collection in one frame. When you are taking the great view, the grand palace, look around at the immediate vicinity too. You will be surprised at what you find. All the pictures here were originally such 'secondary' shots, but they have all made it into various publications. One of them even became a magazine cover.

● BELOW The pattern of these woven African pots makes a pleasing picture in itself. Grouping them produces an interesting composition.

● RIGHT A detail of the ceiling of St Paul's Cathedral in London. In many churches the details of the decoration – mosaics, frescos, mouldings – are the most interesting thing. These can often be lost in one overall view of the interior.

● RIGHT This was taken while photographing the town of Sante Fé in New Mexico. It works as a composition because the vivid blue of the pot complements the terracotta of the wall. Both textures sit well together. As a vignette it would fit well into a mosaic of small shots of the town.

● ABOVE A sequence taken in a vineyard called not only for shots of the sweeping rows of vines but also for details of the grapes. They were shaded by the vine leaves, so a small reflector was used to bounce light back on to them. This has made them glow, so that they look even more succulent.

● LEFT Going in close to this locomotive wheel gives a strong geometrical pattern. The well-defined paintwork adds to the effect. Imagine this in a group with other details of the engine. It would make an interesting presentation of fine engineering.

COLLAGE

There are endless ways of making a photographic collage. The simplest can be made from a single image, which can be either a negative or a transparency. Alternatively, a highly complex design can be made from a large number of images.

To take the simplest case first, two prints could be made of a single image. Then the negative or transparency might be flipped over and another two prints made as a mirror image. The four prints could then be fitted together with a normal one the right way up at the top left, a mirror-image one the right way up at the top right, the other mirror image turned upside-down at bottom left, and the remaining normal one upside-down at bottom right. This will make a design with fourfold symmetry for a kaleidoscope effect. There are in fact four symmetrical ways of arranging these prints, and all could

be tried to see which looks best. Such a collage could be enlarged endlessly by adding more prints to the outside, using the same image or a different one.

A more complicated design could be produced by cutting up the prints diagonally and fitting them together to make a radiating design. Again, more pieces of the same image or different one could be added in rings around the central circle.

Naturally there is no need to stick to a symmetrical design. A free-form collage can also give a stunning result.

● **LEFT AND ABOVE** Often the best kaleidoscopic collages are made with normal and reversed prints of a single image. This works particularly well with a landscape where there is strong detail on one side of the picture.

● BELOW Any image can be used to make a kaleidoscopic collage. The more detailed it is, the more complicated the final effect. These collages were made from a single photograph of a detail of the carving around the doorway of the cathedral in Orvieto, Italy. Even an image that is uninteresting in its own right can create a fascinating effect when treated in this way.

JOINER PICTURES

Joiner pictures were made famous by the artist David Hockney. They consist of a cluster of images joined together by quite literally sticking them to a board. Almost any subject lends itself to this treatment. All that is needed is imagination and a good eye for composition.

When making a joiner picture, it is important to remember that the aim is to create an imperfect join between images. They may be of different sizes or taken through different lenses. It is not even necessary for all the images to have been taken at the same session. A joiner could be made of shots taken outdoors of parts of the same scene over a period of hours. This would show different lighting and shadows as the sun moved across the sky.

Have the film processed at a laboratory which does borderless prints. Lay them out loosely at first and experiment with arrangements. Discard any prints that do not enhance the overall effect. When the design has crystallized, stick the prints down on a mounting board, bearing in mind that the picture will have irregular edges around which the board will be visible. A board that picks out one of the colours in the pictures might give the best effect.

Gradually-changing light is only one of the time effects that can be exploited in a joiner. For example, a city scene might show the changing traffic. The final image should show the viewer the scene as a series of different glances, much in the same way as it is seen by the eye in real life.

● BELOW This joiner picture of the River Thames and the Houses of Parliament in London was made from shots taken on colour print film. All the pictures were taken in a fairly short space of time, and all on the same film. Even so, variations in print density have occurred. Instead of being a distraction, these help to draw the eye to certain sections of the picture.

● RIGHT Building up joiner pictures enables the photographer to include the same person in different positions. In this picture the young boy appears on both sides of the shot and the photographer's feet can be seen in the bottom of the frame.

SANDWICHING TRANSPARENCIES

Montages can be made not only with prints, but also by sandwiching together transparencies made with colour reversal film. A reasonable-sized collection of transparencies will probably yield quite a few pictures that would benefit from being combined.

Pictures discarded for being slightly overexposed are likely to be just the ones for this technique; so are correctly exposed pictures with plenty of highlights or a prevailing light tone. Do not try to put two dark subjects together: they will just absorb most of the light and the result will be muddy.

Skies, tree bark, water, leaves, even mud, can be used as an overlay for a more defined image such as a portrait, which should preferably be one taken against a white or pale background.

Try the combinations on a light box. When a good one is found, fix the two transparencies together with a narrow strip of clear tape wrapped around the blank edge of the film and put them in a plastic slide mount for projection or viewing. A really good image made by this method is worth having copied, though good copies of transparencies are quite expensive.

With some experience of sandwiching transparencies, it should be possible to see opportunities for shots which may not be too interesting on their own but will be ideal as part of a sandwich. These can be made into a collection for use when a suitable pair presents itself.

● LEFT The wheel of an army truck and a tree trunk form this sandwich.

● BELOW This girl was photographed against a white background. This image is combined with one of a dry river bed.

● LEFT Superimposing a portrait of a girl against a shot of a hedgerow has formed some interesting patterns.

● BELOW A girl's face is used against a photograph of a mushroom taken with a macro lens.

● BELOW LEFT One transparency was of a group of logs on end. The other was a section of a dry stone wall.

● BELOW RIGHT A combination of a girl's face photographed against a white background and part of a car window covered in raindrops produces this stylish image.

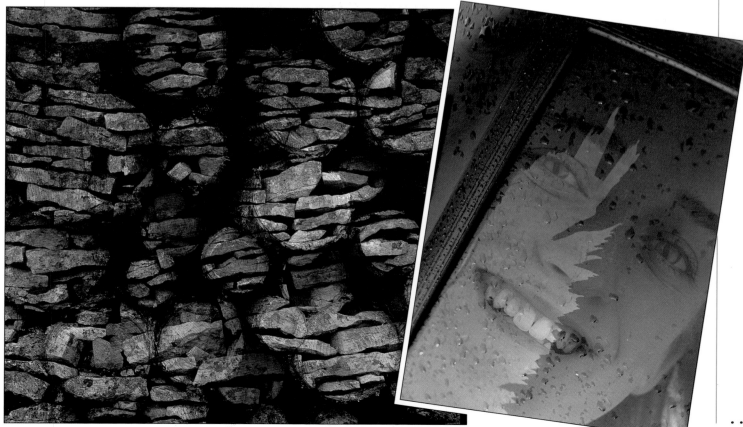

227

SHOOTING A STILL LIFE

Still life photography can be rewarding in more ways than just ending up with a pleasing image. Taking such pictures calls for patience and an eye for a good composition and theme. Still lifes are among the best of visual exercises. Innumerable famous painters, past and present, have turned to the still life at some time. Much of their work has in turn inspired photographers.

Almost any object can form part of a still life. There may be a collection of things with a particular link – for example, objects brought back from visits to a particular country. Such a collection could be interesting simply because everything came from that place. But everyday objects from home and around can be made into an equally satisfactory assemblage. When positioning the items, always check the view through the camera. When photographing flowers, which can wilt, or other fragile objects, add them to the arrangement last.

Equally, it is vital to pay attention to lighting. This conveys mood. A still life can be photographed in daylight, but shooting indoors gives far better control of lighting. There is no need for an elaborate studio or lots of lights; many pictures can be taken with a single light and a few reflectors and diffusers. A tiny adjustment of one of these, or of the position of an object, can make a great difference to the way a shadow falls and change the effect.

The shot will be taken from quite close in, probably using a standard lens or a medium telephoto. Every little detail will show up – a crease in a tablecloth, dust on a plate.

Undoubtedly the best camera to use for such work is a medium or large format one such as 5 × 4; but adequate results can be obtained on 35 mm if the composition is strong.

● LEFT Some of the best still life arrangements are the simplest. This one was constructed with a piece of rough marble. The two ceramic pieces are by the same potter. A drape of shiny cotton material completes the ensemble.

● LEFT The seashells and rocks were collected over some time, and photographed at home. They were laid on a slab of rough stone and the composition was arranged while constantly checking through the viewfinder. One light with a diffuser and two reflectors was used, and just before the shot was taken the whole area was lightly sprayed with water, using a fine houseplant mister.

● RIGHT This shot uses a black backdrop. A single light was placed above the pears, shining down on them from slightly behind. A large white reflector was placed in front of the camera, with a hole cut in it for the lens. A lens hood was used to keep stray light from falling on the lens itself. The reflector throws back a little light onto the pears so that they are softly illuminated.

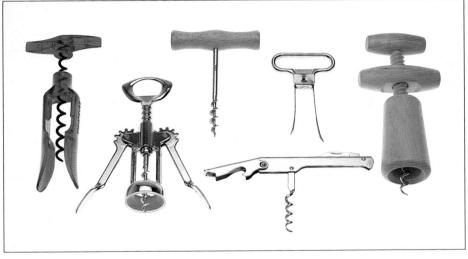

● LEFT Backlighting still life collections gives a very clean effect and can make the objects – in this case a collection of corkscrews – seem to float in space. They were laid on a piece of acrylic sheet lit from underneath, with another light directed down on them from above.

● LEFT These Mexican crafts objects had been collected over repeated visits to the country. A simple backdrop of rough timber was specially made. Two rugs were laid on a table and the assemblage built up, taking care that each item could be seen clearly. The two pictures were hung on the backdrop. A small light bulb was put in the lamp to create a realistic glow. The exposure time was 1 second to pick up this light; the rest of the picture was briefly lit by flash during this exposure.

FINDING PICTURES

There are many places where good pictures can be found, but it is easy to overlook them. Often they are camouflaged by their surroundings, or they need to be looked at from a different angle. Sometimes the chance of a picture appears suddenly, and if the camera is loaded and ready the opportunity can be seized.

When the picture is of a person, producing a camera may inhibit them and the chance of a great shot may be lost. But sometimes seeing the camera will make them strike a pose, and this may produce an image even better than the one that first caught the eye.

Simple and apparently uninspiring things can also be the basis of a great picture. It could be a wall, a fence or a door – perhaps the texture of peeling paint or weathered stone, or torn posters or graffiti.

To find these pictures what is chiefly required is constant awareness. There is usually no need for special or expensive equipment. Sometimes a picture is waiting to be taken, but this is not apparent from normal eye level. It may need a high or low viewpoint, or the different field of view given by a wide angle or telephoto lens to fit the composition into the frame.

Take time to evaluate the surroundings. Look at them selectively. With practice, even the most ordinary places and objects can be made to yield striking images that most people simply overlook. Even if the first attempts largely fail it is worth persevering. And even then, a collection of images that are not particularly interesting in themselves can often make a successful collage or series of pictures on a theme.

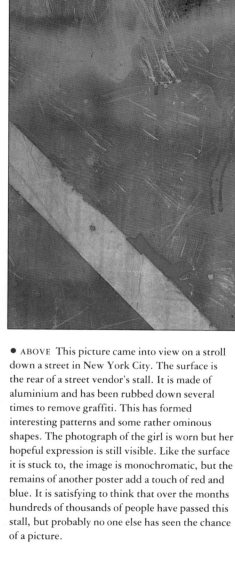

● RIGHT Looking for different angles can often result in original and unusual pictures. This one was taken while lying on the ground and looking upwards. The train couplings form a strong shape that seems to be a strange mechanical mating ritual. Always try a different viewpoint before giving up an idea as unpromising.

● ABOVE This picture came into view on a stroll down a street in New York City. The surface is the rear of a street vendor's stall. It is made of aluminium and has been rubbed down several times to remove graffiti. This has formed interesting patterns and some rather ominous shapes. The photograph of the girl is worn but her hopeful expression is still visible. Like the surface it is stuck to, the image is monochromatic, but the remains of another poster add a touch of red and blue. It is satisfying to think that over the months hundreds of thousands of people have passed this stall, but probably no one else has seen the chance of a picture.

● LEFT The original idea was to photograph the building, but while this was being done the man leaned out of the window with an enquiring look. He spoke no English, but a little sign language persuaded him to stay put while the lens was changed for a telephoto. He turned out to be a willing subject, and after a few shots suggested including his dog. The dog posed as uninhibitedly as he did. Without these two posturing figures the picture would have been dull, but by seizing a chance opportunity a good picture was obtained.

PETS

Pets are always a favourite subject. Before you start to photograph them, it is most important to realize that although pets cannot speak they do have ways of communicating. If you endlessly try to get a dog to do something it does not want to do, it is never going to look happy and the shot will betray its mood. Eventually it will snap at you or even bite. You do have to take this seriously, especially if you are using pets and children together. Both get bored quickly, and when the session is no longer a game for them, stop.

So you will need to work quickly. An autofocus lens and TTL exposure control will be an asset. Very often it is the fleeting expression that makes the shot. Going in close helps to capture this. A medium telephoto lens, say 100 mm, would be a good choice. This will help to fill the frame without getting too close to your subjects and disturbing them.

Try to avoid dressing animals up. The best shots are natural ones, not dogs wearing dresses or cats in sunglasses.

As well as shots for the album or framing, pictures of pets are ideal for Christmas and birthday cards.

Most animals grow faster than we do. Keep photographing them: taking a shot every month of your puppy or kitten will form an interesting record of its development.

● ABOVE LEFT Children with pets make very good subjects for photographs. But in both cases their attention soon wanders. When you see either tiring or becoming agitated it is time to stop.

● ABOVE RIGHT Some pets are more docile than others. This donkey in Ireland allowed plenty of time to move around and choose the best viewpoint. The background is blurred by using a wide aperture and fast shutter speed. The donkey's face is sharp and crisp, and the shot was taken just as it pricked up its ears.

● RIGHT The dog looks alert and the fishing net makes an interesting prop. Autofocus and TTL exposure metering help you to work quickly when photographing pets.

● LEFT, ABOVE AND BELOW These are ideal shots for a Christmas card. A simple prop such as the holly used here is all that was needed to set the scene. The backdrop is a graduated one shading from white to black, and the scene is lit by flash.

FIREWORKS

Photographs of fireworks are fun to take and good to look at. As with so many successful photographs, a little advance planning is necessary to ensure success. If photographing at a public display, get there early. It makes no difference what the weather is like: even in pouring rain people will flock to see a first-class display. Once in position, try to find out where the fireworks will go off.

Many of the most successful shots of fireworks, especially of rockets or other aerial displays, are in fact multiple exposures. There are two ways to achieve these shots. In either case the camera should be set on a tripod and a cable release fitted. Try to ensure that no one will jostle the camera – this can be difficult in a crowd. Point the camera at the place where the rockets are expected to explode.

If the camera has a multiple exposure device, take two or three shots of the rockets. For 100 ISO film the correct exposure is in the region of 2 seconds at f5.6.

If the camera will not take multiple exposures, set the aperture to the same size but turn the shutter ring to the B or T setting. Have a lens cap or some other device ready for covering the lens. Before the rockets go off, cover the lens and fire the shutter. If using the B setting, keep the cable release depressed. When the rockets explode, take off the cap for about 2 seconds, then replace it. Repeat this two or three times, then close the shutter by letting go of the cable release (for B) or pressing it again (for T).

● RIGHT AND TOP INSET These pictures were taken with multiple exposures – in each case, three pictures from the same position. The film was 100 ISO, and the aperture was f5.6. Each of the exposures was 2 seconds. It was raining, and a large lens hood was used to keep raindrops off the lens.

● ABOVE Photographs of individual fireworks can be quite effective. Depending on the brightness of the firework, an exposure of 2 to 4 seconds at f5.6 will probably be right.

● BELOW Flash can be used for firework shots to light something else in the foreground, in this case the boy. The exposure for this picture was 5 seconds at f8. The flash was set for f8, correctly illuminating the boy, while the rest of the exposure time recorded the trail of the sparkler.

IMPROVING YOUR TECHNIQUE

The ancient Chinese proverb that 'a picture is worth a thousand words' has never been truer than it is today. Even with the rapid growth of on-the-spot television reporting, still images have a key role in conveying the intrinsic nature of a story. In modern history it is the still photograph taken in war, famine or natural disaster that stays in people's memory. On a lighter note, it is very often the photograph on the cover of a magazine that will persuade the consumer to buy it.

Photographs can tell a story in many different ways. The pictures here may not make up what many people would think of as a story, but they tell us quickly what this man is associated

with: ancient music and instruments. On the shoot many pictures were taken of him in his workshop, cutting, chiselling, glueing, polishing, tuning. Further shots showed the craftsman by himself, with his instruments, in his home. And many were taken of the instruments themselves. When it came to editing all these it was decided that a strong portrait with one of his instruments was required. Another decision was to show the detail of many finished instruments, rather than have a story of the making of a single one. Different angles showed the elegant curves of the lutes' bodies. The detail in the frets and roses showed the delicacy of the craftsmanship. Keeping the

lighting low emphasized the featured part of each instrument. Restricting the picture sequence to these shots has let the feeling of precision, sensitivity and sheer art shine through.

When you are planning to photograph a person or their work, or an event, try to see how several shots can be used. You may be photographing a member of your family for the album rather than shooting a sequence for a magazine, but think of how you can create a series of shots that will make an attractive and rewarding layout. It may seem difficult to edit your pictures – even wasteful – but to do justice to your best shots good presentation is vital, and so a wide selection is important.

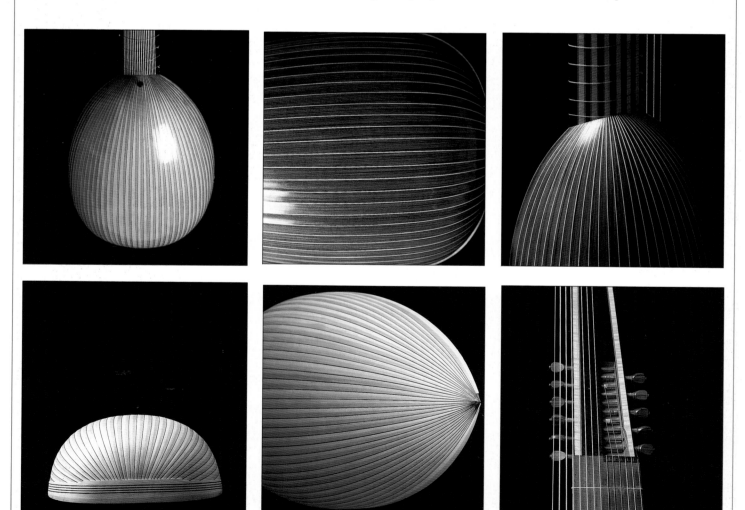

● A sequence of close-up, detailed shots portrays the subject matter, while a larger portrait of the craftsman himself neatly completes the picture story.

In a world where colour photography has become the norm people are often surprised at the power of the images produced by black and white. This is particularly the case where a serious subject or a sombre mood has to be portrayed. Black and white can convey squalor and misery in a way that colour can never do. The memorable images of great documentary photographers such as Don McCullin remain in the mind partly because they are shot in stark black and white.

When telling a story in black and white, the basic ingredients are much as they would be for a colour sequence, but the vital things to look for are tone and texture.

Make a plan of the kind of pictures that are needed before starting to shoot. Look at photo features in a news magazine. The number of pictures used in one story is usually quite small, and each one has a purpose. If the geographical location of the story is relevant, there must be a picture that gives the viewer some idea of what the place looks like.

If the story is one based on people, try to get to know them first. Not only will they supply information, they will take more kindly to a photographer who is interested in them and who seems to be including them in his work, rather than snapping them surreptitiously from behind a tree. People in some regions, or in inner cities, may seem intimidating, but it is better to have them on one's side than to treat them as strangers, which only invites hostility.

Medium speed film, about 400 ISO, is adequate for most situations. If necessary it can be uprated to a higher speed and also given a longer development time.

● LEFT Only by going in really close could this portrait be made to work. This man's leathery skin and tousled hair show what it means to live rough. He gladly accepted a cigarette and talked ramblingly, but sadly he seemed oblivious to what was going on around him.

● BELOW This picture tells us about the location: part of London's East End. The scruffy appearance gives us an indication of the surroundings. Little touches such as the cat sitting on a pile of rubbish add interest to an otherwise bleak scene.

● RIGHT Alcohol can be a refuge for many people, mainly men drinking openly on the streets, in doorways and in the few open spaces. Confronting such people may seem daunting, but sharing the time of day and a cigarette is less likely to arouse suspicion and ill-feeling than lurking behind a wall.

● ABOVE Nobody knew where this woman lived. She would appear nearly every morning at six when the café opened. She always had two cups of tea and a sandwich. She never said a word, but indicated that she did not mind having her picture taken. The viewpoint from one end of the table gives a strong sense of perspective. Many social statements could be read into the surroundings.

● LEFT This shot was taken near a street market. In one section people sell what others have long since discarded. This trader selling just a handful of items stands against a crumbling backdrop. It is a cold day and although he is well wrapped up, he still seems to be clutching himself to keep warm.

● A shot taken on black and white film and printed in the normal way.

P ROCESSING T RICKS

Many areas of photography lend themselves to manipulation. Often such treatment goes completely against what is accepted as normal procedure; it might even be seen as a 'mistake'. Yet the results can be so exciting and dynamic that such mistreatment becomes a valid technique in its own right. Many such techniques do not need any special equipment or even a darkroom: just a camera and film.

For example, colour reversal film, which produces colour transparencies, is processed using a chemical solution known as E6. Colour negative film, which produces prints, is processed using C41. What happens if reversal film is processed using C41 or negative film is processed using E6? The colours go crazy in a completely unexpected way. Some films turn magenta, others bluish green. Start with one type of film and see what happens. Study carefully what has happened to each colour. This may give a pointer to more interesting results. Does the film need more exposure – for example, should 400 ISO film be rated at 100 ISO? Should it also be 'push processed' – given more development time than usual? Only persistence and careful evaluation of the results will give the answer. In any case, the technique will give wild results and these might include some great shots.

Another 'deliberate mistake' is to have black and white negatives printed on a colour printing machine. When a colour negative is printed the light passes through three filters: magenta, cyan and yellow. Asking the printer to print with only one of these filters will give a positive print in that colour. Try each filter in turn, or try two of them – for example, magenta and yellow combine to make red. Of course, a sympathetic processing lab is needed.

● The black and white negative printed on a colour machine, using only the yellow filter.

● The same negative printed through a magenta filter.

● Here the cyan filter was used.

● There are endless variations. This picture was printed through all three filters.

● ABOVE Here 100 ISO colour negative film was rated at 25 ISO and given the E6 process normally used for colour reversal film. The skin tones are quite bleached out, and the effect is much less vibrant.

● RIGHT This picture was taken on 64 ISO colour reversal film rated at 12 ISO and push processed half a stop in the C41 chemicals designed for use on colour negative film. This has increased the contrast and intensified the colour, especially on the floor and the yellow wall. A different type of film would have produced a totally different effect. Only trial and error will perfect the technique.

PHOTOCOPYING

● BELOW The addition of a hand-drawn border around a favourite photograph gives an extra quality to the final image. This border was photocopied and then cut out to accommodate the print. Slightly overlaying the border onto the photograph before re-photocopying it gives the effect of a single image.

One of the simplest yet most effective ways of producing prints from transparencies, photographic prints or 'video still' disk is a photocopying machine. Most large towns now have a photocopying centre with a variety of machines which will produce same-size copies, enlargements or reductions. The prints can be selectively enlarged and the colours manipulated. Sections of prints can be cut up and rearranged to form an instant collage.

As well as making prints onto paper, photocopied images can be transferred onto fabric; many shops offer a T-shirt printing service, for example, and liquid transfer kits are now available so that fabric can be decorated at home using colour photocopies.

Some photocopies produce prints directly from 35 mm transparencies by means of a projector. Positive prints can be produced from negatives, and vice versa. Colours can be greatly manipulated and images can be created by 'dragging'; this is where the original image is moved while the machine is in the process of scanning. Pictures can be

repeated and built up into a mosaic. Details such as jewellery or a hand, for instance, can be scanned individually and used as images on their own or overlaid with other details. By making a copy of a copy, the original image can be broken down to create an abstract graphic picture. Images can be printed using just a single colour or reproduced in black and white.

The obvious attraction of using a photocopier to produce a collage is that the effect can be seen immediately and

adjustments can be made at once without having to wait for the film to be developed. Photocopying is an economical way to print favourite pictures as postcards or greetings cards, or for making a large mural that would be prohibitively expensive if produced using traditional photographic processes. The quality of this form of printing cannot be compared to a proper photographic enlargement but the scope for producing a variety of eye-catching images is endless.

● ABOVE By photocopying two different photographs, interesting collages can be made. The people from one picture were cut out and pasted onto a photocopy of another image. This in turn was re-photocopied. This simple technique means that family and friends can be transported to a totally different environment or country.

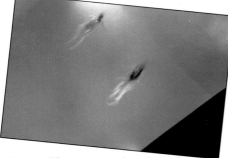

● RIGHT The most surreal results can be achieved by photocopying your holiday photographs. These two photographs, ABOVE, are not particularly interesting by themselves, but when placed together and photocopied the effect is visually intriguing. There appear to be two viewpoints: one of the swimmers under the water, and another from a higher viewpoint looking down on the pool.

● FAR LEFT The original black and white photograph was selectively hand-coloured using fluorescent inks. This was then photocopied; the result is a brightly coloured boat sailing on a monochromatic sea.

THE VIDEO STILL CAMERA

One of the newest innovations in photography is the video still camera. Unlike conventional cameras, the video still records an image on a small floppy disk, exactly like those used in personal computers. Each disk has the capacity to record up to 50 separate photographs. Instead of sending the disk away to be processed, as would be the case with 35 mm film, the images can be played back instantly on a television screen or computer monitor. They can also be recorded on video tape or run out as prints at the majority of photocopying stores, yet the pictures may not be as good as conventional images.

The video still camera itself looks and is operated in much the same way as a compact camera. It comes with a standard lens but has wide angle and telephoto attachments. It has built-in flash and a tripod adaptor. The exposure selection is automatic and the focus is fixed, but there is a macro facility. Single, multi and self-timer shooting modes, back light control and a rechargeable battery are all standard; it is also a very quiet camera to operate. The conventional rechargeable battery is powerful enough to take 50 shots. An additional power pack is available that will enable you to take 4000 shots. The camera can also be worked directly from the mains as a true 'electronic' camera. There is a time lapse facility which allows a picture to be taken at various intervals, for instance either every minute or up to once every hour.

By using a video controller, the shots can be displayed and previewed backwards and forwards. The viewing sequence can be altered to meet different requirements and recorded on video tape for a permanent display.

● BELOW This picture was originally taken on 35 mm transparency film and then copied onto disk. The print was made using a thermal printer.

● BELOW LEFT By looking at the recorded image on a computer screen, selected parts of a picture can be printed in much the same way as a conventional enlargement. This is a detail of a much larger photograph.

ADVANTAGES OF THE VIDEO STILL CAMERA

● Disks can be stored, edited or used repeatedly.

● The image is stored electronically so there is no need for lengthy conventional processing.

● Unlike conventional film, the disk cannot be 'fogged' and can be exposed to light without incurring any damage.

● Images recorded on disk are instantly ready for viewing just as on video tape.

● A range of accessories, including lenses, are readily available.

● ABOVE This strong image originated from a picture taken on a video still camera of a reflection in a shop window. The camera is at its best when shooting close in, but the scope for abstraction when put into the computer is where your creativity can excel.

● LEFT This full-length portrait was shot using available light filtering through an open window; it was recorded on a floppy disk and printed on a computer thermal printer.

● BELOW Colours can be altered or black and white prints made using a video still camera. This almost monochromatic picture was achieved by manipulating the original disk image in a computer. The scope for different variations and experiments from a single image is endless.

ENTERING COMPETITIONS

With growing skill, better equipment and more adventurous photography, it may be time to think of entering some pictures in competitions. There is nothing so encouraging as seeing your own work in print, in a magazine or a newspaper, or simply on display as a prizewinner.

Whatever the medium, there will be hundreds of entries – thousands in a national competition. The judges will be looking for technical excellence and originality of composition, but in the first place they will be looking for an image which exactly fits the theme set for that category. It is amazing how many entrants send in landscapes when the organizers have quite clearly stated that the subject was to be a building or a portrait.

Read the rules carefully. Only a single entry may be allowed in any one category. Prints should be clearly marked on the back with a name, address and telephone number. Sometimes these should be written on the entry form and this should be stuck to the print.

If a photograph really is good enough to enter, it is probably good enough to be made into a professional enlargement. This does not have to be huge; in fact most competitions stipulate a maximum and minimum print size. Discuss the proposed enlargement with the printer. Often a picture can be greatly enhanced if it is cropped, and perhaps angled slightly. Certain areas may benefit from being printed up or shaded.

When entering transparencies it is equally important to read the rules.

There is no point submitting a transparency in a beautiful professional black mask if the organizers want 35 mm slides for projection.

An appropriate caption is vital. A picture may be worth a thousand words, but if it comes to a tiebreak, a single witty or appropriate word can swing the result.

Finally, package entries carefully. A surprising number of pictures arrive creased or bent because they were not properly packed. Often such prints are discarded and not judged.

● LEFT This picture of a cemetery in northern France dedicated to the dead of the First World War has the makings of a worthy competition entry. It is correctly exposed throughout. The clouds in the blue sky are clearly defined. The lines of headstones form a strong composition complemented by the row of trees on the horizon.

● ABOVE Sometimes a shot taken some time ago suddenly fills the brief of a competition perfectly. This graphic image of an imminent storm could fit several competition categories. It was taken just before the sun was masked by clouds. The buildings are caught in a shaft of sunlight which isolates them from their gloomy surroundings.

● RIGHT A competition entry for a picture story or photo documentary is likely to include a character shot of a person. Look for a picture that says the most about the person and their surroundings, taken from an angle that makes the strongest composition.

● LEFT When entering black and white photographs make sure that the print is of the highest quality. Even the best exposed negatives can be further enhanced in the darkroom. Often the winning entry is the simplest of images beautifully printed and presented.

COULD YOU SELL YOUR PICTURES?

If pictures are good enough to enter in competitions they might also be good enough to sell. The right image in the right place and at the right time can sell an idea or product, or stimulate people's interests. Such a picture can be worth a lot of money.

Unlike many products, a picture – or rather, its reproduction rights – can be sold again and again. A single sale may bring in only a modest sum, but repeated sales over several years can notch up a tidy amount.

There are no rules about what makes a picture sell. Often an original and beautiful shot will sit in a drawer for ever because it does not fit into any particular subject area. However, one thing is for sure: a picture that is under- or overexposed, or out of focus, or simply badly composed, will not sell – no matter how interesting its subject may be.

For colour photographs, transparencies are preferred to negatives.

If a picture prominently features a person, a model release form from that person is a necessity. For groups of individuals, there must be a release form from each of them. Agencies will not consider publishing such pictures without the form.

Pictures can be submitted to a photo library, which will assure them wide coverage. A certain amount of trust is required from both parties when entering into such an arrangement. Only apply to a large and well-known library, which will be honest about how many times a picture has been used. It is worth asking other photographers or looking at the picture acknowledgements in books, newspapers and magazines to find out the names of reputable libraries.

● RIGHT These commuters are blurred but they convey the urgent movement of rush hour in a city. Such pictures have editorial and advertising uses. This one has been published many times in magazines and newspapers.

● LEFT This picture of London's famous department store, Harrods, has been published in one form or another all over the world, and has been used literally hundreds of times. Its most important ingredient is that it is instantly recognizable. It is also a good composition and correctly exposed.

● BELOW Good landscape pictures are always needed by local and national travel agencies, and magazines and newspapers running features on a country or region. Good composition, spot-on exposure, well-defined clouds and a strong, immediate point of interest are all vital ingredients in ensuring good and lasting sales.

STOCKISTS AND SUPPLIERS

HEAD OFFICES

Advice on stockists and repairs

UK

Canon UK Ltd
Units 4, 5 & 6
Brent Trading Centre
North Circular Road
London NW10 0JF

Minolta (UK) Ltd
1–3 Tanners Drive
Blakelands North
Milton Keynes MK14 5BU

Nikon UK Ltd
Nikon House
380 Richmond Road
Kingston
Surrey KT2 5PR

USA

Canon USA Inc
1 Canon Plaza
Lake Success
NY 11042

Canon USA Inc
100 Park Boulevard
Itasca
IL 60143-2693

Canon USA Inc
5825 Oakbrook Parkway
Norcross
GA 30093

Canon USA Inc
123 Paularino Avenue East
Costa Mesa
CA 95054

Canon USA Inc
4000 Burton Drive
Santa Clara
CA 95054

Canon USA Inc
3200 Regent Boulevard
Irving
Texas 75063

Canon USA Inc
1020 Auahi Street
Building 8
Honolulu
Hawaii 96814

Canon USA Inc
5701 General Washington Drive
Alexandria
VA 22312

Minolta Corporation
101 Williams Drive
Ramsey
NJ 07446

Minolta Corporation
11150 Hope Street
Cypress
CA 90630

Minolta Corporation
3000 Tallview Drive
Rolling Meadows
IL 60008

Nikon Inc
1300 Walt Whitman Road
Melville
NY 11747-3064

Nikon Inc
19601 Hamilton Avenue
Torrance
CA 90502-1309

Nikon Inc
5355 Oakbrook Parkway
Norcross
GA 30093

CANADA

Canon Canada Inc
6390 Dixie Road
Mississauga
Ontario L5T 1P7

Canon Canada Inc
10652 Côte de Liesse
Lachine
Quebec H8T 1A5

Canon Canada Inc
2828 16th Street
NE Calgary
Alberta T2E 7KY

Minolta Canada Inc
369 Britannia Road East
Mississauga
Ontario 14Z 2H5

Minolta Canada Inc
3405 Thimens Boulevard
St Laurent
Quebec H4R 1V5

Minolta Canada Inc
105–3830 Jacombs Road
Richmond
BC V6V 1Y6

Nikon Canada Inc
1366 Aerowood Drive
Mississauga
Ontario L4W 1C1

Nikon Canada Inc
No 5 13511 Crestwood Place
Richmond
BC V6V 2E9

Nikon Canada Inc
3300 Chemin Côte Vertu
Montreal
Quebec H4R 2B7

AUSTRALIA

Canon Australia Pty Ltd
1 Thomas Holt Drive
North Ryde
NSW 2113

NEW ZEALAND

Canon Optics New Zealand Ltd
Fred Thomas Drive
Takapuna
PO Box 33–336
Auckland

SPECIALIST DEALERS

UK

Fox Talbot Cameras
443 Strand
London WC2R 0QU

Keith Johnson & Pellings
93–103 Drummond Street
London NW1 2HJ

Keith Johnson & Pellings
Unit 8
Barclay Hill Place
Portlethen Industrial Estate
Aberdeen AB1 4PF

Keith Johnson & Pellings
Unit 7
Montpelier Central Station Road
Montpelier
Bristol BS6 5EE

Keith Johnson & Pellings
Unit 3
Loughside Industrial Park
Dargan Crescent
Duncrue Road
Belfast BT3 9JP

Leeds Photovisual Ltd
20–26 Brunswick Centre
Bernard Street
London WC1N 1AE

Leeds Photovisual Ltd
Charlton Place
Downing Street
Manchester M12 6HH

Leeds Photovisual Ltd
2 Newhall Place
16–17 Newhall Hill
Hockley
Birmingham B1 3JH

Leeds Photovisual Ltd
Lovell House
North Street
Leeds LS2 7PN

Leeds Photovisual Ltd
30–30A Lee Way
Lee Way Industrial Estate
Newport
Gwent NP9 0TW

The Studio Workshop
153 Farringdon Road
London EC1R 3AD

USA

Sinar Bron Inc
17 Progress Street
Edison
NJ 08820

CANADA

Lisle-Kelco Ltd
3525 Nashua Drive
Mississauga
Ontario L4V 1R1

AUSTRALIA

Baltronics
Unit 8
Chuter Place
Holt Street
North Sydney
NSW 2060

NEW ZEALAND

CR Kennedy (NZ) Ltd
PO Box 14-058
Panmure
Auckland

SOUTH AFRICA

Photra Photo
PO Box 9072
Johannesburg 2000

ASA
American Standards Association: a series of numbers that denote the speed of a film; now superseded by the ISO number.

APERTURE
Opening at the front of the camera that determines the amount of light passing through the lens to the film.

APERTURE PRIORITY
A metering system in the camera that allows the photographer to choose the aperture while the camera selects the shutter speed.

B SETTING
Indication on shutter speed dial that allows the shutter to remain open for as long as the shutter release is depressed.

BARN DOORS
Attachment that fits on the front of a studio light and allows the photographer to control the spread of light.

BETWEEN-THE-LENS SHUTTER
Usually built in to a lens, this type of shutter allows flash synchronization at any shutter speed.

BRACKETING
Method of exposing one or more exposures on either side of the predicted exposure to obtain the best result.

CDS
Cadmium sulphide cell; used in electronic exposure meters.

CABLE RELEASE
Cable which allows the shutter to be fired with minimum vibration or camera shake; essential for long exposures.

CAMERA MOVEMENTS
Found on large format cameras, these allow the photographer to move the front and back panels of the camera.

CASSETTE
Light-tight container for holding 35 mm film.

COLOUR NEGATIVE FILM
Film that produces negatives for prints.

COLOUR REVERSAL FILM
Film that produces transparencies or slides.

COLOUR TEMPERATURE
A scale for measuring the quality of light in values of kelvin.

CONTACT SHEET
Method for printing negatives the same size as the film so that the photographer can choose the images to be enlarged.

CYAN
Blue-green light; the complementary colour to red.

DIN
Deutsche Industrie Norm; German method of numbering the speed of a film now superseded by ISO numbering.

DX CODE
Bar code on a 35 mm cassette that contains information such as film speed. This is read inside the camera which adjusts itself automatically.

DARK SLIDE
Container for holding a sheet of film; used in large format cameras.

DAYLIGHT-BALANCED COLOUR FILM
Colour film that is balanced for use in daylight light sources at 5400 kelvin.

DEPTH OF FIELD
The distance in front of the point of focus and the distance beyond that is acceptably sharp.

DIAPHRAGM
The adjustable aperture of a lens.

DIFFUSER
Material placed in front of the light source that softens the quality of the light.

EXPOSURE METER
Instrument for measuring the amount of light available that can be read to indicate shutter speed and aperture.

EXTENSION BELLOWS
Extendable device that fits between the lens and the camera body that enables the photographer to take close-up shots with a variable degree of magnification.

EXTENSION TUBES
Tubular device that fits between the lens and the camera body to enable the photographer to take close-up pictures. The degree of close-up available varies with the length of the tube used.

F NUMBER
A scale of numbers that indicate the size of the aperture used i.e. f2.8, f4, f5.6, f8, f11, f16 etc. Sometimes referred to as stops.

FILTERS
Coloured glass, plastic or gelatin that alters the colour of the light falling on the film when placed over the lens.

FIXED FOCUS
Camera that has no means of altering the focus of the lens; usually only found on the cheapest cameras.

FOCAL PLANE SHUTTER
Shutter method that exposes the film to light by using a moving blind in the camera body.

HIGH KEY
Photography where most of the tones are from the light end of the scale.

HOT SHOE
Electrical contact usually found on the top of 35 mm SLR cameras; forms part of the camera's flash synchronization.

ISO
International Standards Organization: the numbering system now used to indicate the speed of a film.

INCIDENT LIGHT READING
Method of taking an exposure meter reading by recording the amount of light falling on the subject.

LIGHT BOX
An illuminated box used for viewing transparencies or negatives.

LOW KEY
Photography where most of the tones are from the dark end of the scale.

MACRO LENS
Lens that enables the photographer to take close-up pictures without the need for extension tubes or bellows.

MAGENTA
Blue-red light. The complementary colour to green.

MONTAGE
Picture made up of a collection of other images.

PANNING
Method of moving the camera in line with a moving subject such as a racing car. This produces a blurred background but keeps the subject sharp, thereby giving a greater effect of movement in the final image.

PARALLAX
The difference between what the camera viewfinder sees and what the lens sees. This difference is eliminated in SLR cameras.

PERSPECTIVE CONTROL (PC) LENS
Lens that can be adjusted at right angles to its axis. This enables the photographer to alter the field of view without moving the camera. Also known as a shift lens.

POLARIZING FILTER
Filter that enables the photographer to darken blue skies and cut out unwanted reflections.

RANGEFINDER CAMERA
System that allows sharp focusing on a subject by aligning two images in the camera viewfinder.

RECIPROCITY FAILURE
Situations where shots requiring exposures of longer than 1 second result in a loss of film speed; this leads to underexposure.

SLR
Single lens reflex; type of camera that allows the photographer to view the subject through the actual lens, via a mirror that moves out of the way when the picture is taken.

SHIFT LENS
Alternative name for perspective control lens.

SHUTTER
Means of controlling the amount of time light is allowed to pass through the lens onto the film.

STOP
Also known as the f number.

T SETTING
Indication on shutter speed dial that allows the shutter to remain open when the shutter release is depressed and close when it is depressed again.

TTL
Camera that assesses the exposure required by taking a reading through the camera lens.

TUNGSTEN-BALANCED COLOUR FILM
Colour film that is balanced for use in artificial light sources at 3400 kelvin.

ZOOM LENS
Lens with variable focal length.